Modeling Ungrammaticality in Optimality Theory

Advances in Optimality Theory

Editors: Ellen Woolford, University of Massachusetts, Amherst, and Armin Mester, University of California, Santa Cruz

Optimality Theory is an exciting new approach to linguistic analysis that originated in phonology but was soon taken up in syntax, morphology, and other fields of linguistics. Optimality Theory presents a clear vision of the universal properties underlying the vast surface typological variety in the world's languages. Cross-linguistic differences once relegated to idiosyncratic language-specific rules can now be understood as the result of different priority rankings among universal, but violable constraints on grammar.

Advances in Optimality Theory is designed to stimulate and promote research in this provocative new framework. It provides a central outlet for the best new work by both established and younger scholars in this rapidly moving field. The series includes studies with a broad typological focus, studies dedicated to the detailed analysis of individual languages, and studies on the nature of Optimality Theory itself. The series publishes theoretical work in the form of monographs and coherent edited collections as well as pedagogical texts and reference texts that promote the dissemination of Optimality Theory.

Consultant Board

Judith Aissen, University of California, Santa Cruz
Daniel Büring, University of California, Los Angeles
Gisbert Fanselow, University of Potsdam
Jane Grimshaw, Rutgers University
Géraldine Legendre, Johns Hopkins University
John J. McCarthy, University of Massachusetts, Amherst
Alan Prince, Rutgers University
Paul Smolensky, Johns Hopkins University
Donca Steriade, MIT, Cambridge, MA
Moira Yip, University College London

Published:

Hidden Generalizations: Phonological Opacity in Optimality Theory
John J. McCarthy

Optimality Theory, Phonological Acquisition and Disorders
Edited by Daniel A. Dinnsen and Judith A. Gierut

Phonological Argumentation: Essays in Evidence and Motivation
Edited by Steve Parker

Conflicts in Interpretation
Petra Hendriks, Helen de Hoop, Irene Krämer, Henriëtte de Swart and Joost Zwarts

Forthcoming:

Understanding Allomorphy: Perspectives from Optimality Theory
Edited by Bernard Tranel

On 'Elsewhere'. Disjunctivity and Blocking in Phonological Theory
Eric Baković

The Phonology of Contrast
Anna Łubowicz

Faithfulness in Phonological Theory
Marc van Oostendorp

Modeling Ungrammaticality in Optimality Theory

Edited by Curt Rice and Sylvia Blaho

Published by
UK: Equinox Publishing Ltd., 1 Chelsea Manor Studios
Flood Street, London SW3 5SR

USA: DBBC, 28 Main Street, Oakville, CT 06779

www.equinoxpub.com

First published 2009

British Library Cataloguing-in-Publication Data
A catalogue record for this book is available from the British Library.

ISBN-13   978 1 84553 215 4   (hardback)
            978 1 84553 216 1   (paperback)

Library of Congress Cataloging-in-Publication Data

Modeling ungrammaticality in optimality theory / edited by Curt Rice and Sylvia Blaho.
    p. cm. -- (Advances in optimality theory)
 Includes bibliographical references and index.
 ISBN 978-1-84553-215-4 (hb) -- ISBN 978-1-84553-216-1 (pb)
1. Speech errors. 2. Grammaticality (Linguistics) 3. Language and languages--Study and teaching--Error analysis. 4. Optimality theory (Linguistics) I. Rice, Curt. II. Blaho, Sylvia, 1979-
 P37.5.S67M63 2009
 415'.0182--dc22
                        2009030081

Printed and bound in Great Britain and the USA

Contents

1 Modeling Ungrammaticality

Curt Rice and Sylvia Blaho
*University of Tromsø and
Research Institute for Linguistics, Hungarian Academy of Sciences*

1   Introduction

Modeling the contrast between grammatical and ungrammatical utterances is the core enterprise for any generative theory of grammar. The heart of a particular model will therefore start with an input to a grammar and pursue the creation or identification of corresponding well-formed outputs.

In syntax, models focus on movements that apply to inputs to satisfy the requirements a particular grammar imposes on its outputs. In phonology, outputs are achieved by manipulating inputs through operations often described as spreading, syllabification, deletion, insertion, on so on. Focus on movements and manipulations in syntax and phonology is a focus on grammaticality.

The studies in this book look at the flip side of the issue, namely *un*grammaticality. The papers collected here focus on cases that fail — cases in which no movement or manipulation is invoked to create a grammatical output for some particular input. This situation goes under various names in the literature. When discussing syntax, the term *ineffability* is commonly used (Pesetsky 1997). In the realm of phonology, the phenomenon is described as *absolute ungrammaticality*, or with a reference to theoretical tools used in analyses, such as *the null parse* or *null outputs*.

We emphasize that the cases under consideration easily *could* be rescued. A little spreading here, a deletion there, and the inputs could be rendered well-formed. But they aren't.

The stations that would be necessary to visit along the road to a grammatical output are obvious and easy to identify. But that isn't enough. The road isn't taken, and the result is an input which has no corresponding well-formed output.

This is absolute ungrammaticality; one of our central claims is that models of grammar must capture this as well. It's not enough to model grammaticality, and assume that by implication one has also modeled ungrammaticality. There are two roads an input can follow, and they both require the theoretician's attention.

1.1   OT's focus on ungrammaticality

With the papers gathered here, we focus on the problem that ungrammaticality presents for Optimality Theory (Prince and Smolensky 1993). The architecture of OT makes the problem of ungrammaticality particularly clear.

At least two aspects of the theory contribute to this clarity. First of all, OT focuses on outputs to a greater extent than other models. OT analyses are permeated with a focus either directly on the candidate outputs themselves (markedness), or on the pairing of a particular input with a set of possible outputs (faithfulness). This contrasts with derivational approaches, in which the focus rests on an input, a set of rules, and the application of those rules to the input, rather than on the output itself. In derivational approaches, the generation of an output is the end of the story; in OT, it's a prerequisite to getting started.

OT's focus on outputs emphasizes a central architectural property of the theory, namely that every input is associated with some output. This property is scrutinized in the collection here. Cases in which some input seemingly has no output challenge the very core of the model. The theory's focus on the output makes a confrontation with this challenge inevitable.

The second aspect of OT which makes clear the need to explicitly model ungrammaticality is the presence and role of violable constraints in the model. Well-formedness — or, grammaticality — as modeled with OT is anisomorphic with constraint satisfaction.

While it is in principle possible to construct a version of OT in which grammatical forms satisfy all constraints of the grammar, no known optimality theoretic model of grammar presents such scenaria. All models include faithfulness constraints, which regulate the input-output relationship. An output which is identical to its input will satisfy all faithfulness constraints.

But all models also include markedness constraints, assessing the performance of a particular output against a set of requirements on surfacing structures. These requirements punish the presence of structure. Some versions of OT include constraints punishing all structure (examples), such that any output will inevitably incur some violations.

Some approaches may envisage true unmarkedness at the nadir of a hierarchy of structural deviance, such that an output like [ti.ti] at first glance will seem to maintain its purity. Even this form, though, will ultimately be sullied by the inevitable violation of constraints on prosodic structure, such as one of two competing alignment constraints drawing stress to the left or the right edge of the word.

The need to model ungrammaticality explicitly is emphasized by the fact that all grammatical outputs violate some constraints. The violation of a constraint is not enough to be eliminated from consideration as a well-formed output; violation is not enough to be characterized as ungrammatical.

Because the grammatical output associated with any input is imperfect, it becomes particularly striking that some inputs have no outputs. Optimality Theory is designed not to yield grammatical forms which are without imperfection, but rather to yield grammatical forms which are good enough — good enough to be best. The cases considered in the following chapters are cases in which no form is good enough; even slight imperfection is enough for complete disqualification.

Two components of OT — focus on outputs, and constraint violability — conspire to emphasize the complete unexpectedness of ineffability, or absolute ungrammaticality. The existence of such phenomena is a confrontation of the architectural structure of OT. Out theoretical work is not complete until this confrontation is met.

1.2   DP's non-focus on ungrammaticality

The study of absolute ungrammaticality is an untilled field in derivational approaches to modeling phonological behavior. In derivational phonology (DP), the focus is on the processes which must be applied to inputs to render well-formed outputs.

Since the cases presented in the book are, as noted, cases in which a solution is easily imagined, derivational approaches will have to prevent that solution from applying. For example, the Norwegian case receiving much attention in the following papers (and presented in section 2.4 below) has inputs which, if syllabified without further segmental modification, would have coda clusters with rising sonority. Potential solutions abound, the most prominent among them being deletion of one of the consonants or epenthesis of a vowel either between or after the consonants. Epenthesis is documented elsewhere in the language, so why doesn't it apply here? Perhaps that question can be answered, such that the structural description of the epenthesis rule can be narrowed down to exclude these cases.

If the structural description is such that a rule of repair does not apply, what happens then? Either the derivation must be stopped, modeling a crashed derivation, or the ungrammatical form makes its way through the derivation, only to be controlled for well-formedness as part of the final packaging prior to delivery to the phonetics.

Derivational approaches to phonology have traditionally taken the latter option. Constraints on outputs are posited, and they must be satisfied. If a coda cluster with rising sonority makes it through the rule application block, then the form must be blocked from surfacing by violating a constraint on syllabic well-formedness.

A derivational approach to phonology must therefore be enhanced with constraints on outputs. The function of these constraints in the theory is to model ungrammaticality. Rules apply to give a set of surface forms. But those candidate surfaces must pass one more test before they can be characterized as grammatical, namely satisfaction of some constraints.

It is these constraints, then, which in derivational phonology might be said to model ungrammaticality. The constraints have no other function. The rules alone could yield grammatical structures as long as there was a strategy for stopping the ungrammatical ones before they emerge from the block of rules. But there is no such strategy, and we therefore need constraints on outputs.

When comparing OT with DP, the role of constraints in DP is important to keep in mind. We would claim, although not without the fear of contradiction, that both approaches will need some specific tool to model ungrammaticality. In DP, that tool is constraints on outputs. What that tool should be in OT, is the topic of this book.

2   Examples

Absolute ungrammaticality is not a major theme in the literature, either in syntax or phonology. For the reader unfamiliar with the phenomenon, we sketch a few cases here. A few brief examples are given, followed by a bit more detail about the Norwegian case, which several of the following papers take up. This section draws heavily on a similar presentation in Rice (2007), where even more examples are given.

2.1   Turkish suffixation

The grammar of Turkish imposes a disyllabic minimality requirement on the output of suffixation (Itô and Hankamer 1989; Orgun and Sprouse 1999; Raffelsiefen 2004), although Inkelas and Orgun (1995) note that there are varieties of Turkish in which the minimality requirement is not observed. When a CV stem in a Turkish dialect with a minimality requirement gets a consonantal suffix, the minimality requirement is not met, and suffixation fails, leaving an incomplete paradigm, as seen in (1a), which has a gap for the genitive singular. Epenthesis is available as a repair in the language, but only to fix phonotactic infelicities, such as the derived [l+m] cluster in (1b). Epenthesis is not available to fix the templatic inadequacy of (1a).

(1)   *Disyllabic minimality for bimorphemic Turkish words*
          a.   (i)   do: 'musical note C'
                 (ii)   *do:-m 'my C'
          b.   (i)   sol^y 'musical note G'
                 (ii)   sol^y-üm 'my G'

2.2   Hungarian CCik verbs

A triconsonantal cluster yielded by the concatenative morphology of Hungarian cannot surface as such; it must either undergo epenthesis, or be avoided (Hetzron 1975; Törkenczy 2002; Rebrus and Törkenczy 2005, this volume). Avoidance is the most popular strategy, cf. Papp (1969), a representative example of which is given in (2).

(2)   *A fragment of a Hungarian verbal paradigm*
          a.   csuklani 'to hiccup'
          b.   csuklottam 'I hiccupped' , csuklik 'he hiccups'
          c.   *csuklhat 'he may hiccup'

The consonant-initial suffix *-hat* cannot be attached to the stem *csukl* 'hiccup', with the result that the form for 'he may hiccup' is left unformed.

2.3   Tagalog infixation

The Tagalog actor-focus morpheme *-um* is much-discussed in the OT literature, including references such as Prince and Smolensky (1993); Orgun and Sprouse (1999); Crowhurst (2001); McCarthy (2003); Klein (2005). As is well known, this morpheme can appear after the first consonant in a word, as in (3a), or even after the first cluster, as in (3b). However, if the initial consonant is a sonorant labial, then affixation cannot occur, (3c). This instance of ineffability is proposed to be motivated by the joint effects of requiring that the affix come early in the word, along with a specific OCP requirement targeting sequential onsets of a particular flavor.

(3)   *Well- and ill-formed affixation in Tagalog*
    a.   sulat — **sum**ulat 'to write'
    b.   preno — pr**um**eno ~ **pum**reno 'to brake'
    c.   mahal — *m**um**ahal 'to become expensive'

2.4   Norwegian imperatives

Consider now imperative formation in Norwegian (Kristoffersen 1991; Rice 2003, 2005). Norwegian imperatives are identical to their roots, while infinitives (for consonant-final roots) show affixation of a final schwa. As a result, we find infinitive-imperative pairs of the variety seen in (4).

(4)   *Well-formed Norwegian imperatives*
    a.   å spise — spis! '(to) eat'
    b.   å snakke — snakk! '(to) talk'
    c.   å løfte — løft! '(to) lift'

However, when a root ends in consonant cluster with rising sonority, there may be a gap for the imperative, as in (5). The expected result from the morphology is an imperative identical to the root. However a monosyllabic expression of the root will be ill-formed. As noted in Rice (2003), and as will be discussed in greater detail below, there is dialectal variation in the response to this situation, but the most common response, to which we here attend, is that the attempt to form an imperative comes to naught.

(5)   *Ill-formed Norwegian imperatives*
    a.   å åpne — *åpn! 'open'
    b.   å padle — *padl! 'paddle'
    c.   å sykle — *sykl! 'bike'

The appearance of a gap in an inflectional paradigm reflects a speaker's synchronic knowledge, and it will therefore be incumbent upon a theory of grammar to speak to these cases. In the case of Norwegian imperatives, there is solid evidence that the phenomenon is properly construed as synchronic and we make a brief digression here to present this evidence here.

The claim above that the imperatives in (5) are unutterable is somewhat imprecise because these imperatives do in fact surface when they are followed by a vowel-initial word. This fact is taken here as evidence that speakers do indeed master the morphology of these words.

Following Golston's (1995) proposal that phonology can select between syntactic options, Rice and Svenonius (1998) note that the negative imperative in Norwegian has two possible word orders. The negator *ikke* can come either before or after the imperative, as in (6).

(6)   *Syntactic variability with Norwegian negative imperatives*

    a.   *Hopp ikke på møblene.*
        jump not on the.furniture
        'Don't jump on the furniture!'

    b.   *Ikke hopp på møblene.*
        not jump on the.furniture
        'Don't jump on the furniture!'

However, when the imperative is of the type in (5), only one of the two syntactic possibilities is well-formed. In this case, *ikke* must follow the imperative if it is to be uttered, assuming that the next word is consonant-initial. Otherwise, the imperative would be followed by a consonant-initial word and would therefore be unutterable, as in (7).

(7)   *Phonology selects among syntactic options*

    a.   *Klatr ikke på møblene.*
        climb not on the.furniture
        'Don't climb on the furniture!'

    b.   **Ikke klatr på møblene.*
        not climb on the.furniture
        'Don't climb on the furniture!'

Note that this is not a fact specifically about negated imperatives; these simply provide a convenient example because *ikke* is vowel-initial. The point could just as well be made with the examples in (8), where the contrast involves prepositions which differ in being vowel-initial or consonant-initial.

(8)   *Phonology forbids a consonant-initial preposition*

    a.   *Sykl opp bakken.*
        bike up   the.hill
        'Bike up the hill!'

    b.   *Sykl ned   bakken.*
        bike down the.hill
        'Bike down the hill!'

And, of course, both options for the negated imperative return if the subsequent word is vowel-initial, as in (9) with the preposition *opp* 'up'.

(9)   *Negative imperative syntactic optionality recovered*

    a.   *Klatr ikke opp på møblene.*
        climb not up on the.furniture
        'Don't climb up onto the furniture.'
    b.   *Ikke klatr opp på møblene.*
        not climb up on the.furniture
        'Don't climb up onto the furniture.'

These data underscore the synchrony of the phenomenon. Speakers can form the imperative, even when the root has a cluster of rising sonority, but only in the correct phrasal environment — specifically, an environment in which the cluster is heterosyllabic. The gaps under consideration here are not merely the reflex of a diachronic development. They are the result of a synchronic process in the grammar, and a model of the grammar must therefore offer a representation of such processes.

We have seen in this section several examples of phonologically motivated gaps in paradigms. Phenomena such as these are the focus of this book.

3   OT approaches to absolute ungrammaticality

Absolute ungrammaticality was early recognized as a challenge for OT and several solutions have been proposed over the hectic life of the theory. The solutions share a general strategy, namely the identification of some candidate which is optimized by the grammar, but which nonetheless is unutterable. The reasons for unutterability vary across approaches.

The first proposal invokes the *null parse* (Prince and Smolensky 1993). The null parse is a candidate which has not been assigned a morphological category and which therefore violates the constraint MPARSE. MPARSE of course is a constraint which specifically requires an output to have a morphological parse. The null parse can be the optimal candidate in a grammar which ranks MPARSE low in the constraint hierarchy. When the null parse is optimal, its lack of a morphological parse makes it "uniquely unsuited to life in the outside world" (Prince and Smolensky 1993: 51). In other words, even though the candidate is optimal in the phonology, it finds no home in a string of morphosyntactically parsed forms, and thereby can never surface. The input to the phonology thus does correspond to some output, but the output cannot be used by the morphosyntax, rendering the input impotent.

One technical challenge with Prince and Smolensky's approach involves the relationship of the null parse candidate to the other constraints of the grammar. If the null parse, for example, is syllabified but simply not assigned a morphological category, then it should violate the relevant markedness constraints. The familiar form of a constraint banning a particular segment, after all, makes no reference to the presence or absence of a morphological category.

To suppress this discussion, McCarthy (2002) offers a development of Prince and Smolensky's proposal, positing instead a *null output*, which has "no structure whatsoever" (McCarthy 2002: 197). Of course, an output with no structure whatsoever is an output in which all elements of the input have been deleted, leading to massive violation of MAX. This problem is circumvented by the stipulation that the null output "always and only" violates MPARSE. For a proposal eliminating this stipulation, see McCarthy and Wolf's contribution to the present volume.

Orgun and Sprouse's (1999) CONTROL theory models absolute ungrammaticality entirely within the phonological domain, albeit an enhanced one. In particular, they posit a CONTROL component of the grammar, which differs from the familiar OT EVAL component insofar as it has *hard* — inviolable — constraints. In familiar OT fashion, an input and a set of outputs are submitted to EVAL, which identifies the optimal candidate. This optimal candidate from EVAL then proceeds to the CONTROL component, which has a subset of the constraints from EVAL. If the output of EVAL fails to satisfy the constraint(s) in CONTROL, then the input has no output. Additional discussion of the CONTROL strategy is found in Fanselow and Féry (2002) and Raffelsiefen (2005).

A third approach tackles the problem of ineffability in the context of the optimal paradigms theory (OP) of McCarthy (2005). OP construes phonology as operating not on individual forms, but on paradigms of related forms, motivated by the claim that the the output of a single form can be influenced by its paradigm kin. When comparing candidates in OP, constraint violations are awarded for each instance of the constraint violation within a paradigm. In a series of articles, Rice extends this approach to model absolute ungrammaticality. A candidate paradigm which includes a member violating a highly ranked constraint will lose in EVAL to a candidate paradigm in which that member is absent. In this way, a particular grammar may prefer an incomplete paradigm to a complete one. Further details about this approach are available in Rice (2003, 2005, 2007).

4 Moving forward

One of the important properties of the well-studied Norwegian example mentioned above is the phrasal effect. Recall that the ineffability of some Norwegian imperatives depends on the phrasal environment. When an imperative ends with a consonant cluster with rising sonority it is ungrammatical. But that ungrammatical depends on a phrasal context. If the imperative is to be uttered in isolation or prior to a consonant-initial word, we encounter absolute ungrammaticality. But when the phrasal context is such that the next word begins with a vowel, the phonology of the phrase is grammatical.

A deep analysis of these facts depends on a conception of the interaction between phonology and syntax. If spell-out in syntax draws from the lexicon, ineffable forms must be stored there, at least in the Norwegian case. In cases such as Turkish or Tagalog, the particular concatenation of (non-null) morphemes creates the circumstances for ineffability, such that a morpho-syntactically well-formed phrase is rendered ungrammatical by the phonology. A theory which reduces phonology to a mere *interpretive component* would thereby seem to fundamentally underappreciate the role of the phonological component in the determination of grammaticality. The earlier works on gaps cited in this chapter do not offer an analysis taking these issues into account. For that reason, we find it fitting to gather a collection of papers which look further into the topic.

The problem described here is important for both syntacticians and phonologists, and this volume includes contributions from both. Géraldine Legendre challenges Pesetsky's (1997) claim that ineffability is evidence against an OT architecture in syntax, and argues that a neutralisation approach to absolute ungrammaticality, although it requires relaxing the assumption that competing candidates have the same LF interpretation, is more economical than the null parse proposal of Ackema and Neeleman (2000). Ralf Vogel discusses the syntax and semantics of wh-islands. He argues that treatments of ineffability should look outside linguistic subdomains and consider the possible and impossible interaction between levels of grammar.

The phonology papers are imprecisely divided into two groups. Three of the papers focus primarily on architectural issues. Matthew Wolf and John McCarthy extend the null output approach, addressing both the phrasal issues mentioned above, and also providing an explicit and precise method for assessing the violation of faithfulness constraints. Marc van Oostendorp discusses the case of diminutive formation in Dutch, identifying a gradual path from grammaticality to ineffability and offering a model of gradient well-formedness. Orhan Orgun and Ronald Sprouse further develop their earlier work on CONTROL theory, offering new examples and addressing some previous criticisms.

The other three phonology papers offer more in-depth studies of some particular cases, with heavy emphasis on morphological paradigms. Adam Albright discusses paradigm gaps without any apparent phonotactic violations, showing that these are not arbitrary, but rather, result from the lack of robust patterns that speakers could use to predict these forms. Outi Bat-El investigates an absolute gap in a class of Hebrew deadjectival nouns, and concludes that it arises due to identity (and similarity) avoidance in the paradigm. Finally, Péter Rebrus and Miklós Törkency present a complex pattern of ineffability that occurs in both the inflectional and the derivational paradigm of Hungarian verbs. Their analysis connects ineffability and optionality, and shows that a satisfactory account of the Hungarian pattern has to uncover the interplay of phonotactic and morphosyntactic factors.

With this collection of papers, we invite our readers into an understudied area which we believe has potentially profound implications for our understanding of the architecture of grammar.

Bibliography

Ackema, P. and Neeleman, A. (2000) Absolute ungrammaticality. In J. Dekkers, F. van der Leeuw, J. van de Weijer (eds.) *Optimality Theory: Phonology, Syntax, and Acquisition* 279–301. Oxford: Oxford University Press.

Crowhurst, M. (2001) Coda conditions and *um*-infixation in Toba Batak. *Lingua* 111: 561–90.

Fanselow, G. and C. Féry (2002) Ineffability in grammar. In G. Fanselow and C. Féry (eds.) *Resolving Conflicts in Grammars: Optimality The-*

ory in Syntax, Morphology, and Phonology 265–307. Hamburg: Helmut Buske Verlag.

Golston, C. (1995) Syntax outranks phonology: evidence from Ancient Greek. *Phonology* 3(12): 343–68.

Hetzron, R. (1975) Where the grammar fails. *Language 51*: 859–72.

Inkelas, S. and C. O. Orgun (1995) Level ordering and economy in the lexical phonology of Turkish. *Language* 71(4): 763–93.

Itô, J. and J. Hankamer (1989) Notes on monosyllabism in Turkish. In J. Ito and J. Runner (eds.) *Phonology at Santa Cruz* 61–69. Santa Cruz: Linguistics Research Center.

Klein, T. B. (2005) Infixation and segmental constraint effects: UM and IN in Tagalog, Chamorro, and Toba Batak. *Lingua* 115: 959–96.

Kristoffersen, G. (1991) *Aspects of Norwegian syllable structure.* Ph. D. thesis, University of Tromsø.

McCarthy, J. J. (2002) *A thematic guide to Optimality Theory.* Cambridge: Cambridge University Press.

McCarthy, J. J. (2003) OT constraints are categorical. *Phonology* 20: 75–138.

McCarthy, J. J. (2005) Optimal paradigms. In L. Downing, T. Hall, and R. Raffelsiefen (eds.) *Paradigms in phonological theory* 295–371. Oxford: Oxford University Press.

Orgun, C. O. and R. L. Sprouse (1999) From MPARSE to CONTROL: deriving ungrammaticality. *Phonology* 16: 191–224.

Papp, F. (1969) *A magyar nyelv szóvégmutató szótára* [Reverse dictionary of Hungarian]. Budapest: Akadémiai Kiadó.

Pesetsky, D. (1997) Optimality Theory and syntax: movement and pronunciation. In D. Archangeli and D. T. Langendoen (eds.) *Optimality Theory, an overview* 134–70. London: Blackwell Publishers.

Prince, A. S. and P. Smolensky (1993) Optimality Theory. Constraint interaction in generative grammar. Technical Report #2, Rutgers University Center for Cognitive Science. ROA 537; Published in 2004 by Blackwell Publishers).

Raffelsiefen, R. (2004) Absolute ill-formedness and other morphophonological effects. *Phonology* 21: 91–142.

Raffelsiefen, R. (2005) Paradigm uniformity effects versus domain effects. In L. Downing, T. Hall, and R. Raffelsiefen (eds.) *Paradigms in phonological theory* 372–454. Oxford: Oxford University Press.

Rebrus, P. and M. Törkenczy (2005) Uniformity and contrast in the Hungarian verbal paradigm. In L. Downing, T. Hall, and R. Raffelsiefen (eds.) *Paradigms in phonological theory* 455–514. Oxford: Oxford University Press.

Rice, C. (2003) Dialectal variation in Norwegian imperatives. *Nordlyd* 31(2): 372–84.

Rice, C. (2005) Optimal gaps in optimal paradigms. *Catalan Journal of Linguistics* 4, 155–70. Special issue on *Morphology in Phonology*, edited by Maria-Rosa Lloret and Jesus Jimenez.

Rice, C. (2007) Gaps and repairs at the phonology-morphology interface. *Journal of Linguistics* 43(1): 197–221.

Rice, C. and P. Svenonius (1998) Prosodic V2 in Northern Norwegian. Ms., University of Tromsø.

Törkenczy, M. (2002) Absolute phonological ungrammaticality in output-biased phonology. In I. Kenesi and P. Síptar (eds.) *Approaches to Hungarian, vol 8. Papers from the Budapest Conference* 311–24. Budapest: Akadémiai Kiadó.

Part I

Architecture

2 Less than zero: correspondence and the null output

Matthew Wolf and John J. McCarthy
University of Massachusetts Amherst

1   Introduction

A central property of Optimality Theory is *competition* (Prince and Smolensky 2004). GEN associates an array of candidate output forms with each input, and these candidates compete against one another. EVAL chooses the winner of this competition, the candidate that satisfies the constraint hierarchy of the language in question better than any other candidate.

But what if some input has no output? What candidate is the winner of the competition? In phonology, this problem arises primarily in paradigmatic gaps. In a paradigmatic gap, some combination of morphemes in the input is ruled absolutely ungrammatical for apparently phonological reasons, leaving a hole in the paradigm that is filled by periphrasis, suppletion, or allomorphy. Absolute ungrammaticality requires, or so it seems, that *all* candidates be ruled out. But this is at odds with the fundamental assumption in OT that all constraints are in principle violable: for any input, one of the candidates supplied by GEN will violate the constraints less seriously than the others, and hence will win. No candidate does so badly that it cannot win except insofar as some other candidate does less badly. Therefore, it is impossible for all candidates to be eliminated from contention, which is what seems to happen when there is a gap.

Prince and Smolensky (2004: 57ff.) propose a solution to this problem: the gap is itself a candidate for every input. Under the appropriate conditions, the gap will be able to win like other candidates. The gap candidate — which they refer to as the *null parse* — is taken to violate only a single constraint, named MPARSE. If the null parse violates no other constraints, any constraint C ranked above MPARSE is effectively inviolable, since any candidate that violates it will lose to the null parse, as shown in (1). Legendre, Smolensky, and Wilson (1998: 257, fn. 9) term this effect of MPARSE a *harmony threshold*: MPARSE is able to set a standard that any viable candidate has to satisfy, so constraints ranked higher than

MPARSE are de facto inviolable. (Throughout, we will represent the null parse with the symbol ⊙. For the comparative tableau format, see Prince (2002). The integers are tallies of violation marks, and W or L indicates whether a constraint favors the winner or a loser.)

(1)   MPARSE harmony threshold

	/in/	C	MPARSE
☞	⊙		1
	out	W_1	L

Our primary goal in this chapter is to rationalize the properties of the null parse or *null output*, as we will refer to it. In particular, how is it possible for this candidate to violate only MPARSE and satisfy all faithfulness and markedness constraints? In section 3, we will argue for a revision of the theory of correspondence (McCarthy and Prince 1995, 1999) from which the null output's faithfulness status follows automatically, and we will also show why the null output violates no markedness constraints. But first we will look at some general properties of the gap phenomenon and some preconditions for an adequate theory of MPARSE.

2   On gaps

The MPARSE model was in some ways anticipated in work on gaps by Hetzron (1975), Iverson (1981), and Iverson and Sanders (1982). Their observations can be summarized as this: some languages have phonological processes that are exceptionless in attested surface forms, and crucially any forms that appropriately condition these processes but fail to undergo them lack any surface realization (rather than simply being exceptions to the process and surfacing without having undergone it). Put somewhat differently, these are cases where some phonologically ill-formed configuration Γ is always eliminated on the surface, and where the phonological process that normally eliminates Γ is disallowed for some defined class of words, forcing the grammar to resort to outright gaps in order to maintain the surface absence of Γ. In OT terms, this situation involves rankings in which some markedness constraint, as well as the conflicting faithfulness constraints, all dominate MPARSE. Retaining the marked structure or making the changes that could eliminate it would both result in more serious violation profiles than having a gap in the paradigm, and so the gap wins.

A particularly fine example comes from Rice (2003, 2005a, 2005b). In Norwegian, the imperative is normally identical to the infinitive, except that the imperative lacks the suffix [-ə]. But verb roots ending in a rising-sonority cluster have no imperative (compare (2) with (3)). The bare root *[åpn] is unpronounceable because of its final cluster, and obvious alternatives like epenthetic *[åpən] are ruled out for most speakers. Hence, those speakers have no imperative of 'open', and so they must resort to circumlocution when they wish to convey this meaning.

(2)   Norwegian imperatives
        å spise   'to eat'   spis!   'eat!'
        å snakke   'to talk'   snakk!   'talk!'
        å løfte   'to lift'   loft   'lift'

(3)   Norwegian imperative gaps
        å åpne   'to open'   *gap*   'open!'
        å paddle   'to paddle'   *gap*   'paddle!'
        å sykle   'to bicycle' *gap*   'bicycle!'

In Rice's analysis, the constraint SONSEQ rules out faithful *[åpn] as the surface realization of the imperative, and faithfulness constraints like DEP prohibit alternatives like *[åpən]. These constraints must dominate MPARSE, as shown in (4). Because retaining or eliminating marked structure would each violate constraints ranked above MPARSE, the MPARSE-violating candidate — that is, the gap — is optimal. Other constraints, also ranked above MPARSE, rule out other imaginable nongapped outcomes, such as obstruentization or deletion of /n/.

(4)   SONSEQ, DEP ≫ MPARSE in Norwegian

	/åpn/	SONSEQ	DEP	MPARSE
	⊙			1
a.	åpn	W1		L
b.	åpən		W1	L

This example illustrates some of the principal properties of the gap phenomenon, properties that any theory of gaps must accommodate. Gaps are typically observed in inflectional paradigms (Rice 2005a, 2005b). As Iverson (1981) points out, derivational processes of the sort discussed by Halle (1973) can independently exhibit significant degrees of idiosyncrasy that often cannot be explained in phonological terms. For example, the adjective *callous* does not take the suffix *-ity* in English, and our understanding of this fact is not significantly advanced by analysis in terms similar to the account of Norwegian imperatives. Formal gaps are also unnecessary in describing restrictions on phonotactics, segmental inventories, and the like. Phonotactic ill-formedness is more typically attributed to neutralizing mappings in which the prohibited structures merge with some other structure that is surface-licit. For instance, it is not necessary that /bnɪk/ map to the null ouput in English; absent alternations, the non-existence of [bnɪk] can as well be accounted for by mapping /bnɪk/ to, say, [nɪk].

Nonetheless, various researchers have used the null output in analyses of derivational gaps (Raffelsiefen 2004) and phonotactic gaps (Prince and Smolensky 2004: 57). Since we will pursue a model in which the null output is among the candidates produced by GEN for *every* input, even monomorphemic ones, mapping to the null output is always one option for the analyst or learner who needs to account for the failure of some known input to surface faithfully. Still, the point remains that it is inflectional gaps that most clearly show the *need* for the null output as candidate. For other examples of phonologically-conditioned gaps in inflectional paradigms, see: Hetzron (1975), Iverson (1981), and Rebrus and Törkenczy (this volume) on Hungarian verbs without jussive forms; Eliasson (1975) and Iverson (1981) on Swedish adjectives without singular neuter forms; Steriade (1988: 112–113) and McCarthy and Prince (1993b: 143–144) on Sanskrit verbs without reduplicated intensives; and Halle (1973), Hetzron (1975), and Iverson (1981) on Russian verbs without first person singular nonpast forms.

The Norwegian example also illustrates an important characteristic of the null output that we have noted previously: it satisfies all markedness and faithfulness constraints. We will examine the markedness properties of the null output below in section 4.2; for now, we will focus on its faithfulness properties. Clearly, the null output must obey DEP, since otherwise in (4) it would lose to candidate (b), which is non-null and violates DEP. An important but less obvious point is the difference between the null output and deletion. Among the candidates supplied by GEN is one in which every segment has mapped to zero. This candidate, which can be symbolized by Φ, violates the anti-deletion constraint MAX once for each segment in the input. Φ is usually non-viable. Φ is non-viable because a candidate with less deletion is more harmonic. For example, in a language that is like Norwegian except that DEP dominates MAX, SONSEQ could in principle be satisfied by mapping /åpn/ to [åp] or to Φ. But since [åp] incurs one MAX violation to Φ's three, Φ is clearly a non-starter.

This point about Φ's usual loser status means that Φ and $\odot$ cannot be the same thing, because then $\odot$ would never win. The challenge is to define the null output $\odot$ in such a way that it is distinct from the candidate that has deleted all of the underlying segments Φ. The foundation is laid in the next section, and then the null output is defined — and the challenge addressed — in section 3.

3   String correspondence and faithfulness

3.1   The nature of candidates

In the McCarthy and Prince (1995, 1999) version of correspondence theory, correspondence is defined as a relation $\Re$ between the segments of an input string i and the segments of an output string o. Requiring that $\Re$ be a relation says very little about $\Re$, since 'relation' is a very general concept. Tighter restrictions on $\Re$ are left up to ranked, violable constraints. For example, the constraint INTEGRITY is violated by one-to-many mappings from input to output (e.g., diphthongization), so INTEGRITY is equivalent to saying that $\Re$ must be a function from i to o. The constraint UNIFORMITY is violated by coalescence processes, in which multiple input segments map to a single output segment. UNIFORMITY is therefore equivalent to saying that $\Re$ is one-to-one from i to o or that its inverse $\Re^{-1}$ is a function from o to i. In deletion, $\Re$ is a partial relation from i to o. Thus, the anti-deletion constraint MAX is equivalent to saying that $\Re$ is a total relation from i to o. In epenthesis, $\Re$ is not onto o, or, equivalently, $\Re^{-1}$ is a partial relation from o to i. Hence, the anti-epenthesis constraint DEP is equivalent to saying that $\Re$ is a relation from i onto o. If all of the aforementioned faithfulness constraints are obeyed, then $\Re$ is a total bijective (i.e., one-to-one and onto) function from i to o.

Our proposal alters these original assumptions about $\Re$. Faithfulness constraints no longer have responsibility for ensuring that $\Re$ is a total bijective function; instead, we leave that up to MPARSE (see section 4). Except for the null output, then, $\Re$ is a total bijective function in all candidates, even candidates with deletion, epenthesis, coalescence, and diphthongization.[1] The faithfulness constraints are redefined accordingly.

---

[1]This is not quite true. As we will see in section 4.3, there are other candidates besides the null output in which $\Re$ is not a total bijective function and in which MPARSE is violated. We will demonstrate, however, that all such candidates are harmonically bounded by $\odot$.

Deletion and epenthesis, which in the old model require $\mathfrak{R}$ or $\mathfrak{R}^{-1}$ to be a partial relation, will now involve mappings between segments and *e*, the identity element under concatenation. We implement this idea by using the notion of a *concatenative decomposition* of a string, which is defined in McCarthy and Prince (1993a). Instead of a relation between the literal input string *i* and some literal output string *o*, as in the earlier theory of correspondence, $\mathfrak{R}$ is now to be understood as a relation between concatenative decompositions of *i* and of *o*, which will be notated as $\langle i \rangle$ and $\langle o \rangle$, respectively.

Concatenative decomposition is defined and explained as follows:

> Dfn. Concatenative Decomposition.
> A concatenative decomposition of a string S is a *sequence* of strings $\langle d_i \rangle_{j \leq i \leq k}$ such that $d_j \frown \ldots \frown d_k = S$.

The concatenative decompositions of a given string are numerous indeed, because any of the d_i may correspond to the empty string *e*, which has the property that $s \frown e = e \frown s = s$, for any string *s*. Compare the role of 0 in addition: $3 + 0 = 0 + 3 = 0 + 3 + 0 = 3$. All these refer to the same number, but all are distinct as expressions. The notion 'concatenative decomposition' allows us to distinguish among the different ways of expressing a string as a sequence of binary concatenations. (McCarthy and Prince 1993a: 89–90)

For example, among the concatenative decompositions of the string *ABC* are the sequences of strings listed in (5).

(5)   Some concatenative decompositions of *ABC*
        $\langle ABC \rangle$
        $\langle e, ABC, e, e \rangle$
        $\langle A, B, C \rangle$
        $\langle AB, C \rangle$
        $\langle A, BC \rangle$
        $\langle A, e, BC \rangle$
        $\langle A, e, B, e, C \rangle$
        $\langle e, ABC \rangle$
        $\ldots$

A concatenative decomposition of a string is a sequence of strings. Because $\mathfrak{R}$ is a relation between concatenative decompositions of strings, $\mathfrak{R}$ maps strings to strings rather than segments to segments. Thus, the new proposal can be referred to as *string correspondence*, to contrast it with the McCarthy and Prince (1995, 1999) version, with its *segmental correspon-*

dence. The difference becomes clear once we look at some of the unfaithful mappings that languages may permit under string correspondence. The hypothetical examples in (6) are representative. In deletion (b) or epenthesis (c), $\Re$ includes a mapping between a monosegmental string and the null string, which we write as # to avoid confounding the more usual notation *e* with phonetic transcriptions. In coalescence (d) or diphthongization (e), $\Re$ includes a mapping between a bisegmental string and a monosegmental string.

(6)   Some unfaithful mappings under string correspondence[2]

     a. Faithful

         $\langle i \rangle = \langle a, p, i \rangle$ /api/

         $\langle o \rangle = \langle a, p, i \rangle$ [api]

         $\Re = \{(a, a), (p, p), (i, i)\}$

     b. Deletion

         $\langle i \rangle = \langle a, p, i \rangle$ /api/

         $\langle o \rangle = \langle \#, p, i \rangle$ [pi]

         $\Re = \{(a, \#), (p, p), (i, i)\}$

     c. Epenthesis

         $\langle i \rangle = \langle \#, a, p, i \rangle$ /api/

         $\langle o \rangle = \langle ʔ, a, p, i \rangle$ [ʔapi]

         $\Re = \{(\#, ʔ), (a, a), (p, p), (i, i)\}$

     d. Coalescence

         $\langle i \rangle = \langle p, an \rangle$ /pan/

         $\langle o \rangle = \langle p, ã \rangle$ [pã]

         $\Re = \{(p, p), (an, ã)\}$

     e. Diphthongization

         $\langle i \rangle = \langle p, ã \rangle$ /pã/

         $\langle o \rangle = \langle p, an \rangle$ [pan]

         $\Re = \{(p, p), (ã, an)\}$

In (6), the correspondence relation $\Re$ is stated explicitly, but this is not usually necessary because $\Re$ is often obvious from inspection of the $\langle i \rangle$ and $\langle o \rangle$ pair. In candidates that obey MPARSE, $\Re$ is a total bijective function: every string in $\langle i \rangle$ has a unique correspondent in $\langle o \rangle$, and every string in $\langle o \rangle$ has a unique correspondent in $\langle i \rangle$. Except for metathesis, in MPARSE-obeying candidates the *k*th string in $\langle i \rangle$ is in correspondence with the *k*th string in $\langle o \rangle$ for all $1 \leq k \leq n$, where *n* is the cardinality of both $\langle i \rangle$ and $\langle o \rangle$. In metathetic candidates, the cardinalities of $\langle i \rangle$ and $\langle o \rangle$ are also identical, but corresponding strings do not occupy identical positions in the concatenative decompositions.

---

[2]In (6) and elsewhere, we omit indices on corresponding strings unless they are necessary for disambiguation.

To sum up the proposal, a candidate for the input i consists of an ordered 4-tuple $(o, \langle i \rangle, \langle o \rangle, \mathfrak{R}(\langle i \rangle) \to \langle o \rangle)$. The output o is evaluated by markedness constraints, as usual. The concatenative decompositions $\langle i \rangle$ and $\langle o \rangle$, together with the correspondence relation $\mathfrak{R}(\langle i \rangle) \to \langle o \rangle$, are consulted by faithfulness constraints. All of the elements of the candidate are freely assigned by GEN, subject of course to the proviso that $\langle i \rangle$ and $\langle o \rangle$ must be possible concatenative decompositions of i and o. $\mathfrak{R}(\langle i \rangle) \to \langle o \rangle$ (usually referred to as just $\mathfrak{R}$) is any relation from $\langle i \rangle$ to $\langle o \rangle$ — that is, it is any subset of the Cartesian product $\{\langle i \rangle\} X \{\langle o \rangle\}$, letting $\{\langle x \rangle\}$ stand for the set of strings in the sequence $\langle x \rangle$. Among the subsets of $\{\langle i \rangle\} X \{\langle o \rangle\}$ is of course the null set $\varnothing$.

3.2   The faithfulness constraints

Since $\mathfrak{R}$ is different in string correspondence than in segmental correspondence, the faithfulness constraints need to be redefined.

The faithfulness constraint MAX militates against configurations in which any string in $\langle i \rangle$ maps to a null string in $\langle o \rangle$. If it is to duplicate the effects of MAX in segmental correspondence, the string-correspondence version of MAX must assign a mark for every segment in an input string if that input string's output correspondent is the null string, #. The new definition of MAX appears in (7), and an example of a MAX-violating candidate is given in (8).

(7)   MAX (new version)
        Given a candidate $(o, \langle i \rangle, \langle o \rangle, \mathfrak{R})$,
                for every string κ in $\langle i \rangle$ where $\mathfrak{R}(\kappa) = \#$
                        for every segment in κ
                                assign a violation mark.

(8)   MAX violation in Lardil /ŋawuŋawu/ → [ŋawuŋa] 'termite'
        $\langle i \rangle = \langle$ ŋ, a, w, u, ŋ, a, w, u $\rangle$
        $\langle o \rangle = \langle$ ŋ, a, w, u, ŋ, a, #, # $\rangle$
        $\mathfrak{R} = \{($ŋ$_1$, ŋ$_1$), (a$_2$, a$_2$), (w$_3$, w$_3$), (u$_4$, u$_4$), (ŋ$_5$, ŋ$_5$), (a$_6$, a$_6$), (w$_7$, #$_7$), (u$_8$, #$_8$)$\}$

The definition of DEP is similar, but it uses $\mathfrak{R}$'s inverse, $\mathfrak{R}^{-1}$. Since $\mathfrak{R}$ is a bijective total function in all MPARSE-obeying candidates, $\mathfrak{R}^{-1}$ is also a bijective total function in those candidates. The new definition of DEP appears in (9), and an example of a DEP-violating candidate is given in (10).

(9)   DEP (new version)
        Given a candidate $(o, \langle i \rangle, \langle o \rangle, \Re)$,

        for every string κ in $\langle o \rangle$ where $\Re^{-1}(\kappa) = \#$
            for every segment in κ
                assign a violation mark.

(10)   DEP violation in /kaŋ/ → [kaŋka] 'speech'
        $\langle i \rangle = \langle k, a, ŋ, \#, \# \rangle$
        $\langle o \rangle = \langle k, a, ŋ, k, a \rangle$
        $\Re = \{(k_1, k_1), (a_2, a_2), (ŋ_3, ŋ_3), (\#_4, k_4), (\#_5, a_5)\}$

The constraint UNIFORMITY (UNIF) exists primarily to regulate segmental coalescence. In segmental correspondence, coalescence is the mapping of two input segments to a single output segment, usually preserving some of the features of each parent segment: $/p_1 a_2 n_3/ →$ [$p_1 ã_{2,3}$]. Under string correspondence, $\Re$ is always one-to-one in MPARSE-obeying candidates. Coalescence must therefore be analyzed as correspondence between a bisegmental string in $\langle i \rangle$ and a monosegmental string in $\langle o \rangle$, as in (12). The definition of UNIFORMITY, which is given in (11), need not be so specific; in fact, it is useful if UNIFORMITY militates against all strings in $\langle i \rangle$ that are longer than a single segment, without even mentioning $\langle o \rangle$:

(11)   UNIFORMITY (new version)
        Given a candidate $(o, \langle i \rangle, \langle o \rangle, \Re)$,

        for every string κ in $\langle i \rangle$
            for every pair of segments in κ
                assign a violation mark.

(12)   UNIFORMITY violation in /pan/ → [pã]
        $\langle i \rangle = \langle p, an \rangle$
        $\langle o \rangle = \langle p, ã \rangle$
        $\Re = \{(p_1, p_1), (an_2, ã_2)\}$

The constraint INTEGRITY (INT) is violated by diphthongization or breaking — that is, it is violated by mappings in which a single input segment maps to two output segments, as in (14). INTEGRITY, defined in (13), is the dual of UNIFORMITY in the same way that DEP is the dual of MAX.

(13)   INTEGRITY (new version)
        Given a candidate $(o, \langle i \rangle, \langle o \rangle, \Re)$,

        for every string κ in $\langle o \rangle$
            for every pair of segments in κ
                assign a violation mark.

(14) INTEGRITY violation in $/\text{p}\tilde{\text{a}}/ \rightarrow [\text{pan}]$
$\langle i \rangle = \langle \text{p}, \tilde{\text{a}} \rangle$
$\langle o \rangle = \langle \text{p}, \text{an} \rangle$
$\mathfrak{R} = \{(\text{p}_1, \text{p}_1), (\tilde{\text{a}}_2, \text{an}_2)\}$

The string-based approach to coalescence and breaking is very different from the approach taken in segmental correspondence theory, and hence it makes different empirical predictions. In string correspondence, coalescence is necessarily local in the sense that it cannot affect two nonadjacent input segments without also affecting any segment(s) intervening between them. Likewise, breaking cannot produce two nonadjacent output segments without also producing any segment(s) intervening between them. In the segmental correspondence model, on the other hand, coalescence and breaking need not be local in this sense. For instance, the mapping $/\text{p}_1\text{a}_2\text{t}_3\text{n}_4/ \rightarrow [\text{p}_1\tilde{\text{a}}_{2,4}\text{t}_3]$ represents nonlocal coalescence and $/\text{a}_1\text{p}_2\tilde{\text{a}}_3\text{t}_4/ \rightarrow [\text{n}_3\text{a}_1\text{p}_2\text{a}_3\text{t}_4]$ represents nonlocal breaking.

To our knowledge, there are no clear examples of nonlocal coalescence or breaking, so the additional descriptive power of segmental correspondence appears to be unnecessary. This power has been used in two more controversial cases, however. De Lacy (1999) proposes that morphological haplology involves merger of segments that need not be (and typically are not) adjacent, such as French $/\text{d}_1\text{e}_2\text{i}_3\text{k}_4\text{s}_5\text{i}_6\text{s}_7\text{-i}_8\text{s}_9\text{t}_{10}/ \rightarrow [\text{d}_1\text{e}_2\text{i}_3\text{k}_4\text{s}_5\text{i}_{6,8}\text{s}_{7,9}\text{t}_{10}]$ 'deixis+ist'. De Lacy and Kitto (1999) propose that in copy-vowel epenthesis a single input segment has two output correspondents that need not be adjacent, such as Selayarese $/\text{p}_1\text{o}_2\text{t}_3\text{o}_4\text{l}_5/ \rightarrow [\text{p}_1\text{o}_2\text{t}_3\text{o}_4\text{l}_5\text{o}_4]$ 'pencil'. There are alternative theories of both phenomena, and pretty good reasons to think that those alternatives are right (Kawahara 2004, 2006, Kurisu 2001, Plag 1998, Russell 1995). Absent solid examples of nonlocal phonological coalescence or true nonlocal diphthongization, it would seem that string correspondence has the upper hand empirically.

In segmental correspondence, the anti-metathesis constraint LINEARITY bans changing the linear order of pairs of correspondent segments. Under string correspondence, the natural move is to define it as in (15), so that it forbids changing the sequencing of strings in the $\langle i \rangle \rightarrow \langle o \rangle$ mapping. The correspondence relation of a LINEARITY violator may be fully faithful, as in (16), but the ordering discrepancy between $\langle i \rangle$ and $\langle o \rangle$ is what triggers the violation. (On reordering of segments *within* corresponding strings, see the next section.)

(15)   LINEARITY (new version)
         Given a candidate $(o, \langle i \rangle, \langle o \rangle, \Re)$,

> For every pair of strings κ_1, κ_2 in $\langle i \rangle$,
>> Assign one violation mark if κ_1 precedes κ_2 but $\Re(\kappa_2)$ precedes $\Re(\kappa_1)$.

(16)   LINEARITY violation in /pra/ $\rightarrow$ [par]
         $\langle i \rangle = \langle p, r, a \rangle$
         $\langle o \rangle = \langle p, a, r \rangle$
         $\Re = \{(p_1, p_1), (r_2, r_2) (a_3, a_3)\}$

Finally, the constraint IDENT must be revised to reflect the differences between string-based and segmental correspondence. Four situations can be identified that the reformulation will need to address:

(i)   Correspondence between a monosegmental string in $\langle i \rangle$ and a monosegmental string in $\langle o \rangle$. In this case, IDENT is unremarkable; it requires featural identity between the unique segment in each string.

(ii)   Correspondence between a monosegmental (or longer) string and the null string #. In earlier, segmental correspondence, IDENT is defined in such a way that it is not violated in segmental deletion and epenthesis (though MAX- and DEP-feature constraints have been proposed as an alternative; see, for example, Causley (1997) and Lombardi (1998)). If this assumption is to be maintained under string correspondence, then segmental strings corresponding with # should not violate the reformulated IDENT constraint.

(iii)   Coalescence and diphthongization, in which a bisegmental (or longer) string stands in correspondence with a monosegmental string. In segmental correspondence, IDENT requires that each segment be featurally identical to all of its correspondents, with the ranking of various IDENT constraints determining which feature values are treated faithfully in coalescence and diphthongization.

(iv)   Correspondence between bisegmental or longer strings in both $\langle i \rangle$ and $\langle o \rangle$, such as $\langle i \rangle = \langle pat \rangle$ and $\langle o \rangle = \langle pat \rangle$. Since the same results can be achieved with correspondence between monosegmental strings, it would be preferable if candidates like this were harmonically bounded, so as to avoid pointless and confounding analytic ambiguities.

The definition in (17) is intended to cover all of these situations. If, say, a bisegmental string in $\langle i \rangle$ maps to a monosegmental string in $\langle o \rangle$, as in the coalescent mapping $\langle p, an \rangle \rightarrow \langle p, \tilde{a} \rangle$, then each of the segment pairs (a, $\tilde{a}$) and (n, $\tilde{a}$) is required to be featurally identical in every respect, exactly as the earlier version of IDENT worked. Mappings to or from the null string # do not violate IDENT because # contains no segments and therefore no feature values. Candidates that put two multisegmental strings into correspondence, such as ⟨pat⟩ → ⟨pat⟩ or ⟨pan⟩ → ⟨pã⟩, incur pointless violations of IDENT constraints. The mapping ⟨pat⟩ → ⟨pat⟩, for example, violates an IDENT constraint for every disagreeing feature value in the pairs (p, a), (p, t), (a, p), (a, t), (t, p), and (t, a). Since the map ⟨p, a, t⟩ → ⟨p, a, t⟩ produces the same result without these IDENT violations or any UNIFORMITY and INTEGRITY violations either, ⟨pat⟩ → ⟨pat⟩ is harmonically bounded by ⟨p, a, t⟩ → ⟨p, a, t⟩. Hence, there is no ambiguity in the faithful mapping.

(17)   IDENT(αF) (new version)
        Given a candidate (o, ⟨i⟩, ⟨o⟩, $\mathfrak{R}$),

> for every string κ in ⟨i⟩, where $\kappa = \kappa_1 \ldots \kappa_n$ and $\mathfrak{R}(\kappa) = \lambda = \lambda_1 \ldots \lambda_m$,
>> assign one violation mark for every pair (κ_p, λ_q) ($1 \leq p \leq n$, $1 \leq q \leq m$) where κ_p is [αF] and λ_q is [-αF].

IDENT constraints are typically associated with theories of representation in which features are attributes of segments but not representational entities in their own right. A natural question to ask is whether string correspondence can accommodate faithfulness to autosegmental representations, in which features are distinct representational primes and can bear correspondence relations of their own. Superficially, it might appear that string correspondence, dependent as it is on breaking the input and output into a sequence of linearly consecutive substrings, cannot handle faithfulness to nonlinear structure.

On closer inspection, however, such worries prove to be unfounded. In autosegmental theories, the representational primes (features, tones, class nodes, etc.) are regarded as occupying one of a number of tiers, with relations of adjacency and linear precedence defined between pairs of elements on each tier, but not between pairs of elements on different tiers. This means that a nonlinear representation can be regarded as a set of strings — the tiers — with indices pointing from the elements of one string to the elements of another — the association lines. (For much more extensive formal development along the same general lines, see Hayes (1990), Kornai (1994) and Pierrehumbert and Beckman (1988).) For example, the standard feature-geometric representation in (18) is equivalent to (19). The first subscript on each element in (19) is that element's unique index and the second subscript is a (possibly empty) set of indices on the tier to which that element is associated. (The root nodes are shown with empty sets of associations because no further structure is depicted and not for some deeper reason.)

(18)   Autosegmental representations as coindexed strings.

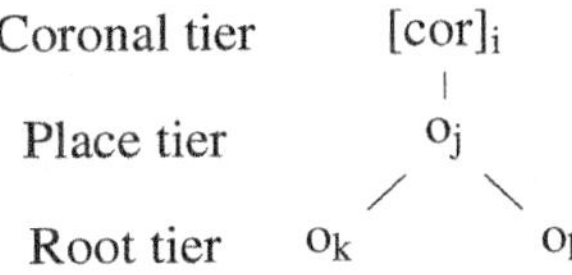

(19)   Example (18) as a set of tiers $\{[\text{cor}]_{i,\{j\}},\ \text{Place}_{j,\{k,\,l\}},\ \text{Root}_{k,\{\}}\ \text{Root}_{l,\{\}}\}$

Once the equivalence between (18) and (19) is recognized, it becomes clear how nonlinear representations can be handled in string correspondence. The input i and output o may be regarded, in a theory with such representations, as consisting of not a single string but as a set of strings, each of which contains all of the structural elements occupying one of the prosodic or autosegmental tiers. Accordingly, $\langle i \rangle$ and $\langle o \rangle$ can be regarded not as concatenative decompositions of a single string, but rather as *sets* of contatenative decompositions, one for each tier, since each tier is a string. Tier-specific faithfulness constraints like $\text{MAX}(\mu)$, DEP(high tone), or MAX(coronal) can then be straightforwardly defined on the appropriate tier-specific concatenative decompositions.

Faithfulness to autosegmental associations can also be defined on these representations, but it is not strictly necessary. We have already defined $\text{IDENT}(F)$ in (17). Spreading is just violation of $\text{IDENT}(F)$ without concomitant violation of $\text{DEP}(F)$ — a segment gains a feature specification, but no feature token is added to the representation. Similarly, delinking is violation of $\text{IDENT}(F)$ without concomitant violation of $\text{MAX}(F)$ — a segment loses a feature specification, but no feature token is removed from the representation. If this approach to spreading and delinking should prove insufficient, we already have the tools in hand to develop a more sophisticated approach within the overall assumptions of string correspondence. For ease of illustration, we will continue for the remainder of this chapter to refer only to strings of segments in our examples, but we emphasize that this is strictly an expository and not a theoretical choice; as we have just argued, string correspondence is entirely compatible with the use of nonlinear representations.

3.3   Harmonic bounding relationships, part I

Harmonically bounded candidates can never win under any permutation of the universal constraint set CON; they are perpetual losers. In the simplest case, one candidate harmonically bounds another by virtue of having a proper subset of the bounded candidate's violation marks. Here and in section 4.3, we show that our proposal entails harmonic bounding of various candidates that would otherwise present problematic ambiguities or typological impossibilities.

In principle, two candidates can have the same input i and output o, but different concatenative decompositions $\langle i \rangle$ and $\langle o \rangle$ and different correspondence relations $\mathfrak{R}$. For instance, instead of the $\langle i \rangle$, $\langle o \rangle$, and $\mathfrak{R}$ in (8), the Lardil mapping /ŋawuŋawu/ → [ŋawuŋa] could be obtained, or so it seems, with the $\langle i \rangle$, $\langle o \rangle$, and $\mathfrak{R}$ in (20). In (8), the monosegmental strings /w/ and /u/ each map individually to #, while in (20) the bisegmental string /wu/ maps to #. The concern, naturally, is that the revised theory has introduced a formal ambiguity: how do learners (or analysts) know whether the correct analysis is the one in (8) or the one in (20)?

(20)   Lardil /ŋawuŋawu/ → [ŋawuŋa] revisited
       $\langle i \rangle = \langle$ŋ, a, w, u, ŋ, a, wu$\rangle$
       $\langle o \rangle = \langle$ŋ, a, w, u, ŋ, a, #$\rangle$
       $\mathfrak{R} = \{$(ŋ$_1$, ŋ$_1$), (a$_2$, a$_2$), (w$_3$, w$_3$), (u$_4$, u$_4$), (ŋ$_5$, ŋ$_5$), (a$_6$, a$_6$), (wu$_7$, #)$\}$

In reality, there is no ambiguity because (8) harmonically bounds (20), so (20) cannot win over (8) under any permutation of the constraints in CON. These two candidates are juxtaposed in (21) for ease of comparison. Both candidates have the same output o, so they have identical markedness violations. Both candidates violate MAX exactly twice, since MAX counts the number of segments in any string in $\langle i \rangle$ that maps to # in $\langle o \rangle$. But candidate (b) also violates UNIFORMITY, which prohibits multisegmental strings in $\langle i \rangle$. Since (a) has no violations that are not shared with (b), and since (b) has a violation that is not shared with (a), (b) is harmonically bounded by (a). There is no ambiguity for learners to unravel, since (b) is not even among the contenders for optimality.

(21)   Harmonic bounding of (20) (=b) by (8) (=a)
       a. $\langle i \rangle = \langle$ŋ, a, w, u, ŋ, a, w, u$\rangle$
             $\langle o \rangle = \langle$ŋ, a, w, u, ŋ, a, #, #$\rangle$
             $\mathfrak{R} = \{$(ŋ$_1$, ŋ$_1$), (a$_2$, a$_2$), (w$_3$, w$_3$), (u$_4$, u$_4$), (ŋ$_5$, ŋ$_5$), (a$_6$, a$_6$), (w$_7$, #$_7$), (u$_8$, #$_8$)$\}$

b.   ⟨i⟩ = ⟨ŋ, a, w, u, ŋ, a, wu⟩
⟨o⟩ = ⟨ŋ, a, w, u, ŋ, a, #⟩
ℜ = {(ŋ₁, ŋ₁), (a₂, a₂), (w₃, w₃), (u₄, u₄), (ŋ₅, ŋ₅), (a₆, a₆), (wu₇, #₇)}

Harmonic bounding of (b) by (a) is surely a desirable result; when bisegmental or longer strings delete, learners should not be forced to choose between two paths to the same end. Harmonic bounding of candidates like (b) ensures that there is no ambiguity: even when several adjacent segments are deleted, the winning candidate maps from a sequence of monosegmental strings to a sequence of instances of #; mapping from a bisegmental or longer string to a single instance of # is never possible.

For a similar reason, candidate (a) in (22) harmonically bounds candidate (b). Both of these candidates violate DEP twice. Furthermore, candidate (b) also violates INTEGRITY. Since they are otherwise identical, (a) harmonically bounds (b). This too is a desirable result; when bisegmental or longer sequences are epenthesized, learners should not be forced to choose among two paths to the same end. Harmonic bounding of candidates like (b) ensures that there is no ambiguity: even when several adjacent segments are epenthesized, the winning candidate maps from instances of # to a succession of monosegmental strings and never from a single # to a bisegmental or longer string.

(22)   Lardil /kaŋ/ → [kaŋka] revisited
a.   ⟨i⟩ = ⟨k, a, ŋ, #, #⟩
⟨o⟩ = ⟨k, a, ŋ, k, a⟩
ℜ = {(k₁, k₁), (a₂, a₂), (ŋ₃, ŋ₃), (#₄, k₄), (#₅, a₅)}
b.   ⟨i⟩ = ⟨k, a, ŋ, #⟩
⟨o⟩ = ⟨k, a, ŋ, ka⟩
ℜ = {(k₁, k₁), (a₂, a₂), (ŋ₃, ŋ₃), (#₄, ka₄)}

Another seeming ambiguity involves metathesis. When two segments metathesize, are monosegmental strings reordered — i.e., ⟨a₁, b₂, c₃⟩ → ⟨a₁, c₃, b₂⟩ — or is there reordering within a multisegmental string — i.e., ⟨a₁, bc₂⟩ → ⟨a₁, cb₂⟩? This question is particularly pressing because LINEARITY as defined in (15) bans reordering of strings but says nothing about string-internal reordering. If ⟨a₁, bc₂⟩ → ⟨a₁, cb₂⟩ were a possible mapping, then it would offer a way of doing metathesis without violating LINEARITY. This would be a problematic result, since it undermines LINEARITY and faithfulness generally.

In reality, there is no ambiguity and no threat to LINEARITY. The mapping $\langle a_1, bc_2 \rangle \rightarrow \langle a_1, cb_2 \rangle$ is harmonically bounded. This mapping violates UNIFORMITY and INTEGRITY, since these constraints prohibit multisegmental strings in $\langle i \rangle$ and $\langle o \rangle$, respectively. Furthermore, this mapping violates all of the IDENT constraints relevant to featural differences in the pairs (b, c) and (c, b). It is harmonically bounded by the mapping $\langle a_1, b_2, c_3 \rangle \rightarrow \langle a_1, c_2, b_3 \rangle$, in which /b/ stands in correspondence with [c] and /c/ with [b]. This candidate has exactly the same IDENT violations incurred by $\langle a_1, bc_2 \rangle \rightarrow \langle a_1, cb_2 \rangle$, but it satisfies UNIFORMITY and INTEGRITY as well as LINEARITY. Since these two candidates have identical markedness violations, as they both represent the output form [acb], the mapping $\langle a_1, bc_2 \rangle \rightarrow \langle a_1, cb_2 \rangle$ has a proper superset of the marks incurred by $\langle a_1, b_2, c_3 \rangle \rightarrow \langle a_1, c_2, b_3 \rangle$, so $\langle a_1, bc_2 \rangle \rightarrow \langle a_1, cb_2 \rangle$ is harmonically bounded. String correspondence thus runs no risk of letting segmental metathesis occur for free.

3.4   Summary

We have proposed a theory of correspondence based on strings rather than segments. The input *i* and the output *o* are represented by their concatenative decompositions $\langle i \rangle$ and $\langle o \rangle$, which consist of sequences of segmental strings rather than sequences of segments. Deletion and epenthesis involve correspondence between monosegmental strings and the null string #, and the constraints MAX and DEP militate against correspondence with #. Coalescence and diphthongization involve correspondence between multisegmental strings and monosegmental strings, and the constraints UNIFORMITY and INTEGRITY militate against multisegmental strings in $\langle i \rangle$ or $\langle o \rangle$. When strings are in correspondence, IDENT requires that all of their constituent segments match pairwise in their featural composition.

The immediate goal of reformulating the faithfulness constraints is to support the proposition that correspondence is a total bijective function from $\langle i \rangle$ to $\langle o \rangle$ even in candidates that are unfaithful by reason of deletion, epenthesis, coalescence, or diphthongization. In segmental correspondence, by contrast, any of these types of unfaithfulness are sufficient to prevent correspondence from being a total bijective function. The larger goal of this reformulation is to identify any departure from a total bijective correspondence function as categorically different from simple unfaithfulness.

One candidate in which $\mathfrak{R}$ fails to be a total bijective function is the null output $\odot$, and in so failing this candidate violates the constraint MPARSE, while satisfying all markedness and faithfulness constraints. Further, the candidate $\odot$ harmonically bounds all other candidates in which $\mathfrak{R}$ is not a total bijective function. In the next section we demonstrate how our theory obtains these results.

4   MPARSE and the null output

4.1   Previous formulations of MPARSE

Prince and Smolensky (2004) suggest two possible means by which the null parse might be defined. One of these is equivalent to what we have been calling Φ: a candidate in which every input segment has been deleted. In terms of their PARSE/FILL model of faithfulness, the null parse would be the candidate that maximally violates PARSE. As we just showed, Φ is problematic: it is unlikely ever to produce paradigmatic gaps, since there will usually be candidates with fewer PARSE violations that equally well satisfy the markedness constraints that motivate the gap.

A more radical and more successful idea is their suggestion that the null output is the result of failure to parse the morphological content of the input into a morphological structure. This candidate violates just a single constraint, the original MPARSE: 'Morphological structure is parsed into constituents.' On this view, the null parse could well still contain phonological structure that is parsed into prosodic constituents (and hence avoid the difficulties faced by Φ) but would be ineffable because it lacks a morphosyntactic category, and hence is unable to participate in syntax or be semantically interpreted. This definition is attractive, since it correctly distinguishes $\odot$ from Φ.

Attributing the violation that the null output $\odot$ incurs to a failure of *morphological* parsing presents other problems, however. First, it is difficult to maintain that all cases of phonologically-conditioned gaps involve a failure in the lexical, word-level phonology, as a morphological interpretation of the null parse would seem to require. The main evidence that gaps are not purely a matter of morphology comes from the observation that the Norwegian imperative gap depends on the phrasal phonological context (section 4.2). Second, even if the null parse is morphologically defective in a way that prevents it from participating as a word in the syntax, it is

unclear why speakers should not be able to produce it as a citation form —
unless the null parse is devoid of surface *phonological* structure as well,
which brings us back to the problem of Φ's nonviable status.

It seems that we will still need a non-stipulative way for the null output $\odot$ to eliminate all input phonological structure without violating the
anti-deletion constraint MAX. McCarthy (2003) moves in this direction by
suggesting in passing that the null output's correspondence relation with
the input is undefined, and that as such it cannot violate any faithfulness
constraints. The next section expands on that idea, while section 6 considers alternative formalizations of Prince and Smolensky's basic insight.

4.2   Defining and using MPARSE

A null output is any candidate that violates MPARSE as defined in (23).

(23)   MPARSE (new version)
        Given a candidate $(o, \langle i \rangle, \langle o \rangle, \Re)$,

            if $\Re$ is not a total bijective function from $\langle i \rangle$ to $\langle o \rangle$,
                assign a violation mark.

The candidate $\odot$ has two related properties: in the $(o, \langle i \rangle, \langle o \rangle, \Re)$
ordered 4-tuple that represents $\odot$, o and its concatenative decomposition
$\langle o \rangle$ are empty, and $\Re$ is undefined for all strings in $\langle i \rangle$ (that is, $\Re = \varnothing$).
Since it is undefined for all strings in $\langle i \rangle$, $\Re$ is the most degenerate type of
partial relation, and so $\odot$ violates MPARSE. An example of $\odot$, the winning
candidate in (4), is given in (24). MPARSE is violated by (24) because $\Re$
is a partial relation from $\langle i \rangle$ to $\langle o \rangle$; indeed, no string in $\langle å, p, n \rangle$ has a
correspondent in $\langle o \rangle$:

(24)   An instance of $\odot$
        $\langle i \rangle = \langle å, p, n \rangle$
        $\langle o \rangle = \langle \ \rangle$
        $\Re = \varnothing$

The discussion of Norwegian in section 2 identified an important characteristic that the null output *qua* candidate must have if it is to suffice
as a theory of paradigmatic gaps: it must satisfy all constraints other than
MPARSE, including the faithfulness constraint MAX. This desideratum for
a theory of the null output is discussed immediately below. Section 4.3
discusses another property of our theory of the null output: there are many

MPARSE-violating candidates in every candidate set, but one of them, $\odot$, harmonically bounds the others. Related topics discussed in that section include the strict categoricality of MPARSE and the effects of having a non-null candidate that nonetheless violates MPARSE.

The candidate $\odot$ violates no faithfulness constraints. Because $\odot$ has no correspondence relations, MAX and all the other faithfulness constraints that mention correspondence relations are vacuously satisfied. Furthermore, INTEGRITY is vacuously satisfied because $\langle o \rangle$ is empty, and UNIFORMITY is satisfied as long as $\langle i \rangle$ contains no multisegmental strings. Thus, the null output represented in (24) satisfies every faithfulness constraint in CON.

A desirable result of string correspondence is that $\odot$ is not the same as the candidate that has deleted all input material. Compare the two candidates in (25). As we noted in section 2, $\odot$ is optimal in paradigmatic gaps, but Φ is rarely if ever optimal — and definitely non-optimal in Norwegian — because some of its MAX violations can usually be avoided while still satisfying all markedness constraints ranked higher than MAX. For this reason, it is important that $\odot$ and Φ be distinct candidates with distinct constraint violations, and they are indeed distinct under string correspondence. Φ violates MAX once for every segment in the input, but it obeys MPARSE, while $\odot$ violates MPARSE but obeys MAX and every other faithfulness constraint in CON.

(25) $\odot$ vs. Φ

    a. $\odot = ([\ ], \langle p_1, a_2, t_3 \rangle, \langle\ \rangle, \varnothing)$
    b. $\Phi = ([\ ], \langle p_1, a_2, t_3 \rangle, \langle \#_1, \#_2, \#_3 \rangle, \{(p_1, \#_1), (a_2, \#_2), (t_3, \#_3)\})$

Furthermore, $\odot$ does not violate any markedness constraints, since it lacks output structure. All markedness constraints either militate against certain structures (e.g., NOCODA: 'there are no codas') or demand that certain structures, if present, have specified properties (e.g. ONSET: 'any syllables have onsets'). Even constraints that seem to require the presence of structure are dependent on the presence of some other structure in order to issue violation marks.[3] For instance, word minimality requirements derive from constraints specifying that every foot must be binary and every phonological word must contain at least one foot. Since $\odot$ lacks even a

---

[3]In general, the highest-scope statement in any markedness constraint is always universal quantification over structures of some type. It is never universal quantification over outputs — no markedness constraint can have the form "$\forall$output$\exists$structure", so no markedness constraint can be violated by the absence of structure. See Gouskova (2003) for related discussion.

phonological-word node, it vacuously satisfies any minimality constraints.

We now have most of the formal tools necessary to analyze the Norwegian imperative gap in terms of string correspondence. In (26), several of the most important candidates are compared with the winner. Candidate (a) is faithful, and it incurs a fatal violation of the markedness constraint SON-SEQ. Candidate (b) has total deletion, and (c) has partial deletion. Either way, high-ranking MAX is violated. The winner is the null output. This candidate satisfies SONSEQ because it has no forbidden tautosyllabic clusters (indeed, no syllables or segments at all), and it satisfies MAX because it places no strings in $\langle i \rangle$ in correspondence with #.

(26)   Norwegian imperative gap with string correspondence

/åpn/	SONSEQ	MAX	MPARSE
☞ ⊙ $\langle i \rangle = \langle å, p, n \rangle$ $\langle o \rangle = \langle \ \rangle$ $\Re = \varnothing$			1
a. åpn $\langle i \rangle = \langle å, p, n \rangle$ $\langle o \rangle = \langle å, p, n \rangle$ $\Re = \{(å, å), (p, p), (n, n)\}$	W$_1$		L
b. Φ $\langle i \rangle = \langle å, p, n \rangle$ $\langle o \rangle = \langle \#, \#, \# \rangle$ $\Re = \{(å, \#), (p, \#), (n, \#)\}$		W$_3$	L
c. åp $\langle i \rangle = \langle å, p, n \rangle$ $\langle o \rangle = \langle å, p, \# \rangle$ $\Re = \{(å, å), (p, p), (n, \#)\}$		W$_1$	L

Tableau (26) shows why deletion is disallowed as a remedy for SON-SEQ-violating clusters. Another logical possibility is epenthesis, producing *[åpən] or *[åpnə]. Interestingly, epenthesis is possible when similar conditions arise in nouns, such as /adl/ → [adəl] 'nobility' (Rice 2005a). This contrast between nouns and imperatives shows that some constraint(s) must have morphologically restricted scope. There are two options to consider: restricting MPARSE or restricting DEP. We will work through both accounts with the aim of showing that the morphological restriction is imposed on DEP and not MPARSE.

A morphologically restricted MPARSE is in the spirit of Rice's (2005b) proposal that the anti-gap constraints require all slots in a paradigm to be filled. (See section 6.1 for further discussion of this theory of gaps.) Suppose that there is a universal set of morphological features, so the set of possible paradigmatic slots is simply the set of morphological feature combinations made possible by UG. For any feature combination, CON would contain an MPARSE constraint that applies when a word bearing those features is submitted as an input to the phonology. In Norwegian, because nouns allow epenthesis, MPARSE$_{\text{NOUN}}$ would be ranked above DEP. But imperatives prefer a gap to epenthesis, so MPARSE$_{\text{Imp}}$ would have to be ranked below DEP.

Difficulties arise when evaluating candidate utterances that contain both a noun and an imperative verb, as will occur in the phrasal phonology. Nouns cannot be gapped because MPARSE$_{\text{NOUN}}$ is undominated. Therefore, the presence of a noun anywhere in the phrase will effectively knock out the null output, and an imperative occurring in the same phrase will not be gapped. Tableau (27) shows the problem; absurdly, the imperative form of /åpn/ is being rescued by the presence of any noun elsewhere in the utterance.

(27)   Unwanted effect of MPARSE$_{\text{NOUN}}$

/…*noun*…åpn…/	MPARSE$_{\text{NOUN}}$	SONSEQ	DEP	MPARSE$_{\text{IMP}}$
…*noun*…åpən…			1	
a. ⊙	W$_1$		L	W$_1$
b. …*noun*…åpn…		W$_1$	L	

This problem with MPARSE$_{\text{Imp}}$ might be avoided by recognizing a separation of word-level and phrase-level phonology. It would not be necessary to go as far as stratal OT, which posits different grammars for words and phrases (see, among many others, Kiparsky 2000); rather, it would suffice to retain the basic idea of Lexical Phonology that the phonological component of the grammar is involved in calculating the contents of the lexicon. At some stage of word-formation, each individual morphosyntactic word would be fed to GEN as an input. If the output of the phonology is ⊙, then no form corresponding to the given set of morphological features would be entered into the lexicon. The syntax therefore would have no access to such items, and so evaluations like (27) could never take place.

Further evidence from Norwegian shows, however, that this approach is incorrect. Norwegian must not have a *lexical* gap for the imperative of verbs like /åpn/, because these imperatives actually occur when the final sonorant can be syllabified as an onset before a following vowel-initial word (Rice 2005a): *Sykl opp bakken* 'Bicycle up the hill!' vs. **Sykl ned bakken* 'Bicycle down the hill!'. This contrast shows that the gap — that is, the victory of the candidate ⊙ — cannot be determined until the phrase-level phonology. We conclude that an analysis with morphologically restricted MPARSE is untenable.

An analysis with morphologically restricted DEP fares much better. Nouns permit epenthesis, but imperatives do not. Therefore, DEP_{IMP} must rank above MPARSE, while DEP_{NOUN} is ranked below MPARSE.[4, 5] The ranking arguments are presented in (28) and (29).

This model has no need to posit a word level phonology that determines the contents of the lexicon. When an utterance would contain both a noun like /adl/ and an imperative verb like /åpn/, the winning candidate is (correctly) the null output (see (30)). But when a following vowel-initial word allows the imperative to be syllabified without epenthesis, there is no gap (see (31)).

The null output is certainly a possible outcome in the phrasal phonology; **Sykl ned bakken* was just cited as an example. More generally, Zec and Inkelas (1990), Golston (1995), and others have argued that phonological restrictions can make sentences ungrammatical. (For the contrary view, that the phonology cannot exert influence on the syntax, see Zwicky

---

[4]Morphological indexation of DEP constraints presents a minor technical challenge. Under Consistency of Exponence (McCarthy and Prince 1993b), epenthetic segments have no morphological affiliation. There is recent work arguing that Consistency of Exponence should be abandoned (Łubowicz 2005, Walker and Feng 2004), as well as a recent defense (van Oostendorp 2007). If Consistency of Exponence is retained, then the effect we desire can be obtained with morphological indexation of the faithfulness constraint O-CONTIG, which prohibits morpheme-internal epenthesis (Kenstowicz 1994, McCarthy and Prince 1995, 1999).

[5]There are cases where the gap is restricted not only morphologically but also lexically. For example, as discussed by Halle (1973), Hetzron (1975), and Iverson (1981), about 100 Russian second-conjugation verbs idiosyncratically lack a first person singular non-past form, thereby avoiding a [d]∼[ʒ] alternation. Since only some verbs meeting these phonological and morphological conditions behave in this way, the appropriate IDENT constraint must be indexed lexically as well as morphologically. Such constraints are required anyway to account for lexical stratification and other patterns of exceptions (as in Itô and Mester 1999).

(28) $\text{DEP}_{\text{IMP}} \gg \text{MPARSE}$

/åpn/$_{\text{Imp}}$	DEP_{IMP}	MPARSE	DEP_{NOUN}
☞ ⊙ $\langle i \rangle = \langle å, p, n \rangle$ $\langle o \rangle = \langle \ \rangle$ $\mathfrak{R} = \varnothing$		1	
a. åpən $\langle i \rangle = \langle å, p, \#, n \rangle$ $\langle o \rangle = \langle å, p, ə, n \rangle$ $\mathfrak{R} = \{(å, å), (p, p), (\#, ə), (n, n)\}$	W$_1$	L	

(29) $\text{MPARSE} \gg \text{DEP}_{\text{NOUN}}$

/adl/$_{\text{Noun}}$	DEP_{IMP}	MPARSE	DEP_{NOUN}
☞ adəl $\langle i \rangle = \langle a, d, \#, l \rangle$ $\langle o \rangle = \langle a, d, ə, l \rangle$ $\mathfrak{R} = \{(a, a), (d, d), (\#, ə), (l, l)\}$			1
a. ⊙ $\langle i \rangle = \langle a, d, l \rangle$ $\langle o \rangle = \langle \ \rangle$ $\mathfrak{R} = \varnothing$		W$_1$	L

(30)   Null output when phrase contains imperative of /åpn/

/…adl…åpn…/	DEP_{IMP}	SONSEQ	MPARSE	DEP_{NOUN}
⊙			1	
a. …adəl…åpən…	W$_1$		L	W$_1$
b. …adəl…åpn…		W$_1$	L	W$_1$

(31)   Nonnull imperative when a vowel follows

Sykl opp bakken	DEP_{IMP}	SONSEQ	MPARSE	DEP_{NOUN}
Sykl opp bakken			1	
a. ⊙			L	

and Pullum (1986), Myers (1987), and Vogel and Kenesei (1990).) For example, according to Zec and Inkelas, Heavy NP Shift in English is only permitted when the postposed NP is realizable as a branching phonological phrase.

It would be beyond the scope of this chapter to give MPARSE analyses of all claimed cases of phonological filtering of syntactic forms. Still, it does seem that the current proposal offers a coherent means of implementing this: when a PF form submitted by the syntax as an input to the phonology yields ⊙, the syntax is forced to 'go back' and try another form. For an example of this mode of analysis, see the discussion of the *–ŋgu/–gu* allomorphy of the Dyirbal ergative suffix in McCarthy and Prince (1993b: Chapter 7).

4.3   Harmonic bounding relationships, part II

Simply by allowing GEN to create candidates where $\Re$ is not a total bijective function — that is, by identifying our revised MPARSE as a violable constraint — we ensure that ⊙ is a member of every candidate set. If we wish to avoid stipulative restrictions on GEN, ⊙ is not the only MPARSE-violating candidate. The candidate ⊙ has a phonologically null output and an undefined correspondence relation. In principle, there can be candidates that violate MPARSE but have phonologically nonnull outputs.

One example of this type is the candidate ([ʔə], ⟨p, a, t⟩, ⟨ʔ, ə⟩, ∅), in which input /pat/ and output [ʔə] are juxtaposed with a completely undefined $\Re$. This candidate has deletion, of a sort, and epenthesis, of a sort, but it violates neither MAX nor DEP, since it posits no mappings to or from the null string #. It doesn't violate IDENT either, since it asserts no correspondence relations between input and output segments. It is, in short, perfectly faithful because it does an end run around the theory of faithfulness. The theory of faithfulness would be completely subverted if such candidates could ever emerge as optimal. This candidate violates MPARSE, of course, but then so does ⊙.

In reality, candidates like ([ʔə], ⟨p, a, t⟩, ⟨ʔ, ə⟩, ∅) pose no analytic worries because they are harmonically bounded by ⊙, so they can never be optimal under any ranking of CON. This is because any candidate with output structure will incur at least one markedness violation, whereas ⊙ incurs none. Even if we adopt Gouskova's (2003) stance against nihilistic markedness constraints like *STRUC ('the output contains no structure'), this still follows because the markedness constraints in CON impose conflicting demands that cannot all be satisfied except in the total absence of structure.

We may illustrate this by attempting to construct a non-null candidate with no markedness violations. If all distinctive features are binary, and for every feature one value is marked and the other unmarked, our first step is to have every vowel and consonant be set to the unmarked value of every feature. Further, the unmarked syllable shape is CV, so presumably [ʔə.ʔə] (or the like) incurs no violations of featural markedness or syllable structure constraints.

But the search for a candidate with no markedness violations fails once we look at higher levels of prosodic structure. If [ʔə.ʔə] is parsed into a single disyllabic foot, then NONFINALITY is violated, because the final syllable in the prosodic word is parsed into a foot. Furthermore, depending on which syllable is stressed, the foot violates either IAMB or TROCHEE. We can satisfy all three of these constraints by creating a non-final monosyllabic foot or no foot at all, but these strategems violate PARSE-SYLLABLE ('All syllables are parsed into feet'). Obviously, if CON were to lack one of these constraints, then this particular avenue would be closed off, but all seem to be well-supported.

We could go on listing other cases of competing markedness demands but will refrain from belaboring the point. We can safely conclude that any candidate that contains phonological structure will have to incur one or more markedness violations, and hence if such a candidate also violates MPARSE, it will be harmonically bounded by $\odot$, which has no markedness violations. The threat from ([ʔə], ⟨p, a, t⟩, ⟨ʔ, ə⟩, ∅) and its kin is illusory, since all such candidates are harmonically bounded by $\odot$.

This assurance of harmonic bounding by $\odot$ crucially depends on MPARSE issuing a categorical assessment: any candidate in which $\mathfrak{R}$ is wholly or partly undefined incurs exactly one violation mark from MPARSE. If MPARSE instead assigned one violation mark for every input segment that is not in the domain of $\mathfrak{R}$ (like MAX in segment-based correspondence), then $\odot$, where $\mathfrak{R}$ is undefined for *every* string in ⟨i⟩, would incur more MPARSE violations than candidates where $\mathfrak{R}$ is undefined for some, but not all, strings in ⟨i⟩. See (32) for an illustration.

(32)   Hypothetical tableau under incorrect definition of MPARSE

/patuki/	MPARSE	MARKEDNESS	MAX
☞ tuki $\langle i \rangle = \langle p, a, t, u, k, i \rangle$ $\langle o \rangle = \langle t, u, k, i \rangle$ $\mathfrak{R} = \{(t, t),(u, u),(k, k),(i, i)\}$	2	1	
a. ⊙ $\langle i \rangle = \langle p, a, t, u, k, i \rangle$ $\langle o \rangle = \langle\rangle$ $\mathfrak{R} = \varnothing$	W_6	L	

Under this incorrect definition of MPARSE, the winning candidate is not harmonically bounded (obviously, since otherwise it could not be the winner). The problem with (32) is that it fundamentally subverts the theory of faithfulness: the mapping /patuki/ → [tuki] seems to involve deletion, but it does not violate MAX. To avoid unwanted outcomes like this, MPARSE must be strictly categorical in its assessments, granting equal status to all candidates in which $\mathfrak{R}$ is not a total bijective function from $\langle i \rangle$ to $\langle o \rangle$. The definition of MPARSE in (23) has exactly this property.

Our argument about ⊙'s ability to harmonically bound all of the non-null MPARSE violators also depends on the assumption that all constraints (besides MPARSE itself) are either markedness or faithfulness constraints. While this assumption is entirely standard, several constraints that may stand outside the markedness/faithfulness typology have been proposed. We will now examine two such constraint types, morpheme realization and antifaithfulness, concluding that morpheme realization constraints are compatible with our proposals but antifaithfulness constraints are not. It should be noted that we do not wish to seem to endorse any of these extra-canonical constraints; our goal is simply to check compatibility.

Some of the various MORPHREAL constraints do stand outside of the basic markedness/faithfulness typology. (References include, among others, Samek-Lodovici (1993), Akinlabi (1996), Gnanadesikan (1997), Rose (1997), and Kurisu (2001).) Many formulations of these constraints demand that all morphemes have overt exponence or realization on the surface, with 'exponence' and 'realization' defined in various ways and with various degrees of explicitness. Such formulations, at an intuitive level, would seem to imply that ⊙ would violate MORPHREAL, since ⊙'s total absence of output structure means that no input morpheme has an exponent.

Somewhat paradoxically, however, ⊙ actually satisfies MORPHREAL in most, if not all, proposed versions of this constraint. Many formulations of MORPHREAL are, in fact, faithfulness constraints: they demand that some piece of every input morpheme be preserved in the output. Under string correspondence, this could be stated as a demand to 'assign a violation mark if every string in ⟨i⟩ containing some unit of structure in the lexical representation of some morpheme stands in correspondence with #'. Since in ⊙ no string in ⟨i⟩ stands in correspondence with # (or with anything else), ⊙ would satisfy MORPHREAL, in just the same way that it vacuously satisfies every other faithfulness constraint.

The version of MORPHREAL proposed in Kurisu (2001) is not a faithfulness constraint. Instead, it demands that the phonological output of *stem + affix* be distinct from the phonological output of *stem*. It thus tests for dissimilarity between two output forms. One of the main arguments adduced by Kurisu in support of this alternative formulation is that certain languages exhibit morphophonological processes that cannot be obviously construed as the result of faithfulness to input structure, such as morphological truncation, deletion of root accents triggered by dominant affixes, or morphological metathesis. These processes remove or alter structure in *stem*, but they do not seem to involve faithfulness to the input structure of *affix*. They do, however, render the output of *stem + affix* different from the output of *stem* — for instance, because *stem* contains segments that are truncated in *stem + affix*.

Under Kurisu's definition, if *stem* is nonnull and *stem + affix* is ⊙, MORPHREAL is technically satisfied. It is certainly counterintuitive that the null output would count as having 'realized' any of its input morphemes, but so long as deletion (as in truncative processes) of some *part* of the input counts as morpheme realization, then so would the deletion of *all* parts of the input, as in the candidate Φ where all strings in ⟨i⟩ map to #. Since Φ and ⊙ are identically structureless at the output level, both will then satisfy Kurisu's version of MORPHREAL, again provided that the output of *stem* does not also yield an output with no structure.

Given the preceding discussion, the claim that ⊙ violates no constraint except MPARSE may be non-stipulatively maintained irrespective of one's position on the presence in or absence from CON of any of the heretofore proposed versions of MORPHREAL. We do not, however, have this luxury of agnosticism regarding a competing theory of morpheme realization, transderivational anti-faithfulness (TAF) constraints (Alderete 2001a, 2001b). As we will now show, TAF conflicts with our proposal in a quite fundamental way. Specifically, TAF constraints would spoil the harmonic bounding of the non-null MPARSE violators.

Under this theory, input morphemes may be associated with one or more TAF constraints, which are literally negations of output-output faithfulness constraints (Benua 1997, Crosswhite 1998, Kager 1999, Pater 2000, and others). Since $\odot$ vacuously satisfies all faithfulness constraints, including output-output faithfulness constraints (see section 4.4), it necessarily violates any anti-faithfulness constraints that might be associated with input morphemes. This fact is not merely an analytic inelegance that causes $\odot$ to violate constraints other than MPARSE — it subverts our result about harmonic bounding because some non-null MPARSE violators will satisfy the anti-faithfulness constraints that $\odot$ violates.

Consider the following hypothetical scenario. Imagine a language identical to Norwegian except that the imperative morphology is associated with the antifaithfulness constraint $\neg\text{IDENT}_{[+\text{low}]}$, which requires mutation of a low stem vowel. If $\neg\text{IDENT}_{[+\text{low}]}$ dominates MPARSE and $\text{IDENT}_{[+\text{low}]}$, as in (33), then a nonnull MPARSE violator can be chosen over $\odot$. Worse yet, once a nonnull MPARSE violator is admitted, then faithfulness constraints can be fully subverted. Hence, the winner in (33) is maximally unmarked — except for the (a, e) correspondence relation that is necessary to satisfy $\neg\text{IDENT}_{[+\text{low}]}$, this form has discarded the input and replaced it with maximally unmarked structure at no cost in faithfulness. This result is obviously disastrous, and it shows the steep price that must be paid for breaking the harmonic bounding of nonnull MPARSE violators.

This argument shows that string-based correspondence is incompatible with antifaithfulness, at least insofar as these theories are developed here and in Alderete (2001a, 2001b), respectively. The presence of antifaithfulness constraints in CON breaks the harmonic bounding of nonnull MPARSE violators, and it thereby vitiates the broader theory of faithfulness. Hence, string correspondence and antifaithfulness cannot both be correct. This is not an entirely unexpected conclusion, since TAF is already far from uncontroversial; see, among others, Apoussidou (2003), Inkelas and Zoll (2003), Kurisu (2001), Trommer (2005), van Oostendorp (2005), and Wolf (2006) for critiques.

To sum up, we have argued that $\odot$ is the most harmonic MPARSE-violating candidate because it violates only MPARSE, whereas all other

(33)   Incorrect victory of non-null MPARSE violator in pseudo-Norwegian

/apn/		SONSEQ	DEP$_{\text{IMP}}$	¬IDENT$_{[+\text{low}]}$	MPARSE	IDENT$_{[+\text{low}]}$
ʔe $\langle i \rangle = \langle a, p, n \rangle$ $\langle o \rangle = \langle ʔ, e \rangle$ $\mathfrak{R} = \{(a, e)\}$					1	1
a.	☉ $\langle i \rangle = \langle a, p, n \rangle$ $\langle o \rangle = \langle \ \rangle$ $\mathfrak{R} = \varnothing$			W$_1$	1	L
b.	apn $\langle i \rangle = \langle a, p, n \rangle$ $\langle o \rangle = \langle a, p, n \rangle$ $\mathfrak{R} = \{(a, a), (p, p), (n, n)\}$	W$_1$		W$_1$	L	L
c.	epn $\langle i \rangle = \langle a, p, n \rangle$ $\langle o \rangle = \langle e, p, n \rangle$ $\mathfrak{R} = \{(a, e), (p, p), (n, n)\}$	W$_1$			L	1
d.	epən $\langle i \rangle = \langle a, p, \#, n \rangle$ $\langle o \rangle = \langle e, p, ə, n \rangle$ $\mathfrak{R} = \{(a, e), (p, p), (\#, ə), (n, n)\}$		W$_1$		L	1

MPARSE violators will incur violations of other constraints. Thus, there is no profusion of MPARSE-violating candidates among the contenders for optimality, and there is no danger of undermining the theory of faithfulness.

The harmonic bounding results that we have shown here and in section 3.3 go a long way toward ensuring that string correspondence does not introduce any novel ambiguities in input-output relations. We have not quite arrived at establishing ☉'s uniquness, however, since for any input there will still be infinitely many null outputs. The reason: ☉ has an empty output, and an empty output has infinitely many concatenative decompositions: $\langle \ \rangle$, $\langle \# \rangle$, $\langle \#, \# \rangle$, $\langle \#, \#, \# \rangle$, and so forth. Outputs like $\langle \# \rangle$ and $\langle \#, \# \rangle$ satisfy MAX as long as the correspondence relation is undefined. Under the constraint system presented above, the candidates ☉, $\langle \# \rangle$, $\langle \#, \# \rangle$, etc. are equally harmonic, since they violate MPARSE and no other constraint.

Strictly speaking, nothing intrinsic to OT rules out the possibility of obtaining an infinity of winners in some evaluations. Samek-Lodovici and Prince (1999) demonstrate that the number of non-harmonically bounded *violation profiles* is finite for every input, but multiple candidate forms can in principle have identical violation profiles. That is the situation with $\odot$, $\langle \# \rangle$, $\langle \#, \# \rangle$, ... Nonetheless, the theoretical possibility of distinct candidates with identical violation profiles has rarely been exploited in actual OT analyses (though see Grimshaw (1997: 410–411) and Hammond (1994)), presumably because the richness of CON makes it almost impossible for two candidates to be equally harmonic on all constraints. Allowing an infinite number of contenders would thus not be a change to the formal properties of OT, but would be empirically unlikely (if not impossible) under previous proposals about the substantive contents of GEN and CON. It would therefore be preferable to distinguish $\odot$ from $\langle \# \rangle$, $\langle \#, \# \rangle$, ... in terms of some constraint.

A similar technical problem arises with nonnull outputs as well: the inclusion of $\# \rightarrow \#$ mappings in candidates that obey MPARSE, so that there are infinitely many equally faithful candidates for any input (see (34)). A $\# \rightarrow \#$ mapping does not violate any of the faithfulness constraints above. Moreover, since markedness constraints only see the literal output o, which does not contain any #s, they cannot militate against the presence of these gratuitous #s. As a result, alongside any given candidate with no $\# \rightarrow \#$ mappings, there are infinitely many candidates with such mappings, all of which tie on all constraints (van Oostendorp 2005).

(34) $\# \rightarrow \#$ mappings

$\langle$p, a, t$\rangle$	$\rightarrow$	$\langle$p, a, t$\rangle$
$\langle$p, a, t, #$\rangle$	$\rightarrow$	$\langle$p, a, t, #$\rangle$
$\langle$p, a, t, #, #$\rangle$	$\rightarrow$	$\langle$p, a, t, #, #$\rangle$
$\langle$#, p, #, a, #, t, #$\rangle$	$\rightarrow$	$\langle$#, p, #, a, #, t, #$\rangle$

...

The most straightforward way of resolving both problems is to introduce a constraint that requires #s in $\langle$o$\rangle$ to have nonnull correspondents in $\langle$i$\rangle$ (see (35)). The null-output candidates in which $\langle$o$\rangle$ equals $\langle \# \rangle$, $\langle \#, \# \rangle$, $\langle \#, \#, \# \rangle$, ... all violate NO-#, while the null output with empty $\langle$o$\rangle$ obeys it. Therefore, the candidate that we have been calling $\odot$, with empty $\langle$o$\rangle$, harmonically bounds all of the null-output candidates with $\langle$o$\rangle$ equal to $\langle \# \rangle$, $\langle \#, \# \rangle$, $\langle \#, \#, \# \rangle$, ... Similarly, the candidate in (34) with $\langle$o$\rangle$ equal to $\langle$p, a, t$\rangle$ harmonically bounds all of the candidates with $\# \rightarrow \#$ mappings, since all of these other candidates also violate NO-#.

(35)   NO-#
        Given a candidate $(o, \langle i \rangle, \langle o \rangle, \Re)$,
                for every string $\kappa = \#$ in $\langle o \rangle$
                    if $\Re^{-1}(\kappa) = \#$ or $\Re^{-1}(\kappa)$ is undefined
                        assign a violation mark.

The constraint NO-# has the unusual property of not conflicting with any other constraint, and hence it is irrelevant where it is ranked. If the reader finds such a constraint to be aesthetically displeasing, other solutions to the same problem can be imagined. For example, on a view in which candidates are produced serially via a succession of harmonically-improving steps (McCarthy 2006, 2007), it may be that candidates with gratuitous $\# \rightarrow \#$ mappings cannot arise, since no constraint favors the presence of such a mapping, and consequently adding one is never harmonically improving.

4.4   MPARSE and other correspondence relations

Correspondence theory recognizes more than one dimension of faithfulness (McCarthy and Prince 1995, 1999). In addition to input-output (IO) correspondence, which has been the focus of our attention thus far, candidates with a reduplicative morpheme in the input also contain a base-reduplicant (BR) correspondence relation. The main thesis of correspondence theory is that all dimensions of correspondence have the same formal properties. It seems desirable to retain this assumption in our revised theory of correspondence, and this means *inter alia* that there will be distinct MPARSE constraints for each dimension of correspondence, just as there are distinct faithfulness constraints for each such dimension. We will therefore investigate MPARSE-BR in some detail. The parallels are not perfect, however, and we will conclude this section with an explanation for why there is no MPARSE constraint on output-output (OO) correspondence.

In reduplicative correspondence, there is a relation between the *reduplicant*, which is defined as the output exponent of the reduplicative morpheme RED, and the *base*, which is the output string to which the reduplicant is affixed. The literal output *o* exhaustively consists of these two substrings, which by hypothesis bear separate correspondence relations to the string *input*. What we have been calling IO correspondence in the discussion so far is thus, strictly speaking, *input-base* correspondence. Since BR and IO are distinct correspondence relations, the string *base* can have different concatenative decompositions as B and as O — e.g., if there is coalescence in the reduplicant but not the base. The concatenative decomposition of *base* which is relevant to IO-correspondence, whose substrings stand in correspondence with substrings of $\langle i \rangle$, can continue to be called $\langle o \rangle$. (The string *reduplicant* is thus entirely outside the scope of the IO-correspondence relation, and so the presence of reduplicated structure violates neither DEP-IO nor MPARSE-IO (McCarthy and Prince 1995, 1999)). The other concatenative decomposition of *base* is used for BR correspondence and can be called $\langle b \rangle$. The substrings in $\langle b \rangle$ stand in correspondence with substrings in the concatenative decomposition of *reduplicant*, which we can call $\langle r \rangle$.[6]

Example (36) illustrates these various concatenative decompositions and the relations between them:

(36)   Illustration of concatenative decompositions in /RED-pamək/ → [pãpam]

Description	Form	Concatenative Decomposition
Input	/pamək/	$\langle i \rangle = \langle p, a, m, ə, k \rangle$
Output	[pãpam]	
Base	[pam]	$\langle o \rangle = \langle p, a, m, \#, \# \rangle$
		$\langle b \rangle = \langle p, am \rangle$
Reduplicant	[pã]	$\langle r \rangle = \langle p, ã \rangle$
IO correspondence relation		$\Re_{IO} = \{(p, p), (a, a), (m, m), (ə, \#), (k, \#)\}$
BR correspondence relation		$\Re_{BR} = \{(p, p), (am, ã)\}$

In this hypothetical example, there is coalescence in the B → R mapping but not in the I → O mapping. Therefore, $\langle i \rangle$ and $\langle o \rangle$ contain only monosegmental (or null) strings, in keeping with our harmonic bounding results in section 3.3. By contrast, the presence of coalescence in the B → R mapping results in [am] forming a bisegmental substring in $\langle b \rangle$, despite these segments belonging to distinct, monosegmental strings in $\langle o \rangle$.

For each of the two relevant correspondence dimensions, $\Re_{IO}$ and $\Re_{BR}$, there exists an MPARSE constraint that tests whether it is a total bijec-

---

[6]If we wish to permit input-reduplicant correspondence, then the strings *input* and *reduplicant* will also each require an additional concatenative decomposition, the substrings of which would stand in IR-correspondence.

tive function. The conditions that produce violations of MPARSE-BR and MPARSE-IO are quite different, however, as we will now show.

Among the output candidates for any RED-containing input is ⊙. This candidate violates MPARSE-IO, of course, but it vacuously satisfies MPARSE-BR. The reason: in the null output, the concatenative decompositions of the base $\langle b \rangle$ and the reduplicant $\langle r \rangle$ are both empty. $\mathfrak{R}_{BR}$, being a relation between empty sequences (or, strictly speaking, from the empty sequence to itself), is vacuously a total bijective function.

The situation is a little more complicated when MPARSE-BR is violated. For concreteness, suppose that MAX-BR and NOCODA dominate MPARSE-BR, as in (37). (We use a violation tableau instead of a comparative tableau because the purpose of (37) is to investigate potential winners rather than locate a specific winner.)

(37)   Potential effects of MPARSE-BR violation

/RED-pam/	MAX-BR	NOCODA	MPARSE-BR
a. pam-pam $\langle b \rangle = \langle p, a, m \rangle$ $\langle r \rangle = \langle p, a, m \rangle$ $\mathfrak{R}_{BR} = \{(p, p), (a, a), (m, m)\}$		**!	
b. pa-pam $\langle b \rangle = \langle p, a, m \rangle$ $\langle r \rangle = \langle p, a, \# \rangle$ $\mathfrak{R}_{BR} = \{(p, p), (a, a), (m, \#)\}$	*!	*	
c. pa-pam $\langle b \rangle = \langle p, a, m \rangle$ $\langle r \rangle = \langle p, a \rangle$ $\mathfrak{R}_{BR} = \{(p, p), (a, a)\}$ (NB: $\mathfrak{R}_{BR}(m)$ is undefined.)		*	*
d. pam $\langle b \rangle = \langle p, a, m \rangle$ $\langle r \rangle = \langle \, \rangle$ $\mathfrak{R}_{BR} = \varnothing$		*	*
e. ʔə-pam $\langle b \rangle = \langle p, a, m \rangle$ $\langle r \rangle = \langle ʔ, ə \rangle$ $\mathfrak{R}_{BR} = \varnothing$		*	*

Candidates (c)–(e) in (37) cannily avoid violating MAX-BR (and, in the case of (e), DEP-BR) by having incomplete and even nonexistent BR correspondence relations. Because all MPARSE-BR failures are treated equally, these candidates are not distinguished by the constraints shown in the tableau. The harmonic bounding relationships among (c)–(e) are instructive, however. Candidate (c) is harmonically bounded by (d) and (e) because (c)'s reduplicated *pa* sequence incurs additional markedness violations that (d) and (e) avoid. Although the reasoning here parallels our argument in section 4.2 there is an important difference: candidate (d), with the null reduplicant, does not harmonically bound candidate (e), where the reduplicant is realized by minimally marked structure. Candidate (e) is favored over (d) by any constraints favoring the presence of phonological material in the reduplicant. MORPHREAL is such a constraint, if indeed it exists (see section 4.2); a constraint like FTBIN (foot binarity) could also have this effect. Conversely (d) is favored over (e) by any constraints that militate against even (e)'s minimally marked reduplicant.

In sum, the existence of MPARSE-BR predicts that there can be a system of reduplication where copying is either exact or doesn't happen at all. In a language with a ranking like (37), the input /RED-ta/ can be copied exactly, yielding [ta-ta], but the input /RED-pam/ cannot be copied at all, so it yields either [pam] or [ʔə-pam], depending on how other constraints are ranked. Significantly, this is not an expansion of the earlier reduplicative typology. The reason is that this system could also be analyzed as emergence of the unmarked (McCarthy and Prince 1994) with crucial domination of MAX-BR (and, in the case of (e), DEP-BR). Close parallels can be found in Cebuano, Tagalog, and Makassarese (Aronoff *et al.* 1987, Carrier-Duncan 1984, McCarthy and Prince 1990, 1994), all of which discriminate between exact and inexact copies.

One final remark about MPARSE-BR: the fact that candidates like (37a) are not harmonically bounded demonstrates that ineffability does not result from the presence of an empty correspondence relation *pre se*. Rather, gaps — instances of the candidate ⊙ — are ineffable for the more simple and concrete reason that they contain no output structure to be phonetically interpreted. Candidates in which $\mathfrak{R}_{BR}$ is not a total bijective function, as (37) shows, can well have overt output structure, and hence, when they emerge as optimal, are entirely utterable.

We might expect there to be an MPARSE-OO constraint as well, but OO correspondence differs in a basic way from IO and BR correspondence. Although IO and BR correspondence relations are freely posited by

GEN, OO correspondence is dependent on IO correspondence and is not free. For example, because the [t] of German [bʊnt] 'federation' and the [d] of [bʊndə] have the same input correspondent in the root /bʊnd/, they must be in OO correspondence with one another. In other words, OO correspondence is a kind of transitivization of IO correspondence from one output via the shared input to another output. Theories of OO correspondence typically do not acknowledge this dependence on IO correspondence (though see McCarthy 2005), but no analysis in the literature known to us relies on positing a fully independent OO correspondence relation.

The dependence of OO correspondence on IO correspondence has two consequences that are relevant to our current concerns. First, it means that MPARSE-OO can be dispensed with: there can be no OO correspondence relation if there is no IO correspondence relation because of OO correspondence's dependent status. Second, it supports the claim made earlier (section 4.3) that ⊙ obeys *all* faithfulness constraints, including OO faithfulness constraints. Because ⊙ has an empty IO correspondence relation with the input, it cannot have any OO correspondence relations with the surface forms of morphologically related inputs either, given the dependence of OO correspondence on IO correspondence. And because ⊙ has no OO correspondence relations, OO faithfulness constraints like MAX-OO or DEP-OO are not violated by it.

5 MPARSE and learning

Gaps present an obvious challenge to the language learner. If grammars are learned only from positive evidence, then learners cannot discover the existence of gaps or the constraint rankings that produce them. This means that learners must assume gaps until proven otherwise — they must go from a grammar that allows only gaps to a grammar that disallows some gaps. This is in accordance with the Subset Principle, which requires learning to proceed from the maximally restrictive grammar to successively less restrictive ones (Baker 1979, Berwick 1985, Gold 1967).

In the OT literature, learning in accordance with the Subset Principle is taken to mean that there is a durable bias toward ranking markedness constraints over faithfulness constraints (Hayes 2004, Prince and Tesar 2004 and references cited there). Learners assume that markedness constraints are unviolated unless they observe noncompliant forms in the primary data.

Our theory requires another ranking bias: faithfulness is ranked over MPARSE. This means that learners only permit unfaithful mappings that are supported by alternations in the primary data, and otherwise they assume a gap. This ranking bias follows from the same reasoning as the markedness over faithfulness bias: learning from positive evidence must be driven by that which occurs rather than that which does not occur. Henceforth, we will refer to these combined ranking biases as M-F-MP.

As we delve into this matter, we adopt certain assumptions that are by now standard in the OT literature on learning phonological grammars. (For references to this extensive work, see McCarthy (2002: 202–216, 230–232) and Kager, Pater, and Zonneveld (eds.) (2004).) Early learning is focused on phonotactics: which structures are allowed or disallowed in the target language? The phonotactic learner's goal is a grammar that performs an identity map from perceived adult forms to the learner's own productions. Later, in morphophonemic learning, the learner's goal is to obtain a unique underlying representation for each morpheme and a grammar that maps these underlying representations to the observed surface forms.

For the phonotactic learner, the M-F-MP bias is overridden by experience with marked structures in the ambient language. For example, the Egyptian Arabic learner who hears [ʔibn] 'son' has evidence that SONSEQ must be ranked below MPARSE and the relevant faithfulness constraints MAX and DEP. This ensures that /ʔibn/ maps to [ʔibn] and not to *⊙, *[ʔib], or *[ʔibin]. But the Norwegian learner's experience does not include coda clusters that violate SONSEQ, so he/she never has reason to demote SONSEQ below MPARSE and the faithfulness constraints. Since the M-F-MP bias puts MPARSE at the bottom until proven otherwise, the Norwegian phonotactic learner's grammar would most harmonically map hypothetical /ʔibn/ to ⊙.

At the conclusion of phonotactic learning, the Norwegian learner's grammar includes the ranking SONSEQ $\gg$ DEP $\gg$ MPARSE. The target grammar was shown in section 4.2: SONSEQ $\gg$ DEP$_{\text{IMP}}$ $\gg$ MPARSE $\gg$ DEP$_{\text{NOUN}}$. For the morphophonemic learner to get to this target, he/she must proceed in maximal compliance with the M-F-MP ranking bias. This means that unfaithfulness is allowed in a particular paradigmatic slot only when required by alternations observable in the primary data. When a particular morphosyntactic feature combination MS exhibits epenthesis, the DEP$_{\text{MS}}$ constraint proper to MS will be demoted below MPARSE. Absent such alternations, forms in the MS category would map to ⊙ if the alternative is violation of SONSEQ. Since the morphosyntactic features are presumably universal, every DEP_{MS} constraint may be immanent in CON or it (and its complement) may be constructed on the fly by learners — how this is done is unimportant. What is important is that learners need not discover gaps because they presume gaps everywhere until they encounter evidence to the contrary.

To sum up, this analysis shows that gaps do not present special difficulties to learners equipped with a theory that includes a null output candidate and MPARSE. The resources required to learn systems with paradigmatic gaps are no different from the resources required to learn OT grammars generally, so we were able to call on familiar ideas from the OT learning literature.

This situation stands in stark contrast to the problem of learning gaps in a theory based on inviolable constraints, Orgun and Sprouse's (1999, this volume) CONTROL model. This model posits a grammatical component called CONTROL that inspects the output of EVAL and may reject it as ill-formed. The constraints in CONTROL come from CON; on a language-particular basis, constraints in CON can be lifted out of the regular constraint hierarchy and placed in CONTROL. A paradigmatic gap occurs when the most harmonic candidate chosen by EVAL is found to violate a constraint in CONTROL. The CONTROL constraints are inviolable, then, because they are outside of and posterior to the system of comparative evaluation.

The empirical arguments for CONTROL have been discussed and reanalyzed in MPARSE terms by McCarthy (2003) and, most extensively, Raffelsiefen (2004). We will not dwell on this empirical material here, but rather we will look at learning in the CONTROL model in comparison with MPARSE.

Learners have two tasks in the CONTROL model: they have to determine the language's regular constraint hierarchy, and they also have to figure out which unviolated constraints belong in CONTROL. Reasoning from the Subset Principle, we might suppose that all constraints start out in CONTROL and then some are moved into the regular hierarchy as the learner observes violations of them. But this simple approach will not work: it has the effect of keeping all unviolated constraints in CONTROL, when in reality only some unviolated constraints produce gaps. In a CONTROL-style analysis of Norwegian, for instance, SONSEQ_{Imp} has to be in CONTROL because it causes a gap, but SONSEQ_{Noun} needs to end up in the regular constraint hierarchy so that it can favor epenthetic [adəl] instead of causing a gap. Since both SONSEQ_{Imp} and SONSEQ_{Noun} are unviolated in the primary data, a learner proceeding from only positive evidence has no way of knowing which constraint belongs where.

For this reason, learning in the CONTROL model requires learners to discover any gaps, and that cannot be done from positive evidence alone. Orgun and Sprouse (1999: 219–221) sketch an approach based on so-called indirect negative evidence. The idea is that each time the learner encounters a paraphrase or other alternative to the gap, he or she receives a hint that there is a gap for which the paraphrase has been substituted. A sufficient accumulation of such hints is a prerequisite to moving a constraint into the CONTROL component.

This approach could perhaps be made to work when there is a consistent substitute for the gap, such as English *more violet* for *violeter.* But it is difficult to imagine a learning mechanism powerful enough to identify diverse expressions in Norwegian as paraphrases of or circumlocutions for 'open!' or 'bicycle!', and then to connect this with the absence of 'open!' and 'bicycle!' from the primary data. It would seem to be necessary for learners to scrutinize every phrase and ask whether it could be paraphrased with a single word using the language's morphological resources, and then to check whether that word has been previously heard.

This is clearly not a workable learning algorithm, and this failure suggests that the CONTROL model is on the wrong track. From an OT perspective, that is a welcome result, since the CONTROL model is at odds with several of OT's most basic premises.

6   Other theories of the null output

In section 4.1, we described Prince and Smolensky's (2004) two original ideas about the null output and MPARSE: failure to parse any input phonological structure, and failure to parse any input morphological structure. In 4.2, we showed why and how nonparsing or deletion of all input phonological structure (the candidate Φ) is distinct from and an inadequate substitute for the null output $\odot$. Below, section 6.2 looks at Walker and Feng's (2004) interpretation of what nonparsing of morphological structure means. But first section 6.1 considers an idea closer to ours, Rice's (2005a, 2005b) proposal to replace MPARSE with constraints requiring paradigm slots to be filled.

6.1 MAX(CATEGORY) constraints

Rice (2005a, 2005b) proposes an alternative to the null output based on the idea that whole morphological paradigms are evaluated as candidates, as in McCarthy's (2005) Optimal Paradigms theory. Rice employs a family of MAX$_{\text{CATEGORY}}$ constraints, which assign a violation mark if no form fills the paradigm slot labeled by *category*.

In Norwegian, for example, plurals are marked by a suffix *–er* and infinitives with a suffix *–e*, but normally the singular noun and imperative verb forms are identical to the bare root. When the root ends in a rising-sonority cluster, as we have seen, the result is epenthesis in the singular noun (*adel*) but a gap for the imperative verb. Rice's proposal captures this difference by having the MAX$_{\text{CATEGORY}}$ constraints for the singular noun and imperative verb be ranked differently with respect to DEP. DEP dominates MAX$_{\text{IMPERATIVE}}$ (38), but DEP is itself dominated by MAX$_{\text{SINGULARNOUN}}$ (39).

(38)   SONSEQ, DEP ≫ MAX$_{\text{IMP}}$

/åpn+{INF, IMP}/	SONSEQ	DEP	MAX$_{\text{IMP}}$
{[åpne]$_{\text{INF}}$}			1
a. {[åpne]$_{\text{INF}}$, [åpn]$_{\text{IMP}}$}	W$_1$		L
b. {[åpne]$_{\text{INF}}$, [åpən]$_{\text{IMP}}$}		W$_1$	L

(39)   SONSEQ, MAX$_{\text{SGN}}$ ≫ DEP

/adl+{SG, PL}/	SONSEQ	MAX$_{\text{SGN}}$	DEP
{[adəl]$_{\text{SG}}$, [adler]$_{\text{PL}}$}			1
a. {[adler]$_{\text{PL}}$}		W$_1$	L
b. {[adl]$_{\text{SG}}$, [adler]$_{\text{PL}}$}	W$_1$		L

Rice argues that this approach to gaps is conceptually superior to one that employs the null output because there is no need to augment the candidate set with a special object that is interpreted as meaning 'no output.' On closer examination, however, it is not so clear that this proposal is able to avoid the need for such a candidate. The problem has to do with affixation: what is the source of the affixes that appear on the plural and infinitive forms in these tableaux? The MAX$_{\text{CATEGORY}}$ approach depicts the input as consisting of a bare root and a set of slots for which inflected forms of the root are to be computed, but affixes are not shown in the input.

Under an item-based theory of morphology, it is necessary to assume that affixes are present in the input. There are two main reasons for this. First, since the relationship between affix form and function is arbitrary, the phonological shape of affixes is unpredictable and therefore must be present in underlying representation. Second, the order of affixes relative to one another respects a number of universals and near-universals, and moreover affix-order has been observed to often (if not necessarily always) bear a non-trivial relationship to the constituent structure of the syntax, as required by the Mirror Principle (Baker 1985 and much subsequent work). The fact that such generalizations exists suggest that affixes must be (preliminarily) ordered before the phonology gets underway, as argued by Horwood (2002).

Under an item-based morphological theory, then, the input to an Optimal Paradigms-type phonology would have to consist not of a root plus a set of categories for which output forms can be constructed, but of a number of collections of the root plus affixes, each serving as the input to one paradigmatic slot: e.g., Latin {/am-oː/, /am-aːs/, /am-at/, ... }. Under such a set-up, however, the MAX$_{\mathrm{CATEGORY}}$ approach runs directly into the same difficulty faced by the original version of MPARSE: producing no output form for a given paradigmatic cell would involve eliminating all of the structure present in the input for that cell, and, in order to avoid a gapped paradigm being harmonically bounded by one with partial deletion in the relevant cell, the MAX$_{\mathrm{CATEGORY}}$-violating gap must be stipulated not to violate phonological MAX (i.e., MAX$_{\mathrm{SEGMENT}}$).

On the other hand, the MAX$_{\mathrm{CATEGORY}}$ approach does appear to be compatible with a process-based theory of morphology in which affixes are not regarded as actual objects in some lexical list, but rather are simply introduced into the output by rules or constraints that specify how certain morphosyntactic properties are to be expressed phonologically. OT approaches that adopt versions of this view of morphology include Hammond (1995), Russell (1999), and MacBride (2004); they are subjected to critical scrutiny in Bonet (2004). The main problem: without affixes in the input, affixes are not subject to faithfulness constraints, and so explanations for language typology based on (positional) faithfulness are not possible.

6.2   Gaps as morpheme deletion

The original version of MPARSE proposed in Prince and Smolensky (2004) demands that the morphemes in the input be parsed into morphological constituents. The null parse, in this formulation, consists of just the input morphemes with no tree structure linking them. The victory of this candidate results in a gap because unstructured morphological content cannot enter the syntax. The fate of morphemes in the null parse candidate, as originally conceived, is thus parallel to that suffered by deleted segments, which, under the PARSE/FILL theory, were not literally deleted but rather not parsed into *prosodic* constituents, and hence rendered unpronounceable.

With the supplanting of the PARSE/FILL model of faithfulness by correspondence, a number of researchers have proposed adapting the original conception of MPARSE to the new faithfulness regime, by replacing underparsing of morphemes with literal deletion of morphemes. Kager (2000), for example, recasts MPARSE as M-MAX: 'every morpheme in the input has a correspondent in the output.' A more elaborate model along the same lines is presented in Walker and Feng (2004). They propose that there are three correspondence relations relevant to the phonology/morphology interface; they are defined in (40) along with the MAX constraints that operate on each dimension of correspondence. The idea is that both input and output have separate phonological and morphological structure. PP-correspondence constraints (a) require input-output faithfulness to phonological structure; MM-correspondence constraints (b) require input-output faithfulness to morphological structure; and MP-correspondence constraints (c) require an affiliation between morphological and phonological structure in the output. We will henceforth refer to this theory as Ternary Morphology-Phonology Correspondence, or TMPC.

(40)   Correspondence relations in Walker and Feng (2004)

    a.   PP-Correspondence (= input-output correspondence on phonological structure)
        MAX-PP: Every segment in the input has a correspondent in the output.

    b.   MM-Correspondence (= input-output correspondence on morphological structure)
        MAX-MM: Every morpheme in the input has a correspondent in the output.

    c.   MP-Correspondence (=affiliation of phonological structure with morphemes)
        MAX-MP: Every morpheme in the output is indexed with some phonological element in the output.
        MAX-PM: Every phonological element in the output is indexed with some morpheme in the output.

In TMPC, paradigmatic gaps are analyzed as follows. Assume that faithful realization of the phonological content of some affix Af would result in violation of some markedness constraint MARK. If the ranking is MARK ≫ MAX-PP, then Af's phonological content will be deleted. (This is equivalent to MARK ≫ MAX in conventional correspondence theory.) If the grammar also contains the ranking MAX-MP ≫ MAX-MM, then (by MAX-MP) every morpheme is required to have some overt phonological exponence, and (at the expense of violating MAX-MM) Af is removed from the output *morphological* structure because it has no output *phonological* structure.

For illustration, consider how a paradigmatic gap in Swedish would be analyzed in TMPC. (For this phenomenon, see Eliasson (1975) and Iverson (1981).) In Swedish, the indefinite neuter singular suffix on adjectives is /-t/: *et rysk-t barn* 'a Russian child'. But adjectives whose stem ends in /dd/ have no neuter singular form: **et rädd-t barn* 'a scared child' (cf. masculine *en rädd pojke* 'a scared boy'). The ranking MARK ≫ MAX-PP, where MARK rules out **dd-t*, favors deletion of /-t/ from the output phonological structure. (This assumes that /-t/ rather than /dd/ deletes, perhaps because of greater faithfulness to root segments.) The ranking MAX-MP ≫ MAX-MM further favors deletion of INDEFNEUTSG from the output morphological structure (indicated here in small caps). The result, shown in (41), is a paradigmatic gap: an output without the morphological structure of an indefinite neuter singular adjective.

(41)   Swedish gap in TMPC

/rädd+t/ /SCARED+INDEFNEUTSG/	MARK	MAX-MP	MAX-PP	MAX-MM
rädd SCARED			1	1
a. rädd-t SCARED+INDEFNEUTSG	W₁		L	L
b. rädd SCARED+INDEFNEUTSG		W₁	1	L

This analysis of Swedish illustrates a key property of TMPC: because the only constraint in the theory that conflicts with MAX-MM is MAX-MP, deletion of morphological structure (that is, paradigmatic gapping) can only occur when some markedness constraint forces deletion of *all* of the phonological content of a morpheme, so the continued presence of that morpheme's morphological structure would violate MAX-MP.

This property proves to be the empirical Achilles' heel of the theory, because it means that TMPC cannot induce paradigm gaps involving morphemes that have no phonological exponent to begin with (i.e., zero affixes). The Norwegian imperative is an example. Because Norwegian has a zero affix in the imperative, the ranking MAX-MM ≫ MAX-MP must hold in the language, in order to prevent the imperative from being gapped across the board. But then there can be no imperative gaps whatsoever since, as (41) shows, the opposite ranking of these constraints is a prerequisite for paradigmatic gaps.

Another reason why TMPC cannot handle the Norwegian facts is that deleting the exponentless imperative morpheme does nothing to remedy the phonological markedness that motivates the gap in the first place. In other words, [åpn-∅//OPEN IMP] and [åpn//OPEN] receive exactly the same marks from the constraint against rising-sonority coda clusters, and indeed from every phonological markedness constraint, since their phonological output shapes are identical. As one may see in (41), the TMPC account works only if deleting the affix's phonological structure improves performance on MARK. That is not the case in Norwegian, since the affix had no phonological structure to start with.

The TMPC analysis of Swedish relies on the fact that MARK can only be satisfied by deleting *all* of the affix's phonological content, so that MAX-MP will be violated unless the affix's morphological structure is also deleted. The Swedish affix in question is monosegmental, but what about longer affixes, where partial deletion would suffice to satisfy MARK? Hungarian (Hetzron 1975, Rebrus and Törkenczy this volume) is a case in point. Certain verbs whose stem ends in a cluster, such as *csukl-* 'hiccup', have gaps for the following categories: the jussive (normally marked by *–j* plus a person marker), the potential (marked by *–hat/het*), and the verbal adverb (marked by *–va/ve*). What all of these affixes have in common is that, if they are concatenated to *csukl-*, a triconsonantal cluster would be created. In the case of the potential affix *–hat/het* and the verbal adverb affix *–va/ve*, though, the triconsonantal cluster could be eliminated by deleting just the initial consonant of the suffix: /csukl-hat/ → *[csuklat]. Since the affix is not completely deleted, MAX-MP is satisfied without further ado, and the gap is unanalyzeable under TMPC's assumptions. In an MPARSE-based theory, on the other hand, it would suffice to simply rank the constraint against triconsonantal clusters and all relevant faithfulness constraints above MPARSE. For this and all of the other reasons discussed in this section, it is clear that morpheme-deletion-based approaches like TMPC are simply not empirically adequate as theories of phonologically-motivated paradigm gaps.

7 Conclusion

In this chapter, we have argued for a revision of correspondence theory in which strings rather than segments are the formal objects that stand in correspondence. In this revision, well-behaved unfaithful mappings do not alter ℜ's status is a total bijective function. Candidates with a less orderly ℜ violate MPARSE; among these candidates there is one that harmonically bounds all of the others, the null output ⊙. The primary goal of this project is to explain why ⊙ uniquely violates no constraints except MPARSE, making it suitable for the analysis of phonologically-conditioned gaps. Along the way, we have also discussed the general properties of MPARSE, the locality of coalescence and breaking, and alternative theories of gaps.

References

Akinlabi, A. (1996) Featural alignment. *Journal of Linguistics* 32: 239–89. ROA 185, http://roa.rutgers.edu.

Alderete, J. (2001a) Dominance effects as transderivational anti-faithfulness. *Phonology* 18: 201–53.

Alderete, J. (2001b) *Morphologically Governed Accent in Optimality Theory*. New York & London: Routledge. [1999 Doctoral dissertation, University of Massachusetts, Amherst. ROA 309, http://roa.rutgers.edu.]

Apoussidou, D. (2003) The deformity of anti-faithfulness. In Jennifer Spenader, Anders Eriksson, and Östen Dahl (eds.) *Proceedings of the Stockholm Workshop on Variation in Optimality Theory* 15–24. Stockholm: Department of Linguistics, Stockholm University. [Available at http://www.fon.hum.uva.nl/diana/The%20Deformity\ %20of%20AntiFaithfulness.pdf.]

Aronoff, M., Arsyad, A., Basri, H., and Broselow, E. (1987) Tier configuration in Makassarese reduplication. In A. Bosch, E. Schiller, and B. Need (eds.) *CLS 23: Parasession on Autosegmental and Metrical Phonology* 1–15. Chicago: Chicago Linguistic Society.

Baker, C. L. (1979) Syntactic theory and the projection problem. *Linguistic Inquiry* 10: 533–81.

Baker, M. (1985) The Mirror Principle and morphosyntactic explanation. *Linguistic Inquiry* 16: 373–415.

Benua, L. (1997) *Transderivational Identity: Phonological Relations between Words*. Ph. D. thesis. Amherst, MA: University of Massachusetts Amherst. ROA 259, http://roa.rutgers.edu [Published (2000) as *Phonological Relations Between Words*, New York: Garland. Excerpted in *Optimality Theory in Phonology: A Reader*, ed. by John J. McCarthy, Malden, MA and Oxford, Blackwell (2004).]

Berwick, R. (1985) *The Acquisition of Syntactic Knowledge*. Cambridge, MA: MIT Press.

Bonet, E. (2004) Morph insertion and allomorphy in Optimality Theory. *International Journal of English Studies* 4: 73–104.

Carrier-Duncan, J. (1984) Some problems with prosodic accounts of reduplication. In M. Aronoff and R. T. Oehrle (eds.) *Language Sound Structure* 260–86. Cambridge, MA: MIT Press.

Causley, T. (1997) Identity and featural correspondence: The Athapaskan case. In K. Kusumoto (ed.) *Proceedings of the North East Linguistic Society 27* 93–105. Amherst, MA: GLSA Publications.

Crosswhite, K. (1998) Segmental vs. prosodic correspondence in Chamorro. *Phonology* 15: 281–316.

Eliasson, S. (1975) On the issue of directionality. In K.-H. Dahlstedt (ed.) *The Nordic Languages and Modern Linguistics 2* 421–45. Stockholm: Almqvist & Wiksell.

Gnanadesikan, A. (1997) *Phonology with Ternary Scales*. Ph. D. thesis. Amherst, MA: University of Massachusetts at Amherst. ROA 195, http://roa.rutgers.edu.

Gold, E. M. (1967) Language identification in the limit. *Information and Control* 10: 447–74.

Golston, C. (1995) Syntax outranks phonology: evidence from Ancient Greek. *Phonology* 12: 343–68.

Gouskova, M. (2003) *Deriving Economy: Syncope in Optimality Theory*. Ph. D. thesis. Amherst, MA: University of Massachusetts Amherst. ROA 610, http://roa.rutgers.edu.

Grimshaw, J. (1997) Projection, heads, and optimality. *Linguistic Inquiry* 28: 373–422.

Halle, M. (1973) Prolegomena to a theory of word formation. *Linguistic Inquiry* 4: 3–16.

Hammond, M. (1994) An OT account of variability in Walmatjari stress. Unpublished manuscript. Tucson, AZ: University of Arizona. ROA 20, http://roa.rutgers.edu.

Hammond, M. (1995) There is no lexicon! Unpublished manuscript. Tucson, AZ: University of Arizona. ROA 43, http://roa.rutgers.edu.

Hayes, B. (1990) Diphthongization and coindexing. *Phonology* 7: 31–71.

Hayes, B. (2004) Phonological acquisition in Optimality Theory: The early stages. In R. Kager, J. Pater, and W. Zonneveld (eds.) *Fixing Priorities:*

Constraints in Phonological Acquisition 158–203. Cambridge: Cambridge University Press. ROA 327, `http://roa.rutgers.edu`.

Hetzron, R. (1975) Where the grammar fails. *Language* 51: 859–72.

Horwood, G. (2002) Precedence faithfulness governs morpheme position. In L. Mikkelsen and C. Potts (eds.) *Proceedings of the 21st West Coast Conference on Formal Linguistics* 166–79. Cambridge, MA: Cascadilla Press. ROA 527, `http://roa.rutgers.edu`.

Inkelas, S. and Zoll, C. (2003) Is grammar dependence real? Unpublished manuscript. Berkeley, CA and Cambridge, MA: University of California and MIT. ROA 587, `http://roa.rutgers.edu`.

Itô, J. and Mester, A. (1999) The phonological lexicon. In N. Tsujimura (ed.) *The Handbook of Japanese Linguistics* 62–100. Oxford: Blackwell.

Iverson, G. K. (1981) Rules, constraints, and paradigm lacunae. *Glossa* 15: 136–44.

Iverson, G. K. and Sanders, G. (1982) On the government of phonological rules by laws. *Studies in Language* 6: 51–74.

Kager, R. (1999) Surface opacity of metrical structure in Optimality Theory. In B. Hermans and M. van Oostendorp (eds.) *The Derivational Residue in Phonological Optimality Theory* 207–45. Amsterdam: John Benjamins.

Kager, R. (2000) Stem stress and peak correspondence in Dutch. In J. Dekkers, F. van der Leeuw, and J. van de Weijer (eds.) *Optimality Theory: Phonology, Syntax, and Acquisition.* Oxford: Oxford University Press.

Kager, R., Pater, J., and Zonneveld, W. (eds.) (2004) *Constraints in Phonological Acquisition.* Cambridge: Cambridge University Press.

Kawahara, S. (2004) Locality in echo epenthesis: Comparison with reduplication. In K. Moulton and M. Wolf (eds.) *Proceedings of the North East Linguistics Society 34* 295–309. Amherst, MA: GLSA.

Kawahara, S. (2006) Copy and spreading in phonological theory: Evidence from echo epenthesis. In L. Bateman, A. Werle, M. O'Keefe, and E. Reilly (eds.) *University of Massachusetts Occasional Papers in Linguistics 32: Papers in Optimality Theory III.* Amherst, MA: GLSA.

Kenstowicz, M. (1994) Syllabification in Chukchee: A constraints-based analysis. In A. Davison, N. Maier, G. Silva, and W. S. Yan (eds.) *Proceedings of the Formal Linguistics Society of Mid-America 4* 160–81. Iowa City: Department of Linguistics, University of Iowa. ROA 30, `http://roa.rutgers.edu`.

Kiparsky, P. (2000) Opacity and cyclicity. *The Linguistic Review* 17: 351–67.

Kornai, A. (1994) *Formal Phonology*. New York: Garland. [Preface available at `http://www.kornai.com/Papers/sel97.pdf`.]

Kurisu, K. (2001) *The Phonology of Morpheme Realization*. Ph. D. thesis, Santa Cruz, CA: University of California, Santa Cruz. ROA 490, `http://roa.rutgers.edu`.

de Lacy, P. (1999) Morphological haplology and correspondence. In P. de Lacy and A. Nowak (eds.) *University of Massachusetts Occasional Papers in Linguistics 25: Papers from the 25th Anniversary* 51–88. Amherst, MA: GLSA.
ROA 298, `http://roa.rutgers.edu`.

de Lacy, P. and Kitto, C. (1999) A correspondence theory of epenthetic quality. In C. Kitto and C. Smallwood (eds.) *Proceedings of AFLA VI* 181–200. Toronto: Toronto Working Papers in Linguistics.

Legendre, G., Smolensky, P., and Wilson, C. (1998) When is less more? Faithfulness and minimal links in *wh*-chains. In P. Barbosa, D. Fox, P. Hagstrom, M. McGinnis, and D. Pesetsky (eds.) *Is the Best Good Enough? Optimality and Competition in Syntax* 249–89. Cambridge, MA: MIT Press. ROA 117, `http://roa.rutgers.edu`.

Lombardi, L. (1998) Evidence for MaxFeature constraints from Japanese. In H. Fukazawa, F. Morelli, C. Struijke, and Y.-C. Su (eds.) *University of Maryland Working Papers in Linguistics*. College Park, MD: Department of Linguistics, University of Maryland. ROA 247, `http://roa.rutgers.edu`.

Łubowicz, A. (2005) Infixaton as morpheme absorption. Unpublished manuscript. Los Angeles: University of Southern California. ROA 773, `http://roa.rutgers.edu`.

MacBride, A. (2004) *A Constraint-based Approach to Morphology*. Ph. D. thesis, Los Angeles: UCLA.
`http://www.linguistics.ucla.edu/general/dissertations/MacbrideAlexPhD2004.pdf`

McCarthy, J. J. (2002) *A Thematic Guide to Optimality Theory*. Cambridge: Cambridge University Press.

McCarthy, J. J. (2003) OT constraints are categorical. *Phonology* 20: 75–138. [Available at
`http://people.umass.edu/jjmccart/categorical.pdf`.]

McCarthy, J. J. (2005) Optimal paradigms. In L. J. Downing, T. A. Hall, and R. Raffelsiefen (eds.) *Paradigms in Phonological Theory* 170–210. Oxford: Oxford University Press.
ROA 485, `http://roa.rutgers.edu`.

McCarthy, J. J. (2006) *Hidden Generalizations: Phonological Opacity in Optimality Theory*. London: Equinox Publishing.

McCarthy, J. J. (2007) Restraint of analysis. In S. Blaho, P. Bye, and M. Krämer (eds.) *Freedom of Analysis* 203–32. Berlin/New York: Mouton de Gruyter.

McCarthy, J. J. and Prince, A. (1990) Foot and word in prosodic morphology: the Arabic broken plural. *Natural Language and Linguistic Theory* 8: 209–83.

McCarthy, J. J. and Prince, A. (1993a) Generalized Alignment. In G. Booij and J. van Marle (eds.) *Yearbook of Morphology* 79–153. Dordrecht: Kluwer. ROA 7, http://roa.rutgers.edu. [Excerpts appear in J. Goldsmith, ed., *Essential Readings in Phonology*. Oxford: Blackwell. Pp. 102–136, 1999 and in J. J. McCarthy, ed., *Optimality Theory in Phonology: A Reader*. Oxford and Malden, MA: Blackwell (2004).]

McCarthy, J. J. and Prince, A. (1993b) Prosodic Morphology: Constraint Interaction and Satisfaction. Report. New Brunswick, NJ: Rutgers University Center for Cognitive Science.
ROA 482, http://roa.rutgers.edu.

McCarthy, J. J. and Prince, A. (1994) The emergence of the unmarked: Optimality in prosodic morphology. In M. Gonzàlez (ed.) *Proceedings of the 24th Annual Meeting of the North East Linguistic Society* 333–79. Amherst, MA: GLSA Publications. ROA 13, http://roa.rutgers.edu. [Excerpted in *Optimality Theory in Phonology: A Reader*, ed. by J. J. McCarthy, Malden, MA and Oxford, Blackwell (2004).]

McCarthy, J. J. and Prince, A. (1995) Faithfulness and Reduplicative Identity. In J. Beckman, L. Walsh Dickey, and S. Urbanczyk (eds.) *University of Massachusetts Occasional Papers in Linguistics 18* 249–384. Amherst, MA: GLSA Publications.
ROA 103, http://roa.rutgers.edu.

McCarthy, J. J. and Prince, A. (1999) Faithfulness and identity in Prosodic Morphology. In R. Kager, H. van der Hulst, and W. Zonneveld (eds.) *The Prosody-Morphology Interface* 218–309. Cambridge: Cambridge University Press. [Excerpted in *Optimality Theory in Phonology: A Reader*, ed. by J. J. McCarthy, Malden, MA and Oxford, Blackwell (2004).]

Myers, S. (1987) *Tone and the Structure of Words in Shona*. Ph. D. thesis: University of Massachusetts Amherst.

van Oostendorp, M. (2005) The theory of faithfulness. Unpublished manuscript. Amsterdam: Meertens Institute. [Available at
http://egg.auf.net/05/docs/handouts/oo{}-io.pdf.]

van Oostendorp, M. (2007) Derived environment effects and Consistency of Exponence. In S. Blaho, P. Bye, and M. Krämer (eds.) *Freedom of Analysis* 123–48. Berlin/New York: Mouton de Gruyter.

Orgun, C. O. and Sprouse, R. (1999) From MParse to control: Deriving ungrammaticality. *Phonology* 16: 191–220.

Pater, J. (2000) Nonuniformity in English secondary stress: The role of ranked and lexically specific constraints. *Phonology* 17: 237–74. ROA 107, http://roa.rutgers.edu.

Pierrehumbert, J. and Beckman, M. (1988) *Japanese Tone Structure*. Cambridge, MA: MIT Press.

Plag, I. (1998) Morphological haplology in a constraint-based morphophonology. In W. Kehrein and R. Wiese (eds.) *Phonology and Morphology of the Germanic Languages* 199–215. Tübingen, Germany: Niemeyer. ROA 344, http://roa.rutgers.edu.

Prince, A. (2002) Arguing optimality. In A. Carpenter, A. Coetzee, and P. de Lacy (eds.) *Papers in Optimality Theory II (= University of Massachusetts Occasional Papers 26)* 269–304. Amherst, MA: GLSA. ROA 562, http://roa.rutgers.edu.

Prince, A. and Smolensky, P. (2004) *Optimality Theory: Constraint Interaction in Generative Grammar*. Malden, MA, and Oxford, UK: Blackwell. [Revision of 1993 technical report, Rutgers University Center for Cognitive Science. ROA 537, http://roa.rutgers.edu.]

Prince, A. and Tesar, B. (2004) Learning phonotactic distributions. In R. Kager, J. Pater, and W. Zonneveld (eds.) *Constraints in Phonological Acquisition* 245–91. Cambridge: Cambridge University Press. ROA 353, http://roa.rutgers.edu.

Raffelsiefen, R. (2004) Absolute ill-formedness and other morphophonological effects. *Phonology* 21: 91–142.

Rice, C. (2003) Dialectal variation in Norwegian imperatives. *Nordlyd* 31: 372–84. ROA 642, http://roa.rutgers.edu.

Rice, C. (2005a) Nothing is a phonological fact: gaps and repairs at the phonology-morphology interface. Unpublished manuscript. Tromsø, Norway: University of Tromsø.
ROA 781, http://roa.rutgers.edu.

Rice, C. (2005b) Optimal gaps in optimal paradigms. *Catalan Journal of Linguistics*: 155–170. [Special issue on phonology in morphology edited by M.-R. Lloret and J. Jiménez. Available at LingBuzz, http://ling.auf.net/buzzdocs/.]

Rose, S. (1997) *Theoretical Issues in Comparative Ethio-Semitic Phonology and Morphology*. Ph. D. thesis, Montréal: McGill University.

Russell, K. (1995) Morphemes and candidates in Optimality Theory. Unpublished manuscript, University of Manitoba.
ROA 44, http://roa.rutgers.edu.

Russell, K. (1999) MOT: Sketch of an Optimality Theoretic approach to morphology. Unpublished manuscript. Winnipeg: University of Manitoba. [available at `http://www.umanitoba.ca/linguistics/russell/mot.ps`.]

Samek-Lodovici, V. (1993) A unified analysis of crosslinguistic morphological gemination. Unpublished manuscript. New Brunswick, NJ: Rutgers University. ROA 149, `http://roa.rutgers.edu`.

Samek-Lodovici, V. and Prince, A. (1999) Optima. Unpublished manuscript. London and New Brunswick, NJ: University of London and Rutgers University. ROA 363, `http://roa.rutgers.edu`.

Steriade, D. (1988) Reduplication and syllable transfer in Sanskrit and elsewhere. *Phonology* 5: 73–155.

Trommer, J. (2005) Against antifaithfulness in Luo. Unpublished manuscript. Leipzig: Institute of Linguistics, University of Leipzig. [Abstract available at `http://www.uni{}-leipzig.de/~jtrommer/05.pdf`.]

Vogel, I. and Kenesei, I. (1990) Syntax and semantics in phonology. In S. Inkelas and D. Zec (eds.) *The Phonology-Syntax Connection* 339–64. Chicago: University of Chicago Press.

Walker, R. and Feng, B. (2004) A ternary model of morphology-phonology correspondence. In B. Schmeiser, V. Chand, A. Kelleher, and A. Rodriguez (eds.) *WCCFL 23 Proceedings*. Somerville, MA: Cascadilla Press.

Wolf, M. (2006) For an autosegmental theory of mutation. In L. Bateman, A. Werle, M. O'Keefe, and E. Reilly (eds.) *University of Massachusetts Occasional Papers in Linguistics 32: Papers in Optimality Theory III*. Amherst, MA: GLSA. ROA 754, `http://roa.rutgers.edu`.

Zec, D. and Inkelas, S. (1990) Prosodically constrained syntax. In S. Inkelas and D. Zec (eds.) *The Phonology-Syntax Connection* 365–78. Chicago: University of Chicago Press.

Zwicky, A. M. and Pullum, G. (1986) The principle of Phonology-Free Syntax: introductory remarks. *Ohio State University Working Papers in Linguistics* 32: 63–91.

3 Dutch diminutives and the question mark*

Marc van Oostendorp
Meertens Instituut, Amsterdam

1   Monostratalism and the null parse

Within a Correspondence framework of faithfulness, there are roughly four ways of treating the problem of ineffability:

1. The 'paradigmatic solution': the Generator function does not generate an individual form, but a paradigm. Ineffability of an individual form means that this particular form is not generated within the paradigm. This type of solution is defended in this volume (in various forms) by Bat-El, Rice, and Rebrus and Törkenczy.

2. The 'null parse' solution: the Generator function generates a candidate in the phonology which does not have a phonetic interpretation, and this is selected as the winner in certain cases; this typo of solution is defended in this volume by Wolf and McCarthy.

3. The 'control' solution: the Generator and Evaluator function conspire to create a (pronounceable) candidate, but a grammatical component outside of the OT system then blocks this candidate. This solution is defended by Orgun & Sprouse in this volume.

4. The 'divergent meaning' solution: we generate a phonologically well-formed form, but one which does not have the intended semantics; the form is therefore unusable. This solution is basically the one proposed by Legendre and by Vogel in this volume for syntax, and will be defended here for phonology.

This article builds on a theory of faithfulness that is different from Correspondence Theory, viz. one which I call Containment Theory, i.e. the version of faithfulness originally propsed by Prince and Smolensky (1993). The idea of the Null Parse was first brought up by these authors within

---

*Thanks are due to Ben Hermans, Anthi Revithiadou, Curt Rice and the participants of the Gaps Workshop in Oslo, May 2006. All errors are mine.

the context of this theory of faithfulness, albeit not in a very formal way. Containment was soon replaced as a theory of input-output relations by Correspondence Theory (McCarthy and Prince 1995), but if I am not mistaken, interest is currently reviving. One important advantage of Containment Theory over Correspondence is that it is theoretically more restrictive, and therefore makes more fine-grained empirical predictions.

Formally, the main difference between Containment Theory and Correspondence Theory is that the former offers a purely monostratal view of linguistic representations. All Containment based constraints, those checking faithfulness as well as those checking wellformedness, only consider one level of representation — the output. We may posit an input to the Gen function, but the constraints of Con are not aware of it, and hence the input representation does not exist for the Eval function. Within Correspondence Theory, on the other hand, there are typically two levels of representation — the input and the output — and constraints refer to properties of one of these levels, if they are wellformedness constraints, or to the correspondence relations between them, if they are faithfulness constraints: both input and output exist both for Gen and for Eval.

If we have only one of level of representation, such as in Containment Theory, we still need to be able to see deleted material, otherwise there is no way to penalize it: we need constraints against deletion, otherwise all deletion will come for free, and since we only consider one representation 'deleted' material still needs to be present in that representation. In classical Containment Theory of Prince and Smolensky (1993) this was accomplished by assuming (i) that all input material would be contained in the output (this was called the principle of Containment, hardwired into the Generator function), but that (ii) the material which was not pronounced is not parsed in the phonological structure: unpronounced features were left unassociated to segments, unpronounced segments are not incorporated into the syllable structure. The phonetics, coming after the phonology, only considered the phonologically parsed material and applied 'stray erasure' to the rest. The phonological derivation thus was monotonic whereas the phonetics was not.

The first theoretical option mentioned above, the one couched in terms of paradigms, is basically impossible to formulate in terms of Containment theory. Paradigmatic relations may be described in terms of Correspondence, but it does not make sense to try to describe the in terms of Containment, since that would involve putting all members of a paradigm into one phonological representation. The null parse solution is also much more problematic for Containment Theory than for Correspondence Theory: if all the material is present in the output anyway, why would we ever choose to not to pronounce any part of that material? This means that the number of theoretical options is reduced by half if we accept Containment, a restrictiveness which might itself considered to be a positive result: we either should choose the control solution or the divergent meaning solution if we accept Containment Theory.

The bigger popularity of Correspondence Theory may account for the fact that almost all of the studies on the issue of ineffability — for instance, all other phonological chapters in this book — are couched in terms of that model of faithfulness. The only Containment attempt at a solution for this problem of which I am aware is Prince and Smolensky (1993: p. 51–52)'s suggestion that the null parse is the form which does not get morphological structure assigned to it. The input of the phonological derivation for some form can be assumed to be { root, affix }, i.e., an unordered set. Gen can decide to assign morphological structure to this set, e.g. [[root] affix] (satisfying a constraint MPARSE), or it can decide to leave the whole structure as it is morphologically unparsed. { root, affix }, however, is something that will not fit into a syntactic structure, and this will cause the crash. See the introduction to this volume for a more detailed explanation.

The discussion of this issue is rather informal in Prince and Smolensky (1993), and it therefore leaves several questions open. For instance, it is not exactly clear where the crash takes place that leads the underlying material to be unpronounced. One way to interpret Prince and Smolensky (1993)'s suggestion is that the null parse is assigned in a morphological module, which is then input to the syntax; here, the word becomes 'uninterpretable' however. Yet, if syntax is also an OT system, — as should be the null hypothesis —, it should not crash on receiving an uninterpretable input, but rather do something else (such as making it interpretable). This is of course even more so if phonology, morphology and syntax work in parallel. It thus still is not completely clear how ineffability works under Prince and Smolensky (1993)'s assumptions. More discussion of this issue will be provided in section 2.

This article aims to fill this gap in the theoretical literature for two reasons. In the first place, I consider Containment Theory a serious alternative to Correspondence, as I will explain in section 2; but as such it needs a worked-out approach of ineffability, among other things, which can compete with the best Correspondence Theory alternatives. In the second place, I believe that Containment Theory puts into a special light an important aspect of all cases of ineffability seen in the literature: that the relation to morphology and to the input plays an important role in it. The results of this investigation may therefore also be of interest for students of ineffability within Correspondence Theory.

I will present my solution to the ineffability problem within Containment in two steps. In section 4, I will develop a 'radical' solution which should be able to compete with Correspondence-based alternatives. However, I will show that often the 'ineffable' cases are actually not completely impossible, and may grow more acceptable to speakers when they hear them repeatedly. In section 5, I therefore set a few additional steps, first embedding my approach into an accepted theory of language variation to be able to describe this pronounceability of 'ineffable' material, and secondly, explaining why lexicalisation helps making a form more acceptable.

Next to these theoretical goals, this article also serves to add some new facts to the discussion about ineffability. These facts are from (Standard) Dutch: it is shown in section 3 that diminutives are difficult to form on the basis of certain proper names and nouns, depending on their phonological shape. The particular relevance of these facts is that diminutive formation seems 'difficult' rather than impossible: while most native speakers agree that these forms are funny, this does not mean that everybody rejects them outright. As a matter of fact, many informants seem to agree that one could use these forms if forced to, even if they sound a little unusual, and a corpus search reveals that they are indeed used, albeit less frequently than forms with a similar meaning but a different phonological shape. In other words, these forms have a question mark rather than an asterisk.

The question mark poses of course a problem to OT which is of the same nature as the problem of ineffability. An OT grammar only knows absolute judgements: there is one candidate output which will win the competition — and therefore be grammatical —, and there are many candidate outputs which will be defeated (and therefore get a star), but there is nothing in between. We argue in section 5 that the question mark indeed is an extragrammatical category, but one which can nevertheless be understood in terms of our Containment based solution and a theory of language variation.

An important difference between the question mark and ineffability is that the latter is a problem mainly for OT and not for other models, such as classical, rule-based SPE-type phonology or Government Phonology: most of these alternatives assign absolute markings to all representations, which can result in some combination of morphemes to be simply impossible. However, the question mark poses serious problems for virtually every (formal) theory of grammar, and maybe even especially so for the theories just mentioned, because of their absolute markings. Given the fact that the study of variation — comparing different forms for one input — is relatively well-developed within OT, the existence of question marks will be argued to actually be an argument in favour of such a model of grammar.

2 Containment

2.1 Containment and Correspondence

In the OT literature, we find roughly two ways of evaluating the relationship between input and output. One is monostratal, and exemplified by Containment Theory: the constraints can see only one representation, the output.[1] The other one is multistratal — usually bistratal: the constraints can see and evaluate input and output and (correspondence) relations between them.[2]

As already pointed out above, within a Containment model we need to be able to see in the output representation which elements are inserted and which elements are deleted. If we would not be able to differentiate an inserted vowel from an underlying vowel at the surface level, there would be no way in which we could block massive epenthesis; and if deleted elements do not leave some trace in the surface structure, there would be no way of preventing massive deletion. The latter point means that input material should still be present in the output representation; hence the generator function is subject to a principle of Containment:

(1)   *Containment.* Every element of the phonological input representation is contained in the output. (There is no deletion.)

Faithfulness constraints are formalized by Prince and Smolensky (1993) in the following way. They assume that 'deletion' means that elements are

---

[1] The fact that Containment Theory is techically monostratal does not imply that it would be incompatible, for instance with Stratal OT (Kiparsky 2000). The 'monostratal' aspect of it involves the relation between input and output, but of course, we can still make the output of one level the input of the next level.

[2] In most versions of Correspondence Theory, there are no constraints evaluating the input structure, but the reason for this is that such constraints would not extend a lot of empirical power, since all candidates in a tableau have the same input, and thus will have the same violations for such constraints. There is no logical ban on constraints on inputs.

'not parsed' into the phonological structure, as outlined above. 'Inserted' segments are supposed to remain empty — there is no insertion of features —, and this is how the phonology can recognize them.

(2)   a.   PARSE: All elements should be 'parsed' in the phonological structure (no deletion.)

          b.   FILL: Do not allow empty elements. (No insertion.)

As already indicated above, an advantage of a Containment approach to faithfulness is that it is theoretically parsimonious: it does not refer to any device which is not needed independently. For instance, the highly abstract correspondence relations are not necessary. Furthermore, the PARSE and FILL families of constraints supposedly are necessary outside the theory of faithfulness proper: we need to say that syllables should be parsed into feet, regardless of whether unparsed syllables are pronounced or not; we thus need PARSE constraints or some equivalent anyway. Similarly, we will want to prevent phonologically 'empty' segments, for instance because they do not seem to occur in all languages; we thus need FILL constraints or some equivalent anyway, even if we subscribe to Correspondence Theory.

This thus poses a problem for many of the proposed alternatives within other phonological frameworks of dealing with faithfulness: we may stipulate that we no longer use PARSE-C or FILL-V, but then we will still need to say something about consonants that are not attached to syllable nodes on the surface, or about vowels that do not have any vocalic feature content. Occam's razor thus seems to run against introducing correspondence relations to accomplish something that can already be done. In that sense, Containment comes very close to the null hypothesis regarding faithfulness theory, given the other theoretical assumptions that were made in Prince and Smolensky (1993); McCarthy and Prince (1993).

However, Containment Theory also has a few problems. One of these is that it seems less well-equipped to deal with interrepresentational relations beyond input-output relations, such as output-output relations (Burzio 1994, 1998, 2000, 2003; Benua 1997; Kager 1999), relations between candidates in a tableau (Sympathy Theory, McCarthy 1999) and, most uncontroversially, for the relations between bases and reduplicants (McCarthy and Prince 1995). However, alternatives for each of these presumed extensions of Correspondence Theory exist, which do not use Correspondence relations. For instance, instead of output-output relations we can use Stratal OT (Kiparsky 2000) or Derivational OT (Rubach 2003); for Sympathy Theory there is a spade of alternatives, and Containment Theory seems particularly suitable to deal with at least certain types of opacity (van Oostendorp 2007); and instead of Base-Reduplicant Correspondence, we can assume that copying in reduplication is governed by the morphology rather than the phonology (Inkelas and Zoll 2005).

Other problems have to do with the specific implementation of the idea of Containment with PARSE and FILL rather than with that idea itself. In particular the theory of epenthesis implied by the FILL constraints is very problematic. It should be the case, for instance, not just that features cannot be inserted, but features should also not be allowed to ever spread to an epenthetic vowel. If ever a vowel which is inserted by Gen would be able to acquire phonological features in whatever way, the epenthetic vowel would no longer be empty, hence it would no longer violate FILL, and the doors would be open to massive unpenalized epenthesis, at least in languages that allow some minimal form of vowel harmony.[3]

For this reason, van Oostendorp (2005b, 2007) develops an alternative implementation of Containment Theory, which evades these problems. This alternative is based on the notion of *Consistency of Exponence*, another classic principle of Optimality Theory which has not been taken sufficiently seriously in my view:

(3)　　*Consistency of Exponence*
　　　　"No changes in the exponence of a phonologically-specified morpheme are permitted." (McCarthy and Prince 1993, 1994)

This principle, assumed to restrict Gen, was explained by McCarthy and Prince (1993, 1994) in the following way:

"[Consistency of Exponence] means that the lexical specifications of a morpheme (segments, prosody, or whatever) can never be affected by Gen. In particular, epenthetic elements posited by Gen will have no morphological affiliation, even when they lie within or between strings with morphemic identity. Similarly, underparsing of segments — failure to endow them with syllable structure — will not change the make-up of a morpheme, though it will surely change how that morpheme is realized pho-

---

[3] The existence of vowel harmony and other types of feature spreading poses problems for the PARSE and FILL model. If spreading can occur, how do we prevent it from happening everywhere in every language? The only reasonable answer to this is: by way of faithfulness constraints against insertion of association lines. But how can we formalize that if constraints against insertion are FILL constraints — what does it mean to say that an association line is empty?

netically. Thus, any given morpheme's phonological exponents must be identical in underlying and surface form."

An important consequence of this principle is that the morphological identity of segments will be visible at the surface structure; in this way our phonological constraints can refer to them even within a monostratal model.

van Oostendorp (2005b) proposes a notation which allows us to see the effects of Consistency of Exponence, and which is based on the metaphor of colouring. It is assumed that every morpheme has its own 'colour' which has been provided by the lexicon and which is distributed over all segments and other material — features, mora's, etc. — lexically present in that morpheme. Assume for instance that we have an input morheme /takp/, and an output candidate which would be pronounced as [tapi]. This candidate would look as follows in the phonological surface (for the sake of reproductional convenience, the colours are reproduced here as subscripts):

(4)

In this simple example, there is only one morpheme with the 'colour' α. The epenthetic segment does not have any morphological colour, which is denoted here by giving $\emptyset$ as its subscript. In terms of colours, Consistency of Exponence states that Gen cannot give colour to epenthetic material, and it cannot alter the colours of underlying material.

(5)   *Consistency of Exponence* (Colour-based version). Gen cannot change the morphological colour of any phonological element.

But given this notational assumption, it becomes easy to determine the status of epenthetic material by checking only the phonological output: epenthetic material is exactly the material which does not have a morphological colour. Epenthetic segments thus do not have to be marked as featurally empty, since they are already empty from a morphological perspective by definition. It now becomes possible to do away with FILL and to define constraints against epenthesis and deletion in a parallel fashion. Deletion means — like in the PARSE&FILL model — that a segment is not incorporated into the phonological structure; epenthesis means that a segment is not incorporated into the morphological structure.

(6) a. PARSE-$\phi(\alpha)$: The morphological element α must be incorporated into the phonological structure. (No deletion.)

    b. PARSE-$\mu(\alpha)$: The phonological element α must be incorporated into the morphological structure. (No insertion.)

Consistency of Exponence has recently come under attack (Walker and Feng 2004; Łubowicz 2005), but van Oostendorp (2007) argues that these attacks are not very convincing, and as a matter of fact that a large literature has to assume Consistency of Exponence, for instance in order to implement morphologically-based positional faithfulness. If that is true, the constraints in (6) come for free, as it were.

The principle of Containment can be seen as a lemma of Consistency of Exponence under the original definition of that constraint in (3): deletion of underlying segments of a morpheme m would mean changing the exponence of m.[4] However, the equation no longer holds under the colour-based definition of Consistency of Exponence given in (5). Consistency of Exponence just states that *if* segments are preserved, they will keep their original morphological colour. This no longer implies that they have to be preserved, just like the principle of Containment does not say anything anymore about the colouring of phonological material. The two principles thus have become logically independent.

2.2 Ineffability in classical Containment Theory

It thus seems useful to take the theoretically parsimonious alternative that Containment poses to Correspondence Theory seriously. This means, however, that we have to provide alternative analyses for theories which have been proposed within Correspondence Theory, such as the analyses of ineffability that are developed in the other chapters of this book.

In order to do this, it is useful to briefly consider Prince and Smolensky (1993)'s discussion of these issues. These authors entertain two slightly distinct possibilities. In the first place, we might assume that in some cases it is better to not assign e.g. a foot or a phonological word label at all. If

---

[4]There are a few marginal cases where the two principles diverge even under PARSE-FILL. We find a concrete example if we consider 'epenthetic' material underlyingly, viz. material that does not belong to any morpheme. This material can be deleted for Consistency of Exponence, but not for Containment. I am not sure that the concept of underlying epenthetic material is a very important one to incorporate into the theory, but it is indeed predicted to exist by the theory developed here.

Latin does not have monomoraic words, this effect may be due to the interaction between FTBIN and the constraint LX≈PR, requiring every lexical word to correspond to a phonological word (this fulfilled a function in the theory which roughly corresponds to that of ALIGN(ω,X_0)).

If FTBIN≫LX≈PR, it may be better not to assign any phonological structure at all in order to prevent monomoraic forms from surfacing:[5]

(7)	/rĕ/	FTBIN	LX≈PR	...	PARSE
	a. rĕ		*	...	*
	b. [(rĕ)$_F$]$_{PrWd}$	*!		...	

Candidate (7b) represents an attempt to parse the structure into phonological constituency, but this results in a non-binary foot. It is then better to not parse the whole structure at all. The result of this is that FTBIN is satisfied vacuously, since there is no foot to violate it. Candidate (7a) will thus win, and handed over to the phonetics. But since the phonetics will only pronounce the material affiliated to a phonological word, the pronunciation of this winning item will be zero.

This solution works well to describe certain Morpheme Structure Constraints (MSCs) for short words ('stems cannot consist of only a short vowel'), viz. precisely in those circumstances in which the relevant markedness constraint, FTBIN in this case, dominates all faithfulness constraints. However, cases of this type are rare and furthermore, MSCs may be derivable by other means (see for instance McCarthy 1998: for a paradigmatic approach). Furthermore, this solution does not work in more complicated cases, where it is not so clear why we could not parse at least a part of the relevant structure. Consider the comparative form of the English adjective *violet*. It is well known that the comparative suffix *-er* can only be attached to Minimal Words of the size of one foot. Now suppose that we input {violet, er} to the grammar: what is the output of that particular set of underlying morphemes? From the point of view of phonology, there can be nothing against an output [$_\omega$ (vio)$_F$ (let)$_F$], since this is a well-formed structure elsewhere in the language, viz. in the simple form of the adjective; so it is not clear why the phonological Null Parse would ever win.

In order to be able to deal with such facts, then, Prince and Smolensky (1993: p. 53) introduce another type of parsing constraint, MPARSE. The

---

[5]A very straightforward, and probably more correct, account for this fact is later on also provided by Prince and Smolensky (1993): an underlying form /rĕ/ would be subjected to vocalic lengthening to [rē]. But if this vowel always surfaces as lengthening, Lexicon Optimisation will cause the long vowel to also be underlying.

idea is that words do not have any morphological structure in the input:

> On this view, then, the underlying form of an item will consist of a very incompletely structured set of specifications which constrain but do not themselves fully determine even the morphological character of the output form. These specifications must be put in relation, parsed into structure, in order to be interpretable.

The constraint MPARSE (M for morphology) requires that in the output all the relevant structure has been assigned. Furthermore,

> Failure to achieve morphological parsing is fatal. An unparsed item has no morphological category, and cannot be interpreted, either semantically or in terms of higher morphological structure.

I have already pointed out in section 1 above that it is not clear how this informal suggestion can be implemented precisely. If semantics or higher-order morphosyntactic structure also work as an OT system, they still cannot crash. If we assume a serial model — if we apply lower-level morphology and phonology first, and feed the results of this to 'higher morphological structure' or semantics, these modules will still try to get a result out of this. The same is true if all modules work in parallel. The only realistic answer therefore should be that it is eventually interpretative modules *outside of (OT) grammar* such as phonetics or pragmatics which will cause the crash.

More importantly, however, notice that the OT system has to be set up in a way which is not fully compatible with the assumption of Richness of the Base, in order for the analysis to work. It is crucial that the input is morphologically and phonologically underspecified. If we would allow inputs which are already parsed underlyingly, these inputs could presumably not be bested by a Null Parse, especially under an architecture of the grammar in which Containment plays a role, i.e. in which no underlying material can be thrown away. It seems therefore necessary to provide a more precise theory of the Null Parse within Containment Theory. This will be attempted in the sections 4 and 5 below, using the concepts of Coloured Containment. But before doing that, I will first provide some data which shed new light on this issue.

3   Dutch diminutives

3.1   The crucial data

The formation of diminutives has been the object of intensive study within Dutch linguistics for a long period of time (see Trommelen 1982; Kooij 1982; van der Hulst 1984; Booij 1995; Gussenhoven and Jacobs 1998; van Oostendorp 2000; Botma and van der Torre 2000; van de Weijer 2002: for some more recent contributions). The process is very productive and can affect all nouns and personal names in principle:

(8)

base form	*diminutive form*	*gloss*
man	man-ətjə	man
maan	maan-tjə	moon
raam	raam-pjə	window
dak	dak-jə	roof
Orhan	Orhan-ətjə	(name)
Geraldine	Geraldiːn-tjə	(name)
Ralf	Ralf-jə	(name)

The diminutive displays a substantial amount of allomorphy, and this is the focus of most phonological work, since this allomorphy is largely determined by prosodic factors. For instance, if a noun ends in a lax vowel plus a sonorant (*man*), the diminutive takes the shape -ətjə, whereas if the noun ends in a tense vowel plus a sonorant (*maan*), the suffix takes the shape -tjə.

Yet a footnote in a recent study in terms of Optimality Theory is particularly interesting. Van de Weijer (2002) notes — as far as I can tell for the first time in the literature — that certain nouns cannot take a diminutive suffix. After having consulted the intuitions of a number of native speakers of Standard Dutch, I conclude that this concerns in particular those ending in -/Tə/, where T is a coronal plosive (/t/ or /d/):

(9)

base form	*diminutive form*	*gloss*
lente	??*lente-tjə	spring
	*lent-jə	
schade	??*schade-tjə	damage
	*schaad-jə	
boete	??boete-tjə	fee
	??boet-jə	
Hilde	??*Hilde-tjə	(name)
	?Hilde-kə	

Note that in the case of names, there is the option of also adding the alternative diminutive suffix *-ke*, which seems to give a more acceptable result for most speakers. This applies only to names, since nouns never get this suffix — they sound dialectal if this is attempted.

If C in -/Cə/ is a different segment, judgments vary, reflecting possibly subtle differences in individual grammars, or the fact that words of this type are almost all proper names and therefore display a slightly different behaviour:

(10)

base form	*diminutive form*	*gloss*
base	??*base-tjə	base
	*baas-jə	
Susanne	?Susanne-tjə	(name)
	*Susan-jə	
	ok Susanne-kə	
Celine	?Celine-tjə	(name)
	ok Celien-tjə	
	ok Celine-kə	
Okke	?Okke-tjə	(name)
Douwe	??Douwe-tjə	(name)
gave	??gave-tjə	gift
	??gaaf-jə	
hetze	??hetze-tjə	innuendo
	*hets-jə	

This is the ineffability fact that will be at the focus of our attention in this paper. In order to properly understand it, we first need some background on the morphophonological status of the diminutive suffix.

3.2   A sketch of the analysis of diminutives

Although this has been phrased in different ways in the literature, the prosodic sensitivity of the diminutive suffix is usually taken to mean that the diminutive needs to be added to a minimal word of a certain shape. In other words, the following constraint applies to the diminutive suffix:[6]

(11)   SUFF-TO-PRWD: The base of suffixation is a bisyllabic word.

Some scholars (e.g. van Oostendorp 2000) assume that tense (long) vowels in Dutch always head an open syllable. The consequence of this

---

[6]This analysis loosely follows van de Weijer (2002).

is that the final consonant of *maan* appears in a separate position, e.g. the onset of an empty-headed syllable. We thus have the following structures for *maan* and *man* respectively:

(12)   a. *maan* 'moon' [maːn]   b. *man* 'man' [mɑn]

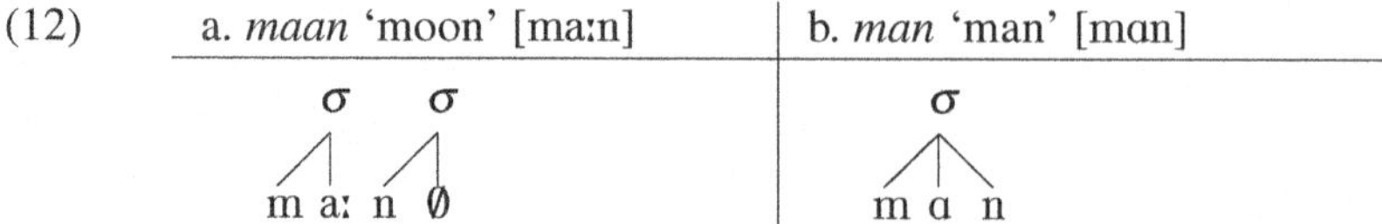

According to SUFF-TO-PRWD, we can affix the diminutive suffix to (12a) without any problems, but — assuming that monosyllabic units do not form minimal words — something needs to be added to the structure in (12b). This may be a schwa, providing the proper prosodic basis for the form in question:

(13)   a. *maantje* 'moon' [maːntjə]   b. *man* 'man' [mɑnətjə]

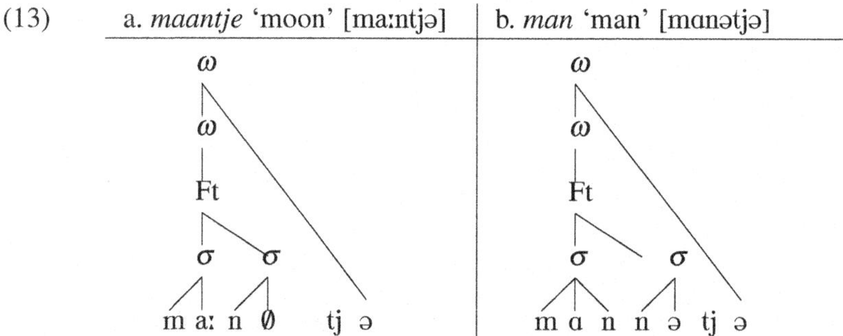

Given this analysis, we can now wonder about the morphological affiliation of the schwa: it does not make sense to say that it is part of an allomorph of the stem, because that would involve positing lexical allomorphy for a (large) natural class of forms; all words ending in a short vowel and a sonorant would have an allomorph with a schwa. There are therefore three options:

1. The schwa has its own morphological status as a separate (binding) morpheme. Such an analysis is possible, because there is independent evidence that Dutch uses schwa in this function. In compounds of a certain shape, we find schwas inserted which are probably not epenthetic: e.g. *vrouw-ə-lichaam* 'female body' from *vrouw* 'woman' and *lichaam* 'body'. As far as I can see, it would however be a novelty in the literature to assume that this binding schwa also shows up in the diminutive, and since nothing seems to bear on the issue for the present discussion, I have decided to assume the standard analysis. See Kooij (1982) for further discussion.

2. The schwa is phonologically epenthetic, and stays without morphological affiliation. Something similar applies to this: Dutch has phonological epenthesis of schwa (van Oostendorp 2000), but this does not normally occur between two consonants with the same place of articulation, such as the two coronals in *mannətjə*; for instance it does not apply in a word like *hand* 'hand', although it does apply in a word like *kalk* 'chalk' ([hɑnt]-*[hɑnət] vs. [kɑlk]-*[kɑlək]).

3. The schwa is part of an allomorph of the diminutive suffix. This seems then the most reasonable solution. A solution for the Dutch diminutive in terms of allomorphy is also suggested in Booij (2002): the suffix can also take the shapes *-kjə*, *-pjə* or *-jə*, and although each of these forms is phonologically conditioned, it is hard to relate them to productive processes of Dutch phonology — for instance, voiceless stops do not otherwise assimilate to neighbouring segments.

It has often been observed that the schwa suffix does not show up after a short vowel followed by an obstruent: the diminutive of *dak* 'roof' is *dakje*, not **dak-ə-tje*. Botma and van der Torre (2000) argue that the reason for this is that obstruents get a different prosodification from sonorants in Dutch: obstruents are always in a separate syllable, even if they are preceded by a short vowel.

(14)

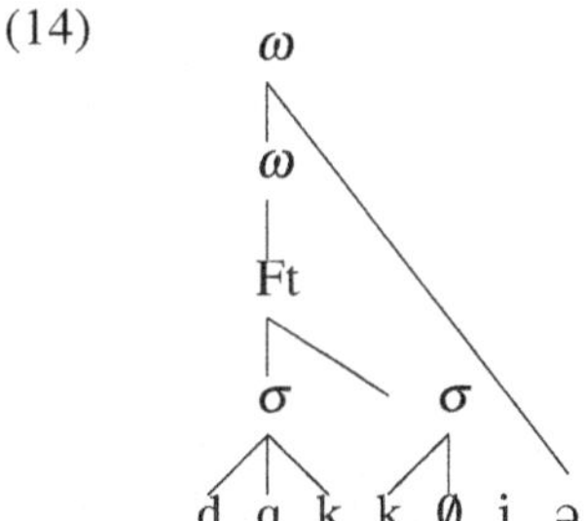

This solution raises the question why the constraint SUFF-TO-PRWD forces the selection of a special allomorph in the case of sonorants rather than using the option of an empty segment. A possible answer is that this is a cyclicity effect. If we assume that *maan* and *dak* are bisyllabic already before attachment of the suffix, we do not have to change anything to adjust to. Yet *bal* needs to be changed, in order to form a minimal word, and for this reason we choose to insert a schwa.

3.3 Why the ungrammatical forms are wrong

Given the rough structure of the diminutive forms, we will now try to find the reasons why diminutives are considered to be ungrammatical if the stem ends in an obstruent. One obvious correlate is the observation that two schwas in a row are dispreferred in Dutch. We will informally call this constraint *əə (van Oostendorp 2000):

(15)   *əə: Two consecutive syllables should not contain schwa.

This constraint is responsible for other forms of allomorphy as well. For instance, the agentive suffix *-er* takes an allomorph *-aar* if the stem ends in a syllable headed by schwa (16a). Also, the allomorphy between the productive plural suffixes *-ən* and *-s* seems to be governed by it at least partly (16b):

(16)   a.   (i)   *denk-ər* 'thinker', *lop-ər* 'walker', ...
              (ii)   *piekər-aːr* 'thinker', *wandəl-aːr* 'walker', ...
        b.   (i)   *berg-ən* 'mountains', *filosof–ən* 'philosophers', ...
              (ii)   *heuvəl-s* 'hills', *denkər-s* 'thinkers', ...

The constraint is not absolutely surface true for Dutch, however. Certain suffixes, such as the comparative, verbal inflection, or one allomorph of the nominal plural, do not seem to be subject to it. We can even combine certain affixes to create longer sequences of schwas as in (17d):

(17)   a.   *groot-ər* 'bigger', *edəl-ər* 'nobler', ...
        b.   *lop-ən* 'walk (PL)', *wandəl-ən* 'walk (PL)', ...
        c.   *kind-ərən* 'children'
        d.   *kind-ər-lək-ər-ə* 'more childish' (child+binding morpheme+ adjectivizing morpheme+ comarative+agreement)

What is more, even the diminutive suffix itself does not always obey the constraint, viz. in those cases in which a special allomorph is chosen after a stem ending in a lax vowel plus a sonorant consonant:

(18)   *bal-ətjə* 'little ball'

Notice also that the effect only holds if the schwa is the last segment in the word, not if it is followed by a consonant: words such as *vadərtjə* 'little father', *tegəltjə* 'little tile' or *bezəmpjə* 'little broom' are unobjectionable.[7]

---

[7] A possible reason for this, suggested by van Oostendorp (2000), is that syllables which are phonetically headed by a schwa and closed by a sonorant, phonologically behave as if

The constraint *əə in (15) should therefore be highly sensitive to morphological information: it clearly is part of lexical rather than of postlexical phonology. Furthermore, it seems that we are dealing with a type of derived environment effect. I will provisionally assume, therefore, that the relevant constraint is formulated as follows:

(19)   *$ə_i ə_j$: Two consecutive syllables with a different morphological colour should not contain schwa.

The constraint should probably more precise in order to deal with the facts mentioned above, but the present format will be sufficient for our purposes. (See section 5, footnote 13 for a suggestion that we can do away with the colours in this constraint.)

Furthermore, another factor plays a role, viz. the quality of the preceding consonant. The fact that the judgements are more equivocal in case the last consonant of the stem is a coronal stop must have something to do with the fact that the diminutive suffix itself also starts with a coronal stop. Now there is some evidence that a constraint of the following type also holds an effect on the Dutch lexicon (van Oostendorp 2000):

(20)   *$C_i ə C_i$: A schwa should not be surrounded by two identical consonants.

Again, it does not seem possible to create structures violating this constraint by morphological derivation or inflection.[8] For instance, the comparative suffix and the agentive suffix both are *-ər*. They can both be attached to stem ending in an /r/, but in this case, they take the allomorph *-dər*:

(21)   *zwaar-dər* 'heavier' (**zwaar-ər*), *boor-dər* 'driller' (**boor-ər*)

An apparent exception is the suffix *-ən* which serves many inflectional functions, like marking plurality on nouns and on verbs, and marking infinitival tense, and which can be added freely to any word ending in /n/: *baan+ən* 'jobs', *wen+ən* '(we/to) adjust'. This may be related, however to the fact that /n/ after schwa is often deleted.[9]

The constraint in (20) may be reduced to the OCP: if we assume that

---

they have a syllabic sonorant in Dutch.

[8]Or, to be more precise, by suffixation. There are forms in which a participial prefix *ge* /ɣə/ can be added to a stem starting in a /ɣ/: *gegaan* 'went' [ɣəɣan].

[9]The deletion takes place in large regions of the Dutch-speaking area, including most of the economically and culturally dominant ones. In the areas in which it does not take place, the suffix is usually realized as a syllabic ṇ.

schwa is a vowel without any features, the two vowels which neighbour to it on the lefthand and on the righthand side are adjacent to each other in a very obvious way.

Of course, the constraints just introduced run against the forms which might otherwise be coming out as the optimal form. They do not explain yet why those candidates are blocked from occurring. It will be our task in the next section to provide that piece of the puzzle.

4   Relativized MPARSE within Coloured Containment

We may conclude from the data in the previous two sections that diminutives in Standard Dutch pose yet another instance of the ineffability puzzle which forms the topic of this book. In the remainder of this chapter, I will first consider a solution which throws out these forms as unwanted; subsequently, this account will be embedded into a theory of language variation to account for the fact that the forms are not completely ungrammatical.

Let us reconsider the constraint MPARSE. We have seen in section 2.2 that Prince and Smolensky (1993) use this constraint in a fairly radical way: underlyingly there is no morphological structure at all, even the morphemes do not have an internal structure. Furthermore, it is assumed that the null parse has no morphological structure assigned to it at all.

Notice, however, that it is reasonable in its own right to have a less radical version of a constraint that says that morphological structure needs to be incorporated in the overall parse of the word, just like phonological structure. Indeed, it seems reasonable, given an (Items-and-Arrangement) theory of morphology withing OT, to assume:

- That the input can be either an unstructured set of morphemes, or a complex word consisting of morphemes arranged into some structure (given the morphological version of Richness of the Base).

- That the optimal output should consist of a morphological word (just like the optimal output will consist of a phonological word).

- That there are (M)PARSE constraints which require that individual morphemes should be part of the morphological structure.

The constraint MPARSE could be formulated as a family of constraints rather than as one monolitihic constraint evaluating all of the morphological structure at the same time:

(22)   MPARSE(M): Every morpheme M has to be parsed into a morphological word.

We assume that instances of this constraint exist for every individual morpheme. Since these are normal OT constraints, they can be violated, and we expect them to be violated sometimes. In the case of the Dutch diminutive, consider for instance an input consisting of a preposition (*aan* 'on') plus a preposition. Dutch does not allow for diminution of determiners, probably for morphological reasons. We could thus set up the following analysis:

(23)   LEXDIM: There is no diminutive of function words.

(24)

{*aan*, DIM}	LEXDIM	MPARSE$_{DIM}$
a. *aantje* (+DIM)	*!	
☞ b. *aan*		*

The winning form in (24a) does not parse the diminutive either morphologically or phonologically. If we have a more precise look at its phonological surface structure, we might observe the following:

(25)

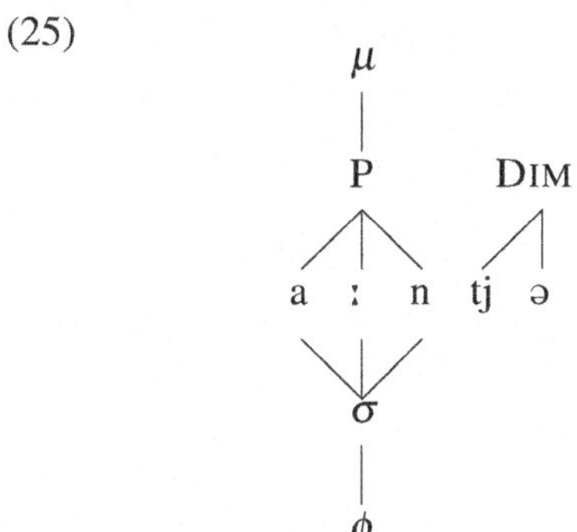

The diminutive suffix is parsed neither in the morphological structure nor in the phonological structure of the output. The reason why it is not parsed in the morphological structure is the constraint LEXDIM: there is no diminutive of the preposition *aan*. This also means that the winner candidate in (24) is not a diminutive, even though its input is (and the diminutive suffix is still hanging around in the output).

What about a candidate with the following structure?

(26)

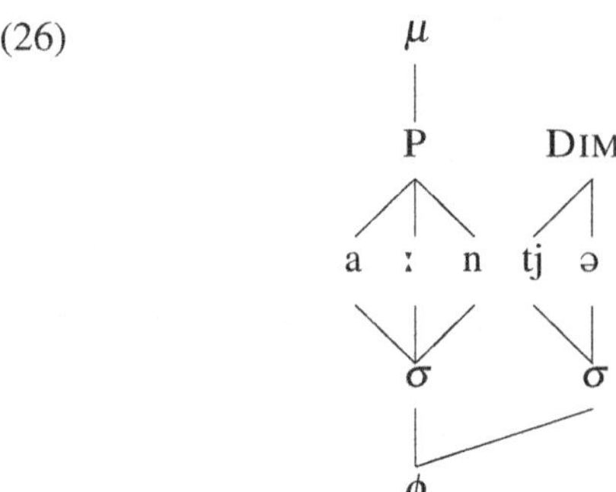

In this case, the segments connected to the diminutive show up in the phonology, but not in the morphology. This is clearly an undesirable result: we have a form which phonologically looks like a diminutive, although it is not a diminutive from a morphological (or semantic) point of view. But indeed it can be shown that forms such as these will never surface: a form such as (26) is harmonically bounded by a form such as (25).

The reasons for this are simple: both forms obviously satisfy all morphological constraints to the same extent; but they also both satisfy all the relevant phonological faithfulness constraints (PARSE-$\phi(\alpha)$). The reason for this is that those constraints require all *morphologically affiliated* material to be parsed into the phonology. Since the material belonging to the diminutive suffix is not part of the morphological structure, these constraints do not apply to them: the phonological parsing of this material in (26) thus is not necessary for reasons of phonological faithfulness.

On the other hand, the segments of the diminutive in (26) will probably violate markedness constraints of the type *STRUC, since they have material which is not present. Furthermore, they violate PARSE-$\mu(\alpha)$, since they represent phonological material which is not incorporated into the morphological structure. In other words, these segments behave like epenthetic material in all relevant respects. Since epenthesis is not required in these cases — we know this because epenthetic material also does not show up in the 'non-diminutive' form of *aan* — we derive that (26) is indeed bounded by (25). The former will therefore never surface (in any language).

In this example, the diminutive is blocked by morphological well-formedness, but of course there is no a priori reason why phonological constraints could not similarly force morphological underparsing (which I have denoted in the following examples by putting the name of the relevant morpheme in parentheses). For instance, if we consider the forms ending in coronal obstruents, we get the following:

(27)

/lentə/+/tjə/	FAITHFUL	OCP$_{[cor]}$	MPARSE(DIM)
☞ lentə (DIM)			*
lentjə	*!		
lentətjəlentjə		*!	

Like in the case of the prepostion just discussed, the relevant output form is not a diminutive in any relevant sense: it just is a non-diminutive form both with respect to its phonological shape as well with respect to its morphological, syntactic or semantic context. This is the sense in which it is not possible to form a diminutive of this word. Even if we set up the input in the most ideal way — with a diminutive morpheme — the output will ignore this input.

If we take into consideration the larger class of cases of words ending in schwa in (10), we only need to replace the relevant markedness constraint:

(28)

/ɣavə/+/tjə/	FAITHFUL	*ə$_i$ə$_j$	MPARSE(DIM)
☞ ɣavə (DIM)			*
ɣavətjə	*!		
ɣaːfjə		*!	

Notice that this solution may be somewhat too strong. It throws out complete forms which speakers indeed consider to be strange or marked, but which nevertheless occur, and are also not necessarily considered to be totally ungrammatical. In other words, we need an analysis of the question mark, and a theory based on the MPARSE does not provide us with one directly (and neither does any other one). We will return to this in section 5.

The following example from Swedish (Iverson 1981; Raffelsiefen 2002; Féry and Fanselow 2003; Rice 2005) is a little bit more complicated. Adjectives get an ending -/t/ in the neuter in attributive position:

(29)　　a.　*en rysk* (MASC) *pojke* 'a Russian boy'
　　　　b.　*et rysk-t* (NEUTER) *barn* 'a Russian child'

However, if the adjectival stem ends in /dː/, the neuter form simply becomes impossible:

(30)　　a.　*en rädd* (MASC) *pojke* 'a scared boy'
　　　　b.　**et rädd-t* (NEUTER) *barn* 'a scared child'

In cases like this, we thus have a gap in the paradigm which is probably due to an OCP effect on the feature coronal. Furthermore, other ('phonological') options of resolving the OCP, for instance deleting the /t/ into one segment, are not available because of high-ranking faithfulness constraints. We then have the following tableau:

(31)

/räd:/+/t/	OCP$_{[cor]}$	PARSE(C)	MPARSE$_{NEUTER}$
☞ räd: (NEUTER)			*
räd:t	*!		
räd:		*!	

Again, the form we have thus created is not marked as bearing neuter agreement. This is why it has become unusuable in (30), given a sufficiently high-ranking syntactic constraint enforcing agreement. A solution will then have to be found in the syntax, e.g. by using the non-inflected form *räd:* in a periphrastic construction.

We will have to assume that MPARSE$_F$ will have a fairly high ranking in all languages for most morphological features F: if an MPARSE$_F$ constraint is low-ranked, it will become virtually unusable, since is would contain many gaps. If too many concepts are pronounced by complete emptyness, most of the imagineable functions of natural language cannot be fulfilled.

5   The question mark and language variation

We are left with one problem to address: why are some of the 'unacceptable' forms generated not completely unacceptable, but rather marked with a question mark? There is some literature on the question mark within the Optimality Theoretic framework, in works such as Anttila (1997b, 2002); Boersma (1998, 2001); Boersma and Hayes (2001); Coetzee (2004). It is important to note that this literature is embedded in work on language variation: the grammar can generate more than one output, of which there are certain less preferred ones.

In the work of Anttila, which we will follow here, the grammar allows for some internal variation. In particular, constraints can be partially ordered. For instance, within the grammar of a language we might find three constraints A, B and C which are not ordered. This means that every ordering of these constraints (A≫B≫C, A≫C≫B) is equally likely. In the case of three constraints there are 3!=6 possible orderings. Now suppose that four of these rankings give output α for some input a, while two give output β. This will then mean that β is in some sense more 'marked' than α as a pronunciation of a; β might get a question mark. With some modifications, irrelevant for our present discussion, similar considerations hold for the view on language variation defended in Boersma (1998, 2001); Boersma and Hayes (2001) and related works. Similarily, in Coetzee (2004), the output of the Evaluation is not a single candidate, but an ordered list, with the preferred candidate in the first position. The phonetics will usually pronounce the first element of the list, but in some cases, it may also pronounce an element with a lower position. These would then be perceived as having one or more question marks.

Combining one of these ideas with MPARSE may give us something similar to the effect we have observed for Dutch: the forms we find are question marked, since they are competing with a form which violates MPARSE. In the following, I choose Anttila's approach for the sake of concreteness, but I suspect that the general idea outlined below could also be applied to the other frameworks. For instance, let us divide the con straint FAITHFUL in (28) into its relevant constituent parts — a constraint against deletion of schwa, PARSE$_\partial$, and a constraint against final devoicing, PARSE$_{[+\text{voice}]}$, and let us assume that these two constraints are unranked with respect to each other and with respect to MPARSE in the sense of Anttila. We then have the six rankings in (28) (assuming that the constraint against sequences of schwas is ranked still on top, and that we therefore do not have to consider [gavətjə]).

The pronounced diminutive form thus sometimes wins, but most of the time it is bested by a form which does not function as a diminutive at all. This describes the ungrammatical feel that the diminutive form has.

An interesting aspect of Anttila's (1997b; 2002) work is that it relates the assignment of intuitive question marks by a native speaker to distribution of forms over a corpus. In this case, such a distribution can also be detected, for instance if we compare the diminutive forms of the names of the four seasons in the Google corpus.[10]

---

[10]The Google-corpus is the corpus of Dutch texts as it is defined by the internet search engine Google.com. According to a fairly recent estimate (van Oostendorp 2005a), the corpus contains 3,000,000,000 Dutch words. This means that the relative percentage of all the diminutives is fairly small. These searches were done on 28.III.2006. The results here have been gathered and normalized in the way described in van Oostendorp (2005a).

(32)

/ɣavə/+/tjə/	PARSE$_ə$	PARSE$_{[+voice]}$	MPARSE
☞ ɣavə (DIM)			*
ɣaːfjə	*!	*	

	PARSE$_ə$	MPARSE	PARSE$_{[+voice]}$
☞ ɣavə (DIM)		*	
ɣaːfjə	*!		*

	PARSE$_{[+voice]}$	PARSE$_ə$	MPARSE
☞ ɣavə (DIM)			*
ɣaːfjə	*!	*	

	PARSE$_{[+voice]}$	MPARSE	PARSE$_ə$
☞ ɣavə (DIM)		*	
ɣaːfjə	*!		*

	PARSE$_{[+voice]}$	PARSE$_ə$	MPARSE
☞ ɣavə (DIM)			*
ɣaːfjə	*!	*	

	MPARSE	PARSE$_{[+voice]}$	PARSE$_ə$
ɣavə (DIM)	*!		
☞ ɣaːfjə		*	*

	MPARSE	PARSE$_ə$	PARSE$_{[+voice]}$
ɣavə (DIM)	*!		
☞ ɣaːfjə		*	*

(33)

	normal form		diminutive		plural of diminutive	
lente	'spring'	6,130,000	*lentetje*	22	*lentetjes*	32
zomer	'summer'	4,580,000	*zomertje*	779	*zomertjes*	236
herfst	'autumn'	2,770,000	*herfstje*	108	*herfstjes*	89
winter	'winter'	8,880,000	*wintertje*	894	*wintertjes*	696

There clearly is a difference between the word for 'spring' and the words for the other seasons. There is no obvious reason in lexical semantics why this could be the case, although a few remarks are in order. In the first place, there are big differences between the occurrences of names of different seasons, for which I have no explanation; notice however that, given the fact *lente* is a season name which occurs more often than *zomer*, for instance, we should expect there to be more instances of its diminutive rather than less, but this is not the case.

In the second place, the fact that the plural form of the diminutive of *winter* is that *(De) Winter* is a farily frequent family name, and that the structure family name+diminutive+plural is a productive way of referring to members of a family:

(34)   Dat de De Wintertjes niks uitvoeren in Amerika, baseer je op een mailtje van een zekere Emma Rose (wie is dat?).[11]
You base the assumption that the family De Winter is not working at all in America, on an e-mail by a certain E.R. (who is that?)

Similar examples are harder to find for the other words, because they occur less frequently as family names. The following data are based on a database of Dutch familynames in 1993; the numbers indicate (roughly) the number of times the name was found in a Dutch register of family names on the internet:[12]

(35)

name	frequency
lente	19
zomer	700
herfst	127
winter	1053

The very low frequency of *lentetjes* may thus be partially ascribed to the infrequency of the family name *Lente*, but this is not true for singular *lentetje*, which has no such direct connection to a name. Notice that this result can be extended to all other theories which describe ineffability effects as the result of a constraint, which can interact with other constraints.

Finally, we have to turn to the observation that the forms can become better if they are repeated over time. I propose that the reason for this is that the forms become lexicalised; which means that the words become analysed as a whole. Suppose, for instance that the word *gavetje* becomes lexicalised. We then obtain the following tableau:

(36)

/ɣavətjə/	FAITHFUL	*əᵢəⱼ	MPARSE_DIM
☞ ɣavətjə		*	
ɣaːfjə	*!		

In this case, the there is no relevant candidate with un 'unparsed' diminutive suffix, since there is no underlying diminutive suffix anymore. Therefore, 'normal' faithfulness decides that it is better to preserve the marked configuration.[13]

---

[11] http://vetvetvet.web-log.nl/log/3858282

[12] The database has been built by Ann Marynissen of the University of Cologne and can be consulted at http://www.familienaam.nl/.

[13] Strictly speaking, there is no issue of violating *əᵢəⱼ anymore, since as we have seen,

Remember from the discussion on page 78 that the archaic suffix *ke* is more acceptable on names: most informants seem to think that *Hildəkə* is more acceptable than *Hildətjə*. I suppose that this is also due to this process of lexicalisation. The fact that it is archaic means that it is not considered to be productive. I therefore suppose that it can only be interpreted as being input to the grammar as a whole.

(37)

/hɪldəkə/	FAITHFUL	$*{\partial}_i{\partial}_j$	MPARSE
☞ hɪldəkə		*	
hɪldə	*!		

One could wonder whether this analysis does not conflict with the principle of Richness of the Base. I do not think it does so in an essential way. Of course, it is possible in principle to posit two underlying morphemes /hɪldə/ and /kə/; the result of the evaluation of such a form would be ineffable, hence not pronounced, or question marked.

6 Conclusion

Representing ineffability seems to come at some cost within any branch of Optimality Theory; as far as I can see, no solution has been proposed which does not invoke some special mechanism that is somehow outside of the core of the OT system. This may be seen to imply that ineffability remains to be one of the real problems for the theory, maybe on a par with the issue of opacity: if only additional patches can be used to describe a phenomenon which is as real as the unpronounceability of certain logically possible forms, the theory may be seen as incomplete at best.

An important technical part of the proposal is that we have implemented a relativised notion of null parse: usually, it will not be the whole input which is left unparsed both from a morphosyntactic and a phonological point of view — thus contributing neither to the morphological structure nor to the sound structure — but only the offending morpheme. If we cannot form a diminutive of a word X, we do not generate complete emptiness, but we generate X without any diminutive connotation. Lexicon Optimisation will eventually give us that it is more optimal then to also not input the diminutive morpheme.

---

this constraint only applies to schwas of different morphological colour (belonging to different morphemes). But if a word is lexicalised, this means that all segments are in the same lexical item together, so they will all have the same morphological colour. But this means that potentially we can do away with the reference to colouring in (19).

I believe that the proposals put forward here form a step forward in a few ways. They do not extend the computational power of the theory in any significant way; to the contrary, they reduce the extra mechanism to a minimum — and even that minimum may be reduced to representational mechanisms which are independently necessary. But more importantly, we have shown how interaction with theories of language variation give us the possibility for describing the question mark.

Bibliography

Anttila, A. (1997a) Deriving variation from grammar. In F. Hinskens, R. van Hout, and L. Wetzels (eds.) *Variation, Change and Phonological Theory* 35–68. Amsterdam: John Benjamins.

Anttila, A. (1997b) *Variation in Finnish Phonology and Morphology*. Ph. D. thesis, Stanford University.

Anttila, A. (2002) Variation and phonological theory. In J. Chambers, P. Trudgill and N. Schilling-Estes (eds.) *The Handbook of Language Variation and Change* 206–43. Oxford: Blackwell.

Benua, L. (1997) *Transderivational Identity: Phonological Relations between Words*. Ph. D. thesis, University of Massachusetts at Amherst.

Boersma, P. (1998) *Functional Phonology*. Ph. D. thesis, University of Amsterdam.

Boersma, P. (2001) Review of Anttila (1997a). *GLOT International* 5(1): 33–40.

Boersma, P. and Hayes, B. (2001) Empirical tests of the gradual learning algorithm. *Linguistic Inquiry* 32(1): 45–86.

Booij, G. (1995) *The Phonology of Dutch*. Oxford: Oxford University Press.

Booij, G. (2002) *The Morphology of Dutch*. Oxford: Oxford University Press.

Botma, B. and van der Torre, E. J. (2000) The prosodic interpretation of sonorants in dutch. In H. de Hoop and T. van der Wouden (eds.) *Linguistics Linguistics in the Netherlands 2000* 17–29. Amsterdam and Philadelphia: John Benjamins.

Burzio, L. (1994) *Principles of English Stress*. Cambridge: Cambridge University Press.

Burzio, L. (1998) Multiple correspondence. *Lingua* 103: 79–109.

Burzio, L. (2000) Cycles, non-derived environment blocking, and correspondence. In J. Dekkers, F. van der Leeuw, and J. van de Weijer (eds.) *Optimality Theory. Phonology, Syntax and Acquisition* 47–87. Oxford: Oxford University Press.

Burzio, L. (2003) Output-to output faithfulness in phonology: The Italian connection. *Lingue e Linguaggio.*

Coetzee, A. W. (2004) *What it Means to be a Loser: Non-optimal Candidates in Optimality Theory.* Ph. D. thesis, University of Massachussets at Amherst.

Féry, C. and Fanselow, G. (2003) Ineffability in grammar. *Linguistische Berichte* Sonderheft 11: 288–310.

Gussenhoven, C. and Jacobs, H. (1998) *Understanding phonology.* London: Arnold.

van der Hulst, H. (1984) *Syllable Structure and Stress in Dutch.* Dordrecht: Foris.

Inkelas, S. and Zoll, C. (2005) *Reduplication. A Morphological Theory.* Cambridge: Cambridge University Press.

Iverson, G. (1981) Rules, constraints, and paradigm lacunae. *Glossa* 15: 136–44.

Kager, R. (1999) *Optimality Theory.* Cambridge: Cambridge University Press.

Kiparsky, P. (2000) Opacity and cyclicity. *The Linguistic Review* 17, 351–67.

Kooij, J. (1982) Epenthetische schwa: processen, regels en domeinen. *Spektator* 11, 315–25.

Łubowicz, A. (2005) Infixation as morpheme absorption. ROA 773, `http://roa.rutgers.edu`.

McCarthy, J. J. (1998) Morpheme structure constraints and paradigm occultation. In M. C. Gruber, D. Higgins, K. Olson, and T. Wysocki (eds.) *CLS 32.*, Volume Part 2: The Panels 123–50. Chicago: Chicago Linguistics Society.

McCarthy, J. J. (1999) Sympathy and phonological opacity. *Phonology* 16, 331–99. Also available as ROA 252, `http://roa.rutgers.edu`.

McCarthy, J. J. and Prince, A. (1993) Prosodic morphology. constraint interaction and satisfaction. ROA 485, `http://roa.rutgers.edu`.

McCarthy, J. J. and Prince, A. (1994) The emergence of the unmarked: optimality in prosodic morphology. *Proceedings of the 24th Annual Meeting of the North East Linguistic Society* 333–79. Amherst, MA: GLSA Publications.

McCarthy, J. J. and Prince, A. (1995) Faithfulness and reduplicative identity. *UMOP* 18, 249–384.

van Oostendorp, M. (2000) *Phonological Projection*. Berlin/New York: Mouton de Gruyter.

van Oostendorp, M. (2005a) *I am feeling lucky* in de taalwetenschap. In J. Engelsman, E. Sanders, and R. Tempelaars (eds.) *Taal als levenswerk. Aspecten van de Nederlandse taalkunde* 101–06. Den Haag: SDU.

van Oostendorp, M. (2005b) The theory of faithfulness. Ms., Meertens Instituut.

van Oostendorp, M. (2007) Derived environment effects and consistency of exponence. In S. Blaho, P. Bye, and M. Krämer (eds.) *Freedom of Analysis?* 123–48. Berlin/New York: Mouton de Gruyter.

Prince, A. and Smolensky, P. (1993) Optimality theory: Constraint interaction in generative grammar. Manuscript, Rutgers University and University of Colorado at Boulder. Published in 2004 at Blackwell, also available as ROA 537, `http://roa.rutgers.edu`.

Raffelsiefen, R. (2002) Gaps in word formation. In U. Kleinhenz (ed.) *Interface in Phonology* 194–209. Berlin: Akademie Verlag.

Rice, C. (2005) Optimal gaps in optimal paradigms. *Catalan Journal of Linguistics* 4: 155-70.

Rubach, J. (2003) Duke-of-York derivations in Polish. *Linguistic Inquiry* 29, 601–29.

Trommelen, M. (1982) *The Syllable in Dutch: With Special Reference to Diminutive Formation.* Ph. D. thesis, University of Utrecht. Published at Dordrect: Foris, 1984.

van de Weijer, J. (2002) An optimality-theoretic analysis of dutch diminutives. In H. Broekhuis and P. Fikkert (eds.) *Linguistics in the Netherlands 2002* 31–42. Amsterdam and Philadelphia: John Benjamins.

Walker, R. and Feng, B. (2004) A ternary model of morphology-phonology correspondence. In A. K. B. Schmeiser, V. Chand, A. K. A. Rodriguez. B. Schmeiser, V. Chand, A. K. A. Rodriguez B. Schmeiser, V. Chand, and A. Rodriguez (eds.) *Proceedings of the 23rd West Coast Conference on Formal Linguistics* 773–86. Somerville, MA: Cascadilla Press.

4 Hard constraints in Optimality Theory

Orhan Orgun and Ronald Sprouse
UC Davis and UC Berkeley

This paper presents the CONTROL approach to morphological gaps, introduced by Orgun and Sprouse (1999). In this approach constraints may belong to either of two components, EVAL and CONTROL. EVAL is the usual ranked constraint component of Optimality Theory (OT; Prince and Smolensky 1993). The EVAL component always proposes an optimal candidate output. This output is grammatical if it satisfies all the constraints in CONTROL. If the optimal candidate violates any constraint in CONTROL, there is no grammatical output.

At the time we made this proposal, gaps had been addressed by few works in OT. The only existing proposal was P&S's MPARSE approach. Since then, ungrammaticality has received more attention in the OT literature. Some researchers (e.g. Beaver and Lee 2004, Fanselow and Féry 2002, Hansson 1999) used and further developed our CONTROL proposal. There have been attempts to defend MPARSE, most notably Raffelsiefen (2004), followed shortly by a defense and further clarification of CONTROL by Bye 2005.

In this paper, we present the original CONTROL proposal, illustrate it with some examples from our earlier work, and include discussion of a new set of data from Rice's work. CONTROL does not address all of the several types of ungrammaticality unearthed in the recent literature; the type of phenomenon it is meant to deal with coincides with the aims of MPARSE: cases where no phonologically wellformed output is possible. Different classes of ungrammaticality where a phonologically well formed output is possible include defective paradigms (where the would-be filler of the empty slot might be well formed in a different context; Rice, this volume), "Buridan's ass" type cases (where multiple possibilities appear more or less equally well formed and the speaker is unwilling or unable to select a specific winner; Albright, this volume), and cases of blocking. It appears that different approaches to these different types of ungrammaticality remain necessary; accordingly, we continue to restrict our attention to the original intended empirical domain of the MPARSE/CONTROL approach.

1 Gaps in Turkish possessives

Orgun and Sprouse (1999), following Itô and Hankamer (1989) and Inkelas and Orgun (1995) observe that some Turkish speakers (five of Inkelas and Orgun's twelve consultants) impose a disyllabic minimal size constraint on suffixed forms.[1]

(1)   Root Suffixed form ($\mu\mu$ min)
         sol^j 'musical note G'   sol^j-ym   'my G'
         do^2 'C'   *do-m   'my C'

Ungrammatical monosyllabic forms are not augmented by epenthesis, as shown in (2), where we have underlined the epenthetic segments:

(2)   Repair by epenthesis is not possible

   a.   *doj<u>u</u>m
   b.   *do<u>u</u>m
   c.   *<u>i</u>dom
   d.   *dom<u>u</u>

However, epenthesis is allowed to avoid vowel hiatus or illicit coda clusters in suffixed forms (3). The form in (b) is especially relevant, since it contains the same possessive suffix as the ungrammatical subminimal form in (1). This shows that epenthesis is possible in forms containing that suffix, making it even more puzzling that the forms in (1) are not augmented by epenthesis:

(3)   a.   /araba + a/   →   arabaja   'car-dative'
         b.   /it + m/   →   it<u>i</u>m   'my dog'

---

[1] There are two standard monosyllabic suffixed forms, *je-r* 'eat-aorist' and *de-r* 'say-aorist'. We do not know what the proper analysis of these forms would be; note that monosyllabic roots generally use the longer *-er* allomorph of the aorist, which would lead one to expect *jijer* and *dijer*, respectively as the aorist forms of these verbs. Indeed, Küntay (pc) reports that children occasionally use these forms.

[2] Inkelas and Orgun report that some speakers have a long vowel in this form, while others have a short vowel. We use the short vowel variety in this paper, though our analysis extends without modification to the long vowel microdialect. It is interesting to note that none of the short-vowel speakers accepted forms such as *do-m*. However, long-vowel speakers did not consistently accept such forms; they were divided more or less evenly in their judgments. Since only 12 speakers in total were consulted, we do not know if this distribution is significant. If it is, it might suggest that some speakers are willing to forgo the two-syllable requirement and settle for one superheavy syllable instead (that is, all speakers impose some form of minimal size requirement on derived forms).

One might wonder whether some other constraint violation could rule out augmentation of *dom. The two most interesting candidates are *do-jum*, with epenthesis of both a vowel and a glide and *doum*, with epenthesis and hiatus. The former candidate could perhaps be ruled out by a conjoined constraint (Smolensky 1995) that rules out a candidate with epenthesis of both a vowel and a glide. For *doum*, Raffelsiefen (2004) suggests that a window constraint against hiatus involving a vowel within the first syllable might solve the problem (Orgun and Sprouse point out that opaque interaction of velar deletion and vowel epenthesis in longer forms can create hiatus). Raffelsiefen's motivation comes from an observation going back to Lees (1961) that (otherwise quite regular) intervocalic velar deletion tends not to apply to monosyllabic roots:

(4)   toprak   'soil'   topra-ɯm   'my soil'
        tak   'arch'   tak- ɯm   'my arch'   *ta-ɯm

This window idea might seem intriguing; however, there are in fact monosyllabic forms that undergo velar deletion as well as polysyllabic forms that do not.[3]

(5)   gøk   'sky'   gø-ym   'my sky'
        tʃok   'many'   tʃo-um   'my many'

        benlik   'identity'   benlik-im   'my identity'
        tetkik   'investigation' tetkik-im   'my investigation'

The irregularity of intervocalic *k*-deletion is an interesting problem in its own right that we don't address here (see Orgun 1997 for discussion); however, the forms in (5) show that a) epenthesis and vowel hiatus can co-exist in forms derived from monosyllabic roots; and b) the window hypothesis fails to explain the lack of *k*-deletion of some polysyllabic roots. The crucial question is how to handle the fact that apparently available repairs are not used to fix ill-formed outputs. The general answer we pro-

---

[3]The TELL database (`http://linguistics.berkeley.edu/TELL`; for a description, see Inkelas et al. 2000) lists 60 polysyllabic k-final forms that do not undergo k deletion in the possessive.

Also, while Raffelsiefen claims that the window approach deals with Inkelas and Orgun's k-deletion data, I&O's analysis actually connects voicing, vowel length, and velar-zero alternations through a minimality-driven syllabification account, and deals as well with some exceptions (monosyllabic roots with deleting velars) through prespecification of morphological stem status. Orgun 1997 extends the analysis to other exceptions (polysyllabic roots with non-deleting velars) through the use of underlying syllable structure—neither type of exceptionality is consistent with a window approach.

pose for this question is that the ranked constraint component EVAL always produces a winning non-null candidate, an optimal form with respect to the given constraint ranking. In order to deal with ungrammaticality, we introduce a new inviolable constraint component, CONTROL. Winning candidates from EVAL must satisfy all constraints in CONTROL in order to be grammatical output forms.[4] This proposal is based on the important but not immediately obvious observation there are two ways in which a constraint may be inviolable. The first type of these is more commonly discussed in the OT literature—constraints that force violation of lower-ranked constraints but are never violated themselves. The Turkish syllable structure constraint causing epenthesis is an example of such an inviolable constraint. The second type of inviolable constraint, which has not received as much attention in the literature, causes ungrammaticality but never repair. In order to be grammatical, an output must satisfy two conditions: (a) it must be the optimal candidate chosen by EVAL; and (b) it must satisfy all constraints in CONTROL.

(6)   Conditions required for all grammatical outputs.
       The output must:
       a.   be the optimal candidate chosen by EVAL;
       b.   satisfy all constraints in CONTROL

We assume that these conditions are evaluated in parallel. They would also work serially; however, if they are to be applied serially, then they must be applied in the order presented.

The resolution to the Turkish constraint-ranking dilemma is in (7). Disyllabic minimality is inviolable. This can result if it is in EVAL and it outranks all conflicting constraints, or if it is in CONTROL, where all constraints are inviolable. High-ranking constraints in EVAL force violation of lower-ranked conflicting constraints. The minimal size condition never forces augmentation of subminimal forms or any other kind of repair. Therefore, minimality constraints belong in CONTROL, not EVAL. In (7) the winning candidate of EVAL is dom, which violates no constraints in EVAL. However, this winning candidate fails to satisfy the minimality conditions in CONTROL and is therefore ungrammatical, as indicated by the ℀ symbol.

---

[4]Control superficially resembles Halle's (Halle) notion of the Filter in that a portion of the grammar overgenerates and another component filters out ungrammatical forms, but the formal mechanism is quite different. Control is more restricted in its use, and, unlike Halle's Filter, cannot alter the phonological, morphosyntactic or semantic properties of its inputs.

(7)   Input /do-m/

a.   EVAL

/do-m/	*V.V	DEP
☞ dom		
doum	*!	*
dojum		*!*

b.   CONTROL

	LEX≈PR, FTFROM
✄ dom	*!

The winning candidate from EVAL is submitted to CONTROL strictly for grammaticality judgments. Unlike EVAL, CONTROL evaluates a single form, and therefore does not choose between candidates. It can only declare the single winning candidate from EVAL grammatical or ungrammatical. Therefore, no repair is possible to satisfy constraints in CONTROL. If the winning candidate from EVAL violates a constraint in CONTROL, ungrammaticality results. Epenthesis, glide insertion, velar deletion, and vowel hiatus may still occur in winning candidates in EVAL if the input contains the appropriate environments.

(8)   Input /it + m/: epenthesis applies.

a.   EVAL

/it + m/	CODACOND	DEP
☞ itim		*
itimi		*!*
itm	*!	

b.   CONTROL

	LEX≈PR, FTFROM
✓ itim	

This example illustrates the important difference between two types of inviolable constraints that our proposal captures. CODACOND is never violated in Turkish. It is always obeyed, even at the expense of violating lower-ranking faithfulness constraints in EVAL. The prosodic minimality condition is also never violated, but forms that violate it are never repaired. Instead, no grammatical output is possible. We account for this by placing the minimal size constraints in CONTROL rather than EVAL. CODACOND, on the other hand, must be in EVAL, since it demonstrably interacts with other constraints in EVAL.

One final question that remains is the restriction of the minimal size condition to morphologically derived forms. Crosslinguistically, nonderived forms are not always immune from prosodic minimality, as shown by Inkelas and Orgun (1995) for a different, bimoraic size condition in Turkish, Mester (1994) for Latin, and McCarthy and Prince (1994) for Axininca Campa. Turkish disyllabic minimality, however, is restricted to derived forms, as is Japanese bimoraic minimality (Itô 1990). For the purposes of this paper, we assume simply that the constraint FTFROM applies in Turkish specifically to derived stems (this is similar to Itô's treatment of Japanese minimality). Monosyllabic roots may thus satisfy LEX≈PR by surfacing with a degenerate foot.[5]

2   English *re*-verb nominalization

This section builds on data first analyzed by Raffelsiefen (1992) concerning zero nominalizations in English.

The construction of interest is what Raffelsiefen calls "stress-shifting nominalization" (henceforth SSN). Essentially, a disyllabic verb with stress on its second syllable is converted to a noun by placing primary stress on the first syllable and secondary stress on the second syllable. This construction is generally unproductive, as the data below show. The verbs on the left hand side have stress-shifted nominals while those on the right hand side do not:

(9)

Verb	Noun	Verb	Noun
accént	àccènt	accòunt	*àccòunt
addréss	àddrèss	arrést	*àrrèst
allòy	àllòy	allúre	*àllùre
abstráct	àbstràct	advànce	*àdvànce
conflíct	cònflìct	consént	*cònsènt
contést	còntèst	concérn	*còncèrn
constrúct	cònstrùct	contròl	*còntròl
decréase	décrèase	deféat	*défeat
discárd	díscàrd	disgúst	*dísgust
discòunt	díscòunt	disdàin	*dísdàin
expòrt	éxpòrt	exhàust	*éxhàust
misprínt	mísprìnt	mistrúst	*místrùst
survéy	súrvèy	surpríse	*súrprìse

---

[5]Inkelas and Orgun (1995) and Orgun (1996) have proposed a more elaborate approach to the immunity of underived forms to prosodic minimality in Turkish, involving cophonologies. Our CONTROL analysis is also consistent with cophonologies.

Even though this stress-shifting nominalization construction is only marginally productive in general, it does have a "niche of productivity", as Raffelsiefen notes. Verbs that contain the prefixf *re-* freely undergo stress-shifting nominalization. Each pair in the left-hand column of the table shows a verb root and its counterpart containing the prefix *re-* (10). Each pair in the right-hand column shows a *re*-verb and its stress-shifted nominalization. It should be noted that some of our *re*-verb examples have homographs that use a different, root level, prefix. This is discussed in more detail below (example (12)). We use a hyphen to distinguish forms containing the word level *re-* from those containing the root level *re-* (e.g., *reform* 'amend for the better' versus *re-form* 'form again' and *remove* 'take away' versus *re-move* 'move again').

(10)	Verb	*re*-verb	Noun
	fill	refíll	réfìll
	do	redò	rédò
	make	remàke	rémàke
	load	relòad	rélòad
	paint	repàint	répàint
	play	replày	réplày
	count	re-còunt	récòunt
	print	represent	répríst
	run	rerún	rérùn
	take	retàke	rétàke

To confirm the productivity of stress-shifting *re*-verb nominalization, we have collected additional data from two native speakers California English. As expected, all the verbs in (11) have stress-shifted nominalizations.[6]

---

[6] Some of these forms sound marginal to some speakers. The sets of stress-shifted nouns that are acceptable and marginal vary from speaker to speaker. This does not mean that the construction is unproductive, but rather is caused by the usual constraint on derivational morphology that forms are acceptable to speakers to the extent that they know what meaning to assign to them. Later in this section we discuss a pragmatic context in which this construction is highly productive.

The stress-shifted nouns are deverbal rather than derived by adding the prefix *re-* to a deverbal noun (fill$_V$ → fill$_N$ → refill$_N$). Although prefix *re-* can be added to noun stems, the resulting word has primary stress on the first syllable of the verb stem (that is, the syllable following *re-*), as in recapture (this claim is supported by the fact that this type of *re-* noun can be found attaching to morphologically marked nominalizations of certain words: *rebaptism* and not *rebaptize$_N$*; *rebirth*, not *rebear$_N$*). The deverbal nouns we are examining in this paper do not have this stress pattern. Rather, they have the stress pattern of stress shifted denominal verbs such as *súrvèy*, which indicates that they are formed by stress shifting nominalization rather than by prefixing *re-* to noun stems.

(11) rebore   recross   rehash   re-pose   re-cede   repass
      rebind   refit   rejoin   reroute   recast   replant
      re-cap   refloat   relay   re-serve rewire   rewrite
      rebuild   re-form   reline   reset   regain   restock
      recharge re-fund   remold   resole   reheat   retool
      re-cite   re-fuse   remount   respray   rehang   retouch
      retread   retrim   revamp   rewind

Although stress-shifting nominalization applies productively to *re*-verbs, it is subject to a number of restrictions. The first restriction is morphological. The verbs shown below do not undergo stress-shifting nominalization.

(12) rĕcount rĕform   rĕport   rĕsign   rĕduce   rĕserve
      rĕceive rĕfuse   rĕpose   rĕsist   rĕfer   rĕsent
      rĕcite   rĕgard   rĕpress rĕsolve rĕfine   rĕside
      rĕcoil   rĕlate   rĕprove rĕsort   rĕflect rĕsign
      rĕcede   rĕlax   rĕpute   rĕsound rĕpeal   rĕstrain
      rĕward   rĕmind   rĕquest rĕspect rĕpel   rĕstrict
      rĕcur   rĕmove   rĕquire rĕspire rĕplete rĕsume
      rĕdeem   rĕnew   rĕsect   rĕstore rĕply   rĕtain
      rĕvive   rĕvoke   rĕvolve rĕtort   rĕtrace rĕtract
      rĕvert   rĕview   rĕvile   rĕvise   rĕverse

What these verbs share is that they all contain the root level prefix *re-*, which can be distinguished from the word level prefix *re-* by its lax vowel (e.g., [ɹɪkoɪl] versus [ɹidu], indicated by a breve in (12)), as well as by semantic considerations (the forms in (11) are semantically compositional, the prefix *re-* signaling repetition. The forms in (12) are noncompositional and *re-* does not make a consistent semantic contribution). We therefore conclude that the "niche of productivity" of stress-shifting nominalization is limited to verbs containing the word-level prefix *re-*. Thus, we need to refer to the specific morpheme in the stem to determine that *re*-verb nominalization may apply productively.

A second restriction involves semantics, although its exact formulation is not clear. One of our informants rejected stress-shifted nominalizations of the verbs below because they could not assign any specific meaning to them.

(13) rebind   rename
      repot   reseat
      re-sign   retell
      reword

In later elicitations, we asked two informants (including the original informant who at first rejected the forms above) to imagine a context like: *"this didn't work too well, we're going to have to do a ..."* where a nominalized verb can be inserted. Both informants could use *re*-verb nominalizations of all disyllabic stems, including those previously rejected, in this context.

The restrictions on SSN that we have discussed so far are not germane to the ungrammaticality issues discussed in this paper. However, there is a third, phonological, restriction on SSN that does concern us directly. SSN does not apply to verbs that contain more than two syllables (Orgun 1996), whether the verbs are derived (14) or underived (9). For derived verbs, the syllable count includes the prefix. None of the verbs in (14) have stress-shifted nominalizations.[7]

(14)	redistribute	re-embark	re-enter	reinter	re-cover
	reconfigure	recriminate	re-establish	reinterpret	re-create
	reascend	recycle	re-examine	reinvest	re-emerge
	reassemble	redecorate	re-export	reissue	re-enact
	rebaptize	recuperate	refashion	rekindle	reinsert
	rebroadcast	redeploy	reforest	remilitarize	reinsure
	reforecast	redial	regenerate	remodel	repolish
	repredict	reduplicate	rehabilitate	remonetize	repopulate
	recoalesce	re-echo	reimburse	reoccupy	reunite
	recapitulate	re-edit	reimport	reorient	revalorize
	recapture	re-educate	reignite	reorientate	revisit
	recommit	re-elect	reinforce	repaper	revivify
	reproduce	requicken	restudy	resurface	resurvey
	retranslate	revaccinate	revalue	repeople	

The SSN size restriction provides the crucial example of ungrammaticality that will be discussed in the next section. However, we first address some apparent counterexamples to the phonological restriction. Since the forms in (15) contain three syllables, they appear to violate the size restriction we have just proposed. However, these forms all share the property that the verb stem (without *re*-) has its own zero nominalization. As we have already described (fn 8), *re*- can attach to deverbal nouns. Our con-

---

[7]Some of these verbs have other nominalized forms than SSN (e.g., *redistribution*), suggesting that a blocking account might be considered. However, this proves not to be feasible, for two reasons. First, some of the already existing nominalizations have restricted meanings (e.g., *revisitation*) and therefore should not block the default SSN construction. Second, some of the verbs listed do not have a lexicalized nominalization at all (e.g., *re-polish*, regular nominalization repolishing) and therefore blocking is not applicable.

clusion is that SSN applies productively to any verb formed by attaching *re-* to a monosyllabic stem. For a noun containing *re-* to exist for longer verbs, some other process (which may or may not be productive) needs to be called upon.

(15)   rebroadcast   re-edit
           remodel   re-export
           re-echo   reimport

In summary, stress-shifting nominalization is unproductive in general. It applies to a seemingly arbitrary class of verbs that do not share any semantic, morphological, or phonological properties. However, there is one class of verbs to which SSN applies productively, namely disyllabic verbs containing the prefix *re-*. The fact that the SSN construction refers to the presence of a specific morpheme (*re-*) is interesting in its own right. Orgun 1996 and Orgun and Inkelas 2002 present a detailed account of this sensitivity in terms of his mechanism of reference to lexical types. Here, we are concerned solely with the phonological restriction on SSN: verbs that contain more than two syllables do not give rise to grammatical stress-shifted nominals.

3   Analysis of the maximum size condition in *re*-verb nominalization

The analysis here is restricted to the productive nominalization of *re*-verbs by the SSN construction. The forms listed in (9) are lexicalized and as such do not necessarily indicate the existence of a disyllabic maximal size condition on nominalizations of verbs other than those containing the prefix *re-*.

The main insight is that ungrammaticality results from two incompatible conditions. First, stress-shifted nominals must have a characteristic stress pattern — initial primary stress and peninitial secondary stress (*rédò*). Second, stress clash is not allowed in forms that contain more than two syllables (in disyllabic forms, stress clash is unavoidable since there are as many stresses as there are syllables).

The phonological restriction to disyllabicity presumably has to do with the foot assignment to stress-shifted nominals (Orgun 1996). A disyllabic stress-shifted nominal has two monosyllabic feet adjacent to each other:

(16)   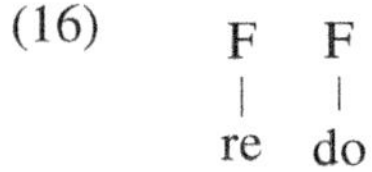

When we attempt to apply SSN to verbs containing more than two syllables there is no grammatical output. For the English *re*-verb problem, the inviolable constraints responsible for ungrammaticality are the ones that require the special stress patterns of stress-shifted nominals.[8] The constraints responsible for the SSN stress pattern are summarized below. Note that these are all standard OT constraints, taken either directly from McCarthy and Prince (1994), McCarthy and Prince (1995), Prince and Smolensky (1993) or modified slightly from their versions.

(17)   LEX≈PR   The output must have a stress foot ("a lexical word must be a prosodic word")

ALIGN HEAD   ALIGN(Word, L, Head, L)
The first syllable of the output must bear the primary stress.

MAXHEADFOOT   The head foot in the input must have a corresponding foot in the output (the primary stress must not be deleted, though it might be shifted or demoted to a secondary stress)

HEAD IDENT   A syllable that is stressed in the input must be stressed in the output (no stress shift)

*CLASH   Adjacent syllables must not be stressed

The major intuitions concerning *re*-verb nominalization are repeated below:

1. Stress clash is avoided whenever possible.

2. Disyllabic inputs cannot avoid stress clash since there are only as many syllables as stresses.

---

[8]One could handle the facts by just stipulating directly that the input to the SSN construction should contain exactly two syllables. This kind of subcategorization approach was commonly used before the advent of OT. However, as mentioned above, the OT program attempts to derive linguistic generalization from the interaction of wellformedness and faithfulness constraints. Therefore, the subcategorization approach is less than satisfactory. Similarly, stipulating that the output of SSN must contain exactly two syllables is hardly better. The interesting question is why there should be such a two syllable maximum. Our analysis answers this question: when a verb contains more than two syllables, it can, and therefore must, avoid stress clash. However, this prevents the characteristic stress pattern of SSN forms from being realized. Thus there is no grammatical output.

3. Inputs with more than two syllables can, and therefore must, avoid stress clash.

4. However, avoiding stress clash prevents the characteristic primary-secondary stress pattern of SSN from being realized. Therefore, there is no grammatical output.

The intuitions developed above are easily captured in the CONTROL framework. EVAL always produces a winning candidate that is optimal with respect to faithfulness and stress clash avoidance. CONTROL eliminates winners that fail to satisfy the SSN stress pattern. Thus, we assign SSN-STRESS to CONTROL. All other constraints are in EVAL. In (11) the inputs are *re*-verbs (*rèdò, rèuníte, rèággregàte*), and the outputs are SSNs, the grammaticality of which is determined in CONTROL.

(18) EVAL

		MAX-H-F	*CLASH	HEAD-ID
☞	rédò		*	
	rédo	*!		
☞	réunìte			
	réùnite		*!	*
	réunite	*!		
☞	réaggregàte			*
	réàggregate		*!	
	réaggregate	*!		

The winners of EVAL must be checked against the inviolable constraint component, CONTROL. This is shown below, where redo$_N$ is accepted but reunite$_N$ and revivify$_N$ are correctly rejected:

(19) CONTROL

		SSN-STRESS
✓	rédò	
✂	réunìte	*!
✂	*réaggregàte	*!

4   Norwegian imperatives

In our original paper introducing CONTROL we assumed that ungrammaticality-causing constraints applied at the lexical level. In each of our case studies — Turkish minimality, Tagalog *-um-* infixation, Tiene stem maximality, and English *-ize* suffixation — we examined word outputs that either were or were not grammatical in their language, as governed by the parochial well-formedness constraints found in CONTROL. The grammaticality of these words does not vary in different phrasal contexts.

Rice (Rice 2005) presents an important set of facts from Norwegian imperative formation that does not follow this pattern. Grammaticality of monosyllabic imperatives depends in part on the phonological context provided by the syntactic phrase. Norwegian imperatives consist of a bare root, and the addition of a final schwa forms the infinitive (all examples from Rice 2005):

(20)   **Imperative**   **Infinitive**
       spis   eat!   å spise   to eat
       snakk   talk!   å snakke   to talk
       løft   lift!   å løfte   to lift

Infinitives with final -CC clusters of rising sonority are unpronounceable in isolation, however:

(21)   **Imperative**   **Infinitive**
       åpn!   open!   å åpne   to open
       padl!   paddle! å padle   to paddle
       sykl!   bike!   å sykle   to bike

In showing that the ungrammaticality of the imperatives in (21) is a synchronic process Rice observes that these forms are grammatical if a vowel-initial word follows, but not if a consonant-initial word follows:

(22)   Sykl opp bakken.
       bike up the.hill
       'Bike up the hill!'

(23)   *Sykl ned   bakken.
       bike down the.hill
       'Bike down the hill!'

The same facts apply to the negative syntactic context, in which the negator *ikke* normally may appear either before or after the imperative, but must appear after the imperative if a consonant-initial word would come immediately after the imperative otherwise:

(24)   Klatr ikke på møblene.
       climb not on the.furniture
       'Don't climb on the furniture!'

(25)   *Ikke klatr på møblene.
        not   climb on the.furniture
        'Don't climb on the furniture!'

The negator *ikke* creates the right environment for these imperatives when it follows the verb, as in (24), but that environment is missing when it precedes the verb, as in (25).

Clearly, a hard constraint in CONTROL cannot declare these imperatives as ungrammatical. If such a constraint were active, there would be no possibility of forming the syntactic constructions in (22) and (24) with those lexical items. Instead, an imperative like *padl* must be: a) the optimal output of EVAL; and b) must not be ruled as ungrammatical by CONTROL at the lexical level. We propose that hard constraints must be active at the phrasal level as well, and that Norwegian rules out phrasal outputs that contain word-final clusters of rising sonority that do not resyllabify across a word boundary. Such a constraint will prevent the syntactic constructions in (23) and (25) from being produced whenever these imperatives precede a consonant-initial word or are utterance final, as in the simple imperatives in (21). Fanselow and Féry 2002 attribute ineffability of syntactic structures to mechanisms independent of CONTROL, which they take to be the source of lexical ungrammaticality only. Norwegian imperatives constitute another class of ungrammaticality in which CONTROL operates at the phrasal level.

An additional complication arises from Norwegian nouns, which sometimes have identical noun and verb roots. Singular formation, like imperative formation, involves zero affixation of the root. Unlike imperative formation, however, singular nouns may be formed from roots ending in clusters of rising sonority (examples from Rice 2005):

(26)   ***Root***   ***Singular***   ***Imperative***
        sykl   'bike'   sykkel   *sykl!/*sykkel!
        adl   'nobility'   adel   *adl!/*adel!
        hindr   'hinder'   hinder   *hindr!/*hinder!
        ordn   'arrange'   orden   *ordn!/*orden!

Singular forms undergo epenthetic schwa insertion to repair the final cluster, but imperatives are simply ungrammatical.

The question is why singular nouns undergo repair while imperatives do not. We are used to seeing different repairs resulting from the same underlying ill-formedness in different contexts, but ordinarily these different repairs emerge as a result of the interplay of constraint rankings in EVAL and faithfulness to the input. Since the hard constraint that rules out Norwegian imperatives is in CONTROL, not EVAL, it has no possibility of influencing the outcome of EVAL. It either declares the optimal output to be grammatical or not. Norwegian singular and imperative formations must therefore differ in their EVAL components such that epenthesis is favored in nouns but not in verbs. We favor an approach that provides separate cophonologies (Inkelas et al. 1997, Itô and Mester 1995a, Itô and Mester 1995b, Orgun 1996) in which DEP ranks lower than syllable well-formedness constraints in nouns but not in verbs.

5   Conclusion

CONTROL provides a principled answer to an important question: how can a form be ungrammatical when there are available repairs used elsewhere in the language in different environments. Our answer is that the job of the generative component EVAL is to identify the optimal candidate. Grammaticality is determined by a separate component, CONTROL, which has no generative capacity. The job of CONTROL is simply to accept or reject the optimal candidate. If the optimal candidate is rejected, ungrammaticality is the result.

While this idea seems to have gained wide acceptance on conceptual as well as empirical grounds, there has been at least one attempt, by Raffelsiefen, to defend its precursor, MPARSE. One of Raffelsiefen's criticisms is based on the possibility that every constraint in CONTROL will also be needed in EVAL, resulting in duplication of constraints. If constraints are universal, it is not clear why this duplication should be considered a problem (in our original proposal, we suggested that in the course of language learning, constraints may be moved from EVAL to CONTROL, but if Raffelsiefen's hunch is correct, we see nothing wrong in assuming that constraints are instead copied to CONTROL). This criticism has been addressed and dismissed by Hansson and Bye, who, independently, propose that EVAL contains universal (and phonologically reasonable) constraints, while CONTROL contains arbitrary language specific constraints.

Raffelsiefen's second criticism is based on predictiveness in English: she seems to suggest that the fact that CONTROL makes possible the existence of a particular type of affix in English (one that can shift stress to the right on its base to make main stress two syllables back, but cannot shift stress leftwards to avoid clash if base is final stressed) is fatal. But surely one would hardly think that English is representative of all possibilities available to UG! The real question is: could there be a morphological construction that repairs one type of unacceptable form while rejecting another type? This is what CONTROL can do in Raffelsiefen's hypothetical example as well as generally. And indeed, Rice shows that this is exactly what one finds. He has examples from Norwegian where one kind of repair is found along with gaps in the same construction, for different inputs.

References

Beaver, D. and Lee, H. (2004) Input-Output Mismatches in OT. In R. Blutner and H. Zeevat (eds.) *Optimality Theory and Pragmatics* 112–53. Palgrave: Macmillan.

Bye, P. (2005) Allomorphy — selection, not optimization. In S. Blaho, P. Bye and M. Krämer (eds.) *Freedom of Analysis?* 63-92. Berlin/New York: Mouton de Gruyter.

Fanselow, G. and Féry, C. (2002) Ineffability in grammar. In G. Fanselow and C. Féry (eds.) *Resolving Conflicts in Grammars: Optimality Theory in Syntax, Morphology, and Phonology* 265–397. Hamburg: Buske.

Halle, M. (1973) Prolegomena to a theory of word formation. *Linguistic Inquiry* 4:3–16.

Hansson, G. Ó. (1999) "When in doubt...": intraparadigmatic dependencies and gaps in Icelandic. Paper presented at North Eastern Linguistic Society, Amherst.

Inkelas, S. and Orgun, C. O. (1995) Level ordering and economy in the lexical phonology of Turkish. *Language* 71: 763–93.

Inkelas, S. Orgun, C. O. and Zoll, C. (1997) Implications of lexical exceptions for the nature of grammar. In I. Roca (ed.) *Constraints and Derivations in Phonology* 393–418. Oxford: Clarendon Press.

Inkelas, S., Küntay, A., Orgun, C. O. and Sprouse, R. (2000) Turkish Electronic Living Lexicon (TELL). *Turkic Languages* 4: 253–75.

Itô, J., and Hankamer, J. (1989) Notes on monosyllabism in Turkish. In J. Itô and J. Runner (eds.) *Phonology at Santa Cruz 1* 61–69. Santa Cruz: University of California, Santa Cruz Syntax Research Center.

Itô, J. (1990) Prosodic minimality in Japanese. In M. Ziolkowski, M. Noske and K. Deaton (eds.) *Papers from the Twenty-sixth Regional Meeting of the Chicago Linguistics Society. Volume 2: the parasession on the syllable in phonetics and phonology* 213–39. Chicago: Chicago Linguistics Society.

Itô, J. and Mester, A. (1995a) The core-periphery structure of the lexicon and constraints on reranking. *University of Massachussets Occasional Papers in Linguistics* 18. Amherst, MA: GLSA.

Itô, J., and Mester, A. (1995b) Japanese phonology: constraint domains and structure preservation. In J. Goldsmith (ed.) *The Handbook of Phonological Theory* 817–38. Cambridge, MA: Blackwell.

Lees, R. (1961) *The Phonology of Modern Standard Turkish*. Bloomington: Indiana University Publications.

McCarthy, J. J. and Prince, A. (1994) Generalized alignment. In G. Booij and J. van Marle (eds.)*Yearbook of Morphology 1993* 79–153. Dordrecht: Kluwer.

McCarthy, J. J. and Prince, A. (1995) Faithfulness and reduplicative identity. In J. Beckman, L. Dickey and S. Urbanczyk (eds.) *University of Massachusetts Occasional Papers in Linguistics 18: Papers in Optimality Theory* 249–384. Amherst, MA: GLSA. Mester, Armin. 1994. The quantitative trochee in Latin. Natural Language and Linguistic Theory 12:1-61.

Orgun, C. O. (1995) Correspondence and identity constraints in two-level OT. *WCCFL*. ROA 62. http://roa.rutgers.edu/

Orgun, C. O. (1996) *Sign-based Morphology and Phonology: with Special Attention to Optimality Theory*, University of California, Berkeley: PhD.

Orgun, C. O. (1997) Syllable faithfulness and privative [voice]. Paper presented at Southwest Workshop on Optimality Theory, University of California, Los Angeles.

Orgun, C. O. and Sprouse, R. (1999) From MPARSE to CONTROL: deriving ungrammaticality. *Phonology* 16:191–224.

Orgun, C. O. and Inkelas, S. (2002) Reconsidering Bracket Erasure. In G. Booij and J. van Marle *Yearbook of Morphology* 115–46. Dordrecht: Kluwer.

Prince, A. and Smolensky, P. (1993) Optimality theory: constraint interaction in generative grammar. Ms., Rutgers University.

Raffelsiefen, R. (1992) A nonconfigurational approach to morphology. In M.Aronoff (ed.), *Morphology Now* 133–62. Albany: State University of New York Press.

Raffelsiefen, R. (2004) Absolute ill-formedness and other morphophonological effects. *Phonology* 21: 91–142.

Rice, C. (2005) Optimal gaps in optimal paradigms. *Catalan Journal of Linguistics* 4: 155–70.

Smolensky, P. (1995) On the internal structure of the constraint component CON of UG. Ms., Johns Hopkins University.

Part II
Paradigms

5 Lexical and morphological conditioning of paradigm gaps

Adam Albright
MIT

1 Introduction

Although paradigm gaps are an analytical puzzle for all linguistic theories, until recently they have received only sporadic discussion in the literature. Since the advent of Optimality Theory, however, gaps have gradually become the subject of more systematic attention. This is certainly due in part to the particular mechanical challenge that gaps pose for OT; hence, a major focus has been on providing a mechanism for all overt candidates to be eliminated, rather than the more usual outcome of one emerging as optimal (Prince and Smolensky 2004, p. 57; Orgun and Sprouse 1999; Fanselow and Féry 2002, Raffelsiefen 2004; Rice 2005, 2006; McCarthy and Wolf this volume). Equally important, though, is the fact that OT provides a natural way to formalize an intuition expressed in some earlier discussions, that gaps often appear when the expected form would violate a surface-true phonotactic constraint, and that silence is simply one part of a larger conspiracy to avoid illegal configurations (Hetzron 1975; Iverson 1981). For this reason, discussions in the OT literature have focused primarily on cases that appear to have clear phonotactic motivation, in that the expected faithful candidates would involve illegal configurations like stress lapse, OCP violations, sonority sequencing violations, and so on (Orgun and Sprouse 1999; Raffelsiefen 2004; Rice 2005).

Not all cases of paradigm gaps involve such obvious phonotactic violations, however. The focus of this paper will be on gaps that affect only certain words, while other, seemingly parallel words surface as expected. For example, many speakers of American English find the past participles of certain irregular verbs to be problematic (Pinker 1999: 68–71):

(1)   Problematic past participles in American English

    a.   *dive ~ dove ~ ???*

"He has diven, dived, dove, doved, doven or whatever … in every major and most minor bodies of water on this planet"[1]

    b.   *stride ~ strode ~ ???*

"I have strode (stridden? strided?) into the backyard, boots strapped on…"[2]

    c.   *smite ~ smote ~ ???*

"It's like you're smitten by God. Smote? Smoten? Smoted? Smited? Well, whatever."[3]

"So I think I've been smote. Smited? What is the past tense of 'to smite'? Anyway, God got me!"[4]

"…the Arab planes are smote (smited? smut? smeet?) mysteriously from the sky to the bafflement of everyone"[5]

    d.   *strive ~ strove ~ ???*

"I've stroven/strove/striven to escape this insanity…"[6]

The problematic forms in (1) do not suffer from irreparable phonotactic violations — in fact, all of the possible options find parallels in other, non-problematic verbs: *arrived* [əɹaɪvd], *driven* [dɹɪvn̩], *ridden* [ɹɪdn̩], *woven* [woʊvn̩], *written* [ɹɪtn̩]. For this reason, such cases have sometimes been referred to as *lexically arbitrary paradigm gaps* (Hetzron 1975; Albright 2003). The aim of this paper is to understand why such gaps arise, and why they affect particular words in particular parts of the paradigm. I claim that they are neither arbitrary not lexical, but that their occurrence is in large part predictable: namely, gaps occur when speakers know that an inflected form must stand in some defined relation to another inflected form, but the language does not provide enough data to be sure what that relation should be.

To preview how the account works at an intuitive level, consider the case of *diven/doven/dove*. For most verbs in English, the form of the past

---

[1]4/05/2006:   `http://www.scubaboard.com/archive/index.php/t-4550.html`

[2]4/05/2006:   `http://spanglemonkey.typepad.com/spanglemonkey/2006/01/the_what_the_fu.html`

[3]4/12/2006:   `http://favorabledicta.blogspot.com/2004/12/my-name-is-espat-and-im-addicted-to.html`

[4]4/12/2006: `http://heather.tadma.net/archives/00000661.html`

[5]4/12/2006: `http://www.trashcity.org/ARTICLES/IBFS0007.HTM`

[6]4/05/2006: `http://raven.utc.edu/cgi-bin/WA.EXE?A2=ind0202&L=scuba-se&P=29779`

participle can be predicted fairly accurately by looking at the form of the simple past: if the simple past is suffixed with [d]/[t]/[əd], the past participle is identical to it; otherwise, it is created using a set of vowel changes, with or without additional suffixation ([æ] → [ʌ] (*drank* → *drunk*); [ʊ] → [eɪ]+*en* (*shook* → *shaken*); [u] → [oʊ]+*n* (*grew* → *grown*); etc.). In the case of irregular pasts with the vowel [oʊ], however, there are several different competing patterns:

(2)   Participle formation for verbs with [oʊ] pasts

> •No change: *shone*
>
> •Suffix -*n*: *worn, torn, sworn, born(e), broken, woken, spoken, stolen, frozen, woven, chosen*
>
> •[oʊ] → [ɪ], and suffix -*n*: *written, driven, risen, ridden*

Not only do these patterns compete with one another, but they are also based on relatively small amounts of data. Even the most robust pattern has just eleven examples, while the others involve a few verb roots each. The observation at the core of the analysis is that generalizations that cover so few forms — and suffer from exceptions at that — are not well enough supported to be trustable. This means that for verbs with irregular past tense forms in [oʊ], speakers do not have any usable generalization that lets them confidently predict the past participle. In most cases, this is not a problem, since the verbs in (2) are generally common enough that speakers can memorize their participles, and need not use their grammar to derive the output. For relatively uncommon verbs like *stride* or *strive*, however, speakers may not have sufficient exposure to be sure of the participle, and are forced to resort (unsuccessfully) to their grammar.[7] The grammar provides several possibilities (*stroven, striven, strove*), but all are poorly supported. In such cases, speakers have no way to produce a past participle; they lack a lexically listed form, and the grammar does not provide any way to derive one.

In order to formalize this intuition, we need two components. First, it is crucial for this analysis that forms in the paradigm are projected from particular other forms — e.g., that past participles in English are generated with reference to the simple past forms, and cannot be projected directly from present tense forms. To see why this is necessary, consider the mapping from presents to past participles. Here, we find an overwhelmingly

---

[7]The verbs *smite* and *dive* are missing past participles for different reasons: *smitten* has undergone semantic drift and is no longer clearly associated with *smite*, while *dive* was historically regular, so did not inherit a participle that corresponds to irregular *dove*.

strong generalization, namely, that verbs of any shape can take past participles with *-ed*. In fact, this pattern is extremely likely and well-supported, because most verbs in English are regular. If speakers had access to this robust pattern, they could use it to confidently derive past participles like *strided, strived, dived*, and *smited*, without regard for the fact that the past tense forms are irregular. The fact that they do not do this indicates the computation of the participle makes crucial reference to the irregular past forms (*strode, strove, dove, smote*). A major challenge in the analysis of lexically arbitrary paradigm gaps is to understand why certain statistically well-supported generalizations (such as the highly regular present → past participle mapping) are unavailable to speakers. The approach taken here is to say that generalizations about the relation between the present form and the past participle cannot be used because the grammar of English simply does not derive past participles directly from present tense forms. Naturally, in order to give this claim substance, we need a theory of how relations are established between different parts of the paradigm. One goal of this paper, therefore, is to show how a model of paradigm organization can predict the occurrence of paradigm gaps in certain parts of the paradigm.

The second thing that is needed to develop this account is an understanding of what constitutes sufficient evidence for a trustable grammatical generalization. Looking at the participle forms of [oʊ] pasts in (2), we see that two factors seem to be important: the inconsistency of the data (three competing patterns), and the paucity of the data (less than a dozen forms for each pattern). In order to make use of this observation, we need a theory of how and why these factors influence grammar. Developing such a theory raises numerous questions: how much data is required? Must it be both sparse and inconsistent to create uncertainty, or is one alone enough? What is the tradeoff between these factors? How is this information stored, and how does the grammar make use of it? A second goal of this paper is to provide a preliminary model of how learners decide which generalizations can be confidently extended, by evaluating the consistency and abundance of data.

The organization of the rest of this paper is as follows: in section 2, I review the details of a lexically arbitrary paradigm gap in the Spanish verbal system (Albright 2003). I show why this data cannot be satisfactorily explained using mechanisms that have been successful elsewhere, such as MPARSE relativized to particular morphological categories (McCarthy and Wolf, this volume) or lexical conservatism (Steriade 1997; Pertsova

2005), and why a model that relates members of the paradigm to particular other forms is needed. Next, I sketch a model of grammatical learning that attempts to discover an optimal set of relations between members of the paradigm, based on considerations of predictability and contrast maintenance (Albright 2002a). This model has two important properties for the analysis of paradigm gaps: first, it correctly predicts which forms in the paradigm may potentially suffer from gaps. In addition, it learns grammars that take into account both the reliability of generalizations, and also the amount of data that supports them. Under this system, generalizations receive higher confidence to the extent that they are based on many forms, and do not vie with competing patterns. When competition is fierce, or when data is sparse, there may be no high-confidence generalizations, leaving the speaker to resort to word-specific knowledge. After showing how this model has the potential to explain key aspects of the cases discussed in section 2, I sketch the outline of an OT analysis of lexically arbitrary gaps. Finally, I consider the relation between these lexically arbitrary cases, and the more clearly phonotactically motivated gaps discussed by Orgun and Sprouse, Raffelsiefen, Rice, McCarthy and Wolf, and others.

2   Some challenges for a theory of paradigm gaps

In this section, I lay out a set of explicanda for a theory of lexically arbitrary paradigm gaps. As an illustration, I use data from two types of gaps in Spanish present tense paradigms, described in more detail in Albright (2003). After this backgound, I will then show in sections 2.2-2.4 why current mechanisms for licensing gaps or alternations in OT do not capture the full range of facts.

2.1   Gaps in Spanish present tense paradigms

Spanish verbs exhibit a wide variety of lexically idiosyncratic properties, but the ones that will relevant for this discussion are those that are seen specifically in the present indicative paradigm. The first major division concerns the choice of theme vowel, which shows up between the verb stem and the person/number endings: *-a-* (class 1), *-e-* (class 2) or *-i-* (class 3; /i/ reduces to [e] when stressless).

(3)   Spanish conjugation classes

a. *hablár* 'speak' (Class 1)

hábl-o	habl-**á**mos
hábl-**as**	habl-**á**is
hábl-**a**	hábl-**an**

b. *comér* 'eat' (Class 2)

cóm-o	com-**é**mos
cóm-**es**	com-**é**is
cóm-**e**	cóm-**en**

c. *vivír* 'live' (Class 3)

vív-o	viv-**í**mos
vív-**es**	viv-**í**s
vív-**e**	vív-**en**

The paradigms in (3) also show that stress (indicated here by V́) falls on the root in the 1SG, 2SG, 3SG and 3PL forms, and the suffix elsewhere. The first singular suffix is always *-o*, while the remaining suffixes reveal the conjugation class to varying degrees. Class 1 (*-ar*) is the productive class for derived verbs, neologisms, and loanwords, and the majority of Spanish verbs belong to this class.

Another source of unpredictability comes from the fact that some verbs that contain mid vowels (*e, o*) in the final syllable of the stem undergo lexically conditioned changes in stressed forms. In some verbs, *e* and *o* diphthongize to *jé, wé* (4a), while in others, *e* raises to *í* (4b); in yet others, no change occurs (4c).

(4)   Lexically conditioned mid-vowel alternations

a.   Diphthongization of *e, o*

i. *sentar* 'seat'

s[**jé**]nt-o	s[e]nt-ámos
s[**jé**]nt-as	s[e]nt-áis
s[**jé**]nt-a	s[**jé**]nt-an

ii. *contar* 'count'

c[**wé**]nt-o	c[o]nt-ámos
c[**wé**]nt-as	c[o]nt-áis
c[**wé**]nt-a	c[**wé**]nt-an

b.   Raising of *e*

i. *pedir* 'request'

p[**í**]d-o	p[e]d-ímos
p[**í**]d-es	p[e]d-ís
p[**í**]d-e	p[**í**]d-en

c.   Neither

i. *rentar* 'rent'

r[**é**]nt-o	r[e]nt-ámos
r[**é**]nt-as	r[e]nt-áis
r[**é**]nt-a	r[**é**]nt-an

ii. *montar* 'mount'

m[**ó**]nt-o	m[o]nt-ámos
m[**ó**]nt-as	m[o]nt-áis
m[**ó**]nt-a	m[**ó**]nt-an

There are significant interactions between conjugation class and mid-vowel alternations. Diphthongizing verbs occur in all three classes, but they are a minority in class 1, somewhat more prevalent in class 2, and a majority in class 3. Raising occurs only in class 3, and in that class, virtually every mid-vowel verb either diphthongizes or raises (Harris 1969: 108–116). There is also an effect of vowel backness: the front mid vowel *e* undergoes both diphthongization and raising, while back *o* diphthongizes but does not raise in the standard language. Furthermore, the segmental contexts that encourage diphthongization differ substantially between *e* and *o*, and the rate of *o* diphthongization is overall lower than that of *e* (Albright et al. 2001). In sum, it is difficult to form any language-wide generalizations about mid-vowel alternations, since they depend heavily on the particular vowel involved, the segmental context, and the inflectional class of the verb.

Another alternation is seen in the 1SG, in which some verbs in classes 2 and 3 show a process of velar insertion: [k] or [g] added between the stem and the suffix. Voiceless [k] is frequently added after stem-final [s]/[θ] (depending on the dialect), while [g] often occurs after stem-final [l] or [n].

(5)   Velar insertion in the 1SG

a. *crecer* 'grow'		b. *valer* 'be worth'	
cré[s**k**]-o [8]	cre[s]-émos	vál-**g**-o	val-émos
cré[s]-es	cre[s]-éis	vál-es	val-éis
cré[s]-e	cré[s]-en	vál-e	vál-en

There are a number of other minor patterns affecting 1SG or stressed forms, which I will not discuss here. What matters for present purposes is that the major unpredictable properties of verbs include (1) conjugation class, (2) diphthongization and raising of mid vowels, and (3) velar insertion.

With this in mind, we now turn to the two patterns of present tense paradigm gaps reported by Spanish grammars (de Gámez 1973; Butt 1997). The first involves verbs that lack all of the inflected forms in which stress would fall on the root:

(6)   Missing stressed forms: *abolir* 'to abolish' (Butt 1997, p. 185)

—	abol-ímos
—	abol-ís
—	—

The second pattern of gaps involves verbs that lack specifically the 1SG:

(7)　　Missing 1SG forms: *asir* 'to grasp' (Butt 1997, p. 194)

—	as-ímos
ás-es	as-ís
ás-e	ás-en

Significantly, verbs with gaps also meet the conditions for undergoing stem alternations: *abolir* contains a potentially diphthongizing mid vowel, while *asir* contains a stem-final strident associated with velar insertion. More generally, verbs missing stressed forms typically belong to the *-ir* class, in which nearly all mid vowel verbs are irregular in some way, while verbs missing the 1SG belong to the *-er* and *-ir* classes, where velar insertion often occurs. Moreover, affected verbs are missing just those forms where the alternation would apply. Finally, when speakers are asked to inflect the verb *abolir*, they frequently utter both diphthongized and non-diphthongized possibilities (e.g., 3PL *abolen, abuelen*), before eventually settling on one or rejecting both. (Exactly parallel facts are also remarked on for Russian by (Hetzron 1975: p. 861).) I take this as very strong evidence that the gaps in these cases involve uncertainty about whether to employ an alternation or not. The connection between irregularity and uncertainty in creating lexically arbitrary paradigm gaps is important, and must be accounted for.

What is the source of this uncertainty? Unlike cases such as Norwegian imperatives (Rice 2005: et seq.), where speakers are forced to choose between a faithful form that is unpronounceable (*[sikl]) and forms that employ repairs not otherwise seen in verbs ([sikl̥]? [sikkəl]? [siklə]?), in Spanish the competing choices both find at least some degree of support from parallel verbs: 3PL *abuelen* would parallel *cuentan* 'count', *suelen* 'are accustomed to', *huelen* 'smell', *duelen* 'are in pain', *vuelan* 'fly', etc., while 3PL *abolen* would parallel (somewhat more distantly) *controlan* 'control', *violan* 'violate', *tremolan* 'flutter', and so on. A major analytical challenge of such cases, therefore, is to explain why certain words suffer from gaps, while others are permitted to surface with one pattern or another. I will call this property LEXICAL SELECTIVITY.

A closely related problem is the MORPHOLOGICAL SELECTIVITY of gaps — namely, the fact that only certain parts of the paradigm are affected. In principle, speakers could be uncertain about other properties of verbs as well, leading to gaps in other parts of the paradigm. For example, uncertainty about which conjugation class a verb belongs to might lead to gaps in forms other than the 1SG, or gaps specifically in the infinitive, 1PL and 2PL (where classes 2 and 3 diverge). Even restricting the discussion to stem vowel alternations, the paradigms in (8) show that in the *-ir* class of verbs, the difference between underlying /i/ vs. "raised /e/" leads to ambiguity in those forms in which the root is stressed (*vivir* ∼ *vive* vs. *pedir* ∼ *pide*).

(8)   Ambiguity in stressed forms: invariant *i* vs. raising *e* ∼ *i*

a. *vivir* 'to live'		b. *pedir* 'to request'	
vív-o	viv-ímos	p[í]d-o	p[e]d-ímos
vív-es	viv-ís	p[í]d-es	p[e]d-ís
vív-e	vív-en	p[í]d-e	p[í]d-en

In principle, this *e/i* neutralization in stressed forms could lead to uncertainty, if a speaker has only encountered a particular verb in stressed forms before — a not unlikely scenario, given that the 3SG, 1SG, and 3PL forms are generally among the most frequent parts of the paradigm, both for adults and children (Rodríguez Bou 1952; Juilland and Chang-Rodríguez 1964; Bybee 1985, p. 71). Yet strikingly, there are no *-ir* verbs with stem vowel [i] in stressed forms, but gaps in all stressless forms (where the vowel could be either [i] or [e]). This is reminiscent of the fact noted by both Rice (2005) and McCarthy and Wolf, that even in more phonotactically motivated cases, only certain morphemes or morphological categories are affected. This is handled in their analyses by stipulating that MPARSE or MAX{MCAT} be relativized to different morphological categories, and ranked lower for some than for others. Something we would like to explain here is *why* certain morphological forms are selectively singled out by gaps, while others never are.

Another feature of the Spanish data that is not evident from grammatical descriptions is the fact that uncertainty about gapped forms is GRADIENT. Albright (2003) reports results of an elicitation study showing that ratings of potentially gapped forms fall along a continuum from very certain to not at all certain. This raises an important question about the object of analysis, since when speakers' intuitions are consulted, there is no obvious watershed of uncertainty that corresponds to a criterion for declaring the verb to be gapped. A similar point is made by Sims (2005) in a study of genitive plural gaps in Greek. One factor that plays an obvious role is lexical frequency — unsurprisingly, the greatest uncertainty surrounds low frequency items. In fact, many of the verbs listed as gapped by grammars are now used only in the infinitive or participial forms, or have switched conjugation classes, or have fallen out of the language completely. Low frequency alone is typically not sufficient to cause inflection to break down, however. In the usual case, speakers are willing to inflect rare or even nonce ("wug") words. Thus, we must account for additional sources of gradient uncertainty that cannot be attributed solely to the effect of lexical frequency.

A fact that goes hand in hand with gradient uncertainty is the relation between gaps and variability. In Albright (2003), I showed that when speakers report uncertainty about inflected forms, they also tend to produce divergent forms (i.e., one speaker says *abolen*, another says *abuelen*, but both profess uncertainty). A plot demonstrating this correlation is reproduced in Figure 1. In more naturalistic settings, this seems to translate into considerable individual variability in whether speakers are willing to utter an odd-sounding form, or whether they seek a periphrastic solution. In some cases, such as Sims' Greek example, an obvious alternative is available and speakers can easily avoid the gap. In the Spanish case, a more serious maneuver is required, and apparently speakers sometimes simply fill the gap — as can be seen from significant numbers of Google hits for both *abole* and *abuele*, sometimes even side by side on the same page.[9] A similar point is made by Rice (2003) concerning Norwegian imperatives, for which many speakers have a gap, but some speakers settle on a solution to avoid periphrasis. Rice argues that in Norwegian, this constitutes a grammatical difference between speakers (some have a grammar that provides a pronounceable solution, others do not). In Spanish we see a different pattern, in which speakers widely agree that the form is uncomfortable (i.e., there is a common grammar which does not derive any form with any degree of certainty), but speakers differ, for possibly non-grammatical reasons, about whether they are willing to venture one of the unappealing possibilities.

Finally, the fact that communal uncertainty manifests itself as variability raises perhaps the deepest and most difficult challenge in explaining lexically arbitrary paradigm gaps: frequently, uncertainty persists in spite of the fact that the repair is (at least somewhat) attested elsewhere in the language. This is true at several different levels. In cases where the gap affects all relevant lexical items for some speakers, others speakers are apparently uttering repaired forms (e.g., Rice's speakers who are willing to

---

[9]E.g., the chronicles listed on `http://cenaculo.org/cenaculo/ius/cuarto.htm` use both forms within just a few lines of each other.

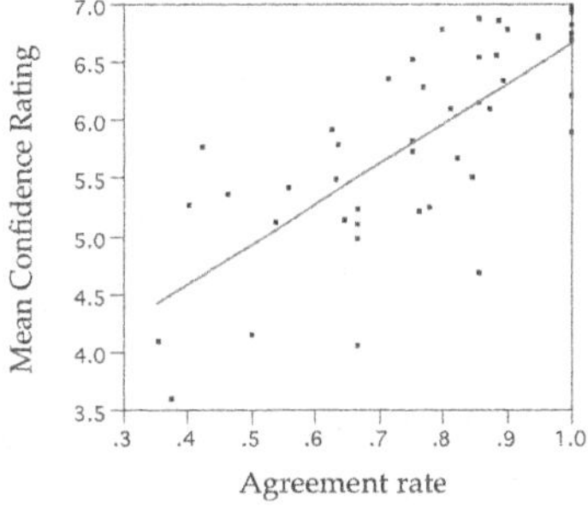

Figure 1. Relation between certainty and between-speaker agreement

devoice to [sykl̥]) — yet these repairs are unable to propagate through the entire population to fill the gap. Across morphological categories, the fix may be attested in one part of the grammar (e.g., for nouns), but this does not automatically carry over to other morphological categories. And at the level of the individual word, we see that gaps persist even though speakers are able to inflect other words, and are even occasionally willing to inflect a supposedly gapped word. For some reason, neither the existence of undiphthongized *controla, tremola, viola,* nor the the 15,000 Google hits for *abole* itself (20 March 2006) are sufficient to guarantee that speakers are willing to accept it. The same issue is also seen from a historical point of view, since gapped forms were often attested as expected at earlier stages of the language. Evidently, this type of sporadic attestation is not enough to ensure the survival of a previously attested solution; gaps are AGGRESSIVE. This property is puzzling, since the gaps themselves provide no positive evidence to "defend themselves" against the occasional data provided by speakers who are willing to utter [sykl̥] or [abole] — and, more generally, there is no overt evidence showing that such forms cannot be used. Given that there do exist small amounts of evidence *against* gaps, the challenge is to explain why these solutions do not take over. One possibility is that the level of attestation for the fixes is simply too low to be learned. An alternative possibility that I will pursue here, however, is that there is a more active force involved: gaps follow from a deeper issue, which sporadic pieces of data are not able to alleviate.

To summarize, then, lexically arbitrary paradigm gaps (and perhaps phonotactically motivated ones to some extent too) exhibit the following set of properties which must be explained: they are morphologically and even lexically selective, they are marked by gradience and variability, they are modulated by lexical frequency, and they emerge in spite of a lack of direct, overt evidence for their existence. In the next few sections, I consider the extent to which existing proposals are able to explain these facts.

2.2   Semantic implausibility, or homophony avoidance?

Descriptive grammars and native speakers frequently rationalize non-occurring forms by declaring them to be semantically implausible or potentially homophonous with unrelated words. It is certainly true that individual cases may suffer from one or more of these problems: for example, the diphthongized candidate for the 1SG of *abolir* 'abolish' is *abuelo*, which also happens to mean 'grandfather', while the 1SG of *pacer* 'graze' would normally be said only by livestock. These factors alone are not enough to explain the gaps, however. Speakers are often comfortable forming semantically or pragmatically improbable inflected forms (*lluevo* 'I am raining', *descaffeíno* 'I decaffeinate'), and they are generally not bothered by homophony (*creo* 'I believe' or 'I create'). Many authors have commented on the fact that these types of explanations do not lend themselves to a viable and explanatory theory of paradigm gaps — see, e.g., Halle (1973) regarding Russian, and Albright (2003) for Spanish. I will not consider such explanations further here.

2.3   Blocking by null?

One approach to arbitrary gaps, put forward by Halle (1973), posits that gapped forms are individually blocked by lexically specific surface filters, which he accomplishes by marking the relevant forms as [−LEXICAL IN-SERTION]. This is equivalent to saying that speakers have learned that the affected form (exceptionally) does not exist — that is, its phonological form is unexpectedly ∅— and that this listed irregular null form blocks the creation of the otherwise expected overt form. In OT, an equivalent account could perhaps be constructed by letting MPARSE constraints be relativized not only to different morphological contexts, but even to different lexical items: $\text{MPARSE}_{asir\text{-}1\text{SG}}$.

This approach runs into several problems with the Spanish data. First and most important, it raises a learnability issue. As noted above, the words most strongly affected by gaps are the lowest frequency words in the relevant classes. This is unexpected under Halle's account, since ordinarily, the words that provide the strongest evidence about their irregularity are *high* frequency words. How do speakers know that for these particular low frequency words, an unattested 1SG form is a true gap, and not an accidental gap? McCarthy and Wolf (this volume) suggest a conservative learning strategy for the ranking of MPARSE when it is relativized to specific morphological contexts: the learner assumes that all MPARSE constraints start low, and rerank to allow pronouceable fixes only in response to positive evidence about the context in question. That is, hearing the answer for one morphological context does not automatically permit the same fix in a different morphological context — each context is assumed to have gaps, until the learner receives overt evidence otherwise. The solution cannot be extended to word-specific MPARSE constraints, however, since it predicts that learners treat every inflected form of every word as a gap until hearing otherwise. This is plainly false; speakers are frequently comfortable constructing inflected forms that they have never heard before, even in cases involving less plausible forms and more frequent verbs (e.g., the 1SG of *llover* 'rain' is widely agreed to be *lluevo*, even if there is little or no occasion to use this form in real life). It is not a safe learning strategy to assume that unattested forms reflect gaps, particularly for low frequency words, which are most susceptible to incomplete sampling. It is hard to see how the existence of gaps could be inferred for these rare words. This is a serious problem for any account that accomplishes lexical selectivity by requiring something to be learned about each affected word.

A blocking account is also unable to explain the morphological selectivity of gaps, since in principle, the same mechanism could be used to prevent any part of any paradigm from surfacing. For example, there is no reason why just a 2SG or infinitive form could not be marked as non-occurring. The fact that there are only two gap patterns (stressed forms, and first singulars), and that these patterns apply only in the irregular conjugation classes, is left unexplained. Lexically-specific blocking is too powerful to predict where gaps actually occur. At the same time, blocking is too weak to capture the observation that gaps are gradient and lead to variability. The experimental results of Albright (2003) suggest that gaps are not an all-or-nothing phenomenon, affecting a limited class of lexical items that can be listed as exceptional.

A "blocking by null" account thus fails to capture the intuition that lexically arbitrary gaps affect potentially irregular forms of word that belong to small and highly irregular inflectional classes, and that the effect is stronger when *less* is known about the word. This is not just a peculiarity of the Spanish example; it also seems to be true for the Russian case discussed by Halle (more on this below).

2.4 A competition-based account?

As noted above, lexically arbitrary gaps frequently target forms with irregular morphophonology. For that reason, it is tempting to suppose that they arise when the language provides two competing patterns, leaving speakers unable to decide between them. Concretely, perhaps the fact that Spanish has both diphthongizing and non-diphthongizing verbs (*vuelo* 'I fly' vs. *violo* 'I violate') creates a tie or a ranking paradox, and when faced with two equally good candidates, speakers are somehow frozen in indecision. There are several reasons to think that the failure is not as simple as "no unique winner", however.

The first obstacle to attributing gaps to indecision among multiple winners is that we would lose a plausible explanation for a different type of data — namely, grammatically licensed variation. Numerous works in OT have linked the availability of multiple surface variants to incomplete or indeterminate grammars (Boersma 1997; Boersma and Hayes 2001; Anttila 2002). In these cases, the response to multiple winning candidates is to allow all of them as possible outputs, rather than none of them. Even in cases of irregularity, variation between happily coexisting competing patterns can be observed (e.g., doublets like *shrunk* ~ *shrank* or *pleaded* ~ *pled* in American English; see also Zuraw (2000) for examples of competition leading to variation). It is natural to suppose that when the grammar produces two outputs, both should be pronounceable. The widely attested phenomenon of side-by-side variants lends support to this idea. Thus, there is a fundamental contradiction between the idea that variation should be modeling via multiple winners on the one hand, versus the idea that ties might cause paralyzing uncertainty on the other. The use of multiple winners to model variation appears to have the upper hand conceptually, and we must look elsewhere to explain gaps.

There is another reason to think that irreconcilable competition between two equally good candidates is not the appropriate analysis of paradigm gaps. In all of the cases to be discussed here, gaps affect those morphological classes where the incidence of irregularity is highest, affecting not just some, but *nearly all* relevant lexical items. We see that gaps are strongest in cases where irregularity nears 100%. This is unexpected if gaps stem from inability to resolve competition between two evenly matched patterns, since competition would be fiercest in a class that is 50% regular and 50% irregular.[10] The fact that gaps can occur even the

---

[10]Hansson (1999) points out that the irregular pattern may exert its influence through

in absence of strong competition from a second pattern shows that evenly matched competition is not a necessary precondition for lexically arbitrary paradigm gaps. The fact that when evenly matched patterns do occur they sometimes lead to free variation shows that such competition is also not sufficient to cause gaps. This serves to strengthen the conclusion that there is no promising easy solution involving a contradiction between two insufficiently distinguished candidates.

Given the discussion in section 2.1 above, it must be acknowledged that empirically, variation and gaps can mimic each other to a certain extent. When there's a gap, people tend to arrive at different solutions (leading to variation in responses), and when variation is brought to people's attention, they sometimes begin to worry about which form is normatively correct (leading to reported uncertainty). Nonetheless, the distinction between peaceable free variation and uncomfortable gaps appears to be a real one. I conclude that the uncertainty that leads to gaps must be modeled not as competition between two equally *good* outputs, but as the attempt to pronounce one or more *bad* outputs. This conclusion is by no means novel; it is, in fact, assumed without argument in all current approaches to phonotactically motivated gaps in OT cited above, which distinguish "bad" outputs as those that lose to the null parse or are eliminated in the Control component.

2.5   Faithfulness to listed allomorphs?

A different intuition, which drives most current analyses of paradigm gaps in some fashion, is that the alternation needed to repair a markedness violation would require an illicit faithfulness violation — encoded, for example, by FAITH ≫ MPARSE (McCarthy and Wolf) or FAITH ≫ MAX{MCAT} (Rice). Applying this to the case of Spanish anti-stress verbs, we might posit that mid-vowel verbs are subject to a markedness constraint that bans stressed mid vowels (stated here, in ad hoc fashion, as *V́-MID), but that all possible fixes (diphthongization, raising, lowering) are ruled out be-

---

a different mechanism than the regular pattern (analogical vs. grammatical mechanisms), and that when irregularity nears 100%, the answers from the two mechanisms would be most at odds with each other. This is an intriguing idea, but I do not know how to reconcile it with results showing that even "irregular" patterns seem to be extended in grammar-like ways (Albright 2002b; Albright and Hayes 2003), and that words that fall under multiple strong patterns, regular and irregular, can plausibly take all of them: *spling* → {*splinged, splung, splang*}.

cause the relevant faithfulness constraints (INTEGRITY ("no breaking"), IDENT$_{[\pm high]}$, etc.) are all ranked above MPARSE:

(9)   A ranking that would produce a 3PL gap

/abol-e-n/	*V́-MID	ID$_{[\pm HI]}$	INTEG	MPARSE
a. abólen	*!			
b. abuélen			*!	
c. abúlen/abálen/…		*!		
☞ d. ⊙				*

Unfortunately, the ranking in (9) predicts that no stressed forms of mid vowel verbs should ever occur. This is patently false: as we saw in (4) above, some Spanish verbs do diphthongize or raise, while others have stressed mid vowels. This leads to several apparent ranking paradoxes, created by the simultaneous existence of verbs that alternate by diphthongization (*V́-MID, IDENT$_{[\pm hi]}$ ≫ INTEGRITY) or raising (*V́-MID, INTEGRITY ≫ IDENT$_{[\pm hi]}$) and verbs that do not alternate (INTEGRITY, IDENT$_{[\pm hi]}$ ≫ *V́-MID), as well as verbs with gaps ($\mathscr{F}$ ≫ MPARSE) alongside verbs without gaps (MPARSE ≫ $\mathscr{F}$).

One way to accommodate the side-by-side existence of alternating, non-alternating, and gapped words is to resort to lexically listed allomorphs. In particular, if we assume that the stressed and unstressed allomorphs of verbs are listed separately, then we do not need to predict mid vowel alternations at all. With the relevant faithfulness constraints (IDENT$_{\text{HEIGHT}}$, IDENT$_{\text{STRESS}}$, INTEGRITY) ranked above *V́-MID, the grammar simply uses whatever stressed allomorph it is given, regardless of whether it is alternating or non-alternating.[11] If a verb happens to lack a listed stressed allomorph, the decision falls to lower ranked constraints — and with MPARSE ranked just below $\mathscr{F}$, it is better to have a gap than to generate a novel stressed allomorph. This is essentially a lexical conservatism account (Steriade 1997), and it is parallel to one proposed by Pertsova (2005) for paradigm gaps in Russian nouns.

The lexical conservatism approach provides a way to describe word-by-word differences, but the solution comes at a steep cost. The grammar in (10) prohibits speakers from projecting any alternations, in effect choking off the generative capacity of the grammar. This prediction is too

---

[11] In theory, this has the potential to allow all sorts of idiosyncratic alternations beyond diphthongization and raising of mid vowels; these would have to be prevented with higher-ranked OO-Faith constraints regulating possible relations between related allomorphs.

(10)   A lexical conservatism approach

a.   Listed non-alternating allomorph

/{viol,viól}-a-n/	$\mathcal{F}$	MPARSE	*V̆-MID
☞ a. viólan			*
b. viuélan	*!		
c. ⊙		*!	

b.   Listed diphthongizing allomorph

/{vol,vuél}-a-n/	$\mathcal{F}$	MPARSE	*V̆-MID
a. vólan	*!		*
☞ b. vuélan			
c. ⊙		*!	

c.   No listed stressed allomorph

/{abol}-e-n/	$\mathcal{F}$	MPARSE	*V̆-MID
a. abólen	*!		*
b. abuélen	*!		
☞ c. ⊙		*	

extreme; in fact, Spanish speakers are often perfectly comfortable generating stressed allomorphs that they have never heard before, including both non-alternating and also diphthongizing ones (Albright et al. 2001). The analysis does not give us any insight into why speakers behave so conservatively in some cases, when equivalent processes apply automatically in other cases — a problem noted also by Pertsova (2005).

In addition, this analysis does not actually do much to explain the lexical selectivity of gaps. There is no reason why verbs that are defectively lacking a stressed allomorph should be limited to the second and third conjugations — or indeed, why they should be restricted to mid vowel verbs, even. In principle, any verb could be missing a stressed allomorph, and the ranking in (10) would prevent a new one from being generated. This account also goes only part of the way towards explaining the morphological selectivity of gaps, since there is nothing that would prevent a verb from defectively missing the stressless allomorph, predicting the possibility of verbs that occur only in stressed forms. It is also difficult to extend this analysis to the 1SG gaps, since this would require stipulating a separate listed allomorph for just this form, even if it is usually identical to the other stressed forms.

Although resorting to lexically listed allomorphs does not explain the particulars of the Spanish data, there are indeed reasons to think that lexical conservatism may nonetheless play a role in shaping lexically arbitrary paradigm gaps. A possibly telling case from Modern Icelandic is documented by Hansson (1999). In Icelandic, both the weak (regular) past tense and the imperative are formed by the addition of a dental -T suffix, which, depending on the preceding context, is realized either as unaspirated *-t* (further lenited to [ð] in some cases), or as aspirated *-t^h*. Abstracting away from some of the details, it can be said that the *-t^h* allomorph occurs when the preceding segment is underlyingly aspirated or when it is itself a /t/, and the unaspirated *-t/-ð* allomorph occurs elsewhere (see Hansson's presentation for a fuller treatment of the distribution). When the *-t^h* allomorph is chosen, its aspiration is typically realized as preaspiration or regressive devoicing of a preceding sonorant.

(11)   Icelandic past/imperative formation

    a.   *-t^h* after aspirated and after /t/

Verb stem	Past/Imp. UR	Past stem	Imp. stem	Gloss
/t^hak^h-/	/t^hak^h-t^h/[12]	[t^haxt-]	[t^haxt-]	'take'
/sɪnt-/	/sɪnt-t^h-/	[sɪn̥t-]	[sɪn̥t-]	'swim'
/mɪrt-/	/mɪrt-t^h-/	[mɪr̥t-]	[mɪr̥t-]	'murder'

    b.   *-t* elsewhere

Verb stem	Past/Imp. UR	Past stem	Imp. stem	Gloss
/sin-/	/sin-t-/	[sint-]	[sint-]	'show'
/mail-/	/mail-t-/	[mailt-]	[mailt-]	'measure'
/heir-/	/heir-t-/	[heirð-]	[heirð-]	'hear'
/hav-/	/hav-d-/	[havð-]	[havð-]	'have'

There are, however, some exceptional verbs that end in sonorants but nonetheless take the *-t^h* allomorph of the past tense (parallel to English irregular pasts like *burnt*, *dwelt*, etc.). Crucially, when the past tense of a verb takes the "wrong" allomorph of the suffix, so does the imperative:

(12)   Exceptional *-t^h* after sonorants

Verb stem	Past/Imp. UR	Past stem	Imp. stem	Gloss
/mail-/	/mail-t^h-/	[mail̥t-]	[mail̥t-]	'speak'
/mein-/	/mein-t^h-/	[mein̥t-]	[mein̥t-]	'mean'

The isomorphism of the past and the imperative is not due merely to some historical accident; in fact, the two relevant imperative forms are relatively recent innovations in Icelandic, formed by reanalyzing the [θ] of the following 2SG pronoun as including a suffix ([sin θu] 'show you' ⇒ [sint θu]). The only way for aspirated *-t^h* to have entered the imperative in these exceptional cases is for it to have been imported directly from the past stem. Stated informally, we could say that the past provides a -T suffixed allomorph, and the imperative parasitically employs whatever is found in the past.

The relevance of Icelandic is clear when we turn to strong verbs, which do not form their past by suffixing $-t^{(h)}$. Here, the imperative is on its own, and in most cases, it takes the contextually appropriate form of the $-t/-t^h$ suffix.

(13)   Imperatives from strong verbs

Verb stem	Past/Imp. UR	Past stem	Imp. stem	Gloss
/trak-/	/trak-t-/	(troː-)	[traɣð-]	'drag'
/halt-/	/halt-t^h-/	(heːlt-)	[hal̥t-]	'hold'

There is one systematic exception to this, however: verbs ending in /nn/ and /ll/ typically do not take either -t or -t^h, but have a gap: /vinn-/ 'work' (past /vann-/) → *[vɪnt-], *[vɪn̥t-]. For these verbs, a different imperative form must be used (periphrasis). What is special about verbs ending in /nn/ and /ll/, that would prevent them from taking the expected -t allomorph? Hansson argues that the problem stems from the fact that among weak verbs, verbs ending in these sequences *usually* take "exceptional" -t^h: [fil̥t], [hɛl̥t], [spɪl̥t], [prɪn̥t], [klɛn̥t], etc. In fact, fully 21/27 of the relevant verbs are exceptional in this way, making "regular" [. . . lt] and [. . . nt] the minority pattern. Hansson's intuition is that speakers know that verbs with this shape are typically irregular, but they are unable or unwilling to assume the "expected irregular" -t^h form. Thus, they are left with an irresolvable clash between the grammatically expected regular form, and the analogically excepted irregular form. This is highly reminiscent of both the Spanish and Russian cases, in which gaps also apply specifically in those inflectional classes where irregularity is the norm.

Strikingly, there is also one exception to the exceptions in Icelandic: the verb /finn-/ 'find' does take the phonologically expected imperative form [fint-] (with unaspirated -t after the sonorant). What makes /finn-/ unique, however, is that it *does* have a -t- in some past tense forms: sg. [fan], [fanst], [fan], pl. [fʏntʏm], [fʏntʏð], [fʏntu]. Historically, the -t- of [fʏntʏm] is part of the verb stem (it is not the dental past suffix), but it appears that speakers nonetheless treat it as evidence that /finn-/ does not take -t^h(*[fʏntʏm]). It is also important to note that the imperative does not simply import wholesale the past plural allomorph /fʏnt-/; rather, it preserves the vowel of the present, and uses the past plural only for evidence about -t/-t^h allomorphy (a *split base* effect; (Steriade 1997)).

The Icelandic data show two lexical conservatism effects: first, the form of the imperative depends on the past allomorph more closely than would be predicted by morpheme concatenation. In particular, there is no reason why the imperative should be bound to take exceptional -t^h when the past does ([mailt-], [meint-]), yet speakers prefer to maintain past/imperative identity rather than creating the regularly expected imperatives [mailt], [meint]. Second, when a regular past allomorph is unavailable and there is uncertainty about whether to use -t or -t^h, speakers look to whatever other allomorphs happen to be present to settle the uncertainty. In the case of [finn-], this yields a -t form, but for other verbs, no such help is available. Hansson (1999) claims that the analysis of the imperative requires reference to the past tense form, and I do not see any alternative.

Lexical conservatism alone is insufficient to provide a complete account of Icelandic, however. First, it is unable to explain why the form of the imperative depends on an attested past stem, and why speakers do not have similar difficulties with the past itself. Hansson observes that -*nn* and -*ll* final verbs never have equivalent gaps in the past; novel verbs are given the regular past tense suffix -*að*-. Lexical conservatism also cannot explain why the problem is confined to -*nn* and -*ll* stems, and why elsewhere, speakers are willing to create new suffixed forms that are unattested in the past. What I conclude from this is that the ability to consult related forms as evidence for the shape of a needed allomorph is indeed important part of the puzzle, and that recourse to listed allomorphs is part of the strategy that speakers use to try to produce potentially gapped forms. What it can't explain is why only certain forms have problems in the first place, where in other parts of the paradigm, speakers are willing to apply a regular default pattern to construct novel allomorphs. The overall picture that this suggests, then, is that if we can find an answer to why certain forms are constructed with reference to other forms, and why this computation sometimes fails to produce a clear winner, then faithfulness to listed allomorphs can help explain why speakers are able to overcome the problem for certain words but not for others. In other words, the machinery of a lexical conservatism account will turn out to be useful in the final formalization, but it cannot not actually explain the core mystery of why gaps occur where they do.

The basic challenge remains, therefore, to explain why the grammar is unable to provide a default winner in cases of gaps.

3   Modeling grammatical confidence with stochastic generalizations

In section 2.1, I argued that in order to understand paradigm gaps, we must understand not only their lexical selectivity, but also their morphological selectivity — that is, why only certain words in certain parts of the paradigm are affected, while parallel structures are fixed or tolerated in other words or other morphological contexts. A key insight is that the forms that suffer paradigm gaps are the ones whose properties are determined with reference to other forms in the paradigm. This is seen very clearly in Hansson's discussion of Icelandic: the imperative is identical to the past stem whenever possible, including even details such as irregular selection of -t^h. It is also seen indirectly for Spanish, since stressed forms (and especially the 1SG) are frequently rebuilt on the basis of other parts of the paradigm, shown by the fact that they have undergone considerable historical restructuring (Penny 2002: p. 183), show a good deal of dialect variation, and exhibit the greatest number of child errors (Clahsen et al. 2002). I take this as evidence that the occurrence of gaps in these parts of the paradigm is not merely a fact about gaps; it is a consequence of the more general morphological organization of the language. If this is correct, then the first step in understanding paradigm gaps is to understand why certain forms are built on other forms.

3.1   Asymmetric relations within the paradigm

In Albright (2002a), a model is proposed that incorporates directionality as an intrinsic part of how paradigms are learned and organized. In particular, it is hypothesized that learners seek to discover which parts of the paradigm are the most INFORMATIVE, or have the greatest power to predict the remainder of the paradigm. These forms are then selected as base forms, from which the remaining forms are projected. In order to be predictive, a form must reveal all idiosyncratic properties of the lexical item. For example, in Spanish, a fully predictive verb form would need to reveal the conjugation class, diphthongization and/or raising, velar insertion, and any other irregular properties that the verb may have. According to this hypothesis, grammars are organized in a way that makes use of predictability relations, by storing the less predictable (more idiosyncratic, or informative) forms and deriving more predictable forms from them.[13]

In the case of Spanish, the most pervasive unpredictable property of verbs is their conjugation class. This can be seen intuitively by inspecting the paradigms in (3)–(5), and observing that every single verb belongs to a conjugation class, while verbs in only certain classes and with certain phonological shapes display alternations like diphthongization or velar insertion. Therefore, the optimal form to memorize in the paradigm is one that clearly reveals conjugation class, such as the infinitive, 1PL, or 2PL, and use this as a base for deriving the remainder of the paradigm. Assuming for the moment that the infinitive is chosen, this makes it very easy to derive the 1PL and 2PL, since for all but a handful of extremely irregular verbs, they simply involve changing the endings. For the stressed forms, however, things are somewhat more difficult, since the forms that most clearly reveal conjugation class also systematically lack information about mid vowel alternations (which occur only under stress), or about velar insertion (which occurs only in the 1SG). For the most part, however, once one stressed form is known, it is straightforward to derive the other stressed forms — for example, starting with the 3SG, the 2SG and 3PL can virtually always be derived correctly by adding *-s* or *-n*. The only remaining ambiguity concerns the 1SG, where velar insertion sometimes creates non-identity with the other stressed forms. This makes the 1SG slightly unpredictable, even given the other stressed forms. In general, this type of reasoning establishes a series of unidirectional relations among paradigm members, and a possible end result of this learning procedure for Spanish in particular is shown in Figure 2. The figure shows that stressed forms are derived from stressless ones (without mid vowel alternations), and the 1SG is derived from a form that shares vowel alternations, but lacks velar insertion. For details of the learning algorithm and the computer simulations that were used to derive this result from a lexicon of Spanish verbs, the reader is referred to (Albright 2002a: chap. 6).

What is crucial about this model is that it establishes asymmetrical dependencies between forms in the paradigm on a language-particular basis. A model of this sort has the potential to explain the morphological selec-

---

[13]This is clearly related to the traditional idea in generative phonology that all lexically arbitrary information is memorized as part of the underlying form, which serves as the input to grammar. The chief difference is that in this model, the input consists of a *surface* form, which cannot combine unpredictable information from multiple parts of the paradigm; see Albright (2002a) for discussion.

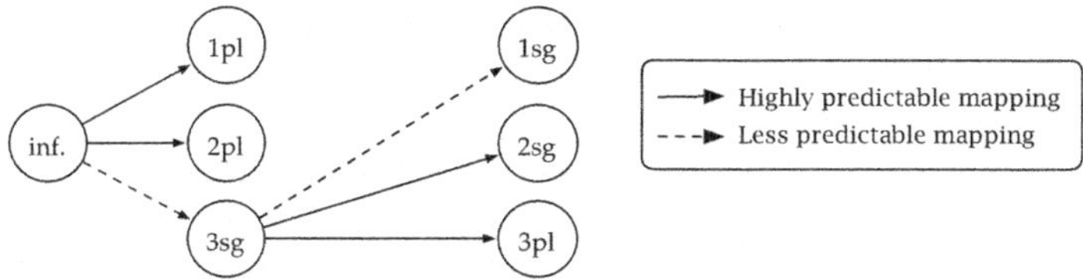

Figure 2. Directionality of mappings in the Spanish present tense paradigm

tivity of paradigm gaps in the following way: building on the observation that gaps occur in parts of the paradigm that are computed with reference to other parts of the paradigm, we can hypothesize that gaps occur when something about the mapping from a base to a derived form fails. This is an important first step in limiting the sets of forms that can potentially suffer from gaps: gaps may independently affect leaf nodes in the derivation structure (the 1PL, the 2PL, the 1SG, the 2SG, or the 3PL), or they may affect whole sets of forms that are derived from the same non-terminal node (e.g., all of the 3SG, 1SG, 2SG, and 3PL). The next step, then, is to understand why mappings fail only for the 1SG and 3SG, and only for particular words in particular inflectional classes.

3.2   Confidence of mappings

The structure in Figure 2 posits six different mappings (infinitive → 1PL, infinitive → 2PL, etc.). Of these, four are nearly 100% predictable across all verbs and all classes:

(14)   Virtually exceptionless mappings in Spanish

INFINITIVE → 1PL	-r → -mos
INFINITIVE → 2PL	-r → -is
3SG → 2SG	Ø → -s
3SG → 3PL	Ø → -n

Looking back to the data in §2.1, we see that the two remaining mappings (infinitive → 3SG and 3SG → 1SG) are also the ones that involve the greatest degree of unpredictability due to the lexically restricted processes of mid vowel alternations and velar insertion. (This is reflected in the dashed lines in Figure 2.) The challenge is to understand why unpredictability leads to uncertainty in just a certain subset of 1SG and 3SG forms.

Table 1. Counts of mid vowel alternations in classes 1 and 3

Unstressed	/e/			/o/		Total
Stressed	é	jé	í	ó	wé	
Class 1 (-*ar*)	916	93	0	588	71	1668
Class 3 (-*ir*)	2	32	42	0	3	79

Let us consider first the mid vowel alternations. Here, it is instructive to compare class 1 (-*ar*) with class 3 (-*ir*). In class 1, there are many verbs that diphthongize (e.g., *sentar*, *contar*; (4a) and many verbs that do not (e.g., *rentar*, *montar*; (4c). Table 1 shows counts of verbs from the LEXESP corpus (Sebastián et al. 2000), categorized according to their "dictionary" alternation pattern (de Gámez 1973; Butt 1997). The counts reveal that overall, mid vowels tend not to alternate in class 1 (just 9% of /e/, and 11% of /o/). Verbs in this class also never suffer from gaps, and when speakers need to project stressed forms, they generally select non-alternating mid vowels as a default. This can be seen in several ways: first, when speakers are given a wug test in which they hear novel class 1 verbs in the infinitive and must produce 1SG forms, they confidently and overwhelmingly choose [é] and [ó] — e.g., novel *rempar* → 1SG *rempo* preferred over *riempo* (Albright et al. 2001). In addition, class 1 verbs have historically tended to lose diphthongization alternations: older *apuerta, entriega, confuerta* ⇒ newer *aporta* 'contribute-3SG', *entrega* 'hand over-3SG', *conforta* 'comfort-3SG' (Penny 2002: p. 183; Morris 2005). If we view such leveling as the replacement of older, irregular forms with newer, grammatically prefered forms (Paul 1920; Kiparsky 1978; Albright 2002b: and many others), then this historical trend confirms that in class 1, diphthongization is irregular, and non-alternation is generally the grammatically preferred option.[14] This seems unsurprising, given the statistical predominance of non-alternating forms, both in class 1 and in the language as a whole. The ability to productively produce non-alternating forms is significant, however, because it shows that in general there is no reluctance to produce novel stressed forms (i.e., lexical conservatism does not hold here).

Of course, a grammar that always predicts non-alternation and never allows diphthongization cannot capture the full set of attested data, since many words do diphthongize. One possibility is that every case of diph-

---

[14]See also Clahsen et al. (2002) for the same claim, made on the basis of data from children's errors.

thongization is simply memorized as exceptional irregularity; Bybee and Pardo (1981), Eddington (1998), and Clahsen et al. (2002) all claim this in one way or another. In the model depicted in Figure 2, this could be captured by saying that speakers have stored an irregular diphthongized 3SG form, which simultaneously blocks the default non-alternating mapping, and at the same time provides a diphthongized input for further mappings to the 1SG and 2SG

There is evidence that such a model is too simple, however. Albright et al. (2001) showed that in addition to the general preference for non-alternation, speakers also have knowledge about particular segmental contexts that tend to favor or disfavor diphthongization. For example, all class 1 verbs that contain *e* before *rr* diphthongize,[15] while class 1 roots containing *e* before *tʃ* never diphthongize. When speakers are presented with novel verbs containing these sequences, their likelihood to select diphthongization varies depending on its attested rate for that context in the lexicon. Albright et al. interpret this result in terms of a grammar with multiple competing rules, at varying degrees of generality. Under this view, the mapping from infinitive to 3SG is not solely an identity map, but rather, contains numerous sub-rules, including extremely general ones (unstressed *e* maps to stressed *é*) and also very specific ones ($e \rightarrow jé$ / ___ *rr*, $e \rightarrow é$ / ___ *tʃ*). These rules compete according to the degree of support they get from the lexicon. A well-supported rule is one which applies with high accuracy (or RELIABILITY), meaning that it should be exceptionless, or as close to exceptionless as possible. A well-supported rule should also be well-attested; generalizations that are based on just a few forms (types) are not terribly impressive, even if perfect. Albright and Hayes (2002) propose a rule evaluation metric called CONFIDENCE, which uses lower confidence limit statistics to combine the reliability and amount of relevant data into a single measure. As can be seen in Figure 3, reliability is the most important determinant of confidence. However, confidence also decreases considerably when there is very little data to go on — especially when there are fewer than ten observations.

In most cases, phonological and morphological processes are seen in more than just a few forms, so the confidence adjustment in Figure 3 is felt only in very small, irregular classes. This turns out to be crucial in the comparison between Spanish class 1 and class 3. In class 1, there are many verbs, and most of them do not alternate (916 + 588, or 1504 out of 1668

---

[15]This includes verbs built from several different roots: *cerr-* 'close', *err-* 'wander', *ferr-* 'grasp', *serr-* 'saw', *terr-* 'bury', *terr-* 'terrify'.

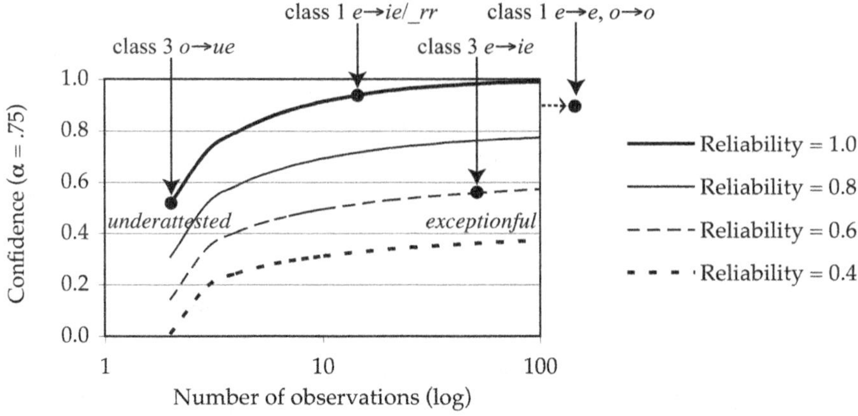

Figure 3. Confidence as a function of size and accuracy

≈ 90%). This means that there is a strong pattern of non-alternation, with a confidence value of .9 (beyond the upper right of Figure 3). In addition, there are a number of subregularities that work perfectly (or close to it) for smaller sets of verbs, including diphthongization of e → jé / ___ rr (100% of about a dozen verbs, or the top line in the middle of Figure 3).

Looking back at Table 1, we see that in class 3, unlike class 1, virtually all verbs with mid vowels alternate. For the back vowel /o/, all existing verbs diphthongize, but actually there are so few of them that it is difficult to form any real generalization: essentially, the data comes from just two verbs, *dormir* 'sleep' and *morir* 'die'.[16] (A prefixed form *premorir* 'predecease' also occurs in LEXESP.) This is similar to the paucity of data seen in the English example in the introduction. This observation forms the core of the current proposal: lexically arbitrary gaps occur in just those cases where there is too little data to be sure about any of the available generalizations. Concretely, there is no *o→ó* rule that would map infinitive *abolír* to 3SG *abóle* (i.e., no non-alternation in class 3),[17] while the *o→ué* rule that would map *abolír* to *abuéle* is supported by only two verbs. For the front vowel /e/, there are relatively more cases, but they are evenly split between diphthongization (32 verbs) and raising (24 verbs). If we look at

---

[16]There is also a verb *oír* 'hear' which has idiosyncratically different stressed forms (1SG *oigo*, 3SG *oye*), and thus provides no evidence concerning diphthongization.

[17]The verb *podrir* 'rot' is sometimes cited in verb tables as a non-alternating class 3 verb; in practice, however, inflected forms of this verb have been replaced by its high vowel doublet *pudrir*.

the curves in Figure 3, we see that the confidence values for these cases are not as different from one another as they might seem: a generalization that works perfectly for 2/2 or 3/3 cases receives a confidence value of around 0.6–0.7 (left edge of the top line), while a generalization that works for 32/56 cases has a confidence value of just under 0.6 (third line down, towards the right of the graph). Thus, generalizations covering both /e/ and /o/ verbs in class 3 suffer from low confidence. Well attested forms like *duerme* 'sleeps' or *muere* 'dies' can survive by lexical listing of the stressed form, but for rarer words like *abolir* a listed form is unlikely to be available, so the only way to synthesize a new form is to use a low-confidence rule.

In order to make use of the observation that there are very few mid-vowel verbs in the third conjugation, it is crucial that the grammar of vowel alternations be subdivided into separate generalization, depending on the particular vowel involved (*e* vs. *o*) and also the particular conjugation class (class 1 vs. that in class 3). This may seem counterintuitive, since there is no obvious formal reason why, for example, diphthongization in class 1 should be treated as a separate process from diphthongization in class 3. There are various reasons to think that native speakers do treat them separately, however. First, we can observe from Table 1 that the overall rates of alternation differ substantially between conjugation classes in Spanish, due partly to the fact that many class 1 verbs have regularized (become non-alternating) over time. The fact that class 2 and 3 verbs have not done the same may indicate that the pressure to diphthongize is not uniform, but rather is assessed separately in different classes. Furthermore, the segmental contexts that encourage diphthongization differ not only from class to class, but also between /e/ and /o/. Albright et al. (2001) found that the best model of likelihood to diphthongize is one that considers diphthongization contexts independently for each vowel and each class. A similar finding is presented by Eddington (1996), who shows that the rate of diphthongization differs substantially across different derivational suffixes, and that speakers respect these differences when producing nonce forms. This fracturing of the grammar for separate segments and separate contexts also mirrors a conclusion of Rice and also McCarthy and Wolf (both this volume), that rankings licensing alternations in one morphological context do not automatically transfer to other morphological contexts.[18] These results

---

[18] In fact, the Swedish example of neuter adjective gaps discussed at the end of McCarthy and Wolf's paper also demonstrates differential treatment of different segments, since as shown by Iverson (1981), the ban on /dd-t/ coalescence that blocks **rädd-t* [rɛtː] 'scared NEUTSG' does not apply to /tt-t/: *rätt-t* 'right NEUTSG' surfaces fine as [rɛtː].

provide converging evidence that the segmental environments and overall rates of alternations are at least sometimes calculated separately for different segments and different morphological contexts.

It is natural to wonder why generalizations should be so fragmented in this case, when in other cases, it can be shown that speakers do form generalizations that cover different morphological contexts and multiple segments. For example, Kiparsky (1965) discusses the innovation of a new umlaut correspondence in the Kesswil dialect of Swiss German, which could not have arisen unless speakers treated umlaut as a unified process across different segments. I conjecture that in the case of Spanish mid vowel alternations, the division of the grammar into separate generalizations for different segments and different classes may be due to the fact that their statistics simply are so different across these different contexts, and for accidental historical reasons, always have been. For a learner seeking the most accurate description of the conditions under which an alternation should occur, it would not be advantageous to throw away information about the particular vowel or conjugation class, since generalizations that ignore this information provide a worse fit to the data. This effect is likely to be greatest in inflectional classes that contain rather small numbers of words; if Spanish classes 2 and 3 had thousands of words each, then the chances of accidental statistical differences between them would be much smaller.

Another obvious question that arises is how much data is enough to support a trustable generalization. The particular confidence limit function shown in Figure 3 suggests that confidence may fall perilously low under only the most extreme of circumstances — a common rule of thumb is about twelve observations or less. (The exact slope of the penalty depends on the particular value of alpha that is chosen — I have shown here a somewhat liberal tolerance of 25% uncertainty.) As the comparison between the class 3 front and back vowels above shows, the claim of this adjustment is that a perfect but poorly attested generalization is no better than an exceptionful but better-attested one. The rationale is that when there is so little data, there is a good chance that additional data might in fact reveal exceptions. Low confidence can also arise when there is more data, but it is hopelessly conflicting (the lower lines towards the right of Figure 3). This, too, is likely to happen only in smallish inflectional classes, however, for the following reasons: first, it rarely happens that a large class of words is evenly split between two conflicting patterns (one almost always predominates, as we seen in class 1 in Spanish). Second, if a large class does happen to be split evenly between two patterns, then this would constitute a major source of unpredictability in the language, and, for reasons outlined above, the grammar would mostly likely not be organized such that it would be attempting to derive it in the first place. (A form that maintains the contrast between the two classes would be favored as the base form.) Thus, by attributing lexically arbitrary gaps to low confidence, we derive a strong prediction: gaps should only occur in small and irregular inflectional classes, in which the number of relevant attested (non-gapped) forms is below some critical threshhold (roughly a dozen to twenty forms?), or the attested cases are extremely inconsistent. This correctly characterizes Spanish class 3, and captures the intuition that there is a deep connection between gaps and morphological irregularity.

3.3 Local summary

In this section, I have outlined a grammatical model that attempts to predict where and when gaps can occur. The features of the model which are essential to the analysis of gaps are: (1) morphological relations are directional, (2) the direction of relations is not universal, but is established by learners in an attempt to find the most reliable or accurate mappings from one form to another, (3) mappings are probabilistic, and are evaluated in terms of confidence values, (4) mappings are potentially established rather locally, such that generalizations are established independently across different segments and different inflectional classes, and (5) when there is too little data about how a particular segment should behave within a certain inflectional class, the resulting generalizations may have such low confidence as to be untrustable. Naturally, competition between different patterns can compound the problem of untrustable generalizations, but it is not actually necessary; extreme paucity of data is by itself sufficient to create low confidence. When speakers lack a good enough grammatical mapping to derive a form confidently, they are forced to resort to a listed form if it exists, and otherwise, they have a gap.

In the final section, I discuss similar data from Russian, sketch how the analysis of these cases could be recast in OT terms, and consider the relation between these cases and the phonotactically motivated cases that have been discussed in the literature.

4   Extensions, and discussion

4.1   Russian 1SG non-past forms

A well-known case of lexically arbitrary paradigm gaps occurs in 1SG non-past forms of Russian verbs (Shvedova 1970: 412–13; Halle 1973: 7–8; Hetzron 1975: p. 861). In particular, 1SG forms are avoided in certain second conjugation verbs ending in *t*, *d*, *s*, *z*, where consonant alternations are expected to occur. Crucially, however, there exist parallel forms in which alternations occur as expected:

(15)   Alternations in 1SG non-past forms in Russian

    a.   Existing (non-gapped) forms (INF., 1SG)

šutít'	šučú	'jest'
budít'	bužú	'waken'
gasít'	gašú	'strike'
podvozít'	podvožú	'haul'

    b.   Missing (gapped) forms

mutít'	*muču	'stir up'
pob'edít'	*pob'ežu	'beat'
dubásit'	*dubašu	'batter'
lázit'	*lažu	'climb'

As argued by Halle, Hetzron, and others, there is no evident semantic reason why the 1SG should be missing for verbs like *mutit'* but not *šutit'*. There is also no clear phonological reason why non-occurring **muču* would be any worse than occurring *šuču*. As above, the challenge is to explain why structures that are acceptable in some words are not acceptable in others.

The Russian 1SG gaps show several commonalities with Spanish. First, they are morphologically selective: they affect only 1SG non-past forms. There is also a systematicity to the particular lexical items that are selected: they all belong to the second conjugation and end in coronals. It is surely not a coincidence that this class of verbs characteristically undergoes alternations in the 1SG — that is, that gaps are associated with morphophonological alternations, and fall in a highly irregular inflectional class. Finally, although I do not know of any data concerning gradience or variability of gapped forms, some of the forms listed by Shvedova appear to be less problematic for some speakers than for others. (The form *lažu*, in particular, seems to occur not infrequently.)

As discussed above, Halle's analysis of these cases is to prevent gapped forms from surfacing by marking them as [−LEXICAL INSERTION]. Just as for Spanish, this approach is too powerful for the Russian data: it does not explain why gaps are limited to just those cases where they actually occur. If the analysis presented in the previous section is on the right track, it should predict the possibility of gaps in precisely these forms, and no others.

In order to understand why paradigm gaps target the 1SG in Russian, we must briefly consider the major sources of unpredictability in verbal inflection (see, e.g., Garde 1998, pp. 306–13 and 344–92 for an overview). Russian verbs are traditionally classified into two conjugation classes, which, as in Spanish, differ in their theme vowel (class 1 = *e*, class 2 = *i*) (Jakobson 1948; Garde 1998). The different between these two classes is most clearly revealed in non-past tense forms other than the 1SG, but can usually also be inferred from the infinitive. The 1SG suffix of both conjugation classes is -*u*, reminiscent of the invariant 1SG suffix -*o* in Spanish.

In addition to theme vowels, there are also numerous alternations within the verb stem itself. Frequently, the form of the stem that occurs in the infinitive differs from that found in non-past tense forms:

(16)   Russian infinitive ∼ non-past tense differences

Infinitive	3PL	Gloss
ž-ít'	živ-út	'live'
ž-át'	žm-út	'cut'
st-át'	stán-ut	'become'

Within the non-past tense paradigm, various suffixes induce stem-final alternations. All person suffixes except the 1SG and 3PL induce palatalization due to the historical (and in many analyses, synchronic) presence of front vowels: *n'es-ú, n'es'-óš, n'es'-ót, n'es'-óm, n'es'-ót'e, n'es-út* 'carry'; this has the effect of adding secondary palatalization to non-velar consonants (e.g., *p, b, v, t, d, s, z, n, r, l*), and fronting velars ($k \rightarrow č$, $g \rightarrow ž$). In the second conjugation class, the 1SG also induces an additional set of changes, illustrated in (17).

Another alternation that can be observed in (17) is that in some verbs, stress differs between the 1SG (falling on the suffix) and the remainder of the non-past tense paradigm (falling on the root).

The important question for the purpose of predicting paradigm gaps is

(17)   Palatalization in the 1SG

Alternation	INFINITIVE	1SG	2SG	Gloss
p, b, f, m ~ pl', bl', fl', ml'	l'ub'-ít	l'u**bl'**-ú	l'úb'-iš	'love'
s, z ~ š, ž	pros'-ít'	pro**š**-ú	prós'-iš	'ask'
t ~ č	trát'-it'	trá**č**-u	trát'-iš	'waste'
t ~ šč	zapr'et'-ít'	zapr'e**šč**-ú	zapr'et'-íš	'prohibit'
d ~ ž	sl'ed-ít'	sl'e**ž**-ú	sl'ed-íš	'follow'

how these unpredictable properties influence the organization of the Russian paradigm. Intuitively, it is evident that the 1SG is the least predictive of all forms in the paradigm: it does not clearly reveal the conjugation class of the verb, it suffers from neutralizations caused by the alternations in (17), and it frequently differs from the remaining forms in the location of stress. Although computational simulations deriving the full predicted organization of Russian paradigms are beyond the scope of this paper, what is important at present is that the 1SG has a very similar status to that in Spanish: it is predicted to be a derived form, and therefore it must be generated based on some other form in the paradigm that does not show the palatalization alternations in (17). This establishes the correct directionality to predict 1SG gaps, and predicts that speakers may be uncertain about the stress and consonant alternations that apply in the 1SG

The next question concerns the lexical selectivity of the gaps: why are second conjugation verbs ending in coronals specifically targeted? The restriction to the second conjugation is not mysterious; this is the class that exhibits the alternations in (17). What is puzzling is why there should ever be any doubt about whether the palatalization alternations in (17) should apply, since they always apply in this class. It is also mysterious why only the coronals are affected, since labials also alternate. This situation is in some ways reminiscent of Spanish, in which diphthongization does not confidently apply to class 3 verbs in -*o*, in spite of the fact that all attested examples do undergo diphthongization. For Spanish, we hypothesized that although the data was consistent, there were too few examples to support a trustable diphthongization rule. Could it be that Russian second conjugation coronal-final verbs are equally sparse?

In order to answer this question, I started with a database of all of the second conjugation verbs that occur in a comprehensive grammatical dictionary of Russian (Zalizniak 1977), and filtered out all duplicate entries and verbs that did not occur at a rate of at least one instance per million in a corpus of 40M words (Sharoff 2002). Overall, there are quite a few second conjugation verbs ending in all consonants — e.g., 66 ending in /d/, approximately 30 each of /t/ and /s/, and so on, casting doubt on a paucity of data account. Crucially, however, a large number of these verbs are derived from just a few verb roots. For example, among the 46 /d/-final verbs with alternating stress, only 7 unique verb roots are represented;[19] the rest are derived by prefixation, mostly from the two common verb roots *xod'-it'* 'go' and *vod'-it'* 'lead'. Additional prefixed forms of the same verb root arguably do not provide speakers with additional information about how words of that shape and inflectional class behave in general, meaning that raw counts of verbs are likely to greatly overestimate the amount of data available to learners.

In order to get a truer estimate of the amount of data that learners have about each class, I removed from the dataset set all verbs that transparently consisted of a prefix + independently occurring verb root (e.g., *p'er'e-vod'it'* 'transfer' from *vod'it'* 'lead'). This eliminated 75 of the 199 verbs in the dataset that end in one of the mutable consonants in (17). We must also keep in mind the fact that Russian verbs also belong to different stress types, meaning that generalizations about final consonants may well be learned separately for each stress type. (This is parallel to the idea that Spanish speakers maintain separate generalizations mid-vowels for different vowels and conjugation classes, for which evidence was presented in the previous section.) The counts for the Russian second conjugation, divided up by consonant and by stress pattern (fixed vs. alternating), are given in Table 2. It should be noted that the on-line Zalizniak dictionary does not indicate separate inflection patterns for verbs with gaps; therefore, counts from this data set are likely to be slightly inflated, since they include verbs that are claimed elsewhere to include gaps, and therefore could not provide speakers with evidence about alternations.

The table reveals two important facts: first, most cells have just a few examples (a dozen or less), making this a prime area for potential gaps. Interestingly, however, there is also a noticeable interaction between place of articulation and stress pattern, such that labial-final verbs consistently prefer not to have stress alternations, whereas coronal-final verbs tend to be much more divided (in differing proportions from segment to segment). In the previous section, I suggested that one factor that may discourage learners from generalizing across multiple segments and multiple contexts may

---

[19]These are: *xod'-it'* 'go', *brod'-it'* 'work', *vod'-it'* 'lead', *bud'-it'* 'wake', *sad'-it'* 'put', *ud'-it'* 'fish', and *s'erd'-it'* 'anger'.

Table 2. Russian second conjugation verb roots, by final consonant and stress pattern

	Stress fixed	Stress alternating	Total	% alternating
p	12	2	14	14%
b	10	0	10	0%
m	9	2	11	18%
v	12	2	14	14%
t	19	10	29	34%
d	19	7	26	27%
s	7	3	10	30%
z	9	1	10	10%

be differences in the rate of alternation. If this is on the right track, it would imply that labials form a coherent class (all show roughly the same degree of preference), while coronal-final verbs are less consistent (multiple stress patterns, different alternation types, and in some cases, multiple competing outputs). For labials, speakers may form an overarching generalization about the behavior of labials that covers several dozen examples and is strong enough to extend productively — and in fact this confirmed by the fact that palatalization has been extended to new verbs ending in [f] (*grafit'* ~ *grafl'u* 'graph'). For coronals, on the other hand, lack of generalization across different segment types would force speakers to rely on local generalizations, all based on 20 or fewer forms. In sum, although coronals are overall better represented than labials, they are also more fragmented. As with Spanish, this observation appears to provide the needed insight into why gaps occur specifically in this conjugation class, and to verbs with this specific phonological shape.

Clearly, these results for Russian would benefit from experimental work quantifying the reluctance to produce forms of different shapes and across different conjugations, as well as modeling work confirming the directionality within the non-past tense paradigm and the effect of different stress patterns and alternation classes on predicted confidence. Nonetheless, the data does seem to support the basic predictions of the current approach to predicting when and where gaps will occur: namely, they should occur in derived forms (those with weak predictive power), and they should affect inflectional classes that are small and fragmented by various irregularities.

4.2   Sketch of an OT formalization

The focus of the preceding sections has been on identifying principles that predict when and where lexically arbitrary gaps may occur. The crucial elements appear to be the following:

(18)   Components of a explanatory theory of lexically arbitrary gaps

1.   A language-particular set of asymmetric relations between members of the paradigm (more predictable forms based on less predictable forms)
2.   A conservative strategy for learning how to derive forms from their bases that generalizes across different segments and different morphological contexts only in case the evidence suggests that they do indeed pattern identically
3.   An ability to assess strength of generalizations that relies not only on the accuracy of the generalization, but also the number of examples
4.   Listed (lexicalized) forms can be used, even when the grammar itself is uncertain

The requirement that forms in the paradigm be computed with respect to particular other forms is reminiscent of base-prioritizing or transderivational correspondence (Benua 1997; Kenstowicz 1996; Kager 1999). In particular, in the case of Spanish, we need to assume that the 3SG is based on the infinitive. I will assume Benua's TCT formalism, in which the grammar first generates the infinitive and then generates the 3SG with reference to the base infinitive form.

In addition to asymmetric relations, we need a way of allowing word-by-word differences while at the same time generating predictions for unknown or novel forms. I will follow a proposal by Zuraw (2000) for handling such blocking effects in phonology by employing a highly ranked USELISTED constraint, which demands that if a lexically listed form exists, it must be used. (If no form is listed, then USELISTED is vacuously satisfied.) Zuraw actually proposes that USELISTED consists of a set of constraints refering to the strength of listing, so better-instantiated forms have stronger blocking power. This would be crucial in modeling gradient gaps in medium-to-low frequency items, but I will abstract away from it in the current analysis.

The last thing we need is a way to state the formal relation between the infinitive and the 3SG As the forms in (3) above show, the relation between the infinitive and the 3SG sometimes involves simply stressing the root, and sometimes involves diphthongization or raising. The data from Albright et al. (2001) suggest that this relation actually consists of numerous independ statements about these processes in different segmental contexts: diphthongization of *e* → *jé* before *rr*, retaining the monophthong before *tʃ*, etc. Thus, we need to be able to state a relation that is more than just an identity map, and which involves several different changes with different probabilities in different contexts. These relations are very naturally stated in rule terms (*e* → *jé* / ___*rr*), and a straightforward way to accommodate them in OT is by using constraints that essentially recode the relevant rules in the form of anticorrespondence constraints (Hayes 1999). Note that the "anti-" part of anti-correspondence is not crucial here; in some cases, the constraints may actually require identity, but this is just a special case of a defined relation between two surface forms.

(19)   (Anti)correspondence constraints relating Spanish infinitive and 3SG forms

    a.　*err*]$_{\text{Class 1 infinitive}}$ → *jérr*]$_{\text{3SG}}$

    b.　*etʃ*]$_{\text{Class 1 infinitive}}$ → *étʃ*]$_{\text{3SG}}$

    c.　*e* X]$_{\text{Class 1 infinitive}}$ → *é* X]$_{\text{3SG}}$ (default non-alternation)

There are various ways to formalize such constraints, but for present purposes, the following definition will suffice: the constraint *err*]$_{\text{Class 1 INF.}}$ → *jérr*]$_{\text{3SG}}$ means that if the infinitive of a class 1 verb ends in *-err*, the 3SG must end with *-jérr*. Such constraints are in many cases quite arbitrary and language-specific. It seems likely that they are learned inductively from the data of Spanish and ranked stochastically in order to produce the gradient and variable pattern that is observed for nonce words; see Albright and Hayes (2006) for a preliminary proposal for how this might be done.

Thus far, we have a grammar of the following form: high-ranking UseListed requires that lexically listed forms be used when available, and otherwise, the choice of the 3SG form falls to a set of stochastically ranked constraints describing the mapping between the infinitive form and the 3SG This is shown for both diphthongizing and non-diphthongizing 1st conjugation forms in (20). For ease of exposition, I simply show the most general "default" constraints demanding alternation and non-alternation for *o* in class 1. Mapping constraints are abbreviated by what class they refer to (class 1 or class 3), and they specify how the final vowel of the root in the infinitive is mapped to the corresponding vowel in the 3SG (e.g., Class 1: *o*→*ó*).

(20)   Lexically arbitrary diphthongization
  a.   *vuela* 'fly-3SG'

/FLY-inf/ (listed: *volar*)	UseListed	Class 1: *o→ó*	Class 1: *o→ué*
☞ a. volár			
b. vuelár	*!		

/FLY-3SG/ (listed: *vuéla*)	UseListed	Class 1: *o→ó*	Class 1: *o→ué*
a. vóla	*!		*
☞ b. vuéla		*	

  b.   *viola* 'violate-3SG'

/VIOLATE-inf/ (listed: *violar*)	UseListed	Class 1: *o→ó*	Class 1: *o→ué*
☞ a. violár			
b. viuelár	*!		

/VIOLATE-3SG/ (listed: none)	UseListed	Class 1: *o→ó*	Class 1: *o→ué*
☞ a. vióla			*
b. viuéla		*!	

In (20a), we see that when verbs have a listed 3SG with diphthongization, this form must be faithfully used (*vuéla*, not **vóla*). In (20b), we see
that if no 3SG form is listed, the default pattern of non-diphthongization
applies (*vióla*, not **viuéla*). Note that it is not crucial to assume that *violar*
has no listed 3SG form — the same surface form would result if the regu-

lar 3SG *vióla* had been redundantly listed. The point here is to demonstrate that for regular, rare, or unknown class 1 verbs, the grammar successfully produces the default pattern of non-alternation.

Next, we need a way of capturing the fact that there is sometimes no trustable mapping from the infinitive to 3SG In the analysis sketched above, this was stated by giving the mapping a low confidence value. As the literature on gaps in OT has pointed out repeatedly, however, this is difficult to translate into a competition-based framework in which the best available candidate is chosen as optimal. As suggested already in section 2.5, I will follow Prince and Smolensky (2004), Raffelsiefen (2004), McCarthy and Wolf, and others, in formalizing gaps as selection of a null output (⊙). The real issue at hand is what motivates the selection of the null parse in the case of lexically arbitrary gaps.

One way to accomplish this using MPARSE would be to stipulate that the mapping constraints for class 1 are ranked lower than MPARSE, while the mapping constraints for class 3 are above it. This has the effect of requiring an overt output with the default vowel for class 1 verbs (21), but prefering the null parse for class 3 verbs (22).

(21)　　*viola* 'violate-3SG'xs

/VIOLATE-inf/ (listed: *violar*)	UseListed	Class 3: $o\to\acute{o}$	Class 3: $o\to u\acute{e}$	MParse	Class 1: $o\to\acute{o}$	Class 1: $o\to u\acute{e}$
☞　a.　violár						
b.　viuelár	*!					

/VIOLATE-3SG/ (listed: none)	UseListed	Class 3: $o\to\acute{o}$	Class 3: $o\to u\acute{e}$	MParse	Class 1: $o\to\acute{o}$	Class 1: $o\to u\acute{e}$
☞　a.　vióla						*
b.　viuéla					*!	
c.　⊙				*!		

(22)   **abole/*abuele* 'abolish-3SG'

/ABOLISH-inf/ (listed: *abolir*)	USELISTED	CLASS 3: $o{\rightarrow}ó$	CLASS 3: $o{\rightarrow}ué$	MPARSE	CLASS 1: $o{\rightarrow}ó$	CLASS 1: $o{\rightarrow}ué$
☞ a. abolír						
b. abuelír	*!					

/ABOLISH-3-sg/ (listed: none)	USELISTED	CLASS 3: $o{\rightarrow}ó$	CLASS 3: $o{\rightarrow}ué$	MPARSE	CLASS 1: $o{\rightarrow}ó$	CLASS 1: $o{\rightarrow}ué$
a. abóle			*!			
b. abuéle		*!				
☞ c. ⊙				*		

This system correctly describes the basic pattern in a more restrictive fashion than the lexical conservatism analysis outlined in (10), but it raises a learnability issue. Given that the mapping constraints employed here must be learned inductively from the data and added to the constraint set gradually, is there a ranking procedure would be able to arrive at the ranking in (21)–(22)? Note that in this ranking, the constraints that refer to class 3 must be ranked above MPARSE, in spite of the fact that this class provides very little positive data. This is consistent with McCarthy and Wolf's claim that MPARSE must be ranked low by default — class 1 provides sufficient evidence to rerank MPARSE above the relevant mapping constraints, but class 3 does not, leaving gaps.

Unfortunately, although this scenario is fully compatible with the assumed initial state of MPARSE, it is not clear that the ranking of the language-particular mapping constraints is so easy to achieve. In fact, there are reasons to think that inductively learned language-particular constraints start low and rise only in response to positive evidence (Boersma 1997; Albright and Hayes 2006). In brief, the quandary is that small-scale, inductively learned constraints are frequently accidentally exceptionless in the data, but this is not enough to guarantee their productivity in the grammar. A ranking procedure that is biased to put small-scale idiosyncratic constraints high in the ranking often overestimates the role that they should play in the final grammar. Boersma (1997) proposes that such constraints should actually start at the bottom of the grammar, and Albright and Hayes (2006) propose a ranking procedure using the Gradual Learning Algorithm that implements this by imposing a bias against small-scale inductively learned constraints. In the present case, this would favor an analysis in which all mapping constraints start out extremely low in the grammar, and class 1 constraints rise farther than class 3 constraints do.

Interestingly, it is possible to flip the constraint ranking to be consistent with this "climb from the bottom" approach to ranking inductively learned constraints, to arrive at a ranking in which better-supported constraints are ranked highest and unsupported constraints stay at the bottom. The intuition beyond this approach is that better supported constraints clamor more strongly to have their mappings applied; small, barely attested classes do not pull much weight in enforcing their mappings. In order to implement this, however, we need a force that counteracts small-scale mappings and demands that their mappings *not* be used. That is, instead of MPARSE, we need a constraint that militates against generating previously unheard outputs: this could be a version of *STRUC (Prince and Smolensky 2004; Zoll 1996), or more simply, a constraint against novel formations: LEX (Steriade 1997).[20] In addition, we must now assume that the null parse violates the anticorrespondence mapping constraints. This is actually more consistent with their definition in any event, since the null parse does not contain the corresponding material that the mapping constraint requires.

(23)　　*viola* 'violate-3SG'

/VIOLATE-inf/ (listed: *violar*)	USELISTED	CLASS 1: $o{\to}\acute{o}$	CLASS 1: $o{\to}u\acute{e}$	LEX	CLASS 3: $o{\to}\acute{o}$	CLASS 3: $o{\to}u\acute{e}$
☞　a.　violár						
b.　viuelár	*!					

---

[20]Gouskova (2003) presents a number of compelling arguments that *STRUC is not the correct way to formalize general economy conditions in OT. In the present context, it would act simply as a cover term for the reluctance to produce any form that is not licensed by faithfulness to a listed form, not as a way of deriving specific economy effects.

/VIOLATE-3Sg/ (listed: none)	UseListed	Class 1: o→ó	Class 1: o→ué	Lex	Class 3: o→ó	Class 3: o→ué
☞ a. vióla			*	*		
b. viuéla		*!		*		
c. ⊙		*!	*			

(24)   *abole/*abuele* 'abolish-3Sg'

/ABOLISH-inf/ (listed: abolir)	UseListed	Class 1: o→ó	Class 1: o→ué	Lex	Class 3: o→ó	Class 3: o→ué
☞ a. abolír						
b. abuelír	*!					

/ABOLISH-3Sg/ (listed: none)	UseListed	Class 1: o→ó	Class 1: o→ué	Lex	Class 3: o→ó	Class 3: o→ué
a. abóle				*!		*
b. abuéle				*!	*	
☞ c. ⊙					*	*

The intuition behind this account, then, is that speakers are biased against constructing novel forms unless they have sufficient evidence that the mapping employed to generate the form is trustable enough to outrank LEX. This assumes also a constraint ranking procedure which is able to decide when enough data has amassed to motivate ranking a mapping above LEX (presumably mirroring the confidence function seen in Figure 3). Crucially, the mapping constraints shown in (23)–(24) are schematic stand-ins for a much larger set of stochastically ranked constraints, reflecting the relative likelihood of different mappings in different segmental contexts, and within different classes. Finally, it is worth reiterating that one of the most important aspects of this analysis for predicting the morphological selec-

tivity of gaps is the directionality of the mapping constraints from basic →
derived forms. This does not follow from anything in the OT formalism,
but is assumed to have been established in the early stages of learning by a
procedure such as the one described in Albright (2002a).

4.3   Relation to phonotactically motivated gaps

In the analysis of lexically arbitrary gaps, directionality of mappings and
strength of generalizations both play a crucial role in predicting where gaps
will occur. In cases of phonotactically motivated gaps on the other hand,
neither of these factors has been invoked to date. This immediately raises
the question of whether the two types of gaps are fundamentally different,
as has sometimes been claimed (Albright 2003; McCarthy and Wolf, this
volume), or whether directionality of mappings and scarcity of data might
play a role in other cases as well.

It seems possible that directionality of mappings could help to shed
light on why certain phonological alternations are learned as general processes that can extend across multiple morphological contexts, and why
others are morphologically restricted. Consider, for example, the example of Norwegian imperative gaps discussed by Rice (this volume): *sykl*.
Here, the mystery is framed as why epenthesis is not employed, even
though it is attested in nouns: /sikl/ → [sikkəl] 'bike'. But how do speakers know that the noun *sykkel* involves epenthesis from underlying /sikl/?
Rice points out that the major source of evidence is the plural [siklər]; the
side-by-side occurrence of words without a schwa in the plural (*sykler*)
and those that retain the schwa (*Mikkeler* 'guys named Mikkel') motivates
an underlying contrast between /kl/ words and /kəl/ words. Suppose, however, that the organization of Norwegian noun paradigms was such that
plurals are obligatorily formed with reference to singulars and not vice
versa. In this case, speakers would be forced to decide whether or not the
plural form has a schwa (*sykkeler* or *sykler*) based directly on the singular
form (*sykkel*). This would effectively require speakers to analyze plurals
like *sykler* as involving irregular syncope, rather than epenthesis. If this
scenario is right, then the only way to learn that there is an epenthesis process is from a part of speech than contains derived *kl*# clusters. In Norwegian, these appear to occur only in the imperatives, with no other possible
source of evidence about the fate of such clusters. In Albright (2002a), I
discuss additional cases from Latin and Lakhota in which the directionality

imposed by the learning procedure determines which alternations can be learned as productive phonology, and which become morphologized. The implication for the analysis of gaps is that perhaps the restriction of phonological processes to particular morphological contexts is a consequence of the direction in which the mappings are applied, rather than an arbitrary failure to generalize repairs across different morphological contexts.

The amount of data that is available to motivate a trustable generalization also appears to be important in some cases of phonotactically motivated paradigm gaps. Rice (2003) notes, citing data from Iverson (1981), that the set of Swedish adjectives that lack neuter forms (chiefly, those ending in [dd]) happens to be a very small class, containing just a handful of words. Iverson (1981) also mentions another class of adjectives that lack gaps in Swedish, namely, those ending in *-id*: *rapid* does not have a neuter form **rapitt/*rapidt*. Here, too, the number of relevant lexical items is small (under a half dozen in ordinary use[21]). Neither Iverson nor Rice makes use of this fact in their analyses, but it suggests that the amount of data may well play a role in creating phonotatically motivated gaps, as well.

It is also of interest to note that such cases involve not only small classes of words, but sometimes also a certain amount of exceptionality or competition. There is, in fact, one Swedish *-id* adjective that does have a widely used neuter form (*solid* 'solid' → *solitt*), and also at least one *-dd* adjective that is attested with a *-tt* neuters (*högljudd* → *högljutt* 'loud'). This shows that individual words may sometimes use lexical listing to avoid more phonotactically motivated gaps, as well (i.e., USELISTED may apply in these cases, too). A fundamental prediction of the current account is that any case of gaps may have sporadic, "exceptionally filled" existing forms. As long as there are only a few of listed forms, however, they will not reach critical mass to let a general pattern emerge and fill in all remaining cases of the gap. The origin of these exceptionally non-gapped forms seems to be somewhat haphazard. In some cases, they consist of inherited forms (Swedish adjectives in *-id* used to take *-itt* neuters more generally but lost them, perhaps precisely because the class was so small and the necessary generalization could not be learned). In other cases, one imagines that a particular innovative speaker was willing to take the plunge and create an otherwise uncomfortable form, which listeners were then able to lexicalize and use.[22] What I conclude from this is that further empirical work is also

---

[21]Namely: *rapid, morbid, gravid, stupid, rigid, solid.*

[22]Raffelsiefen (2004) points out that Turkish musicians have a lexicalized 1SG posses-

needed on phonotactically motivated paradigm gaps to determine in what respects they truly differ from or are parallel to lexically arbitrary gaps.

5   Conclusion

In this paper, I have laid out some basic principles that attempt to predict which parts of the paradigm, and which particular lexical items, may be affected by paradigm gaps. Specifically, it is hypothesized that gaps affect only those forms that are computed with reference to another base form in the paradigm, and occur only in cases where the mapping between the base and the derived form requires an inference over small amounts of possibly conflicting data. Although the principle is an extremely simple one, it makes strong predictions about what types of languages and inflectional classes gaps should occur in, and why gaps appear to be so restricted. Data from Spanish and Russian show that these predictions coincide quite closely with the places where gaps actualy occur. Finally, although the primary purpose has been to provide an analysis of "lexically arbitrary" cases, further inquiry is needed to determine to what extent the mechanisms proposed here may also play a role in shaping other, phonotactically motivated gaps.

Bibliography

Albright, A. (2002a)   *The Identification of Bases in Morphological Paradigms.*   Ph. D. thesis, UCLA.   http://www.mit.edu/~albright/papers/AlbrightDiss.html.

Albright, A. (2002b) Islands of reliability for regular morphology: evidence from Italian. *Language* 78(4): 684–709.

Albright, A. (2003) A quantitative study of Spanish paradigm gaps. In G. Garding and M. Tsujimura (eds.) *Proceedings of the 22nd West Coast Conference in Formal Linguistics* 1–14. Somerville, MA: Cascadilla Press.

Albright, A., Andrade, A. E. and Hayes, B. (2001) Segmental environments of Spanish diphthongization. In A. Albright and T. Cho (eds.)

sive form *dom* from the musical note *do* which is subminimal and would be a gap for many speakers (Orgun and Sprouse 1999). Presumably they use it with high enough frequency to ensure that it remains lexicalized among this particular community of speakers.

UCLA Working Papers in Linguistics, Number 7: Papers in Phonology 5 117–51. UCLA. `http://www.linguistics.ucla.edu/people/hayes/Segenvspandiph/SegEnvSpanDiph.pdf`.

Albright, A. and Hayes, B. (2002) Modeling English past tense intuitions with minimal generalization. *SIGPHON 6: Proceedings of the Sixth Meeting of the ACL Special Interest Group in Computational Phonology* 58–69.

Albright, A. and Hayes, B. (2003) Rules vs. analogy in English past tenses: A computational/experimental study. *Cognition* 90: 119–61.

Albright, A. and Hayes, B. (2006) Modeling productivity with the Gradual Learning Algorithm: the problem of accidentally exceptionless generalizations. In G. Fanselow, C. Féry, R. Vogel, and M. Schlesewsky (eds.) *Gradience in Grammar: Generative Perspectives* 185–204. Oxford: Oxford University Press.

Anttila, A. (2002) Morphologically conditioned phonological alternations. *Natural Language and Linguistic Theory* 20(1): 1–42. ROA 425, `http://roa.rutgers.edu`.

Benua, L. (1997) *Transderivational Identity: Phonological Relations Between Words*. Ph. D. thesis, University of Massachusetts, Amherst.

Boersma, P. (1997) How we learn variation, optionality, and probability. *Proceedings of the Institute of Phonetic Sciences of the University of Amsterdam 21* 43–58. `http://fon.hum.uva.nl/paul/`.

Boersma, P. and Hayes, B. (2001) Empirical tests of the Gradual Learning Algorithm. *Linguistic Inquiry* 32(1): 45–86.

Butt, J. (1997) *Spanish Verbs*. Oxford: Oxford University Press.

Bybee, J. (1985) *Morphology: A Study of the Relation Between Meaning And Form*. Amsterdam: John Benjamins Publishing Company.

Bybee, J. L. and Pardo, E. (1981) On Lexical and morphological conditioning of alternations: a nonce-probe experiment with Spanish verbs. *Linguistics* 19: 937–68.

Clahsen, H., Aveledo, F. and Roca, I. (2002) The development of regular and irregular verb inflection in Spanish child language. *Journal of Child Language* 29: 591–622.

de Gámez, T. (ed.) (1973) *Simon and Schuster's International Dictionary: English/Spanish Spanish/English*. Simon and Schuster.

Eddington, D. (1996) Diphthongization in Spanish derivational morphology: an empirical investigation. *Hispanic Linguistics* 8: 1–35.

Eddington, D. (1998) Spanish diphthongization as a non-derivational phenomenon. *Rivista di Linguistica* 10, 335–54.

Fanselow, G. and Féry, C. (2002) Ineffability in grammar. In G. Fanselow and C. Féry (eds.) *Resolving Conflicts in Grammars: Optimality Theory in Syntax, Morphology, and Phonology*, Number 11 in Linguistische Berichte Sonderheft 265–307. Hamburg: Helmut Buske Verlag. `http://www.ling.uni-potsdam.de/~fery/pdf/ineffability.pdf`.

Garde, P. (1998) *Grammaire Russe: Phonologie et Morphologie*. Paris: Institut d'études slaves.

Gouskova, M. (2003) *Deriving Economy: Syncope in Optimality Theory*. Ph. D. thesis, University of Massachusetts Amherst.

Halle, M. (1973) Prolegomena to a theory of word formation. *Linguistic Inquiry 4*: 3–16.

Hansson, G. O. (1999) 'When in doubt…': intraparadigmatic dependencies and gaps in Icelandic. In P. Tamanji, Hirotani, M. and Hall, N. (eds.) *Proceedings of the 29th meeting of the North Eastern Linguistic Society* 105–19. Amherst, MA: GLSA Publications. `http://www.linguistics.ubc.ca/People/Gunnar/GH_NELS29_Gaps.pdf`.

Harris, J. W. (1969) *Spanish Phonology*. Cambridge, MA: MIT Press.

Hayes, B. (1999) Phonological restructuring in Yidin^y and its theoretical consequences. In B. Hermans and M. van Oostendorp (eds.) *The Derivational Residue in Phonological Optimality Theory* 175–205. Amsterdam: John Benjamins.

Hetzron, R. (1975) Where the grammar fails. *Language* 51: 859–72.

Iverson, G. (1981) Rules, constraints, and paradigm lacunae. *Glossa* 15: 136–44.

Jakobson, R. (1948) Russian conjugation. *Word* 4: 155–67.

Juilland, A. and Chang-Rodríguez, E. (1964) *Frequency dictionary of Spanish words*. The Hague: Mouton.

Kager, R. (1999) Surface opacity of metrical structure in Optimality Theory. In B. Hermans and M. van Oostendorp (eds.) *The Derivational Residue in Phonological Optimality Theory* 207–47. Amsterdam: Benjamins.

Kenstowicz, M. (1996) Base identity and uniform exponence: alternatives to cyclicity. In J. Durand and B. Laks (eds.) *Current Trends in Phonology: Models and Methods* 363–94. Salford: University of Salford. ROA 103, `http://ruccs.rutgers.edu/`.

Kiparsky, P. (1965) *Phonological Change*. Ph. D. thesis, MIT.

Kiparsky, P. (1978) Analogical change as a problem for linguistic theory. In *Linguistics in the Seventies: Directions and Prospects*, Number 8:2 in Studies in the Linguistic Sciences. Urbana, IL: Dept. of Linguistics, University of Illinois.

Morris, R. E. (2005) Attraction to the unmarked in Old Spanish leveling. In D. Eddington (ed.) *Selected Proceedings of the 7th Hispanic Linguistics Symposium* 180–91. Somerville, MA: Cascadilla Proceedings Project. http://www.lingref.com/cpp/hls/7/paper1097.pdf.

Orgun, C. O. and Sprouse, R. (1999) From MPARSE to CONTROL: Deriving ungrammaticality. *Phonology 16*: 191–224.

Paul, H. (1920) *Prinzipien der Sprachgeschichte* (5th ed.). Tübingen: Niemeyer.

Penny, R. (2002) *A History of the Spanish Language* (2nd ed.). Cambridge: Cambridge University Press.

Pertsova, K. (2005) How lexical conservatism can lead to paradigm gaps. In J. Heinz and K. Pertsova (eds.) *UCLA Working Papers in Linguistics, Number 11: Papers in Phonology 6* 13–38. UCLA.

Pinker, S. (1999) *Words and Rules: The Ingredients of Language*. New York: Basic Books.

Prince, A. and Smolensky, P. (2004) *Optimality Theory: Constraint Interaction in Generative Grammar*. Cambridge, MA: Blackwell.

Raffelsiefen, R. (2004) Absolute ill-formedness and other morphophonological effects. *Phonology 21*: 91–142.

Rice, C. (2003) Dialectal variation in norwegian imperatives. *Nordlyd 31*: 372–84.

Rice, C. (2005) Optimal gaps in optimal paradigms. *Catalan Journal of Linguistics 4*: 155–70.

Rice, C. (2006) When nothing wins: gaps and repairs at the phonology-morphology interface. In C. Davis, A. R. Deal, and Y. Zabbal (eds.) *Proceedings of the 36th meeting of the North Eastern Linguistic Society*. Amherst, MA: GLSA Publications. ROA 781, http://roa.rutgers.edu/.

Rodríguez Bou, I. (1952) *Recuento de Vocabulario Español*. Río Piedras, Puerto Rico: Universidad de Puerto Rico.

Sebastián, N., Cuetos, F. Martí, M. A. and Carreiras, M. F. (2000) *LEXESP: Léxico informatizado del español. Edición en CD-ROM*. Barcelona: Edicions de la Universitat de Barcelona (Colleccions Vàries, 14).

Sharoff, S. (2002) Meaning as use: exploitation of aligned corpora for the contrastive study of lexical semantics. In *Proceedings of Language Resources and Evaluation Conference (LREC02). May, 2002, Las Palmas, Spain*. Available for download at: `http://www.artint.ru/projects/frqlist/frqlist-en.asp`.

Shvedova, N. J. (ed.) (1970) *Grammatika Sovremennogo Russkovo Literaturnogo Jazyka*. Moscow: Nauka.

Sims, A. (2005) Paradigmatic gaps and paradigmatic content: a study of the Greek genitive plural. Paper presented at the Annual Meeting of the Linguistic Society of America in San Francisco, CA, January 2005.

Steriade, D. (1997) Lexical conservatism. In *Linguistics in the Morning Calm, Selected Papers from SICOL 1997* 157–79. Linguistic Society of Korea, Hanshin Publishing House.

Zalizniak, A. A. (1977) *Grammaticheskij Slovarj Russkogo Jazyka*. Izdatel'stvo Russkij Jazyk. Available for download in electronic form at: `http://starling.rinet.ru/download.htm`.

Zoll, C. (1996) *Parsing below the Segment in a Constraint-based Framework*. Ph. D. thesis, University of California, Berkeley.

Zuraw, K. (2000) *Patterned Exceptions in Phonology*. Ph. D. thesis, UCLA.

6 A gap in the feminine paradigm of Hebrew: a consequence of identity avoidance in the suffix domain*

Outi Bat-El
Tel-Aviv University

1 Introduction

Hebrew tends to avoid surface forms where a string of suffixes has identical consonants. The feminine paradigm is a wild battleground for such strings, since it involves four *-Vt* suffixes: the singular suffixes *-it*, *-et*, and *-ut*, and the plural suffix *-ot*. Forms ending with any of the singular suffixes are usually pluralized with *-ot*, thus giving rise to potential identity in the suffix domain (e.g. /map-ít-ot/ 'serviettes', */rakáv-et-ot/* 'trains', */tarb-út-ot/* 'cultures').[1] Different singular suffixes may also co-occur (e.g. */tarb-út-it/* 'cultural FMSG'), which in turn can be pluralized with *-ot* (e.g. */tarb-ut-ít-ot/* 'cultural FMPL'). In addition, the *-Vt* suffixes can be non-adjacent (e.g. */tarb-ut-í-ut/* 'civility', */map-ít-on-et/* 'little serviette', *rakáv-et-on-et/* 'little train').

Some surface forms preserve the identity (e.g. *tarb-út-it* 'cultural FMSG'), while others are amended, either by eliminating the non-final -*Vt* suffix (e.g. */rakáv-et-ot/* → *rakav-ót* 'trains') or by replacing the *t* of the non-final suffix with *y* (e.g. */tarb-út-ot/* → *tarb-uy-ót* 'cultures').

There is one case where the amended form is the null output, i.e. the input does not have a surface phonetic realization. This case arises in the plural paradigm of *-ut* nouns derived from adjectives ending in *-i*. As observed in Schwarzwald (2002), inputs like */sod-i-út-ot/* 'secrecies' (singular */sod-í-ut/* → *sod-iy-út*) do not have a corresponding surface form.

---

*I would like to thank Charles Kisseberth, John McCarthy, Ora Schwarzwald, and the participants of the Ineffability Workshop (Oslo 2006) for helpful comments.

[1] Throughout the paper, the input is enclosed in slashes. Stress is marked on the input and the output, where in the input it indicates the position of stress in the surface base of the rightmost suffix. For clarity of exposition, a morpheme boundary is provided in both the input and the output.

The input forms presented above are similar to those resulting in morphological haplology in other languages, whereby two identical strings of segments in adjacent morphemes are reduced to one (Stemberger 1981). In the data discussed here, only the consonants of the morphemes have to be identical, the morphemes must all be suffixes (i.e. not a stem plus a suffix), and not necessarily adjacent, and the reduction to one string is found only with the suffix *-et*. Nevertheless, as in haplology, the function of the various strategies amending the strings of suffixes with identical consonants is identity avoidance.

Identity (and similarity) avoidance is a common phenomenon, for which the Obligatory Contour Principle (OCP) is responsible. The domain of the OCP can be the stem, as in Semitic co-occurrence restrictions (McCarthy 1988; Frisch et al. 2004), across morpheme boundaries, as in various cases of haplology (Yip 1998, Plag 1998), and across the board (van Oostendorp this volume). In the case studied here, the OCP is restricted to the suffix domain, i.e. it triggers alternation only when the identical consonants are segments of suffixes.[2]

In this paper, I present the various strategies Hebrew employs in amending inputs with identical consonants in the suffix domain. The constraint hierarchy that will be developed on the basis of surface forms that eliminate identity will lead to the null output without further stipulation. While the null output will be obtained with no cost, the forms that preserve the identity will require manipulating the distinction between contextual and inherent inflection in one case (Anderson 1992 and Booij 1996), and the proximity hierarchy in the other (Suzuki 1998).

The gap discussed in this paper is "absolute", in the sense that speakers are reluctant to fill it even upon request. It differs from the "unstable" gap in the feminine diminutive plural paradigm of Hebrew (Bat-El 1997), as well as other gaps discussed in this volume, for which speakers are willing to provide a substitute for the null output. I claim that speakers strive to fill the gaps, and thus unstable gaps are unmarked. An absolute gap arises when the language does not have a form similar to the expected filler form, and thus does not support it.

Data and generalizations are provided in §2, starting with a brief over-

---

[2]Hebrew stems can be preceded by one prefix only, which in turn can be preceded by one or more clitics. Therefore, reference can be expanded to affixes (rather than suffixes) in the morphological word, assuming that clitics are within the phonological, but not the morphological word. This restriction allows identical consonants belonging to a prefix and a clitic, as in *mi-me-nahél* 'from a manager', where *mi-* is a clitic and *me-* is a prefix.

view of Hebrew feminine suffixes (§2.1). The interaction of the suffixes is then presented, distinguishing among three types of forms: those where input (adjacent and non-adjacent) identity is resolved in the output (§2.2), the one case where the null output is the optimal candidate (§2.3), and the cases where identity is maintained in the output (§2.4). A summary of the data is then provided (§2.5). The analysis begins in §3 with the constraint ranking responsible for identity resolution, via elimination of the suffix segments when the suffix vowel is mid (§3.1) and replacing one of the identical consonants with another segment when the suffix vowel is high (§3.2). It is then shown in §4 that this same ranking accounts for the null parse without further stipulations. The constraint ranking developed up to this point predicts no identity in the suffix domain. Therefore, the forms exhibiting surface identity, analyzed in §5, require adhering to the distinction between inherent and contextual inflection (§5.1) and manipulating the proximity hierarchy for the OCP (§5.2). For both cases, it will be explained why the null output is not selected. The distinction between absolute and unstable gaps is raised in §6, accompanied by a brief overview of the unstable gap in the feminine diminutive paradigm of Hebrew. The concluding remarks in §7 advise further research on the identity form (the one identical to the base), which could replace the null output, and thus avoid a gap.

2　Data and generalizations

2.1　Hebrew feminine suffixes

Hebrew has four feminine *-Vt* suffixes: three singular, *-et*, *-it*, and *-ut*, and one plural *-ot*. The suffixes *-et* and *-it* serve for both derivational and inflectional purposes in nouns and adjectives (Bat-El 1989), and the suffix *-ut* is a derivational suffix usually denoting an abstract feminine noun (Bolozky and Schwarzwald 1992). The plural suffix *-ot*, attached to nouns and adjectives, is not specified for gender, but rather subcategorized for feminine nouns and adjectives (see §3.1), though with quite a few exceptions in nouns (Schwarzwald 1991). All the singular suffixes are added to free as well as bound stems. The plural suffix is added to surface forms (stems as well as stems plus suffixes), but due to some phonological processes (to be discussed later on) there are surface plural forms where the suffix *-ot* follows a bound stem (see *taxan-ót* 'stations' in (1) below).

(1)   Hebrew *-Vt* (feminine) suffixes

	-Vt noun		Free stem/base[3]	
-et	ʃotér-et	'policewoman'	ʃotér	'policeman'
	maxbér-et	'notebook'		
-it	ʔezrax-ít	'citizen FMSG'	ʔezráx	'citizen MSSG'
	xav-ít	'barrel'		
-ut	ʔezrax-út	'citizenship'	ʔezráx	'citizen MSSG'
	tarb-út	'culture'		
-ot	ʃutaf-ót	'partners fm.	ʃutaf-á	'partner FMSG'
	taxan-ót	'stations'	taxan-á	'station'

There is one more feminine suffix (see the base of *-ot* in (1)), whose
-Vt form appears only in construct state (e.g. *taxan-at ʔótobus* 'bus station') and before a possessive clitic (e.g. *taxan-at-í* 'my station'). In word
final position, where the other feminine suffixes surface as *-Vt*, it surfaces
as *-a* (e.g. *taxan-á* 'station'), and when the plural suffix is added, the *-a*
disappears (e.g. /*taxan-á-ot*/ → *taxan-ót* 'stations'). Therefore, *-a* does not
endanger identity in the suffix domain.

Adjectives and verbs agree with the noun in gender and number (verbs
also agree in person). With the exception of *-ut*, all the suffixes mentioned
above also appear in adjectives (and participles, which may function as
nouns, adjectives, or verbs), where they indicate agreement with the noun.

(2)   Gender and number agreement (FM = feminine; ACC = accusative, PL =
       plural)
       a.   ha-ʃotér-**et**   ʔacr-**á**   ʔet   ha-nahég-**et**
             the-policewoman stopped-FM ACC the-driver-FM
             ha-ʔavaryan-**ít**
             the-offending-FM
             'The policewoman stopped the offending (female) driver'
       b.   ha-ʔezrax-**ít**   ha-zar-**á**   ʔohév-**et** tarb-**uy-ót**
             the-citizen-FM the-foreign-FM loves-FM culture-FM-PL
             maʔarav-**iy-ót**
             western-FM-PL
             'The foreign (female) citizen loves western cultures'

Forms ending in the suffix *-et* always bear penultimate stress (see §3.1).
All the other *-Vt* suffixes are stressed when in word final position, unless attached to an accented stem (Bat-El 1993), in which case the stress stays on

---

[3]The term 'stem' refers to the residue of affix stripping, parallel to the term 'root' in
non-Semitic languages. A 'base' of a suffix can be a stem or a stem plus a suffix.

the stem (e.g. *atóm* 'atom' – *atóm-it* 'atomic FMSG' – *atóm-iy-ot* 'atomic FMPL').

2.2   Forms resolving identity

When the plural suffix *-ot* is attached to a form ending in one of the singular *-Vt* suffixes, the suffix with the mid vowel, *-et*, disappears (3a), while the suffixes with high vowels, *-it* and *-ut*, surface as *-Vy* (3b).[4]

(3)   Resolution of adjacent identity

	Input	Output		Cf. Singular
a.	/rakáv-**et**-ot/	rakav-ót	'trains'	rakév-et[5]
b.	/xav-**ít**-ot/	xav-**iy**-ót	'barrels'	xav-ít
	/tarb-**út**-ot/	tarb-**uy**-ót	'cultures'	tarb-út

The motivation for the alternations in (3) is avoiding identical consonants, commonly attributed to the OCP. However, there are two other relevant properties here: (i) identity avoidance is restrictcd to the suffix domain, and (ii) adjacency among the identical consonants in the suffixes is not required (though, as shown in §5.2, adjacency plays a role).

Restriction to the suffix domain is crucial, since identical consonants within the stem and across the stem–suffix boundary are possible (e.g. *me-xatét-et* 'picks FMSG', *xamim-ím* 'warm MSPL'). An interesting segmentally (but not morphologically) identical pair is the surface form *xavit-ót* 'omelets', which is the output of */xavit-á-ot/*, and the input */xav-ít-ot/*, which surfaces as *xav-iy-ót* 'barrels'. In *xavit-ót* 'omelets', the two *t*s are across the stem-suffix boundary (since the *-a* of *xavit-á* 'omelet' is deleted

---

[4]I assume that the base of *-ot* consists of a stem plus *-et*, rather than the stem only, which could be assumed given that *-et* does not surface in the plural form (the same goes for *-a*). There are several supporting arguments for this assumption. (i) Since the plural suffix does not assign gender (i.e. *-ot* is not specified for feminine but rather subcategorized for feminine), the feminine suffix is required for the gender specification of the plural form; the stem is not specified for gender. (ii) The feminine suffix is not always predictable and therefore must be part of the input (e.g. *beyc-á* 'egg' – *beyc-ít* 'ovule', *xavit-á* 'omelet' – *xavit-ít* 'blintz', */tabáx-it/* → *tabax-ít* 'cook FMSG' – */zamár-et/* → *zamér-et* 'singer FMSG' – */ravák-a/* → *ravak-á* 'bachelor FMSG'). (iii) Had the stem been the base of *-ot*, it would have been a coincidence that the base is a stem when the suffix has a non-high vowel (*-a* and *-et*) but a stem plus a suffix when the suffix has a high vowel (*-it* and *-ut*). The phonological distinction between these two types of suffixes, i.e. the height of the vowel, suggests a phonological account for the elimination of the suffixes with the non-high vowel (see §3).

[5]See §3.1 for the *a-e* alternation in *rakév-et* – *rakav-ót* 'train(s)'.

before *-ot*) and thus not affected by the OCP. In /*xav-ít-ot*/ 'barrels', however, the two *t*s are in the suffix domain, and thus do not survive in the output.

The restriction to the suffix domain can be obtained by assuming that stem faithfulness constraints outrank suffix faithfulness constraint (McCarthy and Prince 1995), i.e. FAITHSTEM ≫ OCP ≫ FAITHAFFIX. In addition, in order to account for OCP violation across a stem-suffix boundary (e.g. *xavit-ót* 'omelets'), faithfulness constraints referring to the edge must outrank the OCP, i.e. FAITHEDGE ≫ OCP (see §3.1 for the FAITHEDGE constraints).

I assume a general OCP, specified for identical consonants without requiring adjacency. Indeed, not only are the identical consonants not adjacent (given the vowel of each suffix), but the suffixes too do not have to be adjacent. As shown below, the alternations appearing when the suffixes are adjacent (3) also appear when they are not. When the diminutive suffix *-on* is flanked by two *-Vt* suffixes, the suffix *-et* disappears (4a) and the *-Vt* suffixes with the high vowels surface as *-Vy* (4b).[6]

(4)　　Resolution of non-adjacent identity

		Non-adjacent identity		Cf. Adjacent identity (3)	
a.	/rakáv-et-on-et/	rakav-ón-et	/rakáv-et-ot/	rakav-ót	
		'little train'		'trains'	
b.	/map-ít-on-et/	map-iy-ón-et	/map-ít-ot/	map-iy-ót	
		'little serviette'		'serviettes'	
	/xan-út-on-et/	xan-uy-ón-et	/xan-út-ot/	xan-uy-ót	
		'little shop'		'shops'	

Following Suzuki (1998), among others, I assume that the OCP is a family of universally ranked constraints specified for proximity. I discuss this issue in §5.2, where I compare forms in which non-adjacent identity is resolved (e.g. /*xan-út-on-et*/ → *xan-uy-ón-et* 'little shop') with those where it remains surface true (e.g. /*tarb-ut-í-ut*/ → *tarb-ut-iY-út* 'civility').[7]

---

[6]When the nominal suffix *-on* (not the diminutive one) is attached to a noun ending in *-it*, we do not expect alternation, since there are no two *-Vt* suffixes. Indeed, as expected, we get the derivationally related pair *zav-ít* 'angle' – *zav-it-ón* 'angle-bar' (cf. *zav-iy-ót* 'angles'). However, we also get the pair *map-ít* 'serviette' *map-iy-ón* 'serviette holder' (cf. *map-iy-ót* 'serviettes'). This suggests that all the forms of the paradigm are listed in the lexicon, allowing exceptional selection of a base, as is often the case in derivational morphology.

[7]Another case of identity avoidance in the suffix domain is found in the dual paradigm of Hebrew (Paz 2006). When the dual suffix *-aim* is attached to a feminine noun, its base

2.3   The null output

In addition to the *y* corresponding to the *t* in the *-Vt* suffixes with a high vowel (e.g. */map-ít-ot/* → *map-iy-ót* 'serviettes', */xan-út-ot/* → *xan-uy-ót* 'shops'), there is another source of *y* in the suffix domain. When the adjectival suffix *-i* is followed by a vowel initial suffix, a *y* is inserted to avoid an onsetless syllable. Onsetless syllables are allowed within the stem, but not across a suffix boundary, with the exception of masculine plural forms whose base ends in the adjectival suffix *-i*, as in *tarb-ut-i-ím* 'cultural MSPL' (see §2.4). For clarity of exposition, the *y* following the adjectival *-i* is transcribed as *Y*, thus visually (but not phonetically) distinguished from the *y* corresponding to *t*.[8]

(5)   *y* Epenthesis (*Y*)

Base	MSADJ *-i*	FMADJ *-a*	Abstract N *-ut*
sod 'secret'	sod-í 'secretive MSSG'		sod-iY-út 'secrecy'
musár 'moral'	musar-í 'moral MSSG		musar-iY-út 'morality'
	agresív-i 'aggressive'		agresív-iY-ut 'aggressiveness'
dat 'religion'	dat-í 'religious MSSG'	dat-iY-á 'religious FMSG'	dat-iY-út 'religiousness'
carfát 'France'	carfat-í 'Frenchman'	carfat-iY-á 'Frenchwoman'	carfat-iY-út 'Frenchness'

Given that */sod-í-ut/* surfaces as *sod-iY-út* 'secrecy' (5) and */xan-út-ot/* as *xan-uy-ót* 'shops' (3b), we would expect */sod-i-út-ot/* 'secrecies' to surface as **sod-iY-uy-ót*. That is, we expect an epenthetic *y* after the *-i* and another *y* replacing the *t* of *-ut*. However, **sod-iY-uy-ót* has two *y*s in the

---

usually includes the feminine plural suffix -ot (e.g. *map-ít – map-iy-ót* 'serviette(s)' – *map-iy-ot-áim* 'two serviettes'; **map-it-áim*). However, when the dual suffix is attached to a masculine noun, its base never includes the plural suffix *-im*, since a sequence of the plural and the dual suffixes will incur two *m*s in the suffix domain (e.g. *xodaʃ-ím* 'months' – *xodʃ-áim* 'two months; **xodaʃ-im-áim*). As is with the case of two *t*s, two m's across the stem–suffix boundary are allowed (e.g. *yam-im* 'days', *yom-áim* 'two days'), supporting the observation that the OCP is restricted to the suffix domain.

[8] There is another distinction between *t–y* and ∅*–y*; in the former, the *y* takes an available prosodic position (the one occupied by *t* in the input) while in the latter, a new prosodic position must be added to host the *y*. In the analysis to be provided later on, I assume two DEP constraints, one for a segment and another for a prosodic position. The latter one will be ignored due to its low ranking.

suffix domain, and thus it violates OCP, just like the input */sod-i-út-ot/*, which has two *t*s in the suffix domain. In this case, as opposed to the cases discussed in §2.2, Hebrew does not provide any resources to amend the illformed structure, and the null output (⊙) is thus obtained.

(6)   The null output: */X-i-ut-ot/* input

Stem/Base	ADJECTIVE -*i*	NOUN -*ut*	PLURAL -*ot* – ⊙
sod	sod-í	sod-iY-út	*sod-iY-ut-ót
'secret'	'secretive MSSG'	'secrecy'	*sod-iY-uy-ót
dat	dat-í	dat-iY-út	*dat-iY-ut-ót
'religion'	'religious MSSG'	'religiousness'	*dat-iY-uy-ót
prat	prat-í	prat-iY-út	*prat-iY-ut-ót
'item'	'private MSSG'	'privacy'	*prat-iY-uy-ót
musár	musar-í	musar-iY-út	*musar-iY-ut-ót
'moral'	'moral MSSG'	'moraliy'	*musar-iY-uy-ót
medin-á	medin-í	medin-iY-út	*medin-iY-ut-ót
'state'	'political MSSG'	'policy'	*medin-iY-uy-ót

Note that substrings of **sod-iY-uy-ót* are possible; *iYu* appears in *sod-iY-út* 'secrecy' and *uyo* in *tarb-uy-ót* 'cultures'. That is, it is the identity in the suffix domain, rather than a constraint on the substrings, that renders **sod-iY-uy-ót* and **sod-iY-ut-ót* impossible.

As Schwarzwald (2002) notes, many abstract nouns, with or without -*ut*, do not have a plural form for semantic reasons (e.g. *cédek* 'justice', *rigúl* 'espionage', *ʔabah-út* 'fatherhood', *ʔalim-út* 'violence'); Schwarzwald reports that 92.2% (1829/1983) of the -*ut* nouns listed in Even-Shoshan's dictionary do not have a plural form. However, among the -*ut* nouns that are pluralized, there is not even one noun where the -*ut* is preceded by the adjectival -*i*. This, of course, is not a coincident.

Moreover, while speakers can easily provide a plural form for abstract nouns that do not have a plural form for semantic reasons, they are reluctant to provide one for nouns ending in -*i*-ut (see further discussion in §6). Notice that while the string *iYuy* is not found anywhere in the language, *utot* is not uncommon (e.g. *nexut-ót* 'inferior FMPL'). Nevertheless, both **sod-iY-uy-ót* or **sod-iY-ut-ót* are not acceptable even upon request.

2.4   Surface identity

Much less success in avoiding identity is obtained when a -*Vt* suffix with a high vowel is followed by -*it* (there are no such sequences with -*ut*). In this case, the identity remains surface true.

(7)   Surface adjacent identity
     Input   Output
     /tarb-ut-it/   tarb-ut-it   'cultural FMSG'
     /tavn-it-it/   tavn-it-it   'structural FMSG'

Given that *-Vt*, where *V* is high, becomes *-Vy* before another *-Vt* suffix (3b), we would expect /tarb-út-it/ to surface as *tarb-uy-ít and /tavn-ít-it/ as *tavn-iy-ít. However, these forms are ruled out because Hebrew, like some other languages (e.g. Klamath; Clements and Keyser 1983) does not allow tautosyllabic *y* and *i*. Reference to the syllable is crucial, since heterosyllabic *y* and *i* are possible (e.g. *ci.yur* 'painting', *so.di.yut* 'secrecy'). This is a general restriction in Hebrew, as evident by the deletion of *y* in /cafúy-im/ → *cfuím* 'predictable MSPL' and the absence of *y* epenthesis, and thus the presence of an onsetless syllable in *tarb-ut-i-ím* 'cultural MSPL'. I argue in §5.1 that an OCP violation is tolerated in *tarb-ut-ít* 'cultural FMSG' but not in *sod-iY-uy-ót or *sod-iY-ut-ót because they belong to different types of inflectional paradigms.

In addition to the surface adjacent identity in (7), there is also surface non-adjacent identity. Recall that in (4), non-adjacent identity is amended (e.g. /xan-út-on-et/ → *xan-uy-ón-et* 'little shop').

(8)   Surface non-adjacent identity
     Input   Output[9]
     /tarb-ut-í-ut/   tarb-ut-iY-út   'civility'
     /tavn-it-í-ut/   tavn-it-iY-út   'structuralism'

When two *-Vt* suffixes with a high vowel have the suffix *-i* between them, the *t* of the internal *-Vt* suffix does not surface as *y* since the output, *tarb-uy-iY-út, would violate OCP as well as the above mentioned restriction against tautosyllabic sequence of *y* and *i*. As in (7), we do not get the null output but rather a surface form violating OCP at a distance (where 'at a distance' here means across another suffix).

---

[9]I assume that the base of these *-ut* nouns is the masculine adjective (with the suffix *-i*) rather than the feminine one (with the suffix *-it*). However, phonologically, either one could serve as a base since the *y* between the two *-Vt* suffixes could either correspond to the *t* of the adjectival feminine suffix *-it* (e.g. /tarb-ut-ít-ut/ → *tarb-ut-iy-út*), or be an epenthetic *y* inserted after the adjectival masculine suffix *-i* (as in (8)).

2.5 Summary

As summarized below, input identity is resolved when a -*Vt* suffix is adjacent (9a-i) or non-adjacent (9a-ii) to another -*Vt* suffix. Input identity remains surface true when two -*Vt* suffixes with a high vowel are adjacent (9b-i) or non-adjacent (9b-ii).

(9)　　a. Identity resolution

i. Adjacent identity (3)		ii. Non-adjacent identity (4)	
/-et-ot/	-∅-ot	/-et-on-et/	-∅-on-et
/-it-ot/	-iy-ot	/-ut-on-et/	-uy-on-et
/-ut-ot/	-uy-ot	/-it-on-et/	-iy-on-et

　　　　b. Surface identity

Adjacent identity (7)		Non-adjacent identity (8)	
/-ut-it/	-ut-it	/-it-i-ut/	-it-iY-ut
/-it-it/	-it-it	/-ut-i-ut/	-ut-iY-ut

The null output and its morphological relatives are provided below. In all surviving forms, the rightmost suffix is faithful to its input (see §3.1) and the adjectival -*i* is followed by an epenthetic *y* (in non-final position), A -*Vt* suffix with a high vowel surfaces as -*Vy* before another -*Vt* suffix, unless this suffix begins with *i* (i.e. either -*i* or -*it*), in which case it remains -*Vt*. The null output, ⊙, arises when a sequence of two -*Vt* suffixes, the first of which has a high vowel, is preceded by -*i*.

(10)　　The null output and its morphological relatives

Stem/Base	In=Out	∅–y	t–y	⊙
	ADJFM	NOUN	PLURAL	PLURAL
sod 'secret'		/sod-í-ut/ sod-iY-út	/sod-ít-ot/ sod-iy-ót	/sod-i-út-ot/ ⊙
tarb-út 'culture'	tarb-ut-ít	/tarb-ut-í-ut/ tarb-ut-iY-út	/tarb-út-ot/ tarb-uy-ót	/tarb-ut-i-út-ot/ ⊙
tavn-ít 'pattern'	tavn-it-ít	/tavn-it-í-ut/ tavn-it-iY-út	/tavn-ít-ot/ tavn-iy-ót /tavn-it-ít-ot/ tavn-it-iy-ót	/tavn-it-i-út-ot/ ⊙

With the data and generalizations at hand, the analysis begins in the following section.

3 Identity resolution

3.1 The suffix *-et* (-et-Vt → ∅-Vt)

The suffix *-et* is unique not only due to the fact that it is the only *-Vt* suffix that disappears before another suffix. Unlike the other suffixes discussed here, *-et* requires the preceding syllable to be stressed and headed by a mid vowel.[10] Consequently, a low vowel in the stem final syllable is raised to *e* when followed by *-et* (e.g. *zamár – zamér-et* 'singer MS-FM'). High vowels, however, resist alternation (see §3.2) and therefore *-et* cannot be added to a base with a high vowel in the final syllable. When *-et* disappears (3a), there is no surface context for vowel raising, and the input *a* appears (e.g. *zamér-et – zamar-ót* 'singer FMSG–PL'). Since the *a–e* alternation also appears when *-et* follows a bound stem, as in *rakév-et – rakav-ót* 'train(s)', I assume that the input of *rakév-et* is with *a*, i.e. */rakav-et/*.

As described in §2.2, when a form ending in *-et* is pluralized, the *-et* disappears and only the plural suffix *-ot* surfaces (3a). Such a strategy is employed without exception, whether the base of *-et* is a free morpheme (11a) or a bound one (11b).

(11)   *-et* followed by *-Vt*

		MSSG	FMSG *-et*	FMPL *-ot*	
a.		toʃáv	toʃév-et	toʃav-ót	'inhabitant'
		zamár	zamér-et	zamar-ót	'singer'
b.			któv-et	ktov-ót	'address'
			rakév-et	rakav-ót	'train'

First, there is a morphological issue here. As noted in §2, the plural suffix does not assign gender (Bat-El 1997). Evidence to this claim is drawn from irregular plural forms, where a masculine noun takes the plural suffix *-ot*, which is subcategorized for feminine (e.g. *xalon-ót* 'windows', *kir-ót* 'walls'). Such plural forms remain masculine, as evident from the masculine plural suffix *-im* appearing on the adjective via agreement (e.g. *xalon-ót gdol-ím* 'big windows', *kir-ót levan-ím* 'white walls'). The agreement test also tells us that the plural forms in (11) are feminine (e.g. *rakav-ót mehir-ót* 'fast trains'), despite the facts that the plural suffix does not as-

---

[10]This behavior of *-et* probably stems from its form in earlier stages of the language, which is argued to be *-t*. The *e* corresponds to a historical epenthetic ε, which according to traditional analyses, is inserted to break up the word final consonant cluster created by the addition of the suffix *-t* to a stem ending in a consonant.

sign gender and that there is no surface feminine singular suffix. I thus assume, that the morphological structure of the plural forms in (11) is STEM]∅]_FM-ot]_FMPL, where ∅ indicates the absence of an overt feminine marker (not a zero morpheme). What is crucial for the ensuing analysis is whether the singular suffix *-et* vanishes via morphological deletion, i.e. truncation, or phonological deletion, i.e. an independent deletion of each segment in the suffix.

I claim that the target of deletion in the plural form is not the suffix as a unit (morphological), but rather its segments (phonological). In a rule-based approach (Bat-El 1989) it can be viewed as *t*-deletion due to the OCP (*/zamár-et-ot/* → **zamar-e-ot*) followed by *e* deletion due to ONSET (**zamar-e-ot* → *zamar-ót*). This claim is supported below by two cases of vowel deletion: the first case shows that the vowel of *-et* can be deleted leaving the *t* behind, and the second shows that ONSET can trigger vowel deletion.

When the suffix *-et* is followed by the adjectival suffix *-i*, OCP is not relevant since there are no identical consonants in the suffix domain; therefore the *t* of *-et* survives. In this case, however, the *e* of *-et* is deleted (e.g. */kacáf-et-i/* → *kacaf-t-í* 'creamy' (cf. *kacéf-et* 'cream'), */bikór-et-i/* → *bikor-t-í* 'critical' (cf. *bikór-et* 'criticism')). This type of deletion is familiar from the paradigms of verbs and adjectives, where *e* is deleted in a two-sided open syllable (e.g. */xivér-im/* → *xivr-ím* 'pale MSPL', */gidél-a/* → *gidl-á* 'she raised'). Evidence that ONSET triggers vowel deletion across a suffix boundary, as argued for (*/rakáv-et-ot/* →) **rakav-e-ot* → *rakav-ót*, is drawn from nouns with the feminine suffix *-a*, which is deleted when followed by the plural suffix *-ot* (e.g. */matan-á-ot/* → *matan-ót* 'gifts', */miʃpax-á-ot/* → *miʃpax-ót* 'families'). These two cases support the phonological deletion of *-et*, i.e. that its two segments are deleted independently. This approach will also be relevant for the analysis of *-Vt – -Vy* correspondence (§3.2), where I argue that *t* is deleted and *y* is inserted (rather than *t* changes to *y*).

Before proceeding with the analysis, it should be noted that it is never the case that the rightmost suffix is altered to accommodate OCP, or any other constraint for this matter. I thus assume two inviolable faithfulness constraints referring to the segment at the right edge of the word (FAITH-EDGE). ANCHORR, which requires the segment at the right edge of the input to correspond to that at the right edge of the output (no deletion) and IDENTR, which requires the segment at the right edge of the output to be identical to its correspondent in the input (no alternation). Candidates violating these two constraints will not be considered in the analysis.

In addition to the OCP, which prohibits identical consonants, the relevant constraints are as follows: ONSET, which may trigger vowel deletion or consonant epenthesis to avoid an onsetless syllable, DEP, which penalizes for having an epenthetic consonant, and MAX, which incurs a violation mark for every deleted segment. The constraint violated by the null candidate (☉) is MPARSE (Prince and Smolensky 1993), which, in its current version, following Wolf and McCarthy (this volume), is violated only when the candidate has no phonological material. Consequently, all other candidates respect MPARSE, even when they do not preserve all input morphemes (i.e. when -*et* does not surface).

(12)   -et – ∅: /rakáv-et-ot/ → rakav-ót 'trains'

rakav-et-ot	ONSET	DEP	OCP	MPARSE	MAX
a. rakav-e-ot	*!				*
b. rakav-eC-ot		*!			*
c rakav-et-ot			*!		
d. ☉				*!	
e. ☞ rakav-ot					**

Candidate (a), where the *t* of -*et* is deleted, violates ONSET, and candidate (b), where the *t* is replaced by another consonant (whose nature is not relevant here), violates DEP. Notice that in candidate (b), I assume "replacement", i.e. violation of DEP and MAX, rather than "alternation", i.e. violation of IDENT; this issue will come up again in §3.2, in the discussion on the *t*–*y* correspondence. Candidate (c), the faithful candidate, violates the OCP, since it has two *t*s in the suffix domain, and candidate (d), the null output, does not violate any constraints, except MPARSE. The winning candidate (e) has two violation marks for MAX for the two deleted segments of -*et*, but it does not violate all the other constraints outranking MAX.

As noted in §2.1, the OCP does not require adjacency among the suffixes, and therefore the ranking in (12) also accounts for forms where the -*Vt* suffixes are not adjacent (4a), as in */rakáv-et-on-et/ → rakav-ón-et* 'little train'. I will return to non-adjacent identity in §5.2.

3.2   The suffixes with a high vowel ($/\text{-V}_{[+high]}\text{t-Vt}/ \rightarrow \text{-V}_{[+high]}\text{y-Vt}$)

When a form ending in a *-Vt* suffix with a high vowel is pluralized with *-ot*, the suffix is not deleted but rather the *t* is replaced with *y*. Here too, free stems (13a) and bound stems (13b) are equally affected.[11]

(13)   *-it/ut* followed by *-Vt*

	MsSg	FmSg *-it* / *-ut*	FmPl *-ot*	
a.	rakdán	rakdan-**í**t	rakdan-i**y**-ót	'dancer'
	manhíg 'leader'	manhig-**ú**t	manhig-u**y**-ót	'leadership'
b.		tavn-**í**t	tavn-i**y**-ót	'pattern'
		tarb-**ú**t	tarb-u**y**-ót	'culture'

Given that the segments of *-et* are deleted before *-ot* to resolve an OCP violation, the question is why *-it* and *-ut* are not deleted in this context? The answer comes from other paradigms, which show that high vowels in Hebrew resist morpho-phonological alternations, including deletion.

There are three cases demonstrating the resistance of high vowels to morpho-phonological alternations: (i) In the verb paradigm, *e* is deleted in a two-sided open syllable (e.g. */ti-ʃév-i/* → *ti-ʃv-í* 'you FMSG will sit'), while *i* and *u* survive (e.g. */ta-ʃír-i/* → *ta-ʃír-i* 'you FMSG will sing', */ta-kúm-i/* → *ta-kúm-i* 'you FMSG will get up'); when the vowel is not deleted, it keeps its stress. (ii) A non-high vowel in the stem final syllable of verbs alternates with *e* when the penultimate syllable is closed and the suffix is vowel initial (e.g. */nixnás-a/* → *nixnes-á* 'she entered'),[12] while a high vowel in the same environment does not alternate with e (e.g. */hitxíl-a/* → *hitxíl-a* 'she started'); again, a vowel that does not alternate preserves its stress. (iii) Polysyllabic feminine singular participles with non-high vowels take the suffix *-et*, which requires a mid vowel in the preceding syllable (see §3.1). A mid vowel in the preceding syllable stays as is (*/mevakéʃ-et/* → *mevakéʃ-et* 'she asks') and a low vowel is raised to e (e.g. */mevukáʃ-et/* → *mevukéʃ-et* 'she is wanted'). However, since high vowels resist alternation and *-et* requires a mid vowel in the preceding syllable, *-et* cannot follow a participle stem with a high vowel in the final syllable. As claimed

---

[11]Following traditional generative phonology, both allomorphs should get an equal chance to be considered as the base. I take the *-Vt* form, rather than the *-Vy*, to be the input, as the latter appears in a limited environment, only when another *-Vt* suffix appears in the suffix domain.

[12]This alternation does not appear in the participles (e.g. */nixnás-im/* → *nixnas-ím* 'they enter'), since the morphology and the morpho-phonology of participles tell us that they are adjectives rather than verbs (Bat-El 2006b).

in Bat-El (2006b), this is the reason why participles with a high vowel in the stem final syllable are the only polysyllabic participles that take the feminine suffix *-a* (e.g. /ʃamúr-a/ → ʃmur-á 'she is preserved', /matxíl-a/ → *matxil-á* 'she is starting').

The resistance of the high vowels is also revealed in the suffixes *-it* and *-ut*, which, unlike *-et*, do not disappear when followed by the plural suffix *-ot*. I assume a high ranked constraint MAXV$_{[+high]}$, which prohibits the deletion of high vowels. The preservation of the high vowel in the suffix does not mean that the consonant has to be preserved as well, since, as argued in §3.1 with regard to *-et*, the phonology affects the segments of the suffix, rather than the suffix as a morphological unit. The *t–y* correspondence in the *-Vt* suffixes with the high vowels could be viewed as an IDENT violation, i.e. that *t* "changes" to *y* after a high vowel, to rescue an OCP violation. Although this alternation is not unreasonable, since both *t* and *y* are coronal, I advocate the "replacement" approach here, i.e. that *t* is deleted, to rescue the OCP and *y* is inserted to rescue ONSET, which cannot be rescued by vowel deletion (as is the case with *-et*) due to MAXV$_{[+high]}$. First, ONSET rescuing *y* epenthesis after the high vowel of the adjectival *-i* is independently motivated within the feminine paradigm (§2.2). Second, by assuming *t* deletion, the analysis of the fate of *-V$_{[+high]}$t* is on a par with that of *-et* (§3.1).[13]

Therefore, I assume that the *t–y* correspondence violates MAX, due to the deletion of *t*. The appearance of *y* instead of *t* is not cost-free. Here again, the epenthetic *y* could be viewed as a DEP violation. However, given that *y* is inserted only after high vowels, it is reasonable to assume that it gets its [+high] feature from the preceding high vowel (*i* or *u*) via spreading.[14] Therefore, the epenthetic *y* violates *SPREAD, and thus the *t–y* correspondence violates MAX and *SPREAD.

---

[13]Instead of relying on the resistance of high vowels, it is possible to account for the distinction between the suffixes on the basis of the fact that only high vowels can be rescued by an epenthetic *y* due to the shared features (i.e., the addition of a feature is not necessary). That is, /rakáv-et-ot/ → *rakav-e-ot → *rakav-ey-ot is impossible since *e* does not have the feature [+high], and therefore we get *rakav-ót* 'trains'.

[14]Since Hebrew does not have a back glide, a [+high] in a syllable margin can be nothing but *y*. It should be noted, however, that *w* is not entirely absent from the language. It appears in onomatopoeic names imitating animal sounds, usually associated with child language (e.g. *kwa kwa* 'duck's sound', *haw haw* 'dog's sound', but also *hav hav*), as well as in the interjections *waw* and *wála*. In old loan words, a source *w* corresponds to *v* in Hebrew (e.g. *víski* 'whisky' and *váfla* 'waffle') but the younger generation freely produces *wála* 'Walla (the internet search engine)' and *wíski* 'whisky'. Thus, even if we accept *w* as a phoneme in Hebrew, it is certainly highly marked, and thus the markedness hierarchy *w ≫ *y will account for the epenthetic *y* after both *i* and *u*.

(14) $-V_{[+high]}t --V_{[+high]}y$: /tarb-ut-ot/ → *tarb-uy-ot* 'cultures'

tarb-ut-ot		ONSET	MAXV$_{[+hi]}$	DEP	OCP	MPARSE	*SPREAD	MAX
a.	tarb-u-ot	*!						*
b.	tarb-ot		*!					**
c.	tarb-uC-ot			*!				
d	tarb-ut-ot				*!			
e.	⊙					*!		
f. ☞	tarb-uy-ot						*	*

All candidates except (d) resolve the identity in the suffix domain, and thus respect the OCP. However, candidate (a), where only the *t* is deleted, violates ONSET (and MAX), and candidate (b) where both the high vowel and the *t* are deleted (as in the case of *-et*), violates MAXV$_{[+high]}$ (and MAX twice). In candidate (c), the *t* is replaced by any consonant other than *y*, and it thus violates DEP. Candidate (d) is the faithful candidate, but it violates the OCP, and candidate (e), the null output, violates MPARSE. In candidate (f), the identity is eliminated by replacing *t* with *y*. This replacement, as argued above, involves a MAX violation for the deletion of *t* and a *SPREAD violation for the spreading of [+high] from the high vowel to the following consonant. Since MAX and *SPREAD are crucially ranked below all the other constraints, (f) is the optimal candidate.

The ranking in (14) also accounts for cases where the two *-Vt* suffixes are not adjacent (4b), as in /*map-ít-on-et*/ → *map-iy-ón-et* 'little serviette' and *xan-út-on-et* → /*xan-uy-ón-et*/ 'little shop', since the OCP does not demand adjacency among the suffixes. I will return to non-adjacent identity in §5.2.

4   The null output

As described in §2.2, the null output arises when the plural suffix *-ot* is attached to a noun where the suffix *-ut* is preceded by *-i*, as in /*sod-i-út-ot*/ 'secrecies'. As shown below, the null output is derived by the same constraint ranking deriving the amended outputs analyzed so far. However, it provides evidence for the crucial ranking OCP ≫ MPARSE, which was not relevant in the earlier cases, where a candidate respecting both of them was available.

(15)   /sod-i-út-ot/ → ⊙

sod-i-ut-ot		ONSET	MAXV$_{[+hi]}$	DEP	OCP	MPARSE	*SPREAD	MAX
a.	sod-i-ut-ot	*!			*			
b.	sod-i-uy-ot	*!					*	
c.	sod-iY-ut-ot				*!		*	
d.	sod-iY-uy-ot				*!		**	*
e.	sod-uy-ot		*!				*	*
f.	sod-iY-ot		*!				*	**
g.	sod-iY-u-ot	*!					*	*
h.	sod-iY-uC-ot			*!			*	*
i. ☞ ⊙						*		

Candidates (a–d) stand for the four possible forms, the given the two processes: *y* epenthesis after *-i* and *t* replacement by *y*. In candidate (d), both processes take place, in (c), only epenthesis, in (b), only replacement and in (a), none of the above (i.e. the faithful candidate). Candidates (e–h) involve deletion of the suffix segments, as is the case with /rakáv-et-ot/ → *rakav-ót* 'trains' and /kacáf-et-i/ → *kacaf-t-í* 'creamy' (§3.1). In candidate (e), *-i* is deleted, and in (f), *-ut* is deleted. In (g), the *t* of *-ut* is deleted, and in (h), the *t* of *-ut* is replaced by another consonant (other than *y*). All the candidates, except the null one, violate the constraints outranking MPARSE, and therefore the null candidate is optimal. The hierarchy below accounts for all cases of identity resolution, including the null output.

(16)   ONSET, MAXV$_{[+high]}$, DEP, OCP ≫ MPARSE ≫ *SPREAD, MAX

5 Surface identity

There are two unrelated cases of surface identity (§2.3), involving adjacent and non-adjacent *-Vt* suffixes with a high vowel. The ranking OCP ≫ MPARSE cannot account for these cases, since it predicts that the null output (which violates MPARSE) will always win over the candidate with surface identity (which violates the OCP). Therefore the hierarchy in (16) must be revised.

5.1   Adjacent surface identity

As shown in (7), the OCP is violated when a *-Vt* suffix with a high vowel is followed by *-it* (e.g. *tarb-ut-ít* 'cultural FMSG', *tavn-it-it* 'structural FMSG').[15] Since *-ut* and *-it* surface as *-uy* and *-iy* respectively before *-ot* (e.g. *tarb-uy-ót* 'cultures', *tavn-iy-ót* 'patterns'), we would also expect them to have the same allomorph before *-it*, i.e. **tarb-uy-ít* and **tavn-iy-ít*.

The illformedness of these forms is due to the constraint $*[_\sigma yi$, which prohibits tautosyllabic *y* and *i*. Independent evidence for this constraint is drawn from masculine adjectives ending in *-i* when followed by the masculine plural suffix *-im*. Due to the constraint $*[_\sigma yi$ epenthesis is blocked and the form remains onsetless (thus $*[_\sigma yi \gg$ ONSET), though in casual speech the onsetless syllable may disappear (e.g. *tarb-ut-i-im ~ tarb-ut-im* 'cultural MSPL').

The constraint $*[_\sigma yi$ must be ranked above the OCP, to allow *tarb-ut-ít* to win over **tarb-uy-it*.

(17) $*[_\sigma yi \gg$ OCP – */tarb-ut-it/* → *tarb-ut-it* 'cultural FMSG'

tarb-ut-it	$*[_\sigma yi$	OCP
a. tarb-uy-it	*!	
b. ☞ tarb-ut-it		*

Recall, however, that MPARSE is crucially ranked below OCP. The question is then why the output of */tarb-út-it/* is not the null output, as would be predicted by the ranking $*[_\sigma yi \gg$ OCP $\gg$ MPARSE.

The relevant distinction between inputs */tarb-út-it/* and */sod-i-út-ot/*, where the latter results in the null output, is their lexical category, adjective and noun respectively. Indeed, in both forms, the rightmost suffix is inflectional; *-it* assigns gender (fm.) and number (sg.) to the adjective and *-ot* assigns number (pl.) to the noun (recall that the plural suffix does not assign gender). However, they differ in the type of inflection; that of the adjectives is contextual inflection while that of the nouns is inherent inflection. This distinction, drawn in Anderson (1992) and Booij (1996), isolates the paradigms of categories that "trigger" inflection (inherent inflection) from those which are "assigned" inflection by syntactic context (in our case agreement).[16] In Hebrew, an adjective agrees in number and

---

[15] In addition, there are a few lexical exceptions where *-it* remains surface true when the plural suffix is added (e.g. *xan-ít – xan-it-ót* 'spear(s)'; cf. *xav-ít – xav-iy-ót* 'barrel(s)'). There are no such examples with *-ut*.

[16] As noted in Bat-El (2006a), this distinction is also manifested with respect to redupli-

gender with the noun it modifies (2), and thus the noun is the "trigger" of inflection while the adjective is "assigned" inflection.[17] Further evidence for this distinction is drawn from the regularity of the paradigms. There are quite a few exceptions in the nominal paradigm, where a masculine noun takes the plural suffix subcategorized for feminine (e.g. *xalón – xalon-ót* 'window(s) ms.'), and to a lesser extent when a feminine noun takes the plural suffix subcategorized for masculine (e.g. *ʃoʃan-á – ʃoʃan-ím* 'rose(s) fm.'). There are no such exceptions in the adjectival paradigm (nor in the verbal paradigm).

I thus assume, as in Rice (2007) and Wolf and McCarthy (this volume), that MPARSE is a morphologically conditioned family of constraints, specified for the type of inflectional paradigm. The more specific constraint MPARSE$_{CI}$, which prohibits the null output in contextual inflection (CI), is ranked above OCP, while the general (not specified) MPARSE, as in (16), is ranked below OCP.

(18)   MPARSE$_{CI}$ ≫ OCP ≫ MPARSE

tarb-ut-it	$*[_\sigma yi$	MPARSE$_{CI}$	OCP	MPARSE
a. tarb-uy-it	*!			
b. ☞ tarb-ut-it			*	
c. ⊙		*!		*

If we incorporate derivational paradigms into the study of gaps (Raffelsiefen 2004, Rebrus and Törkenczy this volume), the MPARSE family can be expanded to the universal ranking MPARSE$_{CI}$ ≫ MPARSE$_{II}$ ≫ MPARSE (where II stands for inherent inflection). This ranking is based on a lexicalization scale (in the spirit of Bybee 1985): contextual inflection >

---

cation, which, in Hebrew, only characterizes derivational relations. Therefore, reduplication is never found in the verb tense paradigm, which is contextual inflection, but there are a few nouns, i.e. inherent inflection, whose plural form is reduplicated (e.g. *lev – levav-ót* 'heart(s)').

[17] A similar case appears in Hebrew truncated imperatives (derived from the future form), where the null output appears when the expected form violates the SSG (though the base can serve as a filler; see §6). However, if the masculine form exists, there must also be a feminine form (Bat-El 2005).

Masculine		Feminine		
Base	Imperative	Base	Imperative	
tiftax	ftax	tiftexi	ftexi	'to open'
tilmad	⊙ (*lmad)	tilmedi	⊙ (*lmedi)	'to learn'
teʃev	ʃev	teʃvi	ʃvi	'to sit'
telex	lex	telxi	lexi (*lxi)	'to go'

inherent inflection > derivation. Each type of morphology can be further expanded to specific categories, as proposed in Rice (2007) and Wolf and McCarthy (this volume). That is, the more lexical the paradigm is, the more likely it is to have gaps. A paradigm with gaps is traditionally referred to as a defective paradigm (Rebrus and Törkenczy this volume), which entails some type of irregularity. However, this is not an irregularity with respect to the grammar, as shown in the analysis of the null output (§4), but rather with respect to the completeness of the paradigm. Nevertheless, paradigm completeness and grammar regularity follow the same scale, where derivational paradigms exhibit the highest degree of irregularity/incompleteness and contextual inflectional paradigms the lowest degree.

The analysis in this section required the addition of $*[_\sigma yi$ and MPARSE$_{CI}$ above the OCP. Onsetless adjectives such as *tarb-ut-i-ím* 'cultural MSPL' (contextual inflection) suggest that $*[_\sigma yi$ and MPARSE$_{CI}$ also outrank ONSET.

(19)   MAXV$_{[+high]}$, DEP, $*[_\sigma yi$, MPARSE$_{CI}$ $\gg$
                        ONSET, OCP $\gg$ MPARSE $\gg$ *SPREAD, MAX

5.2   Non-adjacent surface identity

The analysis proposed in §3 accounts for adjacent as well as non-adjacent identity avoidance. However, as shown in (8) above, there are cases where non-adjacent identity is preserved in the output (e.g. /tarb-ut-í-ut/ → *tarb-ut-iY-út* 'civility', /tavn-it-í-ut/ → *tavn-it-iY-út* 'structuralism').

This case of identity cannot be attributed to MPARSE$_{CI}$ (§5.1) since these forms do not involve contextual inflectional; these are nouns (rather than adjectives) ending with the derivational suffix *-ut*. Without MPARSE$_{CI}$, the ranking OCP $\gg$ MPARSE would wrongly predict the null output as the optimal candidate, since the two non-null candidates of /tarb-ut-í-ut/, i.e. *tarb-ut-iY-ut* and **tarb-uy-iY-ut*, violate the OCP (the latter also violates $*[_\sigma yi)$.

The difference between /tarb-ut-í-ut/, whose output violates the OCP at a distance and /sod-i-ut-ot/, whose output is null, can be viewed below, taking into consideration, in both cases, the null candidate (iii), the candidates with two *t*s (ii) and those with two *y*s (i). As noted in §4, these are the three candidates that survive all the constraints up to the OCP. The crucial distinction to be observed is whether a candidate exhibits adjacent identity (AI) or non-adjacent identity (NAI).

(20)　　Adjacent vs. non-adjacent identity

a.	/sod-i-ut-ot/		b.		/tarb-ut-i-ut/	
i.	sod-iY-uy-ot	AI	i.		tarb-uy-iY-ut	AI
ii.	sod-iY-ut-ot	AI	ii.	☞	tarb-ut-iY-ut	NAI
iii. ☞ ⊙			iii.		⊙	

The relation between the input and the candidates is identical in the two forms in (20). In all the non-null candidates, there is an epenthetic *y* after the adjectival *-i*. In candidates (i), the *t* of (the non-final) *-ut* is replaced by *y*; in candidates (ii), the *-Vt* suffixes are faithful to the input, and candidates (iii) are the null output. However, due to the different morphological structure of the two forms, there is a surface distinction between the two candidate sets; In (20a), the two non-null candidates exhibit adjacent identity, while in (20b), only one does; the other one (candidate (ii)) exhibits non-adjacent identity. This suggests that the null candidate is better than a candidate with adjacent identity (20a), but a candidate with non-adjacent identity is better than the null candidate (20b). In addition, the cases where non-adjacent identity is amended (4) suggest that no identity is better than non-adjacent identity. The hierarchy of preference is thus as follows:

(21)　　Hierarchy of preference
　　　　No identity > Non-adjacent identity > Null output > Adjacent identity

The role of adjacency, or more precisely proximity, in identity avoidance is familiar from consonant co-occurrence restrictions on Arabic (and Hebrew) $C_1VC_2VC_3$ stems. These restrictions, which prohibit homorganic consonants, are respected to a lesser extent on $C_1\&C_3$ than on $C_1\&C_2$ (Greenberg 1950, McCarthy 1986, 1988, 1994, Mester 1986, Padgett 1995, Frisch et al. 2002). Notice that here too, as in the case of the identity in the suffix domain, the vowels do not play a role. This fact cannot be attributed to the Semitic non-concatenative structure, because the vowels of the suffixes are not morphologically distinct from the consonants. It is not the case that Hebrew vowels are, in general, ignored by the OCP, since identical (and homorganic) adjacent consonants without an intervening vowel are impossible, while non-adjacent ones, as noted earlier, can be found in certain structures. Rather, the vowel is a unit in a proximity hierarchy of the type proposed in Suzuki (1998), which provides a gradient distance (starting with strict adjacency) defined in terms of phonological units (see also Rose and Walker 2004). The proximity hierarchy relevant to the present discussion (extracted from the detailed hierarchy proposed by Suzuki) involves only two types of distances, C_iVC_i, referred to here as adjacent identity, and $C_i\sigma C_i$, which is thus non-adjacent identity.

Given the binary opposition relevant to the present discussion, I distinguish between two OCP constraints here: the specific, and thus dominating, OCP_V (for adjacent identity), which prohibits identical consonants interrupted by one vowel (C_iVC_i), and the general OCP (for non-adjacent identity), which prohibits identical consonants regardless of their distance. Of course, above OCP_V stands $OCP\varnothing$ referring to strict adjacency, which, as noted above, is never violated in Hebrew. To account for the preference of the candidate with non-adjacent identity over the null output, MPARSE has to be ranked between these constraints.

(22)　　$OCP_V \gg$ MPARSE $\gg$ OCP

tarb-ut-i-ut	OCP_V	MPARSE	OCP	*SPREAD	MAX
a. ☞ tarb-ut-iY-ut			*	*	
b.　　tarb-uy-iY-ut	*!		*	**	*
c.　　⊙		*!			

This is the last case under consideration here, and thus the final version of the constraint ranking is as follows:

(23)　　$MAXV_{[+high]}$, DEP, $*[_\sigma yi$, $MPARSE_{CI} \gg$

　　　　　　　　ONSET, $OCP_V \gg$ MPARSE $\gg$ OCP, *SPREAD, MAX

All the cases discussed in the previous section follow from this hierarchy. Adjacent identity is amended when a candidate with no identity is available (§3); otherwise the null output is obtained (§4). As for non-adjacent identity, it is tolerated in the absence of a candidate with no identity (22), but avoided when a candidate with no identity is available (24).

(24)　　Resolving non-adjacent identity

map-it-on-et	OCP_V	MPARSE	OCP	*SPREAD	MAX
a. ☞ map-iy-on-et				*	*
b.　　map-it-on-et			*!		
c.　　⊙		*!			

In (24), the OCP$_V$ is not relevant since there is no candidate with the structure C_iVC_i, and thus MPARSE and OCP get to eliminate the non-optimal candidates.

6   Absolute vs. unstable gap

The gap discussed in this paper is an "absolute" gap, i.e. speakers do not accept any other candidate to fill the empty position in the paradigm. There is another gap in Hebrew, also in the paradigm of the feminine plural, which, unlike the gap discussed above is "unstable". An unstable gap may be filled upon request (in judgment and production), though with a certain degree of hesitation, and with comments such as "possible but does not sound good". Rice, for example, notes that speakers may employ several different strategies to fill the gap in the Norwegian imperative paradigm, and Oostendorp proposes an analysis predicting the various forms that may fill the gap (what he terms "question marked forms") in the diminutive paradigm of Dutch. Albright's analysis of lexical gaps in Spanish verbal paradigm is based on uncertainty in grammar, which allows speakers to produce a form to fill the gap, though not without hesitation. The degree of acceptability is also a matter of processing, where priming may increase acceptability, as it does in regularization of irregular English past forms, primed by the vowel of the preceding nouns (Stemberger 2004). Oostendorp (this volume) proposes that the degree of acceptability of the gap filler is derived from the number of rankings

A brief description of the unstable gap is provided below (see further discussion in Bat-El 1997). Taking into consideration the intuitive assumption that paradigms with gaps are indeed defective, I propose that paradigms are expected to be unstable and provide the condition under which they have to be absolute.

The feminine diminutive forms end with the suffixes *-on* followed *-et*, because the suffix *-on* is specified for masculine, and thus *-et* is added in order to preserve the gender of the base. Without the *-et* after the diminutive -ON, a 'girl' *yald-á* would turn into a 'little boy' *yald-ón* (recall that *-a* disappears before a suffix), a 'serviette' *map-ít* will turn into a 'serviette holder' *map-iy-ón* (there is also a non-diminutive *-on*, functioning as a general nominal suffix), and *xan-út* 'shop' will end up as a non-existing form **xan-ut-ón/*xan-uy-ón* (though it could be some noun related to a shop, but not a 'little shop'). When Hebrew speakers are provided with the plural form of the feminine diminutive, i.e. with the suffix *-ot* (which the dictionary provides), they judge it as "strange", and when asked to provide the plural form, they hesitate, though eventually they produce it. I take these reactions (in judgment and production) as an indication of a gap, though, as will be discussed below, not an absolute gap.

(25)   Feminine diminutives

Base	DIMINUTIVE	PLURAL – ⊙	
matan-á	matan-ón-et	*matan-on-ót	'gift'
magév-et	magav-ón-et	*magav-on-ót	'towel'
map-ít	map-iy-ón-et	*map-iy-on-ót	'serviette'
xan-út	xan-uy-ón-et	*xan-uy-on-ót	'shop'

As argued in Bat-El (1997), the gap in this paradigm is due to gender mismatch, obtained in a morphologically transparent surface structure.

The plural suffixes, as noted in §2, are subcategorized for gender, such that *-ot* selects a base specified for feminine and *-im* selects a base specified for masculine. Crucially, the plural suffixes do not assign gender, and thus the gender of a plural form is obtained via feature percolation, i.e. the gender of the singular base is the gender of the plural form. The gender of the base is either inherent (in the absence of a derivational suffix), or assigned by the suffix attached on the last cycle. Given the morphological structure $[[X]\text{-}\acute{o}n\text{-}et]_{FM}$, where the feminine specification is due to the suffix *-et*, the expected plural form is $/[[[X]\acute{o}n\text{-}et]_{FM}\ ot]_{FMPL}/ \rightarrow [[[X]on]_{FM}\acute{o}t]_{FMPL}$ (recall from §3.1 that *-et* disappears when the plural suffix is added).

The output structure $[[[X]on]_{FM}\acute{o}t]_{FMPL}$ exhibits surface ambiguity, since the suffix *-on* is specified for masculine, but it is the rightmost suffix in a base specified for feminine. The plural suffix thus matches the gender specification of its base (assigned by the suffix *-et*, which does not appear in the output), but it does not match the gender specification of the rightmost suffix *-on* (26c).

There are two other cases of potential ambiguity, but they do not exhibit such a mismatch. The first case involves nouns ending in *-et*, which disappears when the plural suffix is added. Such nouns are pluralized as expected, i.e. with *-ot*, although the suffix assigning the feminine gender does not surface (e.g. *rakév-et – rakav-ót* 'train(s)', *zamér-et – zamar-ót* 'singer(s)'). I assume that the base of such *-et* nouns is not specified for gender. This assumption can hold also for animate nouns, where the base of *-et* is a masculine surface form, since masculine is the unmarked gender in Hebrew (see Berent et al. 2002 for an experimental study supporting this view). That is, the plural suffix does not mismatch the gender of the stem/base, because the latter does not have a gender specification (26a).

The other potential ambiguity is found in nouns ending in the nominal (non-diminutive) suffix *-on*. These nouns are always masculine, as opposed to nouns without a suffix, which can be either feminine (e.g. *xérev* 'sword') or masculine (e.g. *dégel* 'flag'). It is thus assumed that this type of *-on* is also specified for masculine. Although these *-on* nouns are masculine, they usually take the plural suffix *-ot* (e.g. *xalon-ót* 'windows', *dimyon-ót* 'imaginations') though a few take *-im* (e.g. *xelbon-ím* 'egg white, protein', *tilyon-ím* 'medallions'). This irregularity, which must be lexically specified, does not affect the gender of the plural form, i.e. the plural form is masculine (recall that the plural suffix does not assign gender).[18] Therefore, there is no mismatch between the rightmost suffix of the base and the gender subcategorization of the plural form (26b).

(26)   Surface gender (mis)match (input suffixes that do not surface are in bold)

a. FM NOUN no overt FM suffix	b. MS NOUN overt MS suffix	c. FM NOUN no overt FM suffix overt MS suffix
rakav **-et** -ot ∅ FM PL	xal -on -ot ∅ MS PL	matan **-a** -on **-et** -ot ∅ FM MS FM PL
rakav]$_{FM}$ ot]$_{FMPL}$ ∅	xal-on]$_{MS}$ot]$_{MSPL}$ MS	matan]on]$_{FM}$ ot]$_{FMPL.}$ MS

In order to account for the gap in the feminine diminutive forms (26c), I assume the constraint ranking *MISMATCH ≫ MPARSE, where the former is a morphological constraint prohibiting a gender mismatch between the gender of the rightmost morpheme of the base and the gender subcategorization of the plural form. That is, this paradigm, unlike the one discussed earlier, has a morphologically driven gap.

This gap, as noted above, is not absolute. Hebrew speakers are "reluctant" to provide the expected plural form, i.e. $^{?}$*matan-on-ót*, but can produce it if required. They also judge the expected form as "strange" but they do not say that it is absolutely impossible (Schwarzwald 2002). I thus propose that "upon request", speakers reverse the ranking of these two constraints, to provide the expected form. Oostendorp (this volume) also proposes a constraint reranking to account for the gap fillers. However,

---

[18]Becker (2008) argues for the tendency to assign the suffix *-ot* in stems that have *o*, regardless of gender.

in his analysis the reranking is not given upon request, and thus the null output competes with the gap fillers. The null output wins when there are more constraint permutations where it is optimal. This approach wrongly predicts that if only two constraints are involved, as in the present case, the null output and the gap filler have an equal status.

Turning back to the phonologically driven gap discussed in the previous sections, there are three candidates that survive the constraint up to the OCP; the null candidate, and two other candidates that violate the OCP, one with two *y*s and another with two *t*s, and the third one is the null candidate. The reversal of the ranking resulting in the null output, OCP ≫ MPARSE (27a), would allow the candidate with the two *t*s to be optimal (27b).

(27) a. OCP ≫ MPARSE: */sod-i-út-ot/* → ⊙

sod-i-ut-ot	OCP	MPARSE	*SPREAD	MAX
a. sod-iY-ut-ot	*!		*	
b. sod-iY-uy-ot	*!		**	*
c. ☞ ⊙		*		

b. MPARSE ≫ OCP: */sod-i-út-ot/* → **sod-iY-ut-ot*

sod-i-ut-ot	MPARSE	OCP	*SPREAD	MAX
a. ☞ sod-iY-ut-ot		*	*	
b. sod-iY-uy-ot		*	**!	*
c. ⊙	*!			

The question is why **sod-iY-ut-ót* (the optimal candidate in (27b)) is not provided upon request, i.e. why the paradigm is absolute. I propose below that in order to fill the gap with a certain form, speakers search for a form similar to the filler.

A paradigm is a network of words related on two axes, the horizontal axis of the stems/lexemes and the vertical axis of the morphological category (van Marle 1985). Studies in Correspondence Theory are usually concerned with relations on the horizontal axis (i.e. among stems), but actually, there are also relations on the vertical axis.

I propose that speakers are always willing to fill the gap in order to arrive at a perfect paradigm (in the sense that all the cells are filled), and they do so by searching for a form whose phonological structure is identical to the expected form. After arriving at the expected form (via constraint reranking), they look at cross-paradigm relations to support this form. In the case under consideration here, they look for paradigms involving *X-ut-ot*. However, they do not get any support since it is always the case that

-ut (not preceded by *-i*) surfaces as *-uy* before *-ot*. I thus claim that gap fillers must exhibit faithfulness on the vertical axis to a surface form in the language. Note the forms such as *nexut-ót* 'inferior FMPL' do not support *X-ut-ot* since *ut* in *nexut-ót* is not a suffix but rather part of the stem, and thus morphologically different.

In the morphologically-driven paradigm discussed in this section, the form filling the gap gets support from another paradigm. The sequence *-on-ot*, as in the expected form *?matan-on-ót* (26c), appears in *xal-on-ót* 'windows' (26b), as well as in other similar forms, such as *fitf-on-ót* 'floods', *zixr-on-ót* 'memories' and *nicx-on-ót* 'victories'. Indeed, the *-on* in these forms is not the diminutive *-on* that appears in *?matan-on-ót*, but the phonological identity is sufficient to provide support for the gap filler, and thus to make the paradigm unstable. Actually, it is not only the phonological identity, since there are nouns with the non-diminutive *-on* which include the diminutive property, though they do not take the plural suffix *-ot* (e.g. *maxʃév* 'computer' – *maxʃev-ón* 'calculator', *gag* 'roof' – *gag-ón* 'cupola', *séfer* 'book' – *sifr-ón* 'booklet'). These *-on* nouns do not denote 'little X', where X is the base, but rather a Y, where Y is related to and smaller than X.

I thus conclude that an unstable gap is unmarked, since speakers strive to achieve a perfect paradigm. Absolute gaps may arise only when the filler of the gap does not have a supporting similar form. The evaluation of similarity remains a topic for further research, and so does the number of supporting forms required to fill a gap.

7 Conclusion

The feminine paradigm of Hebrew nouns employs various strategies to avoid identity in the suffix domain, one of which is the null output. Given the constraint ranking developed for the surface forms that amend the input identity, the null output is inevitable. That is, the null output is not an exception. Nevertheless the paradigm is exceptional (or defective), since it has a gap.

Inflectional paradigms strive to be complete, and therefore unstable gaps, those which are filled upon request, are more common. Absolute gaps arise only when there are no supporting forms similar to the potential filler.

A potential filler which was not discussed here, nor in the other papers in this volume, is the "identity form", i.e. the one identical to the base. Chimwi:ni, for example, chooses the identity form to avoid a gap in the infinitive paradigm, allowing syncretism instead (Kisseberth and Abasheikh 1976, 2004). The prefix *ku-*, attached to the imperative to form an infinitive, undergoes vowel deletion and spirantization when the stem begins with a voiceless obstruent (e.g. */ku-pik-a/* → *x-pik-a* 'to cook'; cf. *ku-wak-a* 'to build'). However, when the stem begins with *x*, the prefix does not have a surface realization and the infinitive is identical to the imperative (e.g. *xor-a* 'to scratch, scratch!', *xarib-a* 'to corrupt, corrupt!). The identity form can also be a gap filler, as it is the case in Norwegian imperative paradigm, where the infinitive is provided by some speakers when the imperative is the null output (Rice 2007).

That is, the identity candidate competes with the null candidate, and the question remaining for further research is whether the selection of one or the other is just a matter of language specific constraint ranking, or whether it follows from some general principles contingent upon the type of paradigm.

References

Albright, A. (this volume) Lexical and morphological conditioning of paradigm gaps.

Anderson, S. (1992) *A-Morphous Morphology*. Cambridge: Cambridge University Press.

Bat-El, O. (1989) *Phonology and Word Structure in Modern Hebrew*. Ph.D. dissertation, UCLA.

Bat-El, O. (1993) Parasitic metrification in the Modern Hebrew stress system. *The Linguistic Review* 10: 189–210.

Bat-El, O. (1997). On the visibility of word internal morphological features. *Linguistics* 35: 289–316.

Bat-El, O. (2002) True truncation in colloquial Hebrew imperatives. *Language* 78: 651–83.

Bat-El, O. (2005). Competing principles of paradigm uniformity: evidence from Hebrew imperative paradigm. In L.J. Downing, T.A. Hall, and R. Raffelsiefen (eds.) *Paradigms in Phonological Theory* 44–64. Oxford: Oxford University Press.

Bat-El, O. (2006a) Consonant copying and consonant identity: the segmental and prosodic structure of Hebrew reduplication. *Linguistic Inquiry* 37(2): 179–210

Bat-El, O. (2006b) What does the morpho-phonology say about Hebrew participles? Paper presented at the Linguistic Interdisciplinary Colloquium, Tel-Aviv University.

Becker, M. (2008) Phonological Trends in the Lexicon: the Role of Constraints. Ph.D. dissertation, University of Massachusetts, Amherst.

Berent, I., Pinker, S. and Shimron, J. (2002) The nature of regularity and irregularity: evidence from Hebrew nominal inflection. *Journal of Psycholinguistics Research* 31: 459–502.

Bolozky, S. and Schwarzwald, O. (1992) On the derivation of Hebrew forms with the +*ut* suffix. *Hebrew Studies* 33: 51–69.

Booij, G. (1996) Inherent versus contextual inflection and the split morphology hypothesis. In G.E. Booij and J. van Marle (eds.) *Yearbook of Morphology 1995* 1–16. Dordrecht: Kluwer.

Bybee, J. (1985) *Morphology: A Study of the Relation between Meaning and Form.* Amsterdam: John Benjamins.

Clements, G. and Keyser, S. (1983) *CV Phonology: A Generative Theory of the Syllable.* Cambridge, MA: The MIT Press.

Frisch, S., Pierrehumbert, J. and Broe, M. (2004) Similarity avoidance and the OCP. *Natural Language and Linguistic Theory* 22: 179–228.

Greenberg, J. (1950) The patterning of root morphemes in Semitic. *Word* 6: 162–181.

Itô, J. & Hankamer, J. (1989) Notes on monosyllabism in Turkish. In J. Itô and J. Runner (eds.) *Phonology at Santa Cruz* 61–69. Santa Cruz: Linguistics Research Center.

Kisseberth, C. and Abasheikh, M. I. (1976) Chimwiini prefix morphophonemics. *Studies in Linguistic Sciences* 6: 142–73.

Kisseberth, C. and Abasheikh, M. I. (2004) *The Chimwiini Lexicon Exemplified.* Research Institute for Languages and Cultures of Asia and Africa: Tokyo University of Foreign Studies.

van Marle, J. (1985) *On the Paradigmatic Dimension of Morphological Creativity.* Dordrecht: Foris.

McCarthy, J. J. (1986) OCP effects: Gemination and antigemination. *Linguistic Inquiry* 17: 207–63

McCarthy, J. J. (1988) Feature geometry and dependency: a review. *Phonetica* 43: 84–108.

McCarthy, J. J. (1994) The phonetics and phonology of Semitic pharyngeals. In P. Keating (ed.) *Papers in Laboratory Phonology III* 191–283.

Cambridge: Cambridge University Press.

McCarthy, J. J. and Prince, A. (1995) Faithfunless and reduplicative identity. In J. Beckman, L. Walsh Dickey and S. Urbanczyk (eds.) *University of Massachusetts Occasional Paper: Papers in Optimality Theory* 249–384. Amherst, MA: GSLA.

Mester, A. (1986) *Studies in Tier Structure*. Ph.D. dissertation, University of Massachusetts, Amherst.

van Oostendorp, M. (this volume) Dutch Diminutives and the question mark.

Padgett, J. (1995) *Stricture in Feature Geometry*. Stanford: CSLI Publications.

Paz, B. (2006) The dual suffix in Modern Hebrew. Ms., Tel-Aviv University.

Plag, I. (1998) Morphological haplology in a constraint-based morphophonology. In W. Kehrein and R. Wiese (eds). *Phonology and Morphology of the Germanic Languages* 199–215. Tübingen: Niemeyer.

Prince, A. and Smolensky, P. (1993) Optimality Theory: Constraint Interaction in Generative Grammar. Report RuCCS-TR-2. New Brunswick, NJ: Rutgers University Center for Cognitive Science. ROA 537 `http://roa.rutgers.edu`

Raffelsiefen, R. (2004) Absolute ill-formedness and other morphological effects. *Phonology* 21: 91–142.

Rice, C. (2007) Gaps and repairs at the phonology-morphology interface. *Journal of Linguistics* 43(1):197–221.

Rose, S. and Walker, R. (2004) A typology of consonant agreement as correspondence. *Language* 80: 475–531.

Schwarzwald, O. (1991a) Grammatical vs. lexical plural formation in Hebrew. *Folia Linguistica* 25: 577–608.

Schwarzwald, O. (2002) *Studies in Hebrew Morphology*. Tel-Aviv: The Open University of Israel (in Hebrew).

Stemberger, J. (1981) Morphological haplology. *Language* 57: 791–817.

Suzuki, K. (1998) *A Typological Investigation of Dissimilation*. Ph.D. dissertation, The University of Arizona.

Yip, M. (1998) Identity avoidance in phonology and morphology. In S. Lapointe, D. Brentari and P. Farrell (eds.) *Morphology and Its Relation to Phonology and Syntax* 216–46. Stanford: CSLI Publications.

Wolf, M. and McCarthy, J. J. (this volume) Less than zero: correspondence and the null output.

7 Covert and overt defectiveness in paradigms*

Péter Rebrus and Miklós Törkenczy
*Research Institute for Linguistics, Hungarian Academy of Sciences,
Eötvös Loránd University, Budapest*

1 Introduction

Defectiveness, i. e., the occurrence of gaps in a paradigm,[1] is a special
case of absolute ill-formedness (Prince & Smolensky 1993/2004). Defectiveness received only sporadic attention in the pre-OT generative literature
(e.g. Halle 1973, Hetzron 1975, Iverson 1981) although there were occasional references to the phenomenon in works usually focussing on some
other aspect(s) of (morpho)phonological structure.[2] Recent interest in paradigm gaps within phonological theory is primarily motivated by the fact
that — as defectiveness by its nature consists in the lack of any output —
it poses an obvious challenge to Optimality Theory (a problem recognised
as early as Prince & Smolensky 1993/2004).[3] Accordingly, research on

---

*We would like to thank Péter Siptár, András Cser, and Adam Albright, Outi Bat-El,
Sylvia Blaho, Martin Krämer, Geraldine Legendre, Bruce Morén, Marc van Oostendorp,
Orhan Orgun, Curt Rice, Paul Smolensky, Ralf Vogel and Matthew Wolf, the participants
of the gap workshop in Oslo in 2006 for valuable comments. This work was supported by
an Országos Tudományos Kutatási Alapprogramok grant (OTKA49327).

[1] In this paper we use the term *paradigm* in a sense which is not restricted to inflection.
We take it to mean a set of words that share a morpheme, i. e., 'a set of words that share
(i) the same value in some morphosyntactic dimension, or (ii) the same stem.' Rebrus &
Törkenczy (2005a): 265. Note that according this definition not only stems, but also affixes
have paradigms (compare Kenstowicz 2005, Steriade 2000).

[2] E.g. English: Carstairs-McCarthy (1998b); Basque: Stump (1998); Bella Coola:
Bagemihl (1991); Catalan: Cabré & Kenstowicz (1995); Hungarian: Károly (1957), Siptár & Törkenczy (2000), Rebrus (2000); Norwegian: Kristoffersen (2000); Russian: Halle
(1973); Runyankore: Poletto (1998); Spanish: Butt (1997); Swedish: Eliasson (1975);
Tagalog: Schachter & Otanes (1972); Turkish: Inkelas & Orgun (1995).

[3] Defectiveness is actually just as problematic for derivational approaches like SPE or
its later lexical, autosegmental, metrical etc. modifications because they are also biassed to
produce an output (cf. Törkenczy 2001, 2002), but this issue was rarely addressed within
derivational theory (to the best of our knowledge, the only papers directly addressing this
issue within derivational phonology are Hetzron 1975 and Iverson 1981).

paradigm gaps concentrates on the technical tools, components and modifications (such as the *Null Parse* (e.g. McCarthy & Wolf this volume), the constraint MPARSE (e.g. Raffelsiefen 1996, 2004), the *Control* component (e.g. Orgun & Sprouse 1999), the theory of *Optimal Paradigms* (McCarthy 2005, Rice 2005abc)) that OT can utilise to handle defectiveness despite the fact that by definition in OT there is always a winning candidate.

In this paper we take a somewhat different approach and pursue a 'lexically motivated' inquiry into defectiveness which tries to explain the existence of paradigm gaps with reference to the patterns of allomorphs within the paradigm. This approach is different from an analysis that attributes defectiveness to constraint ranking or a filter since it is non-arbitrary in the sense that it attempts to relate paradigm gaps to other paradigmatic patterns found in the language and predict the probability of their occurrence on the basis of these patterns (which is more in the vein of Albright 2003).

Defective behaviour may have a non-phonological motivation. Lexical, semantic, stylistic and aesthetic (!) reasons are also referred to in the literature (e.g. Jensen 1990, Katamba 1993, Mayerthaler 1988, Carstairs-McCarthy 1998a, Baerman & Corbett 2005). For example, English *jeans*, Hungarian *légutak* 'respiratory tract' are *plurale tantum* so they do not have singular forms: **jean*, **légút*.[4] The lack of singular forms cannot be explained by any identifiable phonological, morphological, semantic etc. characteristics of these nouns — it is a truly arbitrary property of these morphemes that they lack singular forms. Crucially for us, defectiveness in this type of cases is unrelated to phonology. In the present paper we only concentrate on phonology-related defectiveness.

In what follows we give a typology of phonology-related defectiveness on the basis of the cases discussed in the literature (cf. Rebrus & Törkenczy 2005b, Törkenczy 2001a, 2002a, Baerman & Corbett 2005) and then compare the properties identified with the general characteristics of the paradigm of defective verbs in Hungarian.

There seem to be two basic kinds of phonology-related gaps: *phonologically motivated* vs. *arbitrary*.

---

[4]Throughout this paper we shall use normal Hungarian orthography unless it is crucially important to give a phonetic transcription, Consonant letters typically have the transparent values, although there are some notable exceptions: e.g. ⟨sz⟩ [s], ⟨s⟩ [ʃ], ⟨cs⟩ [t͡ʃ], ⟨ny⟩ [ɲ]. The doubling of a consonant letter or the first letter of a consonant digraph indicates a geminate consonant. Note that the single or double acute accent above a vowel letter means length and not stress. The phonetic values of non-transparent vowel letters are the following: ⟨í⟩ [iː], ⟨ü⟩ [y], ⟨ű⟩ [yː], ⟨ú⟩ [uː], ⟨ö⟩ [ø], ⟨ő⟩ [øː], ⟨ó⟩ [oː], ⟨e⟩ [ɛ], ⟨é⟩ [eː], ⟨a⟩ [ɔ], ⟨á⟩ [aː]. For glosses of words unexplained in the text, see the Appendix.

Phonologically motivated paradigm gaps arise when a morphological operation (affixation, reduplication, truncation, etc.) is blocked if it should produce a string which is in violation of a phonological constraint. This type of gap can be characterised according to (i) the scope of the phonological constraint that motivates it and (ii) the nature of the inapplicable phonological repair that — if it could apply — would produce a form that would 'fill' it.

According to its scope the phonological constraint motivating a paradigmatic gap may be *specific* or *general*. It is specific if the constraint is lexically restricted to an affix/morphological operation. For instance, specific gaps of this kind occur in English word-formation: e.g. suffixation with deadjectival verb-forming *-en* has gaps with sonorant-final stems (cf. Carstairs-McCarthy 1998b, Raffelsiefen 1996, 2004). The phonological constraint may also hold generally true of the sound pattern of the language in question — such general gap occurs in Norwegian imperative formation, where violation of the general phonotactics/syllable structure constraints results in a gap (cf. Rice 2003, 2005a).

The following types of gaps may be distinguished depending on the nature of the (inapplicable) phonological repair. The phonological repair that could in principle apply to fill a paradigmatic gap may be *absolutely excluded* in the language in which the gap occurs, i. e., it may be missing from the entire system (e.g. consonant deletion in Hungarian). It may be *relatively excluded* and *lexically unconstrained*: this happens when the repair does exist in the system, but it is not available to repair a violation of a given constraint (which results in a gap), while the same strategy is available to repair a violation of another constraint. An example is epenthesis in Turkish, which applies to repair violations of syllable structure constraints and the ban on hiatus, but cannot repair subminimal inflected forms. (cf. Orgun & Sprouse 1999). A repair may be *relatively excluded* and *lexically constrained*, i. e., a particular repair is available for a lexically determined stem/affix class, but is not available for another stem/affix class. This occurs in English where stress movement is available for the affix *-ese* to repair a violation of the ban on stress clash (Japán+ése → *Jàpanése*), but it is unavailable for the affix *-eer* (*batón+éer* → ⊙), cf. Raffelsiefen (2004).

The other type of phonology related gap, which we have called *arbitrary* is not phonologically motivated in the sense that although there is some phonological property that it can be associated with, the gap is not the result of a morphological operation being blocked if it should produce a form that violates a phonological constraint. The non-existing form (the gap) is perfectly well-formed phonologically: there is no specific or general constraint that it violates. The paradigm gaps in Spanish discussed by Albright (2003) are of this kind.

In the case of phonologically motivated paradigm gaps it is the non-application of a process (the repair that would produce an allomorph which is phonologically well-formed) that results in a gap. In the case of arbitrary gaps both the application and the non-application of the process results in a phonologically well-formed alternant. Thus phonologically motivated defectiveness is an *anti-allomorphy* effect, but arbitrary phonology-related defectiveness is not.[5]

Independent of the distinction between phonologically motivated vs. arbitrary gaps, phonology-related defectiveness may be *analogy-bound* or not. In the former case a form is only possible if it is analogically reinforced/licensed, i. e., it contains a string that exists elsewhere in the paradigm. An example occurs in Icelandic, where the gaps in the imperative sub-paradigm of verbs do not occur with stems whose paradigm has a form (expressing some other dimension) that contains an identical allomorph (cf. Hansson 1999).[6] Hungarian also has an analogy-bound gap that occurs in the paradigm of a class of verb stems (Cs-stems, which we do not discuss in this paper — for an analysis see Rebrus and Törkenczy 2007).

Furthermore, phonology-related gaps may be category-bound or category-independent depending on whether or not a gap is restricted to some category in the broad sense, where a category may be a morphosyntactic value/dimension or a morphological category (of stems: noun, verb, etc; or of affixes: derivational, inflectional).

A gap that is restricted to a morphosyntactic dimension/value expressed in a paradigm occurs in Icelandic, where gaps are restricted to the imperative (as opposed to the past, where the same phonological state of affairs license a licit form cf. Hansson 1999).

Identical phonological conditions result in a gap in some morphological category, but not in others in Norwegian, where the violation of a sylla-

---

[5]This was recognised (but overgeneralised) by Iverson (1981): "[...] one characteristic common to all cases [of defectiveness] is that paradigms with gaps show no allomorphy of the root morpheme, but would if the gaps were filled" (p. 141).

[6]Interestingly, there is a minimally different case in Romanian, where a particular alternant is only possible in the derivational paradigm of a stem if it occurs in the inflectional paradigm of the same stem. However, here, unlike in Icelandic, the opposite state of affairs, i. e., the lack of analogical reinforcement by an identical allomorph, does not result in defectiveness as in this case another allomorph occurs (cf. Steriade 2006, 2008).

ble structure constraint results in phonologically motivated gaps in verbs, but not in nouns (cf. Rice 2003, 2005a).

Phonology-related gaps may be restricted to the inflectional or the derivational morphology. The morphological domain of Norwegian phonologically motivated gaps is the inflectional morphology (cf. Rice 2003) while in English gaps are derivational (cf. Raffelsiefen 1996, 2004). The more productive the morphological operation is, the more 'dramatic' defectiveness is (this is why the examples usually cited for defective behaviour tend to be inflectional). The typology discussed above is summarised in figure (1) (where dashed lines represent choices that are not mutually exclusive).

The OT analyses in the literature (and the pre-OT generative analyses too) concentrate on phonologically motivated defectivity and are designed to handle specific subtypes of it (e.g. the Control model (Orgun & Sprouse 1999) is designed to handle relatively excluded and lexically unconstrained gaps).

(1)   Typology of phonology related defectiveness

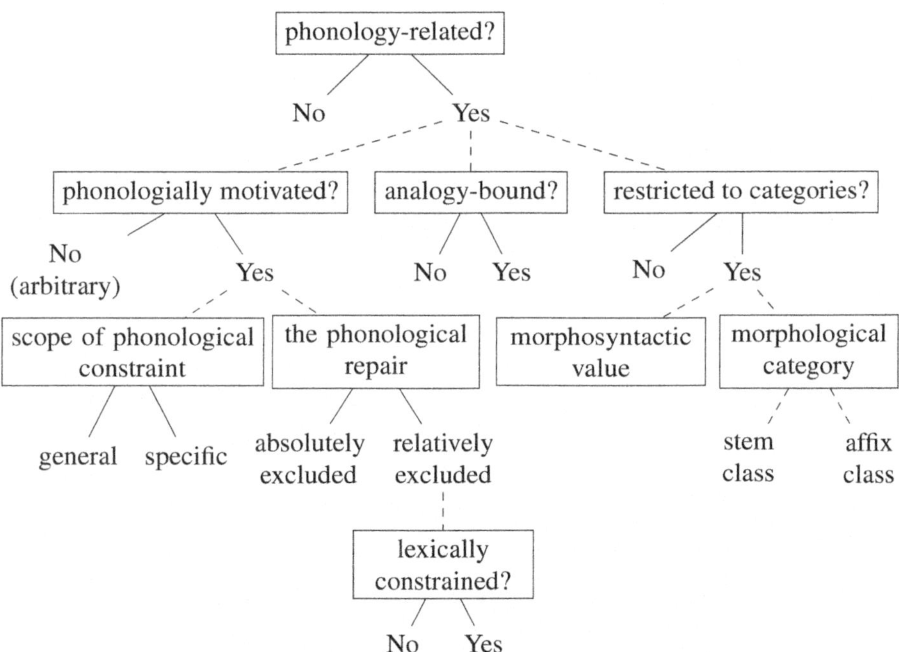

The analyses proposed make predictions about the nature of phonology related gaps and where they can occur. What makes the Hungarian gaps particularly interesting is that they represent a very complex type of defectiveness and there is an imperfect match between its properties and these predictions. We will discuss the Hungarian gaps later in detail (see Section 3.3); here we briefly point out these mismatches.

In Hungarian, the gaps occur in the inflectional and derivational morphology of the verb, and crucially the occurrence of gaps in the *inflectional* paradigm and the *derivational* paradigm of defective stems is determined by exactly the same factors, i. e., it is motivated by the same phonological constraint. This is problematic for an approach like Rice's (2005abc) since it is based on Optimal Paradigms Theory, which is strictly about inflectional paradigms (McCarthy 2005).

The Hungarian gaps are motivated by a phonotactic constraint but are lexically constrained since repair (epenthesis)[7] is only unavailable for a certain class of stems (the 'defective' stems) when they combine with a certain class of suffixes (the 'analytic' suffixes). This presents a difficulty for a Control type of analysis since violations of the same constraint are sometimes repaired, sometimes not by the same repair mechanism and thus the same constraint would have to be in Control and Eval at the same time[8] (cf. Törkenczy 2000, 2001a, 2002a, Rebrus & Törkenczy 2005b).

The distribution of gaps within the Hungarian verbal paradigm is determined by an interaction of (a) *phonotactics*, i. e., the shape of the stem/affix and (b) *'lexical'* or *morphophonological class* membership of (i) the stem and (ii) the affix. The distribution of the gaps is absolutely insensitive to what *morphosyntactic* dimension (value) the affix may express (*contra* Szépe, Gerstner & Szende 2004). Allomorphs of the same suffix (which expresses a specific dimension (value) within the paradigm) may differ as to their morphophonological class membership, which results in an asymmetrical distribution of gaps within the same dimension/value. These properties make Hungarian gaps a challenge to an approach that analyses gaps with reference to the ranking of a constraint that requires a given morphosyntactic dimension (value) to be expressed (cf. Rice 2005abc).

Before we go on to describe the Hungarian paradigm gaps in detail, there is an important theoretical question about defectiveness that we want to discuss.

---

[7]Other conceivable types of repair (like deletion) are out across the board.

[8]This can be handled by 'overkill', if we allow morpheme (class) specific constraint rankings, i. e., permitting a constraint ranking to be associated with a particular affix/stem independently of what the ranking may be for other affixes/stems (e.g. Raffelsiefen 1996, 2004), but that approach can be criticised on theoretical grounds unrelated to the issue at hand (cf. Rebrus & Törkenczy 2005b).

2 Covert defectiveness and the Zooming Effect

The fact that a gap occurs in a paradigm does not mean that the meaning associated with the gap cannot be expressed (cf. Carstairs-McCarthy 1998b). We shall use the term 'masking' to refer to the way(s) in which this is possible (irrespective of whether masking is by a single word or more than one). Masking may be *non-conventionalised* (unsystematic) or *conventionalised* (systematic). In the former case there is not one regular avoidance strategy that systematically applies to mask the gap, in the latter, there is. Non-conventionalised masking in the form of circumlocution is always possible.

For example, the Hungarian verb *csukl-* 'hiccup' is a defective verb, which lacks Subjunctive/Imperative forms (and also other forms, see Section 3.3 for the details). Thus, it is not possible to say **Ne csukolj!* or **Ne csuklj!* 'Don't hiccup!' using the regular imperative marker *-j*. Nevertheless, this meaning can be expressed by non-conventionalised masking. There are many alternative ways in which the gap can be avoided: *Fejezd be a csuklást!* 'Stop hiccuping!', *Nehogy elkezdj csuklani!* 'Don't you begin to hiccup!', etc.

Non-conventionalised masking need not be periphrastic. In English, de-adjectival verb-forming *-en* cannot attach to sonorant-final stems (e.g. Carstairs-McCarthy 1998b), which results in a phonologically motivated specific gap. As can be seen in (2), while periphrastic masking is always possible,[9] morphological ways of masking (e.g. conversion, affixation by some other suffix) are also possible for some adjectives. These gap avoidance strategies, however, are not conventionalised and are unsystematic.

(2)   Deadjectival verbal constructions in English

ADJ	VERB (meaning: 'make sg. ADJ')			
	ADJ+*en*	Conversion	other morphological	Periphrastic (syntactic)
slim	—	*slim*	—	*make sg. slim*
tall	—	—	—	*make sg. tall*
pure	—	—	*purify*	*make sg. pure*
white	*whiten*	—	—	*make sg. white*

The behaviour of the comparative and superlative suffixes *-er, -est* in English is a well-known example for conventionalised periphrastic mask-

---

[9]Note that paraphrase is also possible if there is no gap.

ing. Adjectives longer than two syllables systematically lack forms suffixed with *-er*, *-est*, e.g. **beautifuller*, **beautifullest*, **reluctanter*, **reluctantest*. This is a phonologically motivated specific gap which is systematically filled by the conventionalised periphrastic constructions *more* X_{ADJ}, *most* X_{ADJ}: *more beautiful, most beautiful, more reluctant, most reluctant*.

There is a similar, albeit not phonologically motivated example in Hungarian. Hungarian verbs form the Conditional by taking the suffix *-na/-ná/-ana/-aná*[10]: *akar-na* 'want 3SGINDEFPRESCOND', *akar-ná-d* 'want 2SGDEFPRESCOND'.[11] The conditional morpheme cannot combine with the past morpheme *-t/-tt*[10]: **akar-ná-tt / *akar-t-ana* 'want 3SGINDEFPASTCOND', **akar-ná-tt-am / *akar-t-aná-m* 'want 1SGDEFPASTCOND'. However, there is no overt gap since it is systematically filled by a conventionalised periphrastic construction consisting of the past tense of the verb followed by one of the conditional forms of the copula, viz. *volna* 'be 3SGINDEFPRESCOND': *akar-t vol-na* 'want 3SGINDEFPASTCOND', *akar-t-am vol-na* 'want 1SGDEFPASTCOND'. This is shown in (3):

(3)   Periphrastic expression of Past Conditional forms

	Tense:	PRES. (-∅)	PAST (-*t/tt*)	
Mood:	Pers./Nu.:	morphological		periphrastic
IND. (-∅-)	3. SG. (-∅)	*akar*	*akar-**t***	
	1. SG. (-*m*)	*akar-om*	*akar-**t**-am*	
COND. (-*na/ná-*)	3. SG. (-∅)	*akar-**na***	**akar-t-ana* **akar-ná-tt*	*akar-**t** <u>vol</u>-**na***
	1. SG. (-*m*)	*akar-**ná**-m*	**akar-t-aná-m* **akar-ná-tt-am*	*akar-**t**-am <u>vol</u>-**na***

Gaps may be systematically filled non-periphrastically. In Swedish there is a phonologically motivated gap in the paradigm of /dd/-final verb stems (Iverson 1981). These verb stems (e.g. *rädd-* 'save') cannot be suffixed directly with an ending beginning with a dental stop — which would happen in the second and third conjugations in the past (/-de/), supine (/-t/) and the past participle (/-d/). However, this does not result in an overt gap since they all follow the first conjugation where the inflectional suffixes are preceded by a 'stem-forming vowel /a/' (*räddade* (past), *räddat* (supine), *räddad* (past participle)).

---

[10]The suffix alternation (irrelevant here) is due to the application of some general morphophonological rules and there are other alternants as well cf. Siptár & Törkenczy (2000).

[11]In the examples that follow, the hyphens only appear to facilitate segmentation into morphemes; they are not present in the spelling.

Hungarian provides another, more complex example. There are two copulas in Hungarian, *van/vol-* and *lesz/le-* both of whose paradigms are defective.[12] The gaps are not phonology-related; *van/vol-* does not have Imperative/Subjunctive, Modal and Infinitive forms while *lesz/le-* lacks all Indicative forms. However, the gaps in the two paradigms are complementary and thus conventional masking applies in both: each gap in a paradigm is systematically filled with the corresponding form from the other paradigm. This is shown in (4) below (note that both stems have their own forms in the conditional, i. e., there is variation):

(4)   Suppletive paradigm of the copula

Stem form: Suffixes:	*van / vol-* 'be'	*lesz / le-* 'be'
3SGINDICPRES **3PL**INDICPRES 3SGINDIC**PAST**	*van* *van-nak* *vol-t*	⊙ ⊙ ⊙
3SGIMP-SUBJUNC 3SGINDICPRESMODAL INFINITIVE	⊙ ⊙ ⊙	*le-gy-en* *le-het* *len-ni*
3SGCONDPRES	*vol-na*	*len-ne*

Paradigms in which the meanings of some missing forms are expressed by conventionalised (systematic) periphrastic or non-periphrastic masking are traditionally not considered to be defective — only those paradigms are for whose gaps only non-conventionalised periphrastic or non-periphrastic masking is available. Whether conventionalised masking exists is often accidental and independent of the nature of the gap. For instance in Swedish /dd/-final adjectives (e.g. *rädd* 'scared') lack indefinite singular neuter forms, i. e., they cannot be affixed with a suffix that begins with a dental stop like the indefinite singular neuter suffix /t/ (Iverson 1981). This is obviously the same gap that we have discussed above (and was systematically masked in the case of verbs), however, there is no conventionalised masking for it.

We suggest that all the examples discussed can be seen as instances of *covert* defectiveness, where a given meaning cannot be expressed in a certain formal way (for phonological or other reasons), but where another form is available to express the same meaning (cf. Törkenczy 2002b). If we follow through this idea, it means that *allomorphy* where allomorphs are restricted to appear under complementary conditions is also covert de-

---

[12]The homophonous verb *lesz/le-* 'will be, become' has a complete paradigm.

fectiveness. The paradigm[13] of each allomorph is defective since it has a gap (or it has gaps) where only the other allomorph(s) can appear. Seen from this point of view, defectiveness is actually much more frequent and non-marginal than it is usually thought to be.

The phonologically conditioned allomorphy of the Hungarian 2SGIN-DEFPRESINDIC suffix is a case in point. Disregarding Vowel Harmony this suffix has three allomorphs: -V*l* appears after sibilant-final stems, -*sz* [**s**] after vowel-final stems and non-sibilant consonant-final stems and -V*sz* , i.e., V[**s**(ː)] after cluster-final stems whose final consonant is non-sibilant.

(5)   Lexical allomorphy in the suffix

	Suffixes:		
3SGINDEFPRESINDIC	2SGINDEFPRESINDIC		
Stems:	*-ol*	*-sz*	*-asz*
mos 'wash'	*mos-ol*	⊙	⊙
vonz 'attract'	*vonz-ol*	⊙	⊙
kap 'get'	⊙	*kap-sz*	⊙
bont 'take apart'	⊙	⊙	*bont-asz*

Thus the paradigm of -V*l* is defective because it does not combine with stems like *kap* and *bont* (**kap-ol*, **bont-ol*, etc.) and, on the other hand, the paradigm of *kap* is defective too, because it does not have forms with -V*l* and -V*sz* (**kap-ol*, **kap-asz*). Defectiveness in both cases is covert because there is a systematic way to fill the gaps.

Our point here is that defectiveness is a matter of how fine-grained of a view we are taking, what the level of detail is at which we are calculating defectiveness. 'Viewed from a distance,' at and above the phrasal level, there is no overt defectiveness, i. e., all defectiveness is covert defectiveness, since meanings can be expressed somehow — at worst, by paraphrase. If however we take a very fine-grained view so that allomorphs are taken into consideration, then overt defectiveness is very frequent. At this level there is no defectiveness only if (a) there is no allomorphy or if (b) there is free variation. We call this the 'Zooming Effect': overt defectivity increases with the degree of detail. The Hungarian 2SGINDEF-PRESINDIC suffix (see (5)) is overtly defective if we take the allomorphs into consideration, however, it is *not* (i. e., its defectiveness is covert) at the *morpheme* level. Different instances of overt defectiveness may require a different zooming, i. e., a different detail of analysis. We shall see below

---

[13]Naturally, in this case, paradigm has to be interpreted to mean 'a set of words that share the same *allomorph*'.

that a proper description of the behaviour of Hungarian defective stems requires a zoom to the level of *allomorphs*. Note also that variation, i. e., the existence of alternative expressions shows an interesting parallelism with defectiveness. Like defectiveness, it is also present at every level of detail: at the phrasal level and above, paraphrase may not only mask gaps, but is also available as an alternative to existing expressions (e.g. see Chart (1) above), and free variation may occur at the level of allomorphs. On the other hand, variation too may be unsystematic (e.g. paraphrase) or systematic/conventionalised (e.g. the free variation of allomorphs, or parallel stems/morphemes).

3 Hungarian data

There are several stem and suffix alternations in Hungarian. In this section we discuss those types of stem and suffix allomorphies that are relevant for the analysis of defectiveness, i. e., the analysis of those paradigmatic gaps that can only be masked by (unsystematic) paraphrase.

3.1 Stem types

From a morphophonological point of view it is crucial whether a verbal stem in all its allomorphs ends in one consonant (stable VC-final stems) or in two consonants (stable CC-final stems). (See their different behaviours in section 3.2.) However, there is a third type of stems: these stems show vowel-zero alternation. These *epenthetic stems*[14] have two basic forms: a CVC-final and a CC-final one. Some examples are shown in (6), where the separable CCs are underlined and the 'unstable' vowels are emboldened.

Note that 3SGINDEFPRESINDIC forms (the first column in table 6) can contain two types of suffixes: zero or the marker *-ik*. This is an arbitrary lexical property of the stem. Accordingly, a verb is either an '*ik*-verb' or a 'non-*ik* verb'. This distinction is independent of the semantics and the phonological shape of the stem. There are *ik*-verbs and non-*ik* verbs in all the three stem types in (6a, b, c). We shall see later that the *ik* – non-*ik* distinction has a crucial role in verbal allomorph selection and defectiveness.

---

[14]It is irrelevant to the present analysis if we consider V~zero alternation to be the result of epenthesis, V-deletion or some other phonological process (cf. Siptár & Törkenczy 2000). We shall arbitrarily refer to it as epenthesis here, and call the relevant class of stems 'epenthetic stems'.

(6)   Three stem types

3SgIndef ∅ / -ik	Suffixes: Stem types:		2SgDef -od	1PlIndef -unk	Gerund -ás	2SgDef Imp-Subj	3SgDef -ja	Modal -hat
ápol *rakodik*	a. VC-stem	*– non-ik* *– ik*	*ápol-od* *rakod-od*	*ápol-unk* *rakod-unk*	*ápol-ás* *rakod-ás*	*ápol-d* *rakod-d*	*ápol-ja* *rakod-ja*	*ápol-hat* *rakod-hat*
kotor *ugrik*	b. epenthetic	*– non-ik* *– ik*	*kotr-od* *ugr-od*	*kotr-unk* *ugr-unk*	*kotr-ás* *ugr-ás*	*kotor-d* *ugor-d*	*kotor-ja* *ugor-ja*	*kotor-hat* *ugor-hat*
hord *fingik*	c. CC-stem	*– non-ik* *– ik*	*hord-od* *fing-od*	*hord-unk* *fing-unk*	*hord-ás* *fing-ás*	*hord-d* *fing-d*	*hord-ja* *fing-ja*	*hord-hat* *fing-hat*

There are phonotactic constraints for the last two consonants of these stem types. These limitations are very restrictive for the non-*ik* stems of the stable CC-type, because their 3SgIndefIndicPres forms are identical with the bare stem (see 6c). Epenthetic stems have other restrictions on their last consonants (which are strictly adjacent in one allomorph, and separated by a vowel in the other): e.g. (partial) geminates and some other CC-combinations do not occur in these stems (see 6b).[15] This means that in some cases the type of the two last consonants can be a proper indicator for the actual stem type. However the type of a stem is not completely predictable from this information. There are stems that belong to different stem types, although their last C(V)C is the same, as can be seen in table (7) where each CC type is exemplified. (Suffixes: *-ok/ek/ök*: 1SGINDEF-PRESINDIC, *-ik*: 3SGINDEFPRESINDIC, *-hat*: 'may'.)

(7)   Types of last consonants in different stem classes

Type of C	stable VC-stems	epenthetic stems	stable CC-stems
nasal + plosive	*inog ~ inog-ok*	*inog ~ ing-ok*	*reng ~ reng-ek*
liquid + plosive	*marad ~ marad-ok*	*füröd-het ~ fürd-ök*	*hord ~ hord-ok*
nasal + fricative	*ónoz ~ ónoz-ok*	*ellenez ~ ellenz-ek*	*vonz ~ vonz-ok*
liquid + fricative	*boroz ~ boroz-ok*	*érez ~ érz-ek*	(only nouns: *borz*)
plosive + fricative	*haboz ~ haboz-ok*	*koboz ~ kobz-ok*	*habz-ik ~ habz-ok*
nasal + liquid	*rámol ~ rámol-ok*	*romol-hat ~ roml-ok*	*háml-ik ~ hámlok*
plosive + liquid	*vedel ~ vedel-ek*	*vádol ~ vádl-ok*	*vedl-ik ~ vedl-ek*

As an important consequence we can state the following:

(8)   The ternary distinction (6a, b, c) between the verbal stem types is lexical.

3.2 Morphophonological suffix classes

The stem alternants of epenthetic stems discussed above depend on the suffix that attaches to the stem. The relevant criterion in verbal morphophonology is that the CVC-final allomorph occurs if the suffix begins with a consonant, see the examples in (6). In this way the suffix-allomorphs can be divided into two sets: vowel-initial and consonant-initial. The problem is that in some cases the vowel that can occur between the stem and the suffix is also unstable, i. e., it alternates with zero. The distribution of these *linking vowels* makes it possible to classify the (verbal) suffixes depending on whether the pre-suffix (linking) vowel appears: (i) after all stems (*synthetic* suffixes); (ii) only after some stems, *viz.* the CC-final ones (*quasi-analytic* suffixes); or (iii) never (*analytic* suffixes). This classification of suffixes is relevant for the shape of the whole form (stem+suffix), because the stem

---

[15] See Törkenczy 1992, 2004, Siptár & Törkenczy 2000, Rebrus 2000, Rebrus & Trón 2002 for details.

alternants can also depend on the occurrence of this linking vowel (as in the case of epenthetic stems).

(9)   Three suffix classes

a. occurrence of the pre-suffixal vowel (linking vowel)

BASIC FORM		Suffix classes: linking V					
		I. SYNTHETIC (after all stems)		II. QUASI-ANALITIC (after CC-stems)		III. ANALYTIC (never)	
3SGINDEF	Stem types:	1SGINDEF	FREQUENT	2SGINDEF	COND	IMP-SUBJ	ADVPART
kap	a. stable VC-stem	*kap-ok*	*kap-ogat*	*kap-sz*	*kap-na*	*kap-j*	*kap-va*
old	c. stable CC-stem	*old-ok*	*old-ogat*	*old-**a**sz*	*old-**a**na*	*old-j*	*old-va*

b. occurrence of the stem-internal unstable vowel

BASIC FORM		Suffix classes: stem-internal unstable V					
		I. SYNTHETIC (never)		II. QUASI-ANALITIC (always for non-*ik*) (optional for *ik*-stems)		III. ANALYTIC (always)	
3SGINDEF	Stem types:	1SGINDEF	1PINDEF	2SGINDEF	COND	IMP-SUBJ	ADVPART
kotor	b₁. epenthetic non-*ik*	*kotr-ok*	*kotr-unk*	*kotor-sz*	*kotor-na*	*kotor-j*	*kotor-va*
ugr-ik	b₂. epenthetic -*ik*	*ugr-ok*	*ugr-unk*	*ug**o**r-sz* / *ugr-asz*	*ug**o**r-na* / *ugr-ana*	*ugor-j*	*ugor-va*

As can be seen in (9) there is a tripartite distinction among suffixes: *synthetic* suffixes always get a linking vowel[16] and never trigger the occurence of the unstable V in epenthetic stems (see column (I) in (9a, b)). *Analytic* suffixation is basically concatenative: the linking vowel never appears and the stem-internal unstable V is compulsory in epenthetic stems (column (III) in (9b)). The third class of suffixes is called *quasi-analytic*; the linking vowel can occur, but typically only after CC-final stems and not after VC-final ones (see column (II) in (9a)). For epenthetic stems this creates a bifurcation since epenthetic stems have both CC-final and VC-final stem alternants. This means that potentially both of the following forms could be well-formed: CC-stem + linking vowel (CC+VC) or CVC-stem + no linking vowel (CVC+C). Both these forms are available for some stems, namely, epenthetic *ik*-stems show this *regular optionality* (e.g. *ugor-na/ugr-ana*). Epenthetic non-*ik* stems only have their VC-final forms without a linking vowel (CVC+C), e.g. *kotor-na/*kotr-ana*, see column (II) in (9b).[17]

It is important to see that the class membership of a suffix cannot be characterized on the basis of its *phonological* shape. In each of the three classes there are suffixes that have vowelless alternants -C(C), and in all three classes there are suffixes that have a stable vowel in all their alternants -CV(C). This means that the occurrence of the linking vowel (and the stem alternation) cannot be attributed to phonological rules only, but is mainly lexical (see the examples in (9)).

There are other effects, too. In some cases the suffix alternants cannot be associated with each other by a (generalizable) phonological rule. This can happen in the case of non-phonological (*lexical*, suppletive) allomorphies. Lexical allomorphs do not have a generalizable common ('underlying') shape, in other words the allomorph selection does not fit into the general morphophonological patterns of the language. In most cases lexical allomorphs do not belong to the same morphophonological class. This is shown in (10) where examples in the second line of each cell are epenthetic stems.

This lack of correspondence is also true of the *morphological* (morphosyntactic) character of the suffixes. The morphological class member-

---

[16]There is no linking vowel after stable vowel-final stems, but this only happens after some *suffixed* stem-forms in the case of verbs. They are irrelevant to our topic.

[17]Note that for quasi-analytic forms these generalizations (linking vowel after CC-final stems, optionality in epenthetic *ik*-stems) are approximative; many subregularities and idiosyncratic forms modify this general pattern.

(10)   Suffix allomorphs belonging to different morphophonological classes

Morpheme:	SYNTHETIC	QUASI-ANALYTIC	ANALYTIC
2SGINDEFINDICPRES (-*ol*~-*sz* /*asz*)	*mos-ol* *viszonz-ol*	*kap-sz, old-asz* *forog-sz*	
PAST (3SGINDEF vs. other) (e.g. -*ott*~-*ta* /*otta*)	*kap-ott* *forg-ott*	*kap-ta,* *old-otta* *forog-ta*	
3SGDEFINDICPRES -*i*~-*ja*	*lep-i* *pörg-i*		*lop-ja* *forog-ja*
FACTITIVE (-*at*~ -*tat*)	*lop-at* *forg-at*		*harap-tat,* *üt-tet* *forog-tat*
FREQUENTATIVE (-*ogat*~-*gat*)	*lop-ogat* *ugr-ogat*		*harap-gat* *söpör-get*

ship of a verbal suffix does not determine whether it is synthetic, quasi-analytic or analytic (i. e., it does not determine its morphophonological class) and vice versa. There are some weak tendencies, but they are not definitive. Table (11) summarizes the number of verbal suffixes in each morphological and morphophonological class (in the case of lexical allomorphy, the suffix has been counted twice, i. e., once for each allomorph).

(11)   Number of productive verbal suffixes in each morphophonological and morphological class[18]

Morphological class:		Morphophonological class:		
		SYNTHETIC	QUASI-ANALYTIC	ANALYTIC
Inflection:	Pers/Num/Def	8	4	5
	Tense/Mood	–	2	2
Derivation:	verb → verb	3	–	1
	verb → non-verb	3	1	2

To summarize, suffixes belong to morphophonological classes, which govern the surface shape of the suffixed forms. The same suffix can have allomorphs which do not belong to the same class, and there is no clearly identifiable systematic correspondence between the class membership of a morph and its phonological shape. The mapping between morphophono-

---

[18]Note that Person/Number markers can occur directly after absolute stems and also after Definiteness, Tense/Mood andInfinitive markers, and they can create fusional morphemes. As opposed to non-fusional ones, fusional morphemes were not counted as combinations of the morphosyntactic dimensions/values they fuse, but as separate instances. For details see Rebrus & Törkenczy (2005a).

logical and morphological suffix classes is very complex, largely accidental. So the following generalization holds:

(12)   The ternary distinction (synthetic, quasi-analytic, analytic) between ver-
        bal suffix types is lexical.

3.3 Defective stems

We have seen in section 3.1. that there are two arbitrary morphological
classes of verbs: (i) non-*ik* verbs, which have a zero marker in 3SGIN-
DEFPRESINDIC form, and (ii) *ik*-verbs, which take a suffix -*ik* in 3SGIN-
DEFPRESINDIC '*ik*-ness' is an arbitrary property of the verb: members
of either '*ik*'-class can belong to any stem-type (stable VC, stable CC or
epenthetic, see (6)). A non-*ik* stable CC-stem can occur as a free form at
the surface, consequently the stem-final CC has to occur at the surface as
a word-final cluster. These CC-clusters are severely constrained in verbs:
they have to satisfy sonority sequencing (C_1 must be more sonorous than
C_2).[19] However, in *ik*-verbs and (-*ik* or non-*ik*) epenthetic verbs these strict
phonotactics need not and do not apply since in these verbs the CC-cluster
never occurs word finally at the surface: the 3SGINDEFINDICPRES forms
are CC+*ik* (-*ik* suffixation) or CVC.

This is also true of synthetic and quasi-analytic suffixation: even if
the stem ends in CC, forms with these types of suffixes never violate
(monomorphemic) phonotactics[20] because (i) the stem-final CC never occurs word-finally; (ii) the stem-final CC never forms a CCC-cluster with
the suffix-initial C. This is shown in (13) with stem-final clusters of rising
sonority (where the existing forms are emboldened and the cell(s) in which
they occur have a thicker outside border, non-existing forms are marked
with (one or two) asterisks; phonotactically excluded forms are marked
with two asterisks; and a given box is shaded if both stem alternants are
excluded). Table (13) is a version of (6), but (a) we left out stable VC-
stems because they are irrelevant here, (b) we included the -*ik* vs. non-*ik*

---

[19]There are further restrictions. The relevant CCs can only be: coronal/velar geminates:
[lː], [rː], [dː], [gː], [dzː], [tsː]; certain NO-clusters: [nd], [nt], [ŋg], [nz], [mz], [mt]; coronal RO-clusters: [rt], [lt], [jt], [rd], [ld], [jz]; coronal ST-clusters: [st], [ʃt], [zd]. This is a
more restricted set than that for nominals, see Törkenczy (2004), Rebrus & Trón (2002).

[20]There is a single exception: 2SGINDEFINDICPRES marker -*sz* [s] can attach to VC-
final stem allomorphs without a linking vowel even if the stem-final consonant is less
sonorous than [s], e. g. *kap-sz* 'get'. We disregard this complication here, cf. Rebrus (2000),
Siptár & Törkenczy (2000).

distinction, and (c) we gave the potential CC and CVC stem alternants in a separate line for each stem exemplifying a given stem class.

As opposed to synthetic and quasi-analytic suffixation, analytic suffixation is concatenative, i. e., analytic suffixes always occur without a linking vowel (see column III in 9), so analytic forms can contain clusters that do not exist in the language monomorphemically. This is true of stable VC-final stems and epenthetic stems, and certain CC-final stems as well.[21]

In certain cases, however, the quality of the stem-final CC-cluster is such that it cannot form a CCC-cluster with the suffix-initial C. This happens in the case of stable CC-final stems whose final CC is not allowed word-finally in verbs, essentially where sonority sequencing is violated (*tl, kl, dl, gr, gz* etc.), but there are other banned clusters, too (*rl, ml,* [ɲ]*l,* [ɲ]*z, lz, rz* etc). In these cases the analytic forms never occur, i. e., the stem is *defective* since (a) the CCC cluster is out for phonotactic reasons and (b) it cannot be broken up by a vowel because the stem is a stable CC-stem which does not have a CVC-final allomorph (*CVC-C) and the suffix is analytic one, which cannot have a linking vowel (*CC-VC). See the forms in the shaded boxes in (13).

As can be seen in (13) a paradigm gap occurs if the stem

    (i)   is a stable CC-stem, and
    (ii) ends in an ill-formed CC-cluster, and
    (iii) is suffixed with an analytic suffix.

Note also that the lack of a suffix (a zero suffix) is like an analytic suffix: non-*ik* stable CC-final verbs lack a 3SGINDEFINDICPRES if they end in an ill-formed cluster (since they would have no overt suffix).[22]

The defectiveness of these stems is phonotactically motivated, but two important remarks have to be made. First, the distinction between epenthetic stems and defective (CC-)stems is lexical, i. e. it is not phonotactically motivated (as we pointed out in (8)). We saw in 3.1 that there are stems that belong to different stem types although their last C(V)C is the same. This is true of defective stems, too, as can be seen in (14). (Synthetic

---

[21] This is constrained only by the shape of the analytic suffix and automatic assimilation rules (palatalization, (de)voicing, degemination etc.). Some examples of clusters that never occur monomorphemically in (verbal) forms: intervocalic *p/b+v, p+h, ng+j*; word-final *C+j, b/g/dz+d, jz/nz+d* etc.

[22] There are only two verbs like this in Hungarian: *kétl-* 'doubt' and *sínyl-* 'suffer'. The 3SGDEFINITEINDICPRES of the same two verbs do exist because these forms have a synthetic suffix: *kétl-i, sínyl-i.*

(13)   Allomorphic variations
       (stems with stem-final obstruent+sonorant clusters)

| Basic | Suffix classes: | | I. SYNTHETIC | | II. QUASI-ANALYTIC | | III. ANALYTIC | |
3SGIND	Stem types:	Stem:	1SGDEF	1PLINDEF	2SGINDEF	COND	IMP-SUBJ	ADVPART
****kotr**	b_1. epenthetic	CC	**kotr-od**	**kotr-unk**	*kotr-asz*	*kotra-na*	****kotr-d**	****kotr-va**
kotor	– non-*ik*	CVC	*kotor-od*	*kotor-unk*	**kotor-sz**	**kotor-na**	**kotor-d**	**kotor-va**
ugr-ik	b_2. epenthetic	CC	**ugr-od**	**ugr-unk**	**ugr-asz**	**ugr-ana**	*ugr-d*	*ugr-va*
ugor-ik	– *ik*	CVC	*ugor-od*	*ugor-unk*	**ugor-sz**	**ugor-na**	**ugor-d**	**ugor-va**
****kétl**	c_1. stable CC	CC	**kétl-ed**	**kétl-ünk**	**kétl-esz**	**kétl-ene**	****kétl-d**	****kétl-ve**
kétel	– non-*ik*	CVC	*kétel-ed*	*kétel-ünk*	*kétel-sz*	*kétel-ne*	*kétel-d*	*kétel-ve*
sikl-ik	c_2. stable CC	CC	**sikl-od**	**sikl-unk**	**sikl-asz**	**sikl-ana**	****sikl-d**	****sikl-va**
sikol-ik	– *ik*	CVC	*sikol-od*	*sikol-unk*	*sikol-sz*	*sikol-na*	*sikol-d*	*sikol-va*

suffixes: *-ok/ek/ök*: 1SGINDEFPRESINDIC, *-ik*: 3SGINDEFPRESINDIC; analytic suffixes: *-hat/het*: 'may' .)

(14)   Stem-final CCs of defective stems and in other stem classes

CC	stable VC-stems		epenthetic stems		defective CC-stems		number
kl	okol-ok	okol-hat	haldokl-ok	haldokol-hat	sikl-ok	*sik(o)l-hat	5
tl	hatol-ok	hatol-hat	botl-ok	boto-hat	kétl-i	*két(e)l-het	3
dl	vedel-ek	vedel-het	vádl-ok	vádol-hat	vedl-ek	*ved(e)l-het	2
gl	vendégel-ek	vendégel-het	dögl-ök	dögöl-het	vonagl-ik	*vonag(o)l-hat	4
ʃl	másol-ok	másol-hat	javasl-ok	javasol-hat	fesl-ik	*fes(e)l-het	4
sl	koszol-ok	koszol-hat	foszl-ik	foszol-hat	díszl-ik	*dísz(e)l-het	1
ʒl	duruzsol-ok	duruzsol-hat	varázsl-ok	varázsol-hat	parázsl-ik	*parázs(o)l-hat	1
zl	gázol-ok	gázol-hat	közl-ök	közöl-het	ízl-ik	*íz(e)l-het	3
ml	rámol-ok	rámol-hat	áraml-ik	áramol-hat	háml-ik	*hám(o)l-hat	9
ɲl	gúnyol-ok	gúnyol-hat	vezényl-ek	vezényel-het	fényl-ek	*fény(e)l-het	5
nl	honol-ok	honol-hat	özönl-ik	özönöl-het	hasonl-ik	*hason(o)l-hat	1
rl	porol-ok	porol-hat	bérl-ek	bérel-het	hírl-ik	*hír(e)l-het	5
jl	mo[j]ol-ok	mo[j]ol-hat	hajl-ok	hajol-hat	morajl-ik	*moraj(o)l-hat	7
bz	haboz-ok	haboz-hat	kobz-ok	koboz-hat	habz-ik	*?hab(o)z-hat	1?
gz	ragoz-ok	ragoz-hat	lélegz-ek	lélegez-het	bagz-ik	*?bag(o)z-hat	5?
kz	okoz-ok	okoz-hat	tajtékz-ik	tajtékoz-hat	patakz-ik	*?patak(o)z-hat	1?
lz	élez-ek	élez-het	túlz-ok	túloz-hat	nyálz-ik	*?nyál(a)z-hat	1?
mz	számoz-ok	számoz-hat	hullámz-ik	hullámoz-hat	fogamz-ik	?fogamz-hat	1?
nz	ónoz-ok	ónoz-hat	viszonz-ok	viszonoz-hat	burjánz-ik	?burján(o)z-hat	1?
rz	boroz-ok	boroz-hat	érz-ek	érez-het	elviharz-ik	?elviharz-hat	5?
						Sum:	65

Table (14) is exhaustive in the sense that it contains all the CC-clusters that occur stem-finally in defective stems (see the third column; there are 65 stems altogether, and we have given the number of defective stems for each cluster, question marks indicate that (some of) the relevant verb stems are not defective for some speakers). All the clusters that occur in defective stems also occur in epenthetic and stable VC-stems. The distinction between defective stems vs. these two stem types is lexical.

Second, although all of the 65 stems we classified as defective *are* defective for some speakers of standard Hungarian, not all of them are defective for all speakers. There is a certain amount of variation because some speakers reclassify some stems. There are two strategies of reclassification: (i) into the class of epenthetic stems by inserting a vowel between the two stem-final consonants in analytic forms, and (ii) into the class of (non-defective) stable CC-stems by permitting the concatenation of the CC-final stem and the C-initial analytic suffix (thereby creating a CCC cluster). Of course, reclassification only happens idiolectally: it varies from speaker to speaker which stems they might reclassify (if any). If reclassification does happen, strategy (i) is potentially available for a defective stem ending in any of the clusters in (14), e.g. *%sikol-hat, %burjánoz-hat*.[23] By contrast, strategy (ii) is phonotactically restricted: it is completely excluded for stems whose final CC has a significant sonority rise (the first 11 clusters in (14)): e.g. **sikl-hat, *vedl-het*, but it may be applied if there is no sonority rise: *%morajl-hat, %burjánz-hat*.[24]

We saw that defectiveness only occurs within the class of stable CC-stems. Although there is a phonotactic difference between non-defective and defective CC stems, the nature of stem-final clusters is not a sufficient motivation of defectiveness. One reason is that in the case of some CC-clusters for some speakers both defective and non-defective CC-stems may end in the same CC-cluster. For these speakers, e.g. the non-defective verb *vonz* 'attract' has all its analytically suffixed forms (*vonz-hat, vonz-va, vonz-d*, etc) and thus is non-defective while the stem *burjánz-ik* 'proliferate' does not (**burjánz-hat, *burjánz-va*, etc.) and thus is defective. This holds for stem-final *mz, jl* as well (cf. non-defective *nemz* 'beget', *rejl-ik* 'be latent in' vs. defective *fogamz-ik* 'conceive', *morajl-ik* 'thunder'). Note that none of the relevant clusters violate sonority sequencing.

The other reason is the following: in some cases the CCC-cluster is not derived at all at the surface because a morphophonological rule applies which simplifies it, nevertheless defectiveness *does* occur even though the CCC-cluster simplifies. The Imperative/Subjunctive marker *-j* is analytic. A suffix-initial /j/ always assimilates to a preceding coronal consonant

---

[23]Interestingly, reclassification may not result in homonyms, e.g. forms of the verb *vedl-ik* 'slough' cannot reclassify as a VC-stem (**vedel-het*) because then they would be identical with the corresponding forms of the verb *vedel* 'drink heavily'.

[24]Note that most of the CCC clusters derived in this way do exist in the language elsewhere, either in suffixed verbal forms or suffixed nominal forms e.g. *vonz-hat* 'may attract', *fájl-hoz* 'to (a) file'.

(such as /l/ and /z/), e.g. /ül+j/ → [yjː] 'sit!', /hoz+j/ → [hozː] 'bring!'. As the stem final clusters of defective stems all end in /l/ or /z/ they are subject to this assimilation[25] when followed by a *j*-initial suffix such as the Imperative/Subjunctive marker: Cl+j → Cjː → Cj, Cz+j → Czː → Cz. Thus, for instance, the expected Imperative/Subjunctive forms of the defective stems *sikl-* 'glide' and *fogamz-* 'conceive' are /ʃikl+j/ → ʃikjː → ʃikj → *[ʃikç], /ʃikl+j+on/ → ʃikjːon → *[ʃikjon] and /fogamz+j/ → fogamzː → *[fogɔmz], /fogamz+j+on/ → /fogamzːon/ → *[fogɔmzon].[26] These forms, however, do not exist, i. e., paradigm gaps occur here in spite of the fact that the resulting clusters are not phonotactically ill-formed (in analytically suffixed forms finally and word internally). Consequently, the lack of Imperative/Subjunctive[27] forms of defective verbs in general cannot be explained with reference to (surface) phonotactics.

To sum up, defectiveness in Hungarian is phonotactically motivated, but phonotactics is not sufficient to determine defectiveness because (i) stable (defective and non-defective) CC- stems vs. epenthetic stems cannot be distinguished phonotactically (see (14)), (ii) within the class of stable CC stems (for some speakers) there may be an overlap between non-defective vs. defective stems; (iii) the suffixation of defective stems with all of the analytic suffixes results in defectiveness, although suffixation with some of them does not result in phonotactically ill-formed strings.

(15)   Defectiveness is phonotactically motivated and is sensitive to lexical information referring to stem class (defective CC-stems) and affix class (analytic suffixes).

We have seen above that paradigm gaps occur with defective stems in the case of analytic suffixation (including suffixation with zero). However, an adequate description must zoom to the allomorph level to capture the distribution of gaps in the paradigms of Hungarian verbs. The reason is that analyticity (or non-analyticity) is a property of allomorphs and not morphemes in Hungarian, see (10). Table (16) below shows the distribution of gaps in the Present Indicative paradigm of back and front, *-ik* and non-*ik* defective verbs (the gaps are shaded).

---

[25]And obligatory degemination; note also that /j/ is realised as [ç] after voiceless non-coronal consonants at the end of word, see Siptár and Törkenczy (2000).

[26]Compare the well-formed Imperative/Subjunctive forms of non-defective *rak* 'put' and *nemz* 'beget': /rak+j/ → rakj → [rɔkç], /rak+j+on/ → [rɔkjon], and /nemz+j/ → nemzː → [nɛmz] and /nemz+j+en/ → nemzːen → [nɛmzɛn].

[27]Note that the same argumentation is true of all the other *j*-inital analytic suffixes, see (16) and (17d).

(16)   Paradigmatic gaps in Present Indicative

Tense/Mood:		PRESENT INDICATIVE				PAST	COND.
Person/ Number:	stem vowel:	INDEF	DEF	INDEF	DEF	(no gaps)	
		'ik - verb'		'non ik - verb'			
1. Sg.	f	vedl-ek	vedl-em	sínyl-ek	sínyl-em	.	.
2. SG.	r	vedl-esz	vedl-ed	síny!-esz	sínyl-ed	.	.
3. SG.	o	vedl-**ik**	vedl-**i**	*síny(e)l-∅	sínyl-**i**	sínyl-ett	sínylene
1. PL.	n	vedl-ünk	*ved(e)l-**jük**	sínyl-ünk	*síny(e)l-**jük**	vedlettük	vedlenénk
2. PL.	t	vedl-etek	vedl-**i**-tek	sínyl-etek	sínyl-**itek**	.	.
3. PL.		vedl-enek	vedl-**i**-k	sínyl-enek	sínyl-**ik**	.	.
1. Sg.		háml-ok	háml-om			.	.
2. SG.	b	háml-asz	háml-od			.	.
3. SG.	a	háml-**ik**	*hám(o)l-**ja**	(there are no back-vowel		háml-ott-a	.
1. PL.	c	háml-unk	*hám(o)l-**juk**	non-*ik* defective stems)		háml-ott-uk	.
2. PL.	k	háml-otok	*hám(o)l-**já**-tok			hámlott-á-tok	.
3. PL.		háml-anak	*hám(o)l-**já**-k			háml-ott-á-k	.

Consider the 3SGPRESINDIC forms. There is an asymmetrical gap here in the indefinite: defective non-*ik* verbs do not have a 3SGINDEF-

218 *Modelling ungrammaticality in Optimality Theory*

PRESINDIC form while defective *-ik* verbs do (*síny(e)l* but *vedl-ik*).[28] The reason is that of the two allomorphs expressing the same dimension (value), viz zero and *-ik*, the first one is analytic, but the second one is not. A similar gap occurs in the definite: defective back verbs do not have a 3SGDEFPRESINDIC form while defective front verbs do (*hám(o)l-ja* but *vedl-i*). The reason is the same as before: of the two allomorphs *-ja/-i*, the first one is analytic and the second one is not (only this time the allomorphy is phonologically conditioned[29]). The same asymmetrical gap repeats itself (for the same reason) in the DEFPRESINDIC subparadigm of defective stems in 2PL and 3PL: front stems have the relevant forms while back stems have gaps[30] (the gaps in 1PL are not asymmetrical: both forms are missing because both suffix allomorphs (*-juk/-jük*) are analytic).

In (16) the Past/Conditional forms in the gapped person/number lines are given to show that the location of the paradigm gaps does not depend on the person/number values since the same Person/Number forms of the same verbs always exist in PAST and COND (dots are meant to indicate that the relevant forms exist but have been supressed to keep the table uncluttered). It is only the analyticity of the allomorph that matters. This can be seen in (17) below where we give an exhaustive list of the analytic morphemes/allomorphs in Hungarian. (Note that the analytic/non-analytic character of a suffix (allomorph) is also independent of whether it is inflectional or derivational (see also (11) above).

Thus in Hungarian, defective stems have gaps in their paradigm exactly where an analytic suffix *allomorph* (including zero) would have to be attached irrespective of (i) what dimension(value) the analytic suffix allomorph or zero might express[33] and (ii) whether the suffix is inflectional or derivational. This means that defectiveness in Hungarian cannot

---

[28] We have pointed out above that there are only two non-*ik* defective stems in Hungarian *kétl-* 'doubt' and *sínyl-* 'suffer'. Both of them happen to be front.

[29] Back stems take *-ja*, front stems take *-i* (cf Siptár & Törkenczy 2000, Rebrus & Törkenczy 2005a).

[30] If there were back non-*ik* defective stems, they would lack the corresponding forms. Notice that a hypothetical back non-*ik* defective stem would have neither a definite nor an indefinite 3SGPRESINDIC form (since the suffix of the latter is zero).

[31] Allomorph selection depends on vowel harmony except in e. (see footnote 2).

[32] Allomorph selection depends on the lexical class membership of the stem: '-*ik*-verb' and 'non –*ik* verb'.

[33] Note that the gaps in the imperative paradigm of Icelandic are similar in this respect. The imperative may be expressed in three ways, but gaps only occur in two, the full imperative and the clipped imperative, never in the archaic one (which expresses the same dimension(value)), cf Hansson (1999).

(17)   Types of verbal gap-inducing (analytic) suffixes

Morpheme type	Allomorph shape[31]	Gap-inducing allomorph	Morphological type	Gloss
a. ADVERBIAL markers	*-va-/-ve* *-ván/-vén*	both	Derivational	IMPERFPART PERFPART
b. MODAL	*-hat-/-het-*	both	? (disputed)	POSSIBILITY
c. TENSE/ MOOD	*-j-* *-d-*	all no allomorphy	Inflectional	all IMP-SUBJ 2SGDEFIMP-SUBJ
d. DEFINITE PERSON/NUM markers (PRESINDIC)	*-juk/-jük* *-ja/-i* *-játok/-itek* *-ják/-ik*	both only the back only the back only the back	Inflectional	1PL 3SG 2PL 3PL
e. INDEFINITE PERSON/NUM marker (PRESINDIC)	*-∅/-ik*[32]	only the non-*ik*	Inflectional	3SG

be handled by any approach that (only) uses rules/constraints that target morphosyntactic values/dimensions (like Optimal Paradigms (Rice 2005abc)).

4   Analysis

In this section we examine the patterning of stem allomorphs (according to their CV structure) in the various paradigm types and suggest an analysis of defectiveness (and variation) with reference to these patterns.

4.1   Paradigmatic patterns of stem allomorphs

Table (18) below shows the surface forms of the five main stem classes[34] (stable VC, non-*ik* epenthetic, *-ik* epenthetic, defective stable CC, non-defective stable CC) when combined with the suffix types (synthetic, quasi-analytic, analytic) that we have discussed in section 3.

The lexical stem classes appear in the rows and the lexical suffix types in the columns of (18). In the leftmost column we also included the 'basic form', i. e., the 3SGINDEFPRESINDIC form, which is the traditional dictionary form of the verb[35] and which plays a definitive role as we shall see

---

[34](18) shows the pattern by focussing on *stem* allomorphs. The pattern based on linking vowels (the suffix-initial vowel) is essentially the same, see (9a).

[35]It has a zero or *-ik* marker. Note that the basic form is the unmarked one in several

(18)   Forms defined by stem and affix classes

BASIC FORM (∅/-ik)	Stem classes:	Suffix types		
		SYNTHETIC (-ok)	QUASI-ANALITIC (-na/-ana)	ANALYTIC (-va)
rámol	i. *stable* VC-stem	rámolok	rámolna	rámolva
hajol	ii. *epenthetic*, non-*ik*	hajlok	hajolna	hajolva
omlik	iii. *epenthetic ik*-stem	omlok	omlana/omolna	omolva
hámlik	iv. *defective* (CC-)stem	hámlok	hámlana	⊙
ajánl	v. *stable* CC-stem	ajánlok	ajánlana	ajánlva

later. 1SGINDEFPRESINDIC *-ok*, CONDITIONAL *-na* and ADVERBIAL-PARTICIPLE *-va* exemplify the Synthetic, the Quasi-analytic and the Analytic types respectively. As we saw in section 3, there are two kinds of stem alternants according to their surface shape: a CC-final one and a VC-final one (henceforth we shall refer to the former as the *C-allomorph*, and the latter as the *V-allomorph*). The area of the paradigm space where C-allomorphs occur is framed with a solid line, while the area for V-allomorphs is framed with dashed line. Table (19) is the same as (18) but allomorph types (C and V) are indicated instead of specific examples.

(19)   Patterns of the stem allomorphs

BASIC FORM	Stem classes:	Suffix types		
		SYNTHETIC	QUASI-ANALITIC	ANALYTIC
V	i. *stable* VC-stem	V	V	V
V	ii. *epenthetic*, non-*ik*	C	V	V
C	iii. *epenthetic ik*-stem	C	C/V	V
C	iv. *defective* (CC-)stem	C	C	⊙
C	v. *stable* CC-stem	C	C	C

The labels in the rows and columns represent generalized types of stem and suffix behaviour respectively. Note that each row is different from all others at least in one cell. i. e., each stem class is different from all others in the value it has for at least one suffix type. In other words, for every pair of stems X and Y that belong to different stem classes there is always a suffix type S all of whose members trigger different stem allomorphs when X and Y are suffixed with a member of S. Similarly, each column is different from all others in at least one cell, i. e., for every pair of suffixes A and B that

respects: it is the most frequent one, it is this form that always exists even if some other forms of the verb are missing for syntactic or semantic reasons, and the zero suffix only occurs here in the verbal paradigm.

belong to different suffix types there is always a stem class all of whose members take different stem allomorphs when suffixed with *A* vs. *B*.

The distribution of C-stems and V-stems in (19) shows that there are two 'prototypical' stem classes, namely, stable VC-stems (19i) and stable CC-stems (19v). These are homogeneous in the sense that they show no stem allomorphy and they have complete paradigms. The other three stem classes can be seen as 'mixed', i. e. they are heterogeneous in that they either show stem allomorphy or have paradigm gaps.

Suffix types can be characterised in a similar way. Synthetic and analytic suffixes are prototypical. Synthetic suffixes only have vowel-initial allomorphs and can trigger stem alternations.[36] Analytic suffixation is purely concatenative: analytic suffixes only have consonant-initial suffix allomorphs and never trigger stem alternations[37] (and clusters created by analytic suffixation can typically violate monomorphemic phonotactics). Again, the third type of suffix can be seen as heterogeneous: on the one hand, substrategies for stem/suffix allomorph selection only occur with quasi-analytic suffixes (e.g. the difference between the quasi-analytic forms of -*ik* vs. non-*ik* epenthetic stems,[38] see (18)), and on the other hand, systematic variation in stem allomorph selection (e.g. the two alternative quasi-analytic forms of epenthetic -*ik* stems, see (18)) and any variation in suffix allomorph selection only occurs with quasi-analytic suffixes.[39]

(18) and (19) show that there are two patterns for stem allomorphs: the V-pattern and the C- pattern and that these two patterns partition the 'paradigmatic space' which is defined by the combination of stem allomorphs with suffix allomorphs.

However, the two patterns are not complementary, i. e. V-pattern and C-pattern do not form a proper partitioning (disjoint and full coverage) of the paradigmatic space. In some cases the two patterns overlap (optional forms) and some cases are not covered by any of the patterns (gaps). This is not surprising since C-allomorphs and V-allomorphs have their own partially independent patterns (cf. Section 3).

---

[36]They trigger vowel – zero alternations in epenthetic stems and various other alternations not discussed in this paper (*sz-d* allomorphy, *v*-augmentation, vowel-shortening in nouns etc.) cf. Rebrus (2000), Siptár & Törkenczy (2000).

[37]If we abstract away from automatic, 'post-lexical' processes like Voicing Assimilation or Degemination, cf. Siptár & Törkenczy (2000).

[38]There are other substrategies, e.g. the quasi-analytic Person/number forms behave differently from other quasi-analytic forms in the case of *sz-d* stems, see Appendix 6.1.

[39]E.g. for some speakers there is variation in the linking vowel of quasi-analytic 2SGINDEFPRESINDIC -*sz* for some stable CC-final verbs: *mond-asz* / *mond-sz* 'say'.

(20)　　Optionality and defectiveness are mismatches of two (or more) patterns that govern allomorph selection.

This means that overt defectiveness (a paradigm gap for a combination of two or more morphemes with unsystematic masking only)[40] is a simultaneous non-occurrence of allomorphs, i. e., the situation where all patterns fail to cover a specific combination of morphemes (a morphosyntactically specified form of a stem). In the case of allomorphy non-optional forms always entail covert defectiveness: one of the patterns of allomorphs will be (covertly) defective in a cell which is covered by another one of the patterns of allomorphs, see the cells marked with ⊙ in the bottom left corner of (21a) for the V-pattern and the cells marked with ⊙ in the top right corner of (21b) for the C-pattern. Optional forms are those which do not show defectiveness at the level of allomorphs at all (see section 2), in our case this is the middle area where the two patterns overlap (shaded in (21a, b)).[41]

(21)　　a. Covert defectiveness of V-stem allomorphs

		Suffix types		
BASIC FORM	Stem classes:	SYNTHETIC	QUASI-ANALITIC	ANALYTIC
V	i. *stable* VC-stem	V	V	V
V	ii. *epenthetic*, non-*ik*	⊙	V	V
⊙	iii. *epenthetic ik*-stem	⊙	V	V
⊙	iv. *defective* (CC-)stem	⊙	⊙	⊙
⊙	v. *stable* CC-stem	⊙	⊙	⊙

b. Covert defectiveness of C-stem allomorphs

		Suffix types		
BASIC FORM	Stem classes:	SYNTHETIC	QUASI-ANALITIC	ANALYTIC
⊙	i. *stable* VC-stem	⊙	⊙	⊙
⊙	ii. *epenthetic*, non-*ik*	C	⊙	⊙
C	iii. *epenthetic ik*-stem	C	C	⊙
C	iv. *defective* (CC-)stem	C	C	⊙
C	v. *stable* CC-stem	C	C	C

---

[40]and also those cases of covert defectiveness whose systematic masking is periphrastic.

[41]There is a general condition on what is a possible pattern. It has to satisfy (a version of) closedness. On the general properties of gradual patterns of this kind see Rebrus (2004) (in morphology), and Rebrus & Trón (2002) (phonotactics).

4.2   Overt defectiveness

The problem may be stated informally in the following way. From a functional perspective overt defectiveness is disadvantageous since the expression of the meaning where the gap occurs is only possible by unsystematic masking (paraphrase, see section 2). Nevertheless, it happens to be (rather) stable, i. e., it is not avoided in Hungarian.

Avoidance of a gap means the reassignment of a defective stem to another stem-class. We assume that this repair of a gapped paradigm must be (i) *conservative*, i. e., it is reclassification: the reassignment of a member of a lexical stem class into another existing lexical class and (ii) *minimal / local*: it must be into a minimally different lexical (stem) class so that a change can only target a point in the paradigm where there is something to repair (in our case, a gap).

The fact that this is not possible in Hungarian and that the paradigm of defective CC-stems has overt gaps can be explained with reference to the patterns of stem types discussed above, cf (21). Let us examine the pattern of defective stems and compare it to those stem classes that are minimally different from it. There are two classes whose paradigms are close to that of defective stems: non-defective stable CC-stems and defective *ik*-stems. This is shown in (22) where the relevant rows of (19) are repeated as ⟨synthetic, quasi-analytic, analytic⟩ 3-tuples with values C and/or V:

(22)   The 'closest neighbours' of the defective stem type
      epenthetic *ik*-stems: ⟨C   C/V   V⟩
      defective CC-stems: ⟨C   C   −⟩
      non-defective CC-stems: ⟨C   C   C⟩

Of the two[42] possibilities of reclassification of defective stems, i. e., as epenthetic *ik*-stems or as non-defective CC-stems, the latter one (as ⟨C C C⟩) is conservative and local. However, this is the point where Hungarian defectiveness is phonotactically constrained: the resulting analytical forms are phonotactically ill-formed/disfavoured (e.g. for *háml-ik* 'peel': **hámlva*). The other possibility of conservative reclassification is non-local because it would have to introduce an alternative V-allomorph in quasi-analytic forms in addition to the introduction of a V-allomorph in analytic forms to get the ⟨C C/V V⟩ pattern of epenthetic *ik*-stems (⟨**hámlok hámlana/*hámolna *hámolva*⟩). Finally, simply introducing a V-allomorph

---

[42]The other conceivable conservative reclassifications, i. e., as stable VC or epenthetic non-ik stems, would be into 'distant', i. e., non-local classes, see (21abi, ii).

only in analytic forms yields a lexically non-existing (and thus non-conserva/tive) pattern: *⟨C C V⟩ * ⟨*hámlok hámlana *hámolva*⟩.

To sum up, Hungarian defective stems behave in the way they do because the repair of their gapped paradigm would

    (i)   violate phonotactics, or
    (ii) be non-local, or
    (iii) be non-conservative.[43]

Conservativeness is a key concept in the explanation we proposed above. In what follows we express this in a more formalised way with reference to regularities that are linguistically plausible and apply in the patterns in tables (18/19/21).

It is apparent in (22) that the reason why defective stems cannot be reclassified as epenthetic -*ik*-stems (in a conservative way) is the variation the latter show in the quasi-analytic cells of their paradigm. The locus of this variation/optionality within their paradigm, however is not arbitrary, but follows from the way in which V-stems and C-stems are distributed in the verbal paradigm of the stem classes.

If we examine the pattern of V-allomorphs and C-allomorphs separately (see (21a, b)), the following generalisations can be made about the quasi-analytic forms.

(23)   The stem alternant that appears in the analytic form of a stem always appears as a stem alternant in the quasi-analytic form of the stem.[44]

This can be formulated in the following way. Let A be the set of analytic suffix-allomorphs, Q the set of quasi-analytic suffix-allomorphs, L the set of lexical stems, and $x \in L$ a stem of any stem class. Let s be an arbitrary suffix and $\langle x', s \rangle$, $\langle x'', s \rangle$ etc. the surface forms of x suffixed with a suffix-allomorph s. Let V and C be the set of existing surface forms whose stem

---

[43] In fact, violations of i-iii. do exist sporadically and idiolectally with some interesting preferences of direction. As we pointed out in 2.3 above the few defective stems that end in clusters with no sonority rise (e.g. *burjánz-* 'proliferate', cf. 2.3) tend to be reclassified as stable CC-stems if they are reclassified while defective stems that end in clusters with a significant sonority rise (e.g. *csukl-* 'hiccup' tend to be reclassified as epenthetic stems if they are reclassified. Naturally, wildly non-local reclassifications (e.g. defective reclassified as stable VC) do not exist at all.

[44] Note that this is very similar to the OT constraint that Kenstowicz (2005) discusses which requires that one surface form should preserve the CV-structure of the stem of another designated surface form.

allomorph is a V-allomorph and a C-allomorph respectively. Then (23) can be expressed as the following two generalisations:[45]

(24)   Correspondence between analytic and quasi-analytic stem-allomorphs: $\forall x \in L \ \forall a \in A \ \forall q \in Q$

    i. $\exists x' : \langle x', a \rangle \in C \Rightarrow \exists x'' : \langle x'', q \rangle \in C$
    ii. $\exists x' : \langle x', a \rangle \in V \Rightarrow \exists x'' : \langle x'', q \rangle \in V$

Note that defective stems do not contradict (24i and ii) since the premise does not hold in either case (since there is no analytic form with either a C-allomorph or a V-allomorph). (24) correctly describes the V-allomorph of the optional/alternative quasi-analytic forms, but does not account for the variation. It must be pointed out that this is exactly where and how epenthetic *-ik* stems and epenthetic non-*ik* stems differ: both of them have a V-allomorph in quasi-analytic forms (in accordance with 24ii), but only epenthetic *-ik* stems have an alternative C-allomorph as well. This is non-arbitrary, but can only be explained with reference to what we called the 'basic-form', i. e., 3SGINDEFPRESINDIC [46], since the basic form is the only form in which the stem allomorphs differ in the two stem classes (in addition to the quasi-analytic forms that we want to explain). Note that this is due to the fact that 3SGINDEFPRESINDIC suffix *-ik* is synthetic while zero (which non-*ik* stems have in their basic form) is analytic. This means that basic forms are 'mixed' in the sense that the markers they take do not belong to the same morphophonological suffix class (see (10) and (17e)). There is a correlation between the stem allomorph of the basic form and that of the quasi-analytic forms. This generalisation holds for all stem classes, epenthetic (*-ik* and non-*ik*) and non-epenthetic stems (cf. Rebrus 2000).

(25)   The stem alternant that appears in the basic form of a stem always appears as a stem alternant in the quasi-analytic form of the stem.[47]

---

[45]Note that the implication in (24ii) can be formulated in a more restricted way as an equivalence since every stem that has a quasi-analytic V-allomorph, also has an analytic V-allomorph (see 20a i-iii). (24i) on the other cannot be substituted with an equivalence since epenthetic *–ik* stems have a C-stem allomorph in quasi-analytic forms but not in analytic forms (see 20b iii) and defective stems have a C-allomorph in quasi-analytic forms but not in analytic forms (see 20b iv).

[46]It is important to point out that the basic form of those stems that do not have a 3SGINDEFPRESINDIC form is the definite form, i. e., the only 3SGPRESINDIC form that they have. The only relevant examples are *sínyl-* and *kétl-* (see notes 22, 28).

[47]See footnote 44.

This can be formulated as (26) where $\langle x' \rangle$, $\langle x'' \rangle$ etc. stand for the basic form of the stem x.

(26) Correspondence between basic and quasi-analytic stem-allomorphs
$\forall x \in L \; \forall q \in Q$

    i. $\exists x' : \langle x' \rangle \in C \;\Rightarrow\; \exists x'' : \langle x'', q \rangle \in C$
    ii. $\exists x' : \langle x' \rangle \in V \;\Rightarrow\; \exists x'' : \langle x'', q \rangle \in V$

(24) and (26) together determine the shape of quasi-analytic stem allomorphs. The only point (cell) in the paradigmatic space where they require a different type of allomorph is the quasi-analytic forms of epenthetic *-ik* stems where (24) requires a V-allomorph and (26) requires a C-allomorph. The variation in the cell satisfies both. This is shown in (27).

(27) Factors determining quasi-analytic forms

Stem types:	Suffix types:		
	BASIC FORM	SYNTHETIC QUASI-ANALITIC	ANALYTIC
i. stable VC-stem	V	······V········➤ V ◄·········	V
ii. epenthetic, non-ik	V	·····C········➤ V ◄·········	V
iii. epenthetic ik-stem	C	······C········ ➤C / V◄ ·····	V
iv. defective (CC-)stem	C	······C········➤ C	⊙
v. stable CC-stem	C	······C········➤ C ◄·········	C

Note that the correspondence requirements (24, 26) that determine the shapes of quasi-analytic allomorphs refer to sources of different types. The analiticity that (24i and ii) refer to is a lexical morphophonological property of suffix allomorphs while the basic stem that (26i and ii) refer to is a morphosyntactic property (3SGINDEFPRESINDIC) of morphemes.

With this in mind let us return to the problem of defectiveness. Conservatism means that (24) and (26) must be obeyed in systematic repair. A systematic repair of defectiveness would mean that all the analytic forms of all defective verbs would have to be supplied (i. e., 6–10 forms for 65 stems, see (15) and (17)). A phonotactically possible repair can introduce a C-allomorph in the analytic forms of a few defective verbs and reclassify them as stable-CC verbs ($\langle$C C V$\rangle$, e.g. $\langle$*burjánzok burján-zana* <u>*burjánzva*</u>$\rangle$[48] where the stem allomorphs introduced by repair are underlined). This is only possible for some speakers, with some stem-final CC-clusters (see the explanation following table (14)). However, for the

---

[48]Remember that the order of elements in this notation is $\langle$synthetic_forms, quasi-analytic_forms, analytic_forms$\rangle$.

majority of defective verbs a phonotactically possible repair would have to introduce a V-allomorph in all analytic forms. This entails a V-allomorph in quasi-analytic forms too, in accordance with (24ii). The V-allomorph would have to be introduced there too because defective stems only have C-allomorphs in quasi-analytic forms (e.g. ⟨*hámlok hámlana*/**hámolna* **hámolva*⟩). This means that the (conservative) repair would be non-local. (To put it in another way, the non-introduction of a V-allomorph in quasi-analytic forms, i. e., the strictly local repair of analytic forms, would make repair non-conservative in that the resulting paradigm would violate (24ii) since it would only have a C-allomorph in quasi-analytic forms and we saw that *⟨C C V⟩ is a non-existing paradigm, e.g. *⟨*hámlok hámlana* **hámolva*⟩).

The reclassification of non-*ik* defective stems (*sínyl-* and *kétl-*) fares even worse. The reason is that in this case, the repair of the gaps (where analytic forms would occur) by introducing V-allomorphs (e.g. **kétel-ve*) would also involve the basic form since it is also analytic (e.g. **kétel*). Given (24ii) and (26ii) this entails that the only stem allomorph that could occur in a quasi-analytic form should be a V-allomorph (e.g. **kétel-ne*). However, defective stems (including non-*ik* defective stems) have (only) C-allomorphs in their quasi-analytic forms (e.g. *kétl-ene*). Thus, conservative repair (i. e., the reclassification of non-*ik* defective stems as non-*ik* epenthetic stems (⟨C V V⟩ with a V allomorph basic-form, e.g. ⟨*hajlok hajolna hajolva*⟩, basic form: *hajol*, see (18ii)) would not only have to be non-local (since repair would have to involve quasi-analytic forms in addition to analytic ones e.g. *⟨*kétlek kétlene*/**kételne* **kételve*⟩,[49] basic form: **kétel*), but would also have to be destructive since it would also have to delete the quasi-analytic forms that are based on a C-allomorph in addition to introducing forms based on V-allomorphs to fill the (analytic) gaps to produce an existing paradigm (that of non-*ik* epenthetic stems): *⟨C ~~C~~/V V⟩ with a V allomorph basic form, e.g. *⟨*kétlek* ~~*kétlene*~~/**kételne* **kételve*⟩, basic form: **kétel*. (To put it in another way, the non-introduction of a V-allomorph in quasi-analytic forms, i. e., the strictly local (and non-destructive) repair of analytic forms, would make the repair non-conservative in that the resulting paradigm would violate (24ii) and (26ii) since it would only have a C-allomorph in quasi-analytic forms and *⟨C C V⟩ (with

---

[49]Note that this (⟨C C/V V⟩) is *not* an existing paradigm if the basic form is V (i. e., it is not an existing paradigm for an epenthetic non-*ik* stem), although it is if the basic form is C (i. e., it is an existing paradigm for an epenthetic *ik*-stem).

a V basic form) is a non-existing stem-paradigm, e.g. *⟨*kétlek   kétlene* *kételve*⟩ (basic form: *kétel*). [50]

5 Conclusion

In this paper we distinguished overt vs. covert defectiveness and phonologically motivated vs. phonology related defectiveness. We suggested that the overtness of defectiveness is a matter of detail: at the level of allomorphs defectiveness (and variation) depends on the non-overlap (and overlap) between allomorphic patterns. We argued that (at least) some cases of defectiveness must be described with respect to allomorphs and not morphemes and analysed Hungarian defective stems as a case in point.

We proposed an explanation of the defectiveness of Hungarian defective stems in which we claimed that (a) defectiveness and optionality (systematic variation) are interrelated, and (b) both depend on the ways in which the allomorphs, i. e., C-allomorphs and V-allomorphs of stems that are members of mainly lexically identifiable stem classes (stable VC, epenthetic (*ik* and non-*ik*), stable CC and defective) and suffix allomorphs belonging to only lexically identifiable classes (synthetic, quasi-analytic, analytic) are distributed in verbal paradigms. Defectiveness in Hungarian is a phonotactically constrained conservatism effect. It is a manifestation of the fact that it is not possible to supply forms that would fill the gaps that occur in the paradigm of defective stems, i. e., it is not possible to reclassify the defective verbs into another paradigm in a systematic way which (i) does not violate phonotactics, (ii) is local in that it only targets

---

[50] It is interesting to speculate about back non-*ik* defective stems, which, if they existed (recall that all the non-ik defective stems happen to be front, cf. note 28), would have an incredibly impoverished paradigm. They would lack all analytic forms like all other defective stems, including the 3SGINDEFPRESINDIC (which would have a zero suffix since they are non-ik). Furthermore, they would not have a 3SGDEFPRESINDIC form either since it would have to contain the suffix *-ja*, which is also an analytic allomorph. This means that they would not have 3SGPRESINDIC forms (cf. note 30), i. e., they would not have a basic form at all. Given (24) and (26), which require that a quasi-analytic form should be based on the analytic forms and the base form, this implies that back non-ik defective stems would not have quasi-analytic forms either. This gap (the lack of quasi-analytic forms of hypothetical back non-*ik* defective stems) would be different from the phonotactically motivated gaps (the lack of analytic forms of defective verbs) discussed in this paper since this new type of gap is due to the lack of analytical reinforcement/licensing (cf. Section 1). Unfortunately though, this is entirely hypothetical since back non-*ik* defective stems do not occur. Luckily, however, there is a minor subclass of verbs (Cs stems) that display just this type of phonotactically unmotivated analogy-bound gap, cf. Rebrus and Törkenczy (2007).

gaps and (iii) is conservative in that it does not produce novel paradigms of stem types. We interpreted conservatism as 'faithfulness' to designated allomorphs of the paradigm. These designated allomorphs can be identified in two ways (a) lexically (the stem allomorph that occurs in analytic forms) and (b) morphosyntactically (the stem allomorph that occurs in the basic form). These two faithfulness requirements may converge in the same allomorph or may require two different allomorphs (in which case they require variation).

This analysis may be given an OT interpretation since (i) it is surface-oriented in that it only refers to surface forms; and (ii) OT only has a device to express conservatism: OO-constraints requiring the correspondence of surface forms within the paradigm (e.g. Benua 1995, Kenstowicz 1996, Burzio 1996, Steriade 1997, McCarthy 2005, Rebrus and Törkenczy 2005a). We briefly want to point out the main difficulties / problems it presents for a general OT theory of gaps (with special regard to current OT approaches to defectiveness). In an OT implementation the relevant constraints would have to evaluate allomorphs and not morphemes in order to capture the patterns (this is especially true of the conservatism effect where the two faithfulness requirements do not conflict if they refer to allomorphs, but may if they are stated with reference to morphemes). The faithfulness requirements refer to designated allomorphs of the paradigm (they are 'asymmetrical' in this sense). This is a problem for an OT analysis based on Optimal Paradigms theory (McCarthy 2005) which is inherently symmetrical. The conservatism effect is only partially related to a morphosyntactically identifiable form that e.g. OO or OP constraints could target — this means that it cannot be true that defectiveness is generally analysable with constraints that make reference to some morphosyntactic property only (e.g. Rice 2005abc).[51]

Appendix: Glosses

akar 'want', *állapodik* 'agree', *ápol* 'nurse', *áramlik* 'flow', *bán* 'regret', *bánik* 'treat', *bérel* 'rent', *boroz* 'drink wine', *botlik* 'lose one's footing', *burjánzik* 'proliferate', *csuklik* 'hiccup', *díszlik* 'adorn', *döglik* 'die', *duruzsol* 'hum', *élez* 'sharpen', *ellenez* 'oppose', *elviharzik* 'rush out', *érez* 'feel', *fénylik* 'shine', *feslik* 'become unstitched', *fingik* 'fart', *fogamzik*

---

[51] There may be different kinds of defectiveness that require different kinds of analyses (as Albright 2003 suggests) and some may be analysable that way (see also note 50).

'conceive', *forog* 'revolve', *foszlik* 'fray', *fürdik* 'bathe', *gázol* 'overrun', *gúnyol* 'ridicule', *haboz* 'hesitate', *habzik* 'foam', *hajlik* 'become bent', *hajol* 'bend', *haldoklik* 'die', *hámlik* 'peel', *harap* 'bite', *hasonlik* 'be in conflict', *hatol* 'intrude', *hírlik* 'be rumoured', *honol* 'reside', *hord* 'wear', *hullámzik* 'wave', *inog* 'sway', *ízlik* 'like the taste of', *javasol* 'recommend', *kap* 'get', *kaphat* 'may get', *kapj* 'get!', *kapna* 'would get', *kapogat* 'get repeatedly', *kapok* 'I get', *kapsz* 'you get', *kétli* 'doubt', *koboz* 'confiscate', *koszol* 'make dirty', *kotor* 'scrape', *kotorhat* 'may scrape', *kotorj* 'scrape!', *kotorna* 'would scrape', *kotorsz* 'you scrape', *kotrok* 'I scrape', *közöl* 'inform', *lélegzik* 'breathe', *lep* 'surprise', *lop* 'steal', *marad* 'remain', *másol* 'copy', *morajlik* 'thunder', *mos* 'wash', *mo[j]ol* 'fiddle', *nyálzik* 'salivate', *okol* 'blame', *okoz* 'cause', *old* 'solve', *oldana* 'would solve', *oldasz* 'you solve', *oldhat* 'may solve', *oldj* 'solve!', *oldogat* 'solve repeatedly', *oldok* 'I solve', *ónoz* 'cover with lead', *özönlik* 'swarm', *parázslik* 'smoulder', *patakzik* 'gush', *porol* 'dust', *ragoz* 'inflect', *rámol* 're-arrange', *reng* 'shake', *romlik* 'go wrong', *siklik* 'glide', *sínyli* 'suffer', *számoz* 'number', *tajtékzik* 'foam', *ugorhat* 'may jump', *ugorj* 'jump!', *ugorna* 'would jump', *ugorsz* 'you jump', *ugrana* 'would jump', *ugrasz* 'you jump', *ugrik* 'jump', *vádol* 'accuse', *vedel* 'drink heavily', *vedlik* 'slough', *vendégel* 'receive as guest', *vezényel* 'conduct', *vonaglik* 'writhe', *vonz* 'attract'.

References

Albright, A. (2003) A Quantitative Study of Spanish Paradigm Gaps. *Proceedings of the 22nd West Coast Conference in Formal Linguistics*, G. Garding and M. Tsujimura (eds.) 1–14. Somerville, MA: Cascadilla Press.

Baerman, M. and Corbett, G. (2005) Typological aspects of defectiveness. Paper presented at the Fifth Mediterranean Morphology Meeting, Fréjus, France, September 2005.

Bagemihl, B. (1991) Syllable structure in Bella Coola. *Linguistic Inquiry* 22: 589–646.

Benua, L. (1995) Identity effects in morphological truncation. In J. Beckman, L. Walsh Dickey and S. Urbanczyk (eds.) *University of Massachusetts Occasional Papers in Linguistics 18: Papers in Optimality Theory* 77–136. Amherst, MA: GLSA.

Burzio, L. (1996) Surface constraints versus underlying representation. In

J. Durand and B. Laks (eds.) *Current Trends in Phonology: Models and Methods* 123–41. European Studies Research Institute: University of Salford Publications.

Butt, J. (1997) *Spanish Verbs.* Oxford: Oxford University Press.

Cabré, T. and Kenstowicz, M. (1995) Prosodic trapping in Catalan. *Linguistic Inquiry* 26: 694–705.

Carstairs-McCarthy, A. (1998a) Paradigmatic structure: inflectional paradigms and morphological classes. In A. Spencer and A. M. Zwicky (eds.) *The Handbook of Morphology* 322–34. Oxford: Blackwell.

Carstairs-McCarthy, A. (1998b) Phonological constraints on morphological rules. In A. Spencer and Arnold M. Zwicky (eds.) *The Handbook of Morphology* 144–48. Oxford: Blackwell.

Eliasson, S. (1975) On the issue of directionality. In K.-H. Dahlstedt (ed.) *The Nordic languages and modern linguistics 2* 421–45. Stockholm: Almqvist & Wiksell.

Halle, M. (1973) Prolegomena to a theory of word formation. *Linguistic Inquiry* 4: 1–20.

Hansson, G. Ó. (1999) 'When in doubt ... ' Intraparadigmatic dependencies and gaps in Icelandic. In P. N. Tamanji, M. Hirotani, and N. Hall (eds.) *Proceedings of NELS 29.* 105-19. Amherst, MA: GLSA. `http://www.linguistics.ubc.ca/People/Gunnar/\GH_NELS29_Gaps.pdf.`]

Hetzron, R. (1975) Where the grammar fails. *Language* 51(4): 859–72.

Inkelas, S. and Orgun, C. O. (1995) Level ordering and economy in the lexical phonology of Turkish. *Language* 71: 763–93.

Iverson, G. (1981) Rules, constraints, and paradigmatic lacunae. *Glossa* 15(1):136–44.

Jensen, J. T. (1990) *Morphology: Word Structure in Generative Grammar.* Amsterdam: John Benjamins.

Károly, S. (1957) A csuklik-féle igék ragozása, képzése. *Magyar Nyelvőr* 81: 275–81.

Katamba, F. (1993) *Morphology* London: Macmillan.

Kenstowicz, M. (1996) Base-identity and uniform exponence: alternatives to cyclicity. In: J. Durand and B. Laks (eds.) *Current Trends in Phonology: Models and Methods* 363–93. Salford: European Studies Research Institute, University of Salford Publications.

Kenstowicz, M. (2005) Paradigmatic Uniformity and Contrast. In L. J. Downing, T. A. Hall, R. Raffelsiefen (eds.) *Paradigms in Phonological Theory* 145–69. Oxford: Oxford University Press.

Kristoffersen, G. (2000) *The phonology of Norwegian*. Oxford: Oxford University Press.

Mayerthaler, W. (1988) *Morphological Naturalness*. Ann Arbor: Karoma Publishers.

McCarthy, J. J. (2005) Optimal paradigms. In L. J. Downing, T. A. Hall, and R. Raffelsiefen (eds.) *Paradigms in Phonological Theory* 170–210. Oxford: Oxford University Press. ROA 485, `http://roa.rutgers.edu`.

McCarthy, J. J. and Wolf, M. (2005) Less than zero: correspondence and the null output. Ms., University of Massachusetts, Amherst. ROA 722, `http://roa.rutgers.edu`.

Orgun, C. O. and Sprouse, R. L. (1999). From MPARSE to CONTROL: deriving ungrammaticality. *Phonology* 16: 191–224.

Poletto, R. (1998) *Topics in Runyankore Phonology*. PhD dissertation, Ohio State University.

Prince, A. and Smolensky, P. (1993/2004) *Optimality Theory: Constraint Interaction in Generative Grammar*. Ms., Rutgers University, New Brunswick, and University of Colorado, Boulder. [Revised version published by Oxford: Blackwell, also available as ROA 537, `http://roa.rutgers.edu`.]

Raffelsiefen, R. (1996) Gaps in word formation. In U. Kleinhenz (ed.) *Interfaces in Phonology* 194–209. Berlin: Akademie Verlag.

Raffelsiefen, R. (2004) Absolute ill-formedness and other morphophonological effects. *Phonology* 21: 91–142.

Rebrus, P. (2000). Morfofonológiai jelenségek. In F. Kiefer (ed.) *Strukturális magyar nyelvtan, 3. kötet: Morfológia* 763–949. Budapest: Akadémiai Kiadó.

Rebrus, P. (2004) Gradualitás és önkényesség az alaktanban. Handout from a talk at the Hungarian Academy of Sciences.

Rebrus, P. and Törkenczy, M. (2005a) Uniformity and contrast in the Hungarian verbal paradigm. In L. J. Downing, T. A. Hall, R. Raffelsiefen (eds.) *Paradigms in Phonological Theory* 263–95. Oxford: Oxford University Press.

Rebrus, P. and Törkenczy, M. (2005b) Phonologically motivated defectivity: paradigmatic gaps. Handout from talks presented at the University of Tromsø, April 2005.

Rebrus, P. and Törkenczy, M. (2007) Phonotactically unconstrained paradigmatic defectiveness: the case of s~d alternation in Hungarian. Poster presented at the 4th Old World Conference in Phonology, Rhodes, Greece, January 2007.

Rebrus, P. and Trón, V. (2002) A fonotaktikai általánosításokról: Kísérlet a magyar mássalhangzó-kapcsolatok nem-reprezentációs leírására. In M. Maleczki (ed.) *A mai magyar nyelv leírásának legújabb módszerei V.* 17–63. Szeged: Szegedi Tudományegyetem.

Rice, C. (2003) Syllabic well-formedness in Norwegian imperatives. *Nordlyd* 31: 372–84. [Available as ROA 642 under title 'Dialectal variation in Norwegian imperatives', http://roa.rutgers.edu]

Rice, C. (2005a) Optimal gaps in optimal paradigms. *Catalan Journal of Linguistics*. [Special issue on phonology in morphology edited by M.-R. Lloret and J. Jiménez. Available at LingBuzz, http://ling.auf.net/buzzdocs/.]

Rice, C. (2005b). Nothing is a phonological fact. Paper presented at the 13th Manchester Phonology Meeting, May 2005.

Rice, C. (2007) Gaps and repairs at the phonology-morphology interface. *Journal of Linguistics* 43: 197–221.

Schachter, P. and Otanes, F. (1972) *Tagalog reference grammar*. Berkeley: University of California Press.

Siptár, P. and Törkenczy, M. (2000) *The Phonology of Hungarian. The Phonology of the World's Languages*. Oxford: Clarendon Press/Oxford University Press.

Steriade, D. (1997) Lexical conservatism. In *Linguistics in the Morning Calm, Selected Papers from SICOL 1997* 157–79. Seoul: Linguistic Society of Korea, Hanshin Publishing House.

Steriade, D. (2000) Paradigm uniformity and the phonetics-phonology boundary. In M. Broe and J. Pierrehumbert (eds.) *Papers in Laboratory Phonology 5* 313–34. Cambridge: Cambridge University Press.

Steriade, D. (2006) Avoiding alternations in Romanian. Handout of paper presented at the *MIT Phonology Circle*.

Steriade, D. (2008) A pseudo-cyclic effect in Romanian morpho-phonology. In A. Bachrach and A. Nevins (eds.) *Inflectional Identity* 313–360. Oxford: Oxford University Press.

Stump, G. T. (1998). Inflection. In A. Spencer and A. M. Zwicky (eds.) *The Handbook of Morphology* 134–44. Oxford: Blackwell.

Szépe, J., Gerstner, K. and Szende, T. (2004) Csuklik, kotlik, hámlik. Megjegyzések a hiányos paradigmájú igék módjelezéséről. *Magyar Nyelv* 100: 358–67.

Törkenczy, M. (1992) Vowel~zero alternations in Hungarian: a government approach. In I. Kenesei and Cs. Pléh (eds.). *Approaches to Hungarian, 4: The Structure of Hungarian* 157–76. Szeged: JATE.

Törkenczy, M. (2000) Absolute phonological ungrammaticality: defective paradigms in Hungarian. Paper presented at the 8th Manchester Phonology Meeting, Manchester, UK.

Törkenczy, M. (2001a) Végzetes rosszulformáltság a fonológiában. In: M. Bakró-Nagy, Z. Bánréti and K. É. Kiss (eds.) *Újabb tanulmányok a strukturális magyar nyelvtan és a nyelvtörténet köréből. Kiefer Ferenc tiszteletére, barátai és tanítványai* 274–91. Budapest: Osiris Kiadó.

Törkenczy, M. (2002a) Absolute phonological ungrammaticality in output-biassed phonology. In I. Kenesei (ed.) *Approaches to Hungarian. Volume 8. Papers from the Budapest Conference* 311–24. Budapest: Akadémiai Kiadó.

Törkenczy, M. (2002b) Covert defectivity, alternative and parallel stems in Hungarian. Paper presented at the 6th International Conference on the Structure of Hungarian, Düsseldorf, Germany.

Törkenczy, M. (2004) The phonotactics of Hungarian. Ms., Hungarian Academy of Sciences.

Trón, V. and Rebrus, P. (2005) Re-presenting the past: contrast and uniformity in Hungarian past tense suffixation. In I. Kenesei, C. Pinón and P. Siptár (eds.) *Approaches to Hungarian 9. Papers from the Düsseldorf Conference* 305–27. Budapest: Akadémiai Kiadó.

Part III
Ineffability in Syntax

8 The neutralization approach to ineffability in syntax

Géraldine Legendre
Johns Hopkins University

1 The nature of the debate

Ungrammaticality in syntax comes in two basic flavors which are illustrated below in contexts of wh-extraction. In cases of ungrammatical extraction out of a complement clause in (1)–(2), a minor structural repair (at least on the surface) produces a better alternative without altering its interpretation. For example, the complementizer *that* must be dropped when the subject of the complement clause is extracted in English; in a similar context in French the complementizer *que* [kə] changes to *qui* [ki]. As shown in (3a-b), the counterparts to (1a-2a) are grammatical in Italian and Bulgarian. Patterns of ungrammaticality are language-dependent, and so are the repair strategies.[1]

(1)   a.   *[$_{CP}$Who$_i$ do [$_{IP}$ you believe [$_{CP}$ that [$_{IP}$ t$_i$ came]]]]?
        b.   [$_{CP}$Who$_i$ do [$_{IP}$ you believe [$_{IP}$ t$_i$ came]]]?

(2)   a.   *[$_{CP}$ Qui$_i$ crois$_j$ [$_{IP}$-tu t$_j$ [$_{CP}$ qu(e) [$_{IP}$ t$_i$ est venu]]]]?
        b.   [$_{CP}$ Qui$_i$ crois$_j$ [$_{IP}$-tu t$_j$ [$_{CP}$ **qui** [$_{IP}$ t$_i$ est venu]]]]?
           'Who do you believe that came'   (French)

(3)   a.   Chi$_i$ credi che t$_i$ sia venuto?   (Italian)

---

[1] These repair strategies prevent the ECP/TGOV (Empty Category Principle) from being violated. High-ranked in English and French, TGOV requires that traces be head-governed (Legendre et al. 1995). See also (1997). (1a)–(2a) are ungrammatical because the subject trace t$_i$ fails to be properly governed (complementizers *that* and *que* are functional rather than lexical categories, a defining attribute of proper governors). When *that* is dropped as in (1b), t$_i$ is properly governed by the matrix verb. Rizzi (1990) assumes that French *qui* is the 'agreeing' version of *que*, somehow making the complementizer eligible to serve as a proper governor of t$_i$. Finally, the grammaticality of corresponding Italian and Bulgarian extractions in (3a,b) is accounted for by positing that subject extraction is from a postverbal position, i.e. a position which is by definition properly governed by the embedded verb (Rizzi 1990). This is independently motivated by the fact that both languages freely allow postverbal subjects in non-wh-contexts.

"

  b. Koj$_i$ misliš če t$_i$ e došul?
    Who believe-2SG that is come
    'Who do you believe that came?'   (Bulgarian)

In other cases, ungrammaticality cannot be repaired within the same construction because the grammar of a particular language does not provide a better alternative via a minor structural repair. This is known as absolute ungrammaticality or **ineffability**. A well-known case is that of multiple wh-questions in some languages (another is passive in Hungarian and other languages). Compare single wh-questions in (4) with multiple questions in (5). Both types of wh-questions are subject to requirements on the position and argumental status of wh-phrases. In English single wh-questions, the wh-phrase must appear in clause-initial position, regardless of its argumental status. In multiple wh-questions there is a Superiority effect whereby the highest available wh-phrase on the argument-adjunct scale (*who > what > where, when > how > why*) must appear in clause-initial position; the other wh-phrase must remain in situ (its d-structure position). Multiple wh-questions like (5a) have a multiple-pair interpretation. Adequate answers are of the form: "John ate pizza, Mary ice cream, etc."

(4) a. Who came?
   b. What did John eat?
   c. Why did John come?

(5) a. Who ate what?
   b. *What did who eat?

Ineffability arises in English when *who* is paired with adjunct wh-phrases *why* or *how,* regardless of which wh-phrase is fronted (6a-b). In other languages requiring wh-fronting in single wh-questions, including Italian for some speakers (Calabrese 1984), multiple wh-questions are all ungrammatical, regardless of the position or argumental status of the wh-phrases involved.

(6) a. *Who came why?   (English)
   b. *Why did who come?
   c. *Chi ha mangiato che cosa?
     Who has eaten which thing?
     'Who ate what?'   (Italian)

For Pesetsky (1997) the existence of ineffability is strong evidence that syntax does not operate on the basis of an optimality-theoretic architecture. Rather, ineffability supports the "clash and crash" model embodied in Principles & Parameters/Minimalist theories. On that view, OT constrains spelling out the abstract syntactic structure only, i.e. its pronunciation.

Pesetsky's conclusion is not the only logical and valid conclusion however. Independent evidence for an OT model of syntax comes from the undeniable existence of significant cross-linguistic variation and economy-based generalizations (which require additional formal constructs in Principles & Parameters or Minimalist models of syntax). Moreover, ineffability is merely one aspect of the mismatch between interpretation and form which manifests itself elsewhere as ambiguity, optionality, etc. (Beaver and Lee 2004). Within OT, the question of ineffability reduces to the characterization of the optimal output in an optimization that does not obviously yield a grammatical output.

Various approaches to handling ineffability in syntax have been developed in the OT literature. In Standard OT (Prince and Smolensky 1993/2004) it is clear that language-particular absolute ungrammaticality cannot be located in *Gen,* the component which precedes *H-eval*; if so, it would predict universal ineffability. This leaves two options. One is to locate absolute ungrammaticality in a component (Interpretation/LF) that follows *H-eval.* On this view, all members of the candidate set share the same LF and the optimal candidate output of a syntactic optimization is simply uninterpretable (Grimshaw 1997). Note however that all competitors have a valid interpretation under LF equivalency. To say that the Italian winner [who ate what?] crashes at interpretation, while its English counterpart does not, entails that the competitors are not all interpretively equivalent after all.

The alternative is that absolute ungrammaticality is in fact located in *H-eval.* Whether this is viewed as problematic or not depends on one's view of the role of Input-Ouput faithfulness in syntax. For example, Heck et al. (2002) consider syntax to be an information-preserving system with richly structured output candidates, whereas phonology is a system that loses information, so that reference to an underlying input is necessary in phonological constraints. They argue that I-O faithfulness constraints in syntax can easily be reformulated as output constraints provided output representations are enriched (this invites the question of whether the output-oriented approach is just a notational variant of the I-O faithfulness approach). Note also that the very existence of wh- or scope ineffability is a direct challenge to the view that syntax is an information-preserving system.

Proponents of I-O faithfulness in syntax however disagree on how to handle ineffability in standard OT. Based on the original proposal by Prince and Smolensky ([1993]/2004), Ackema and Neeleman (2000) propose a **null parse** approach: The optimal candidate is empty (it has no syntactic structure): "Sometimes it's better to say nothing". Ackema and Neeleman assume that the null parse candidate is not fed into the interpretational component (because it has no syntactic structure at all). Since it has no interpretation they further assume that the null parse candidate doesn't violate the requirement that all candidates be semantically equivalent.

(7)   The Null Parse approach

Italian	Input	Optimal Ouput
	Q (single wh-question)	Q
	QQ (multiple wh-question)	⊙

By definition the null parse candidate does not contain any of the information contained in the input. Hence, it does not minimally violate I-O faithfulness, contrary to the axiom that OT constraints are violable but **minimally** so. Furthermore, the null parse approach incorporates significant redundancy in the form of relying on both an LF specification in the input and a separate evaluation of the optimal output to check it. Moreover, underparsing is still needed elsewhere in syntax where semantics are not affected (e.g. pro-drop). Finally, for the cases of ineffability at hand, the null parse approach has proven unworkable for a very general reason discussed in Section 3.3 below.

Legendre et al. (1995, 1998) introduce an alternative **neutralization** approach to ineffability, whereby different inputs (interpretations) neutralize to one and the same optimal output because specific input features ([wh]; operator scope) may be underparsed. The optimal candidate is close to the input interpretation but not identical: "Sometimes it's best to say something else".

(8)   The Neutralization approach

Italian	Input	Optimal Ouput
	Q (single wh-question)	Q
	QQ (multiple wh-question)	Q

The neutralization approach differs from the null parse approach in a number of ways. First, the neutralization approach rests on minimal violations of I-O faithfulness; unlike the null parse approach it does not require relaxing a defining property of OT. Second, all candidates are syntactic structures combined with an LF interpretation in the neutralization approach. In contrast, the null parse approach relies on an odd type of candidate (no structure, no interpretation). Third, the neutralization approach is economical: the input contains a target interpretation; the candidates all have a structure and an interpretation; faithfulness constraints are needed elsewhere in syntax to handle, for example, word order tied to discourse status and expletives. There is no additional interpretational component to operate on the output of the syntax.

Both approaches ultimately rely on two alternative conceptions of the candidate set. Ackema and Neeleman (2000) assume that the candidate set may only include candidates that share the same interpretation plus the null parse candidate which doesn't. Legendre et al. (1998) hold that the candidate set includes candidate outputs that do not have the same interpretation although they share **the same target interpretation**. In other words, the interpretation of a candidate may deviate from, while remaining as close as possible to, the intended interpretation specified in the input. This relaxing of an LF-equivalency requirement on the candidate set is often held against the neutralization approach. However, a fair comparison must include all other relevant aspects of the proposal, including the fact that the neutralization approach is a very economical solution to the problem of ineffability, which the null parse approach is not. The neutralization approach is explored in detail in Section 2.[2]

Any solution to ineffability is concerned with the nature of the input to syntax and how much structure in the input is desirable. On the one hand, there is general agreement that the input to syntax must at least include argument structure specification in addition to lexical items. On the other hand, some object to the treatment of ineffability in multiple wh-questions in terms of I-O faithfulness on the basis that it requires positing additional structure in the input, including operator scope relations. For Legendre et al. (1998) this is no different from including discourse features like [contrastive focus], [topic], etc. to account for so-called optionality in word order (e.g. Choi 1996; Costa 2001; Legendre 2001a,b; Samek-Lodovici 2001).

---

[2]Others (e.g. Müller and Sternefeld 2000:51) object to neutralization on the basis that it creates massive derivational ambiguity characterized as a serious problem in language acquisition and parsing which can be avoided only by positing additional meta-optimization procedures (e.g. lexicon optimization). Such comments confound competence and performance and ignore the fact that OT is explicitly formulated as a theory of competence by its founders.

More generally, the I-O faithfulness approach advocated here on the basis of Legendre et al. (1995, 1998, 2006) takes the view that the main function of the input in OT syntax is to define the competition in the context of an **inventory** view of the grammar familiar from pre-existing constraint-based approaches to syntax as well as the Basic CV Syllable Structure Theory of Prince and Smolensky ([1993]/2004). The inventory view implies that the main question to ask is "What is the inventory of all possible syllable shapes or questions in a given language, deduced by considering all possible inputs?" rather than "What is the input-output mapping, given a particular input?" characteristic of some phonology theorizing (Prince and Smolensky [1993]/2004, Ch. 9). On the inventory view, the input to syntax is more appropriately characterized as the **Index** in the mathematical sense of the term, in which each member of a collection is indexed or uniquely labeled by a member of an 'index set'. A member of the collection in question is a particular candidate set, and its Index uniquely specifies it.Henceforth the term Input/Index is used to reflect the mathematical property in question.

The remaining discussion is structured as follows: Section 2 argues for a neutralization approach to ineffability in multiple wh-questions. Section 3 develops an argument against the null parse approach grounded in the need to recognize multiple I-O faithfulness constraints to handle contrasts in wh-extraction out of wh-clauses and *that*-clauses in Chinese and English. Section 4 presents additional evidence for the neutralization approach that is independent of wh-extraction. Section 5 addresses the question of the surface realization of unparsed input features. Section 6 concludes the discussion of neutralization and faithfulness from the perspective of the general architecture of OT.

2 The neutralization approach

2.1 Cross-linguistic variation in multiple wh-questions

In many languages it is possible to extract –overtly (Bulgarian), covertly (Chinese), or a mixture of both (English) — two or more wh-phrases, subject only to positional requirements associated with overt vs. covert extraction and possible restrictions on which wh-phrases may appear first, second, etc.; see (9). The latter superiority effects need not concern us here.

(9)   a.   ***Koj kakvo na kogo*** e   da   ?
              who what   to whom has given
              'Who gave what to whom?'   (Bulgarian, Rudin 1988)
        b.   Lisi zhidao ***shenme shenme shihou***?
              Lisi know   what   what   time
              'What did Lisi know when?'   (Chinese)
        c.   ***What*** did Congress know ***when***?   (English)

However, multiple wh-questions are not universally grammatical. In Irish (McCloskey 1979), Quiegolani Zapotec (Black 2000), and Italian for some speakers (Calabrese 1984), all combinations of argument and adjunct wh-phrases are ungrammatical regardless of wh-phrase order. That is, these languages permit only the fronting of one wh-phrase per question. Inputs/indexes with multiple wh are simply ineffable.

(10)   a.   *Chi   ha mangiato che   cosa?
            Who ate   which thing?
            'Who ate what?'   (Italian)
        b.   *Cé   aL rinne ciadé?
            who that did   what
            'Who did what?'   (Irish)
        c.   *Pa   go   r-laa de lo   txu?
            what thing do   you face who
            'What are you doing to who?'   (Zapotec)

The patterns in (10) have received a lot of attention in OT syntax for the obvious reason that every optimization in standard OT must yield an optimal output which by assumption is grammatical. What are then the grammatical counterparts to (10a-c) in languages with ineffable multiple wh inputs/indexes? More generally, what consequences does the existence of ineffability have for extending OT to syntax?

2.2 Theoretical constructs

The approach to ineffability developed in Legendre et al. (1995, 1998) starts with a structured Input/Index which includes syntactic categories, clausal boundaries, predicate-argument structure plus the **target interpretation** (e.g.[+wh]), thus setting up the prerequisite for Input-Output Faithfulness constraints on interpretation to operate in *H-eval.*

The universal Input/Index to a wh-question depicted in (11) incorporates standard assumptions about the semantics of wh-questions as operator-variable constructions with an abstract operator Q marking scope and a variable x that it binds (May 1985).

(11)   Universal Input/Index for questioning a direct object out of a simple clause: $[Q_j [\ldots x_j \ldots]]$

GEN generates a universal set of candidates with all relevant brackets (in accordance with standard X'-theory) andis also responsible for placing Q in highest Spec position, typically SpecCP. GEN marks as overt Q or x (or both). A candidate with an overt Q looks like English *What$_j$ did he say t$_j$?* where the wh-phrase is fronted to clause-initial position; x is the trace of the overtly moved wh-phrase. A candidate with an overt x looks like an English echo question *He said what?*[3] This in-situ strategy is used in Chinese to express standard information questions, as shown in (7b) above.

GEN also generates candidates that fail to parse some element of the input (e.g. the [wh] feature). An unfaithful parse like (12c) is not interpreted as a question but rather a statement with a [−wh] or unspecified DP in lieu of a [+wh] DP. See further discussion in Section 2.3.

(12)   Candidate set for a single Q in the input
        a. $[Q_j[\ldots wh_j \ldots]]$ faithful parse
        b. $[wh_j [\ldots t_j \ldots]]$ faithful parse
        c. $\langle +Q_j \rangle [\ldots DP/\langle +wh_j \rangle \ldots]$ unfaithful parse

Inputs to multiple wh involve 2 Qs which receive a pair-list interpretation. However, English allows only one wh-phrase to be fronted, the other remains in situ; see (9c). Following Higginbotham and May (1981) English involves a process of **absorption** whereby two wh-operators convert into a single operator in SpecCP marking the scope of two variables ($wh_{i[j]}$; candidate c in tableaux T1-T5). This is reinterpreted as a violation of *ABSORB. In contrast, Bulgarian allows multiple wh-phrases to be fronted because it tolerates violations of *ADJOIN thereby allowing two operators to adjoin to SpecCP (Rudin 1988): wh $_i$+wh$_j$; candidate b in T2 below. See (9a). Chinese (9b) uses covert adjunction (Q_i+Q_k) under the analysis proposed in Legendre et al. (1998) (although an absorption analysis may also be possible).

Summing up, candidates of interest involve two Qs universally, which may be realized as in (13).

---

[3] Echo questions are not requests for new information. They presuppose that the answer is already known; hence, their interpretation depends on a restricted set of values for the wh-variable.They correspond to a distinct input.

(13)   Best candidates:

    a.   Both wh-phrases in situ: Chinese (adjunction of empty Qs in SpecCP)

    b.   Both wh-phrases fronted: Bulgarian(adjunction of overt wh-phrases in SpecCP)

    c.   Only one wh-phrase fronted, the other in situ: English (absorption of two variables by one overt wh-phrase)

    d.   One fronted, the other unparsed: Italian, Irish, Zapotec

    e.   One in situ, the other unparsed: see discussion in section 2.3.

CON incorporates a general constraint on economy of movement (*t, equivalent to Grimshaw's STAY) and a number of constraints which build on various technical proposals arising from extensive GB studies of wh-questions in the 1980's and 90's.

(14)   Constraints:

*t	"No traces" (general economy of movement)
*Q	"No empty Q-operators" (forces wh-phrases to front)
*ABSORB	"No absorption of Q-operators" (only relevant if wh-phrase is fronted; penalizes the absence of a 1-1 correspondence between wh-operators and variables)
*ADJOIN	"No adjunction of Q-operators" (violated by two fronted wh-phrases)
PARSEQ	"[Q] feature must be parsed" (violated by unfaithful candidates)

2.3   A typology of multiple wh-questions

I adopt the following convention initiated in Legendre et al. (1995): A subject is identified by subscript i, a direct object by subscript j, a referential adjunct (e.g. *when, where*) by subscript k, and a non-referential adjunct (e.g. *how, why*) by subscript l. Following Rizzi (1990) **referentiality** is understood as a short name for the universal scale ranging from arguments to adjuncts with core arguments (subjects and direct objects) being most argumental and *how, why* least argumental. While respecting this scale, languages typically impose a cut-off point somewhere along the scale which establishes a binary distinction distinguishing 'arguments' from 'adjuncts' in a number of syntactic contexts.

T1-T5 display the optimizations in the four languages under discussion, each of which exemplifies a different optimal output. Only one possible ranking yielding a given optimal pattern is considered -- with the understanding that other rankings exist which may yield the same results (in each case, further consideration of question patterns in each language is needed to possibly narrow down alternative constraint rankings). Finally, the position of V in T1-T5 candidates reflects word order properties of the target languages with no consequence for the main issue under investigation.

Chinese is an in-situ-wh language: abstract Q operators in SpecCP bind wh-phrases in situ. Chinese permits adjunction of Q operators in violation of *ADJOIN. Given that candidate *a* has to defeat candidate *b* and that *a* violates *Q, a constraint violated by candidate *b* must outrank *Q, namely *t. (Note: The relative ranking of *ABSORB is a factor only when wh is fronted, i.e. when *Q ranks higher than *t; then it decides between candidates *b* and *c*.)

T1. Chinese

$[\ Q_i\ Q_k\ [V\ x_i\ x_k]]$	*t	*ABSORB	PARSEQ	*Q	*ADJOIN
a. ☞ $[\ Q_i{+}Q_k\ [wh_i\ wh_k\ V]]$				**	*
b. $[\ wh_i{+}wh_k\ [t_i\ t_k\ V]]$	*!*				*
c. $[\ wh_{i[k]}\ [t_i\ wh_k\ V]]$	*!	*			
d. $[\ wh_i\langle+Q_k\rangle\ [t_i\ DP/\langle wh_k\rangle\ V]]$	*!		*		
e. $[\ Q_i\langle+Q_k\rangle\ [wh_iDP/+\langle wh_k\rangle\ V]]$			*!	*	

Bulgarian exemplifies the overt counterpart to Chinese, i.e. adjunction of multiple wh-phrases in SpecCP binding wh-traces in situ. The optimal candidate is *b*. Overt movement of two wh-phrases results in two violations of *t and one violation of *ADJOIN. PARSEQ, *Q, and *ABSORB must outrank *t and *ADJOIN in Bulgarian.

T2. Bulgarian

$[\ Q_i\ Q_j\ [V\ x_i\ x_j]]$	*ABSORB	*Q	PARSEQ	*t	*ADJOIN
a. $[\ Q_i{+}Q_j\ [V\ wh_i\ wh_j]]$		*!*			*
b. ☞ $[\ wh_i{+}wh_j\ [V\ t_i\ t_j]]$				**	*
c. $[\ wh_{i[j]}\ [V\ t_i\ wh_j]]$	*!			*	
d. $[\ wh_i\langle+Q_j\rangle\ [V\ t_i\ DP/\langle+wh_j\rangle]]$			*!	*	
e. $[\ Q_i\ \langle Q_j\rangle\ [V\ wh_iDP/\langle wh_j\rangle]]$		*!	*		

English exemplifies the mixed strategy of fronting a subject wh-phrase while leaving an object one in situ. For an input/index containing for example *who* and *what*, the winner is candidate *c*, a single overt wh-phrase in SpecCP co-indexed with both variables (a wh-phrase and a trace in situ). This means that *ABSORB and *t must be outranked by *Q, PARSEQ, and *ADJOIN in English. The ungrammaticality of *Who came why?* will be addressed in Section 3.2. At that point it will become clear why PARSEQ must be outranked by *Q and *ADJOIN in English.

T3. English

	$[Q_i Q_j [V x_i x_j]]$	*Q	*ADJOIN	PARSEQ	*t	*ABSORB
a.	$[Q_i{+}Q_j [wh_i V wh_j]]$	*!*	*			
b.	$[wh_i{+}wh_j [t_i V t_j]]$		*!		**	
c. ☞	$[wh_{i[j]} [t_i V wh_j]]$				*	*
d.	$[wh_i \langle{+}Q_j\rangle [t_i V DP/\langle{+}wh_j\rangle]]$			*!	*	
e.	$[Q_i \langle{+}Q_j\rangle [wh_i V DP/\langle \mid wh_j\rangle]]$	*!			*	

The two basic strategies of multiple wh-questions — fronting vs. in-situ — yield two alternative candidates that fail to parse one input Q feature: *d* and *e*. In Italian the optimal output is *d*: one Q-feature results in a fronted wh-phrase, the other Q feature is unparsed. One possible constraint ranking is the one displayed in T4: The constraints violated by the optimal candidate *d* (*t and PARSEQ) are outranked by *Q, * ABSORB, and *ADJOIN.

T4. Italian

	$[Q_i Q_j [V x_i x_j]]$	*Q	*ABSORB	*ADJOIN	PARSEQ	*t
a.	$[Q_i{+}Q_j [V wh_i wh_j]]$	*!*		*		
b.	$[wh_i{+}wh_j [V t_i t_j]]$			*!		**
c.	$[wh_{i[j]} [V t_i wh_j]]$		*!			*
d. ☞	$[wh_i \langle{+}Q_j\rangle [V t_i DP/\langle{+}wh_j\rangle]]$				*	*
e.	$[Q_i\langle{+}Q_j\rangle [V wh_i DP/\langle{+}wh_j\rangle]]$	*!				*

Under the ranking (*t $\gg$ *ADJOIN $\gg$ *Q $\gg$ *ABSORB $\gg$ PARSEQ), candidate *e* is optimal. See T5. The outcome is an in-situ-wh language which only allows a single Q feature to be realized. No such language has

248 *Modelling ungrammaticality in Optimality Theory*

been discussed in the literature. Yet, a query by Ralf Vogel (LinguistList, 7/3/2001) revealed that Omaha-Ponca (Siouan) may turn out to exemplify this pattern, courtesy of Catherine Rudin who has conducted fieldwork on this language. In particular she reports that Omaha-Ponca does not seem to have multiple questions of the form "who what likes", "you what where did?". Native speakers either drop the second wh-phrase or give "who likes all these things?".

T5. Predicted possible: one wh-phrase in situ only

	[Q_i Q_j [V x_i x_j]]	*t	*ADJOIN	*Q	*ABSORB	PARSEQ
a.	[Q_i+Q_j [wh$_i$ wh$_j$ V]]		*!	**		
b.	[wh$_i$+wh$_j$ [t_i t_j V]]	*!*	*			
c.	[wh$_{i[j]}$ [t_i wh$_j$ V]]	*!			*	
d.	[wh$_i\langle$+$Q_j\rangle$ [t_i DP/$\langle$+wh$_j\rangle$ V]]	*!				*
e. ☞	[$Q_i\langle$+ $Q_j\rangle$ [wh$_i$ DP/$\langle$+wh$_j\rangle$ V]]			*		*

The reader may verify that the present analysis of multiple wh-questions makes the right predictions for single wh-questions in each language. The constraints pertaining to possible combinations of operators, *ADJOIN and *ABSORB, are vacuously satisfied and the ranking of PARSEQ relative to *Q and *t correctly yields wh-fronting in Bulgarian, English, and Italian vs. wh-in-situ in Chinese (and Omaha-Ponca).

3 Why the null parse approach is unworkable

The neutralization approach is grounded in the interplay of markedness and faithfulness constraints. One objection raised against the approach concerns the overall validity of I-O faithfulness constraints in syntax. This section presents evidence that I-O faithfulness plays a role in contexts other than multiple questions, in particular where it interacts with **locality restrictions** on movement: extraction out of [−wh] complement clauses vs.[+wh] complement clauses.[4]

---

[4]Legendre et al. (1995) discuss a pattern of resumptive pronouns under overt DP topicalization which is sensitive to a subject-object asymmetry. In subject position these resumptive elements offset violations of TGOV at the cost of violating the I-O Faithfulness constraint, FILL, penalizing epenthesis of elements not present in the input.

Another objection to the neutralization approach comes from the existence of an alternative approach — the null parse approach – which is often held to have the advantage of not relaxing the LF-equivalency constraint on the candidate set that is required by the neutralization approach. This section discusses evidence that the null parse approach cannot provide an account of the sort we propose below to account for the relative difficulty of extracting out of a selected wh-clause compared with a selected *that*-clause.

3.1   Extraction out of wh-clauses

Since the early 80's much discussion in generative syntax has been devoted to locality or clause-boundedness effects in syntax despite some surface evidence to the contrary. For example, both English and Chinese permit extraction of direct object *what* (15) and a non-referential *how* adjunct (16) from a [−wh] complement clause selected by the matrix verb *think*, although the extraction is covert in Chinese. In both languages, extraction of a wh-phrase out of a [−wh] complement clause embedded under *think* involves long-distance movement (or movement which spans more than a clause). The present discussion assumes that *think* is lexically marked to select an IP complement in both languages, for two reasons: a) Chinese does not have a complementizer, b) independent evidence for an IP analysis is provided in Legendre et al. (1995).

(15)   a.   [$_{CP}$What$_j$ do [$_{IP}$ you think [$_{IP}$ John fixed t$_j$]]]]?   (English)
       b.   [$_{CP}$ Q$_j$ [$_{IP}$ Ni   renwei [$_{IP}$ Lisi yinggai chuli   shenme$_j$]]]?
                you think   L   should handle what
          'What do you think (that) L should handle t?'   (Chinese)

(16)   a.   [$_{CP}$ How$_l$ do [$_{IP}$ you think [$_{IP}$ John fixed it t$_l$]]]]?   (English)

(i)   Zhangsan$_i$, ta$_i$ xihuan kansu.
      Z   he like   reading
      'Zhangsan, he likes reading'
(ii)   *Zhangsan$_i$, t$_i$ xihuan kansu.
      Z   like   reading
      'Zhangsan, likes reading'

b.   [$_{CP}$ Q_l [$_{IP}$ Ni   renwei [$_{IP}$ Lisi yinggai zenmeyang$_l$ chuli
                you think   L   should how   handle
zhe-jian shi]]]?
this-CL matter
'How (manner) do you think (that) L should handle this matter?'

(Chinese)

According to Tsai (1994), Chinese wh-islands display a pattern of covert extraction (as indicated by scope interpretation) which is sensitive to the universal referentiality scale introduced earlier (*who > what > where, when > how > why*). Covert extraction of a referential wh-phrase (*who*) out of a wh-clause is possible, yielding two alternative direct questions or wide scope readings as shown in (17a). In contrast, the target wide scope reading is impossible when covert extraction of a non-referential wh-phrase (*how*) takes place, as shown in (17b). Yet, (17b) is grammatical under the narrow scope reading of an indirect question, as shown in (17b'). A similar situation obtains with (overt) extraction of referential *who* out of a wh-clause in English, as shown in (17c)–(17d).

(17)   a.   [$_{CP}$$Q_i$+$Q_l$ [$_{IP}$ Ni   xiang-zhidao [$_{IP}$ shei$_i$ zai nali$_l$ gongzuo]]]
                      you wonder   who at   where work
              'Who do you wonder where works?'   (Chinese, wide scope)
        b.   *[$_{CP}$ Q_i+Q_l [$_{IP}$ Ni   xiang-zhidao [$_{IP}$ shei$_i$ zenmeyang$_l$ chuli
                      you wonder   who how   handle
zhe-jian shi]]]
this-CL matter
'How (manner) do you wonder who handled this matter?'

(Chinese, wide scope)
        b'.   [$_{IP}$ Ni   xiang-zhidao [$_{CP}$ Q_i+Q_l [$_{IP}$ shei$_i$ zenmeyang$_l$ chuli
                  you wonder   who   how   handle
zhe-jian shi]]]
this-CL matter
'You wonder who handled this matter how' (Chinese, narrow scope)
        c.   *[$_{CP}$ Who$_i$ do [$_{IP}$ you wonder [$_{CP}$ what$_j$ [$_{IP}$ t$_i$ bought t$_j$]]]]?
                      (English, wide scope)
        d.   [$_{IP}$ you wonder [$_{IP}$ who$_{i[j]}$ bought what$_j$]]?
                      (English, narrow scope)

In a nutshell, Legendre et al. (1995, 1998) provide the following account of the Chinese patterns in (16) and (17). The input to wh-island extractions includes a target wide scope specification, e.g. Q_i you wonder [Q_j x$_i$ ate x$_j$]. In (17b) the extraction of the adjunct wh-phrase *how* out of a wh-clause in Chinese is ungrammatical because the chain [Q_l, *how*] is non-referential and too long, as measured in barriers crossed (to be made precise below as the MINLINK power hierarchy) – despite the fact that the non-referential *how*-chain in the [−wh] complement extraction in (16b) is the same length and is grammatical. The selectional restrictions on the matrix verbs *wonder* vs. *think* provide part of the answer. *Wonder* selects for a wh-clause with the result that two candidates with different scope compete: a narrow scope interpretation associated with a shorter chain and a wide scope interpretation associated with a longer chain. The shorter chain may win even though it is unfaithful to the target wide scope specification in the input if PARSESCOPE is lower-ranked than the particular constraint violated by the long extraction, as must be the case in (17b) and (17c). *Think* does not select for a wh-clause, the shorter chain with narrow scope violates the selectional restrictions on *think* (SELECT is high-ranked) and the longer chain with wide scope is optimal despite being disfavored by MINLINK.The relevant optimizations are sketched out for Chinese in T6 (and further elaborated upon in T10 and T12).

T6. Chinese: Comparative covert extraction of a non-referential wh-phrase

input: Q_1 V_{matrix} [... how_1 ...]	SELECT LINK[†]	MIN	PARSE SCOPE
wh-island extraction (*)			
a. Q_1 wonder$_{[+wh]}$[... how_1 ...]		*!	
☞ b. wonder$_{[+wh]}$[Q_1 ... how_1 ...]			*
think complement extraction (✓)			
☞ *a'.* Q_1 think$_{[-wh]}$ [... how_1 ...]		*	
b'. think$_{[-wh]}$ [Q_1 ... how_1 ...]	*!		*
Remarks:	No [+wh] complement for *think*	[†]constraint crucial here: BAR$^{2\,[-ref]}$	For an extraction input, extract

When an input provides a target involving a long non-referential chain link, the output will not be faithful to the wide input scope, provided that a narrow-scope alternative exists which does not violate the selectional restrictions of the matrix verb. This is the case with *wonder*, but not with *think*.

3.2 Locality vs. I-O faithfulness

The complete analysis of extraction out of complement vs. wh-clauses involves an I-O faithfulness constraint modeled on PARSEQ (Section 2), namely PARSESCOPE, as in (18).

(18)   PARSESCOPE: Target scopes of the Input/Index must be realized.

We also need a family of **barrier** constraints, MINLINK, establishing a scale on which longer wh-links are less harmonic (more marked) than shorter ones. MINLINK exploits both the concept of barrier to movement from Chomsky (1986) and a formal technique of OT, Local Conjunction of constraints (Smolensky 1995, 1997), plus one of its consequences, universal Power Hierarchies.

A barrier is a maximal projection (XP) which is not theta-governed (Chomsky 1986). For the extraction cases discussed here, VP as well as IP preceded by a complementizer count as barriers; they are governed by a functional category, Infl or C, which by definition does not theta-mark its complement. CP and IP in the absence of a complementizer are governed and theta-marked by the matrix verb (*wonder* or *think*), hence they do not constitute barriers.

(19)   BAR: A chain link may not cross a barrier.

A question regarding BAR immediately arises. Is a single constraint sufficient or do we need a family of BAR constraints? The comparison in T7 provides the answer. A single BAR constraint cannot differentiate local from non-local movement (each candidate incurs 3 violations of BAR); it therefore fails to characterize one fundamental property of syntactic operations.

T7. Cyclic *vs.* non-cyclic chains: equally marked, according to BAR (β = barrier)

		BAR
a. Cyclic, 2 links	☞ $[X_i \ldots \beta \ldots \beta \ldots t_i \ldots \beta \ldots Y_i]$	***
b. Non-cyclic, 1 link	* ☞ $[X_i \ldots \beta \ldots \beta \ldots \quad \ldots \beta \ldots Y_i]$	***

This is easily remedied by **locally conjoining** BAR with itself (with domain D = link); we thus obtain BAR $\&_l$ BAR / BAR^2. By recursion we then obtain a universal BAR Power Hierarchy. T8 demonstrates that a cyclic chain is universally preferred to a non-cyclic one.

(20)   a.   BAR^2: A single link must not cross two barriers.

          b.   By definition of the Local Conjunction operation, *universally*: BAR^2 $\gg$ BAR.

          c.   By recursion: MINLINK (universal BAR Power Hierarchy): ... $\gg$ BAR^3 $\gg$ BAR^2 $\gg$ BAR^1.

T8. Universal BAR Power Hierarchy

	MINLINK			BAR
	BAR^3	BAR^2	BAR^1	
a. Cyclic [X$_i$ ... β ... β ... t$_i$ ... β ... Y$_i$]		*	*	** *
b. Non-cyclic [X$_i$ ... β ... β ... ... β ... Y$_i$]	* !			***

One additional application of Local Conjunction is needed because not all cyclic chains are equal. Referentiality matters because it interacts with locality as demonstrated by the Chinese patterns in (17). Non-referential chains are good, if short. Long chains are good, if referential. That is, chains violating *both* MINLINK *and* REF are bad.

(21)   REF: Chains are referential.

Using Local Conjunction and recursion we obtain (22).

(22)   a.   BAR^k &$_1$ REF $\equiv$ BAR$^{k\,[-\mathrm{ref}]}$: A link in a non-referential chain must not cross k barriers.

          b.   MINLINK $^{[\mathrm{B\,ref}]}$: ... $\gg$ BAR$^{3\,[-\mathrm{ref}]}$ $\gg$ BAR$^{2\,[-\mathrm{ref}]}$ $\gg$ BAR$^{1\,[-\mathrm{ref}]}$

          c.   BAR$^{k\,[-\mathrm{ref}]}$ $\gg$ BAR^k

We are now in a position to examine the specific optimizations underlying the English and Chinese patterns in (17). Extracting a referential wh-phrase (*who*) out of a wh-clause (i.e. assigning it a wide scope interpretation) is impossible in English: in T11 the narrow scope candidate c wins. In Chinese, a wide scope interpretation is fine in the same context (candidate a wins). In the interest of simplicity, only a subset of candidates informed by earlier optimizations (T1 and T3) are considered in T9-T10. Full brackets ([) represent barriers and hollow brackets ([[) represent non-barriers. Violations are annotated with relevant indices corresponding to argument and adjunct type to facilitate readability. SELECT is undominated and satisfied by all candidates; for space considerations it is omitted in T9-10.

In an English matrix wh-extraction the best faithful candidate involves fronting of one wh-phrase and absorption (see T3). The equivalent in a long-distance extraction is candidate *a* in T9. However the extraction results in a long link violating BAR^3 (B^3). The latter can be obviated by failing to parse Q, as in candidate *b*; this too is suboptimal (see T3). The optimal candidate *c* violates PARSESCOPE instead and incurs a minimal MINLINK violation: BAR^1 (for *what*).

T9. English: Extraction of subject *who* out of wh-clause

	[Q$_i$ [*wonder* [Q$_j$ [V x$_i$ x$_j$]]]	*Q	PQ	B^3	PSc	B^2	B^1	*t	*ABS
a.	[$_{CP}$who$_{i[j]}$ do[$_{IP}$you [$_{VP}$wonder [[$_{CP}$what$_j$ [$_{IP}$t$_i$ [$_{VP}$V t$_j$]]]]]]			*$_i$!		*$_j$ *$_j$		**	*
b.	[$_{CP}$who$_i$ ⟨Q$_j$⟩ do[$_{IP}$you [$_{VP}$wonder [[$_{IP}$t$_i$ [$_{VP}$V DP⟨wh$_j$⟩]]]]]		*$_j$!			*		*	
c. ☞	[$_{IP}$you [$_{VP}$wonder [[$_{IP}$who$_{i[j]}$ [$_{VP}$V what$_j$]]]]				*		*		*

In Chinese the best faithful candidate involves adjunction of two Q operators in violation of *ADJOIN (see T1). In T10, the most faithful candidate with such adjunction is candidate *a* which incurs violations of BAR^3[−REF] (for *how*) and BAR^2 (for *who*). Failing to parse one Q is suboptimal, as in candidate *b*. The optimal candidate *c* violates PARSESCOPE instead and comparatively incurs minimal MINLINK violations: BAR^2[−REF] (for *how*) and BAR^1 (for *who*). The outcome is the same as in English except for the absorption vs. adjunction strategy (and fronting vs. in-situ, of course). To save space in T10 BAR^2[−REF] and BAR^1[−REF] are conflated into one constraint, as are BAR^3 and BAR^2, without altering the outcome of the optimization.

T10. Chinese: Extraction of *how* out of wh-clause

	[Q$_l$[*wonder* [Q$_i$[V x$_i$x$_l$]]]]	*t	PQ	B^{3-ref}	B$^{2-1-ref}$	PSc	B$^{3-2}$	B^1	*Q	*ADJ
a.	[$_{CP}$Q$_l$+Q$_i$[$_{IP}$you [$_{VP}$wonder [[$_{IP}$wh$_i$ [$_{VP}$ wh$_l$V NP]]]]]]			*$_l$!			*$_i$		**	*
b.	[$_{CP}$Q$_l$ ⟨Q$_i$⟩[$_{IP}$you [$_{VP}$wonder [[$_{IP}$ DP/⟨wh$_j$⟩[$_{VP}$ how$_l$ V NP]]]]]]		*$_i$!							
c. ☞	[$_{IP}$you [$_{VP}$ wonder [[$_{CP}$ Q$_l$+Q$_i$ [$_{IP}$ wh$_i$ [$_{VP}$ how$_l$ V NP]]]]]				*$_l$	*		*$_i$		*

Extrapolating from T10, extraction of a direct object wh-phrase (referential *what*) instead of non-referential *how* out of a wh-clause in Chinese would violate BAR³ (instead of BAR³[−REF]) and result in wide-scope candidate *a* (rather than narrow scope candidate *c*) being optimal.

With respect to extraction out of the complement of *think*$_{IP}$the narrow scope candidate *c* in T11 and T12 is not a viable output for either language because it violates the selectional restriction (SELECT/SEL) on the matrix verb: *think* is lexically marked to select a [−wh] complement with the consequence that an operator (Q or wh) cannot appear in the Spec position of the immediate complement of *think* without incurring a fatal violation.[5] A failure to parse Q resulting in a declarative statement rather than an information question is also suboptimal; see candidate *b*. A long link violating BAR³ in English (for *what*) or BAR³[−REF] in Chinese (for *how*) — candidate *a* — is optimal in both languages.

T11. English: Extraction of *what* out of the complement of *think*$_{IP}$

$[Q_j [think_{IP} [Vx_j]]]$	SEL	*Q	PQ	B³	Sc	B²	B¹	*t
a. ☞ [$_{CP}$what$_j$ do[$_{IP}$you [$_{VP}$think [[$_{IP}$John [$_{VP}$fixed t$_j$]]]]]				*				*
b. [$_{CP}$ DP/⟨wh$_j$⟩ do[$_{IP}$you [$_{VP}$think [[$_{IP}$ John [$_{VP}$fixed ⟨t$_j$⟩]]]]]			*!					
c. [$_{IP}$you [$_{VP}$think [[$_{CP}$what$_j$ [$_{IP}$John [$_{VP}$fixed t$_j$]]]]]	*!				*	*		*

T12. Chinese: Extraction of *how* out of the complement of *think*$_{IP}$

$[Q_j [think [Vx_j]]]$	SEL	*t	PQ	B³⁻ʳᵉᶠ	B²⁻¹⁻ʳᵉᶠ	Sc	B³⁻¹	*Q
a. ☞ [$_{CP}$Q$_l$ [$_{IP}$you [$_{VP}$think [[$_{IP}$Lisi [$_{VP}$how$_l$ handle this matter]]]]]				*				*
b. [$_{CP}$⟨Q$_l$⟩ [$_{IP}$you [$_{VP}$ think [[$_{IP}$Lisi [$_{VP}$DP/⟨how$_l$⟩ handle this matter]]]]]]			*!					
c. [$_{IP}$you [$_{VP}$think [[$_{CP}$Q$_l$ [$_{IP}$Lisi [$_{VP}$how$_l$ handle this matter]]]]]	*!					*		*

In sum, it is clear that not all instances of locality effects in syntax can be analyzed in terms of a single constraint stating that shorter links are better than longer links.[6] In particular, it is not the case that Chinese disprefers

---

[5]Candidate *b* also violates faithfulness to the structural specification of the input by realizing a complement CP structure; see discussion of Baković and Keer (2001) in Section 4.

[6] It is important to appreciate how the MINLINK approach differs from related concepts

long links across the board. Rather, a particular type of link in a particular context is dispreferred: A long link of type $\text{BAR}^3[+\text{ref}]$ is better than a failure to parse input/index scope but a long link of type $\text{BAR}^3[-\text{ref}]$ is worse than a failure to parse scope. However, a long link of type $\text{BAR}^3[-\text{ref}]$ is tolerated if the alternative is to violate selectional restrictions.

It is worth emphasizing that the neutralization account of wh-extraction significantly departs from the traditional one based on locality violations. In our terms, it is harder to extract out of a wh-island not because of locality violations caused by the presence of an intervening wh-phrase but because embedded wh-islands offer a competitor (narrow scope interpretation) that other types of embedded complements do not offer.

3.3 A fatal problem for the null parse approach

The comparison between extracting out of a complement of *think* vs. a complement of *wonder* reveals a fatal problem for the null parse approach relying on a single PARSE WH constraint (Ackema and Neeleman 2000). To account for the range of English and Chinese patterns discussed in this paper it is necessary to posit two separate PARSE constraints: PARSEQ and PARSESCOPE. In the wh-extraction contexts discussed in Section 3.2. both constraints are active because two Qs are present in the input. The option of not parsing one Q (on a par with multiple wh-questions discussed in Section 2.2) exists — see candidate *b* in T9-10 — but is dispreferred. What gives instead is wh-scope in complements of *wonder*, an option simply

---

in the Minimalist Program also grounded in economy such as "Shortest Move" (Chomsky 1993) or the Minimal Link Condition (MLC, Chomsky 1995). In the present account there is no need to stipulate that Shortest Move is measured in terms of relativized minimality violations. Relativized Minimality captures the generalization that locality is not an absolute condition on movement but rather is dependent on each type of intervening element ("Don't move α across a place where α could have landed" where potential landing positions are specified for each type of movement: A-bar-, A-, or head-movement). The result is a complex definition of the relevant conditions which incorporate both each type of intervening element and the concept of barrier (Rizzi 1990). In other words, the comparison inherent to evaluating link length is built into the definition of the MLC as well as Rizzi's antecedent government. In the present OT analysis, the relativized minimality effect is a **consequence** of a general MINLINK constraint in which link length is measured simply in terms of barriers/nodes crossed. None of the constraints require 'relativized' distance measurements, or 'minimality' of any kind: Minimality effects arise purely from the constraint **interaction** automatically provided by OT, so the constraints themselves do not refer to 'minimality', and relativization effects (e.g. *wh* is harder to extract over *wh*) are also a derived consequence of constraint interaction.

not available for multiple wh-questions in a single clause. It is evident that a single parse constraint cannot have the two different positions in the hierarchy needed for PARSEQ and PARSESCOPE within a language, e.g.PARSEQ $\gg$ BAR^3 $\gg$ PARSESCOPE in English (T9) and PARSEQ $\gg$ BAR$^{3\text{-}1[-\text{REF}]}$ $\gg$ PARSESCOPE in Chinese (T10).

More generally, since $\odot$ occurs in every candidate set in the null parse approach, it determines a fixed Harmony threshold for the entire language: $\odot$ wins every competition in which the best alternative has lower Harmony. The Harmony of $\odot$ is governed by the ranking of PARSE. PARSE must be ranked so that every parse of every ineffable Input/Index violates a constraint higher than PARSE (and loses to $\odot$). PARSE must also be ranked so that some parse of every effable Input/Index violates no constraint higher than PARSE (and bests $\odot$). However, it is imperative that the relative Harmonies of Input/Index-specific faithful and unfaithful parses be decisive. This can be accomplished by positing multiple Input/Index-specific unfaithful parses in which just an operator scope or just a Q feature is not parsed, depending on the candidate set. This cannot be accomplished by positing a single unfaithful parse ($\odot$) in all candidate sets.[7]

4   Independent evidence for neutralization in syntax

As argued above, neutralization offers a very economical solution to the ineffability problem that takes full advantage of existing OT resources. But neutralization is not a special strategy solely deployed to handle the minimal underparsing of a Q feature or operator scope in syntax. In fact, neu-

---

[7]Ackema and Neeleman (2000:297-9) discuss another problem arising from their null parse approach to ineffability in passive. In particular, when the possibility of failing to parse passive and the failure to parse Q are put together under the ranking PARSEPASSIVE $\gg$ MARKEDNESS CONSTRAINT $\gg$ PARSEWH, strange languages are predicted to exist: multiple wh questions exist except in passive sentences. They save the null parse approach to ineffability by blocking the interaction of multiple PARSE constraints. This is achieved by replacing the standard single procedure of constraint evaluation in OT with a series of evaluation cycles stipulated to involve only one parse constraint at a time. The output of one optimization is taken to be the input for the next, "with the effect that if the null parse is optimal in one evaluation, it will be also be the optimal output of the total procedure" (p. 298). They resort to generic performance considerations to motivate their specific treatment of PARSE constraints "If in general multiple performance of a simple task is preferred over single performance of a more complicated task, the proposed evaluation procedure for PARSE constraints is indeed preferred" (p. 299). It is far from obvious that the additional, unmotivated machinery warrants preserving LF-equivalency of the candidate set.

tralization is a crucial component of the interpretive optimization in Wilson's (2001) Bidirectional Optimization approach to cross-linguistic patterns in anaphoric binding of the sort *Tom said that Sue loves self.*Wilson argues that 'relativized minimality' (or locality) effects on anaphor binding are a consequence of neutralization in the interpretive optimization rather than the effect of a relativized minimality constraint per se. In his terms, the conflict is between a rigid locality constraint (a version of Principle A of the Binding Theory) and I-O Faithfulness. The ranking LOCALITY $\gg$ FAITH maps non-local binding to local binding, resulting in neutralization of a possible contrast.

T13. Neutralization for relativived minimality in anaphor binding (Wilson 2001)

Input	Output
a.$[T_i [S_j \ldots\ldots self_j \ldots]]$	$[T_i [S_j \ldots\ldots self_j \ldots]]$ faithful output
b.$[T_i [S_j \ldots\ldots self_i \ldots]]$	$[T_i [S_j \ldots\ldots self_j \ldots]]$ unfaithful output

Neutralization also offers a solution to another 'unexpected' pattern under OT assumptions, namely optionality of forms. For example, Baković and Keer (2001) propose that the input to clausal complements of the matrix verb *think* be specified as [+complementizer] or [−complementizer] and derive the two patterns in (23a-b) from distinct inputs.

(23) a. I think [$_{CP}$ that [$_{IP}$ the coat doesn't fit him]].
  b. I think [$_{IP}$ the coat doesn't fit him].

(24) a. The coat$_j$ [$_{CP}$ that [$_{IP}$ he always wears t$_j$]] doesn't fit him.
  b. The coat$_j$ [$_{IP}$ he always wears t$_j$] doesn't fit him.
  c. The coat$_i$ [$_{CP}$ that [$_{IP}$ t$_i$ doesn't fit him]] might fit me.
  d. *The coat$_i$ [$_{IP}$ t$_i$ doesn't fit him] might fit me.

Baković and Keer argue that there is optionality (23a-b, 24a-b) precisely where there is no neutralization. When the complementizer is either obligatory or prohibited (24c-d) it is because certain markedness constraints dominate the proposed faithfulness constraints. As a result, markedness constraints, which favor the same output for both inputs, prevail.

In relative clauses with subject extraction (24c-d), the complementizer *that* is obligatory because the requirement that the subject trace (t$_i$) be governed (TGOV, Grimshaw 1997) outranks FAITH[COMP], an I-O faithfulness constraint regulating the input and output value of the input specification [± complementizer]. In (24c) t$_i$ is governed by *that*, satisfying TGOV. See T14. In (24d) TGOV is fatally violated because relative clauses, being adjunct structures, by definition are ungoverned. See T15: The optimal counterpart — which violates FAITH[COMP] is candidate *a*, with complementizer *that*. T14 and T15 are reproduced from Baković and Keer (2001:103).[8]

T14. English: [+comp] relative clause with subject extraction

[+comp]	TGOV	FAITH[COMP]
☞ a. The coat$_i$ [$_{CP}$ that [$_{IP}$ t$_i$ doesn't fit him]] might fit me		
b. The coat$_i$ [$_{IP}$ t$_i$ doesn't fit him] might fit me	*!	*

T15. English: [− comp] relative clause with subject extraction

[− comp]	TGOV	FAITH[COMP]
☞ a. The coat$_i$ [$_{CP}$ that [$_{IP}$ t$_i$ doesn't fit him]] might fit me		*
b. The coat$_i$ [$_{IP}$ t$_i$ doesn't fit him] might fit me	*!	

In contrast, no neutralization takes place in relative clauses with object extraction (24a-b). By definition, the object position is governed by V. The faithful candidate wins for both [+comp] and [−comp] inputs. The result is optionality of the complementizer.

In sum, the Baković and Keer analysis extends the neutralization analysis beyond the realm of interpretational properties — the focus of Legendre et al. (1995, 1998) — to regulating formal properties of syntactic structures in individual languages.

5   The surface realization issue

For many critics of the underparsing approach advocated here the main question is: If the optimal output is a minimally unparsed structure (as

---

[8] Unlike relative clauses, complement clauses are lexically governed by the main verb. Subject traces thus satisfy TGOV whether there is a complementizer or not: (i) *[Which coat]$_i$ do you think t$_i$ doesn't fit?* (ii) **[Which coat]$_i$ do you think that t$_i$ doesn't fit?* (ii) is ungrammatical because t$_i$ violates TLEXGOV (Grimshaw 1997) which outranks FAITH[COMP].

opposed to a null structure ⊙), what is its surface realization? A more substantial question in our view is: What is the interpretation of the optimal candidate for ineffable inputs? Is a separate component, subject to optimization or not, needed to interpret the optimal candidate? In the neutralization approach discussed above, there is no additional component. Candidates have LF in them; a single optimization of the usual sort is all that is needed to yield a solution to the ineffability problem.

It is important to keep in mind that a candidate set in syntax is a set of possible abstract realizations of an input with many surface properties irrelevant to the optimization at hand, in particular their pronunciation. This means that the job of determining the pronunciation of an underparsed structure falls to another optimization subject to lexical, phonological, and pragmatic constraints.

However, the possible patterns of interpretational repairs in ineffable multiple wh-questions cross-linguistically display properties worth taking a look at here. In some languages (e.g. Chinese), wh-phrases share a lexical form with indefinite quantifiers, resulting in a single form interpreted as *what* in wh-contexts but *something* elsewhere. This led Legendre et al (1995, 1998) to suggest that ineffable multiple wh-questions can be repaired by a single wh-phrase plus an (in)definite quantified phrase (the [−wh] counterpart of wh-phrases). The question to be entertained here is the extent to which languages like English and Italian avail themselves of a similar strategy.

English is particularly relevant because multiple wh-questions display a pattern of ineffability that is sensitive to referentiality. Multiple wh-questions are good, if referential (25a). Non-referential extraction is good, if it involves a single wh-phrase (25b). But multiple wh-questions involving at least one non-referential wh-phrase (e.g. *why*) are bad (25c).

(25)   a.   Who ate what?
        b.   Why did John come?
        c.   *Who came why?

(25a) corresponds to optimal absorption candidate *c* which incurs violations of *t and *Absorb in T3. Candidate *c*, in particular, beats candidate *d* which fails to parse Q. At first glance, this appears to be problematic for (25c). According to the present analysis the optimal output of ineffable multiple Qs is a failure to parse. How can a failure to parse Q beat the absorption candidate if ParseQ is high-ranked in English? The solution lies in the conjunctive effect of referentiality and *Absorb. On the model of

BAR^k &$_1$ REF /BAR^k [Bref] in (22a) a Local Conjunction of *ABSORB and REF yields *ABSORB[Bref] which outranks both constraints in isolation. The Local Conjunction captures the generalization that chains violating *both* *ABSORB *and* REF are bad in English.

T16. English: ineffable multiple wh-questions

	$[Q_i Q_l[V x_i x_l]]$	*Q	*ABSORB[-REF]	*ADJOIN	PARSEQ	*t	*ABSORB
a.	$[Q_i+Q_l[wh_i V wh_l]]$	*!*		*			
b.	$[wh_i+wh_l [t_i V t_l]]$			*!		**	
c.	$[wh_{i[l]} [t_i V wh_l]]$		*!			*	*
d. ☞	$[wh_i Q_l [t_i V DP/wh_l]]$				*	*	
e.	$[Q_i Q_l [wh_i V DP/wh_l]]$	*!				*	

In contrast to Chinese, English wh-phrases *who, what*, are lexically distinct from indefinite quantifiers (e.g. *something, anything*). At first glance, a number of alternative wh-questions (26b-d) come to mind as possible repairs for ineffable inputs such as (26a).

(26)   a.   *Who came why?
        b.   Why did each person come?
        c.   *?Who came for each reason?
        d.   Who came for any reason?
        e.   Who came, and why?

In (26b-c) the unparsed Q feature is realized as a definite quantified expression (rather than an indefinite one, as in Chinese). *Each person* and *each reason* are d(iscourse)-linked expressions (Pesetsky 1987). Both presuppose a pre-existing limited set of referents. However, (26c) is pragmatically marked, compared to (26b). While it is easy to conceive of a limited list of people enrolled in a class for example (by consulting a class roster) it is much harder to conceive of a similar list of reasons. This may be the reason why native speakers in fact never volunteer (26c) as a repair for ungrammatical (26a). There is in fact a grammatical and pragmatically natural alternative to (26c), namely (26d), with a characteristic but unfaithful single wh reading.

Note that substituting *each person* for *who* (as in 26b) allows the retention of the multiple-pair reading characteristic of multiple wh-questions. If (26b) were uttered by a professor on the first day of classes then Johnny would give his reason, Martha hers, etc. If so, then English manages to un-parse Q while preserving the characteristic multiple pair reading of multiple wh-questions.

(26d) represents a distinct strategy sometimes offered by native speakers when confronted with (26a). Both Q features are in fact parsed but separately in two single wh-questions joined by a coordinating conjunction itself preceded by an intonational break. What most obviously gives here is the target syntactic structure specified in the input, a simple sentential structure, as well as the target prosodic structure. Native speakers consulted also find that the target multiple-pair interpretation is not the preferred interpretation of (26d). Rather, the most natural answer to *Who came, and why?* associatesa single reason for *why* with a set of referents for *who,* pointing to a distinct input.

The English strategies largely hold for Italian repairs of ineffable (27a). Like English (26b), Italian (27b) retains a multiple-pair reading while failing to parse one Q feature in all multiple wh-questions. According to native speakers, the alternative (27c) has a distinctive yes/no pair list interpretation 'Who ate something? Gianni, yes; Monica no, etc.' (27d) in turn is comparable to English (26e) and involves an unfaithful coordinate structure.

(27)   Italian

      a.   *Chi ha mangiato   che cosa?
          who has eaten which thing
          'Who ate what?'
      b.   Che   cosa ha mangiato ciascuna persona?
          which thing has eaten   each   person
          'What did each person eat?'
      c.   Chi ha mangiato qualcosa?
          Who ate something?
      d.   Chi ha mangiato e che cosa ha mangiato?
          Who ate and what did (they) eat?

In sum, English and Italian are languages in which a Q unparsing repair strategy may result in a surface structure which retains the multiple-pair reading associated with multiple wh-questions. Others strategies likely to lose competition for favored repair involve unparsing of Q with concomitant unparsing of multiple-pair reading on the one hand and unparsing of input syntactic and prosodic specifications without unparsing of multiple-pair reading on the other. The input to wh-questions must therefore contain the target multiple-pair interpretation (left implicit in Section 2) in addition to Q features. The two properties are independent: A Q feature may be unparsed while the target multiple-pair interpretation is preserved. All other things being equal, minimal LF (rather than structural) unparsing is preferred. This in turn confirms a basic assumption of the neutralization approach: the input includes multiple specifications; it is structured.

6   Conclusion

Ineffability is one of the input-output mismatches providing strong evidence for a decisive role of Input-Output Faithfulness in syntax. Structural optionality of the kind discussed in Baković and Keer (2001) is another, which similarly calls for a neutralization approach.

Neutralizing the input-output mapping is a comparatively simple and elegant solution to the challenge of handling ineffable inputs/indexes in an output-optimizing system. At the syntax/semantics interface of wh-questions two separate instances of two inputs (e.g. multiple vs. single wh, wide vs. narrow scope) were shown to be mapped to the same output each, thus eliminating universally possible contrasts from the languages under consideration.

The neutralization approach requires abandoning the assumption that competitors have the same LF interpretation — though they have the same target interpretation. On the neutralization view, an LF unrealizable in a given language is a structure such that every syntactic output with that LF interpretation is less harmonic in that language than a competitor with a (minimally) different LF.

The neutralization approach is grounded in a 'traditional' view of OT. The original concept of input is retained. Much work is done by I-O faithfulness. No additional component (such as an interpretational one) is needed to operate on the output of the syntax. No additional constraint on the candidate set is imposed either.

The debate surrounding ineffability in syntax ultimately bears on one fundamental single question: What defines the candidate set in an OT system? The answer is: the structured input.

References

Ackema, P. and Neeleman, A. (2000) Absolute ungrammaticality. In J. Dekkers, F. van der Leeuw, J. van de Weijer (eds.) *Optimality Theory:*

Phonology, Syntax, and Acquisition 279–301. Oxford: Oxford University Press.

Baković, E. and Keer, E. (2001) Optionality and ineffability. In G. Legendre, J. Grimshaw, and S. Vikner (eds.) *Optimality Theoretic Syntax* 97–112. MIT Press.

Beaver, D. and Lee, H. (2004) Input-output mismatches in Optimality Theory. In R. Blutner and H. Zeevat (eds.) *Optimality Theory and Pragmatics* 112–153. Palgrave: Macmillan.

Black, C. (2000) *Quiegolani Zapotec Syntax: A Principles and Parameters Account*. SIL International and University of Texas at Arlington. Publications in Linguistics 136.

Calabrese, A. (1984) Multiple questions and focus in italian. In W. de Gest and T. Putseys (eds.) *Sentential Complementation* 67–74. Dordrecht: Foris.

Chomsky, N. (1986) *Barriers*. Cambridge, MA: MIT Press.

Chomsky, N. (1993) A Minimalist program for linguistic theory. In K. Hale and S.J. Keyser (eds.) *The View from Building 20: Essays in Honor of Sylvain Bromberger* 1–52. Cambridge, Mass: MIT Press.

Chomsky, N. (1995) *The Minimalist Program*. Cambridge, MA: MIT Press.

Choi, H.-W. (1996) *Optimizing Structure in Context: Scrambling and Information Structure*. PhD dissertation, Stanford University.

Choi, H.-W. (2001) Binding and discourse prominence: reconstruction in =focus= scrambling. In G. Legendre, J. Grimshaw, and S. Vikner (eds.) *Optimality Theoretic Syntax* 143–69. Cambridge, Mass: MIT Press MIT Press.

Costa, J. (1998) *Word Order Variation: A Constraint-based Approach*. PhD dissertation, Universiteit Leiden. Den Haag: HIL Publications.

Costa, J. (2001) The Emergence of unmarked word order. In G. Legendre, J. Grimshaw, and S. Vikner (eds.) *Optimality Theoretic Syntax* 171–203. Cambridge, Mass: MIT Press MIT Press.

Dayal, V. (2006) Multiple wh-questions. In M. Everaert, H. van Riemsdijk, R. Goedelmans, and B. Hollebrandse (eds.) *The Blackwell Companion to Syntax Vol. III.* 275–326. Cambridge, MA: Blackwell.

Fanselow, G. and Féry, C. (2002) Ineffability in grammar. In *Resolving Conflicts in Grammar: Optimality Theory in Syntax, Morphology, and Phonology*. Special Issue 11 of *Linguistische Berichte*. 265–307.

Grimshaw, J. (1997) Projection, heads, and optimality. *Linguistic Inquiry* 28(3): 373–422.

Heck, F, Müller, G., Vogel, R., Fischer, S., Vikner, S. and Schmidt, T.

(2002) On the nature of the input in Optimality Theory. *The Linguistic Review* 19, 345–76.

Higginbotham, J., and May, R. (1981) Questions, quantifiers, and crossing. *Linguistic Analysis* 1, 41–79.

Legendre, Géraldine. (2001) Masked second-position effects and the linearization of functional features. In G. Legendre, J. Grimshaw, and S. Vikner (eds.) *Optimality Theoretic Syntax* 241–78. MIT Press.

Legendre, G., Wilson, C., Smolensky, P., Homer, K. and Raymond, W. (1995) Optimality and wh-extraction. In J. Beckman, S. Urbanczyck, and L. Dickey Walsh (eds.) *Papers in Optimality Theory* UMOP 18: 607-636.

Legendre, G., Smolensky, P. and Wilson C. (1998) When is less more? Faithfulness and minimal links in wh-chains. In P. Barbosa, D. Fox, P. Hagstrom, M. McGinnis and D. Pesetsky (eds.) *Is the Best Good Enough? Optimality and Competition in Syntax* 249–89. Cambridge, MA: MIT Press.

Legendre, G., Wilson, C., Smolensky, P., Homer, K. and Raymond W. (2006) Optimality in syntax II: wh-questions. In P. Smolensky and G. Legendre, *The Harmonic Mind: From Neural Computation to Optimality-Theoretic Grammar Vol. II* 183–230. Cambridge, MA: MIT Press.

May, R. (1985) *Logical Form: Its Structure and Derivation*. Cambridge, MA: MIT Press.

McCloskey, J. (1979) *Transformational Syntax and Model Theoretic Semantics: A Case Study in Modern Irish*. Dordrecht: Reidel.

Müller, G. and Sternefeld, W. (2001) The rise of competition in syntax: a synopsis. In G. Müller and W. Sternefeld (eds.) *Competition in Syntax* 1–68 . Berlin: Mouton de Gruyter.

Pesetsky, D. (1997). Optimality Theory and Syntax: Movement and Pronounciation. In D. Archangeli and D.T.Langendoen (eds.) *Optimality Theory, An Overview* 134–70. Cambridge, MA: Blackwell.

Prince, A. and Smolensky, P. (1993/2004). *Optimality Theory: Constraint Interaction in Generative Grammar.* Cambridge, MA: Blackwell Publishing.

Rizzi, L. (1990) *Relativized Minimality*. Cambridge, MA: MIT Press.

Rudin, C. (1988) On multiple questions and multiple *wh*-fronting. *Natural Language and Linguistic Theory* 6: 445–501.

Samek-Lodovici, V. (2001) Cross-linguistic typologies in Optimailty Theory. In G. Legendre, J. Grimshaw, and S. Vikner (eds.) *Optimality Theoretic Syntax* 315–54. MIT Press.

Schmid, T. (2001) OT accounts of optionality: a comparison of global ties and neutralization. In: G. Müller and W. Sternefeld (eds.) *Competition in Syntax* 283-319. Berlin: Mouton de Gruyter.

Smolensky, P. (1995) On the internal structure of the constraint component CON of UG. Paper presented at UCLA.

Smolensky, P. (1997) Constraint interaction in generative grammar II: Local conjunction, or random rules in UG. Paper presented at HOT, Baltimore, MD.

Tsai, W.-T. (1994) On nominal islands and LF extraction in Chinese. *Natural Language and Linguistic Theory* 12(1):121–75.

9 Wh-Islands: a view from Correspondence Theory

Ralf Vogel
Universität Potsdam

1 Introduction — Ineffability in OT Syntax

Ineffability can arise in various ways in syntax which require a different treatment within Optimality Theory. We can make the following distinction:

1. Some structure S is impossible for all languages of the world.

2. Some structure S is impossible in one group of languages, but possible in others.

The first class of ineffability problems is not answered in OT in a way that differentiates it from other frameworks. To take one example of this kind: as far as I know, there is no language that has multiple relativisation within a single relative clause. Though relativisation and question formation have many properties in common and are treated as instances of the same syntactic movement type, *wh*-movement, this is an aspect where the two differ. An explanation for this restriction will refer to the semantic and syntactic characteristics of relativisation, in any framework. The right place for this restriction in OT is the generator. Its implementation could, in principle, borrow heavily from other frameworks.

As dealing with such phenomena will not help us in figuring out where the particular contribution of OT to the theory of grammar lies, I will not deal with this first type of ineffability phenomena.

The second type of ineffability is weaker. We observe a typological contrast between two groups of languages that lies in whether they allow for structure S or not. The typical OT answer in such cases is constraint reranking. We identify the conflicting constraints that are relevant for our phenomenon and characterise the different language groups by different rankings of the crucial constraints.

In this paper, I will follow the proposals by Legendre et al. (1998), Baković and Keer (2001) and Vogel (2004a) who deal with this second type of ineffability in the standard OT way, by the interaction of markedness and faithfulness. Not all cases of ineffability have to be treated this way, however. A very simple case is the head directionality within the verb phrase. There are OV languages, showing object-before-verb order, and VO languages with the opposite order. For such cases, an opposition of two markedness constraints, for instance, HEADLEFT and HEADRIGHT by Grimshaw (1997a), or HEADBEFORECOMPLEMENT and COMPLEMENTBEFOREHEAD by Schmid and Vogel (2004); Vogel (2006b), is more appropriate. The relative ranking of these two constraints is responsible for the choice for OV- or VO-order.

Syntactic phenomena often receive a semantic, morphological or phonological explanation. OT syntax grammars therefore often imply quite complex interactions between these levels of grammar. Syntactic ineffability not only arises when we find that a certain structure as such cannot be found in a language. It also arises as *expressive ineffability*, that is, a *certain meaning* cannot be expressed by using a *particular* structure S in some language — perhaps contrary to what we find in other languages. While such cases of expressive ineffabilty are frequent, the more general case of semantic ineffability — the absolute impossibility to express a certain meaning in some language — is rather rare. My impression is that there always is some way to express every meaning in every language.

The two interesting cases of syntactic ineffability that will play a role in my discussion in this paper are thus the following ones:

- The impossbility of a particular structure S in some language(s).

- The impossibility to express a particular meaning M by using a particular structure S in some language(s).

I will focus on a family of restrictions on syntactic extraction, so-called *wh*-islands. The analysis will be formulated within the OT syntax model developed in Vogel (2004a,b), where the grammar organises the optimal *correspondence* between semantic, syntactic and phonological representations by means of mapping constraints. The model is inspired by work by Jackendoff (1997), Williams (2003) and Culicover and Jackendoff (2005). The more technical details of the OT model are borrowed from the correspondence theory of faithfulness developed by McCarthy and Prince (1995). For the phenomenon at hand, I will argue that the *wh*-island restriction results from the impossibility to establish a perfect semantics-syntax mapping in the relevant structures.

The — typologically rare — structures that violate the *wh*-island constraint are in general more marked than structures that use a resumptive pronoun as a repair — which are widely spread. Exceptions to the *wh*-island constraint can be found in English. I show that these exceptions are restricted to cases where a resumptive pronoun would occur in a position where it would cause a prosodically problematic situation.

Section 2 introduces the model I am using, and presents examples of some accounts of ineffability which I developed elsewhere. That section also introduces the basics of my treatment of *wh*-movement. Section 3 develops the account of *wh*-islands. Section 4 discusses the exceptions to the *wh*-island restriction that we see in English, and extends my account to handle these cases. The OT implementation of this account is presented in Section 5.

2 Correspondence-based OT syntax

A central question for the design of an OT system is the choice of the objects serving as input and output and their representational formats. OT systems that use the same objects for input and output have to be distinguished from those that use different ones.

In OT syntax, a model that has often been used is that of a mapping from a *semantic* representation in the input to a *syntactic* representation in the output (Grimshaw 1997a). Here, input and output are radically different. The input-output mapping has the character of a *translation*.

But it is sometimes useful to have the same kinds of objects in input and output, for example, if one wants to describe the typology of syntactic constructions: If language L_1 lacks a particular construction C_1 that occurs in language L_2, an OT model could show that C_1 would be mapped onto a different construction C_2 if it was in the input in language L_1.[1]

One example is the typology of free relative constructions as modeled in Vogel (2001, 2002):

(1)   German free relative and correlative construction:

    a.   Wer   einmal lügt, lügt auch zweimal
        who-NOM once   lies   lies also twice

    b.   Wer   einmal lügt, der   lügt auch zweimal
        who-NOM once   lies   that-one-NOM lies also twice

---

[1] The first who proposed a model with such properties for OT syntax, were Legendre et al. (1998) and Baković and Keer (2001), as far as I know.

(1a) contains a so-called "free relative clause" (FR) which serves as the grammatical subject of the whole sentence. In (1b), this FR is accompanied by a resumptive pronoun. Here, the FR is preposed out of the core sentence – so-called "left dislocation" — and we have a corefering resumptive pronoun, *'der'* ('that one') as grammatical subject. This latter construction is an instance of a "correlative construction".

FRs as in (1a) are marked compared to correlative constructions (CR) as in (1b): Languages that have FRs also have CRs, but there are languages with CRs that lack FRs. Also, languages with FRs differ in the contexts which allow for this construction — contexts which allow for free relatives also allow for correlatives, but there are contexts allowing for correlatives that do not allow for free relatives. For example, in German, a FR is ungrammatical, if it would imply the suppression of oblique case (in the following example, dative):

(2)   Wer   einmal lügt, *(dem)   glaubt   man nicht
         who-NOM once   lies   the-one-DAT believes one not

The solution I proposed in the works cited above is an OT system where the syntactic structure (FR or CR) is specified in the input, and where FRs and CRs compete in the output. In cases like (2), a FR in the input is neutralised to a CR in the output. A CR in the input, however, is always mapped onto a CR in the output. That way, it is possible to account for the absence of a syntactic structure in a language, using the standard OT scheme of markedness outranking faithfulness, where faithfulness is understood in terms of OT correspondence theory (McCarthy and Prince 1995).

Which representations does an OT syntax system actually need? I follow Jackendoff (1997) who summarises the traditional point of view of what grammars are doing: he claims that there are three representations, a semantic one, a syntactic one and a phonological one, and it is their *correspondence* that is modeled by a grammar. Let us use the symbols $\mathcal{M}$ (for 'meaning'), $\mathcal{S}$ (syntax) and $\mathcal{P}$ (phonology) for these representations.

A common assumption about the role of syntax is that it *mediates* between 'meaning' and 'sound'. One way of modelling this could be a serialisation of two optimisations, one where $\mathcal{M}$ is mapped onto $\mathcal{S}$, and a second step, where the winning $\mathcal{S}$ is mapped onto $\mathcal{P}$. This would imply that there is no direct correspondence relation between $\mathcal{M}$ and $\mathcal{P}$. But much work on the interaction of information structure and prosody shows that such a direct relation exists. The picture that we get looks more like a triangle: $\mathcal{M}$ is connected with both $\mathcal{S}$ and $\mathcal{P}$, as are $\mathcal{S}$ and $\mathcal{P}$.

The model that I propose for OT syntax combines these different perspectives: a) we specify for syntax in both input and output to account for optionality and ineffability of syntactic constructions in a standard OT fashion, and b) we use a correspondence-theoretic architecture that organises a mapping from meaning to form in the sense indicated above. Both input and output are ordered pairs which combine a syntactic structure with a semantic (input) or phonological (output) structure, respectively. The structure of input and output (candidates) is the following (the two occurrences of $\mathscr{S}$ in input and output are distinguished by subscripts):

(3)   Input and output representations in OT syntax, (see Vogel 2004b):

Input:	$\langle \mathscr{S}_I, \mathscr{M} \rangle$
Output:	$\langle \mathscr{S}_O, \mathscr{P} \rangle$

Some phenomena require the complexity of a bidirectional model. The examples that I discuss in detail in Vogel (2004a) are cases of word order freezing, where a structure that is marked, but well-formed in principle is ruled out because of homophony with a less marked structure. The simple case are German proper names which are ambiguous for nominative and accusative:

(4)   a.   Den   Hans liebt Maria
               the-ACC H.   loves M.
               'Hans, Maria loves'
        b.   Hans liebt Maria
               'Hans loves Maria', NOT: 'Hans, Maria loves'

Unless explicitly marked as accusative, as in (4a), a clause-initial proper name is interpreted as nominative. If object-verb-subject (OS) order for (4b) were to be ruled out in the usual way, then we would have to exclude sentences with OS order in general. We cannot distinguish between (4a) and (4b) in terms of abstract syntax. Furthermore, it is clear that given appropriate syntactic contexts, this freezing effect disappears.[2]

        i.   Den   Peter liebt Sonja, den   Karl liebt Ida, und Hans
               The-ACC P.   loves S.   the-ACC K.   loves I.,   and H.
               liebt Maria
               loves M.
               'Peter is loved by Sonja, Karl is loved by Ida, and Hans is loved by
               Maria.'

---

[2]One example is a coordination of unambiguous object-verb-subject sentences, where ((4b)) as final conjunct would be analysed as having a parallel syntactic structure, i.e., object-verb-subject.

Hence, it is clear that the ill-formedness of OS order for (4b) is due only to non-recoverability of underlying syntactic structure, not because of structural ill-formedness as such. In the model I am advocating, this is implemented by the addition of a second step of optimisation which uses the winning $\mathcal{P}$ of the initial optimisation as input and takes $[\mathcal{M},\mathcal{S}]$ pairs as output candidates. I called this optimisation *feedback optimisation* in Vogel (2004a,b):

(5)   Input and output representations in bidirectional OT syntax:

First optimisation:	Input:	$\mathcal{S}_I, \mathcal{M}$
	Output:	$\mathcal{S}_O, \mathcal{P}$
Feedback optimisation:	Input:	$\mathcal{P}$
	Output:	$\mathcal{S}_I, \mathcal{M}$

In some rare cases, such surface ambiguities even lead to ineffability, and not only to non-recoverability of underlying structure. The example that I discuss in Vogel (2004a) is the following contrast:

(6)   a.   Wem$_1$ hat er abgeraten, sofort   wem$_2$ nach Saloniki
            who-DAT has he dissuaded immediately who-DAT to   Saloniki
            nachzureisen?
            travel-after
            'Who has he dissuaded from travelling after whom to Saloniki?'
      b.   *Wem$_{1/2}$ hat er (t$_1$) wem$_{2/1}$ abgeraten, sofort   t$_2$ nach
            who-DAT has he   who-DAT dissuaded immediately   to
            Saloniki nachzureisen?
            Saloniki to-travel-after
            intended reading: 'Who is the person such that he has dissuaded whom to travel after that person?'
      c.   Wohin$_2$ hat er wem$_1$ abgeraten, der Prinzessin   t$_2$
            where-to has he who-DAT dissuaded the princess-DAT
            nachzureisen?
            to-travel-after
            'What is the place such that he has dissuaded whom to travel there after the princess?'
            (cf. Haider 1996, 2000; Fanselow 1991)

In principle, it is possible to extract a *wh*-phrase out of an embedded infinitive across another *wh*-phrase in the matrix clause in German. This is exemplified by (6c). But if the two *wh*-phrases are homophonous, this option breaks down. (6b) is ungrammatical. Unlike (4b) above, (6b) is not only impossible to interpret with a particular reading. This is derived in the bidirectional model with a definition of grammaticality that combines both perspectives:

(7)   **Grammaticality:**
A triple $[M_i, S_i, P_i]$ is grammatical, if and only if the input $[M_i, S_i]$ yields $[S_i, P_i]$ in first optimisation, and the input $[P_i]$ yields $[M_i, S_i]$ in feedback optimisation.

Under the analysis that I developed in Vogel (2004a), sentence (6b) is not part of any triple $[M_i, S_i, P_i]$ that is grammatical under the definition in (7). In feedback optimisation, (6b) is interpreted such that the initial '*wem*' belongs to the matrix clause, and the second '*wem*', though contained in the matrix clause, belongs to the embedded clause. But when we use this underlying structure as input form in first optimisation, it will be mapped onto a different surface form $\mathcal{P}$, namely the one that conforms to (6a). In order to achieve such a result, the bidirectional perspective is unavoidable.

2.1   Syntactic Correspondence Constraints

The constraints in our correspondence theoretic OT syntax model are requirements on corresponding elements or parts of the representations $\mathcal{M}$, $\mathcal{S}$ and $\mathcal{P}$. To give an example for an $\mathcal{M} \leadsto \mathcal{S}$ mapping constraint, the argument hierarchy given in the argument structure of the verb (as part of $\mathcal{M}$) is required to be translated into asymmetric c-command at $\mathcal{S}$ between the two phrases that correspond to the arguments.[3]

(8) $\mathcal{M} \leadsto \mathcal{S}$ (ARG):
If an argument m_1 precedes another argument m_2 at $\mathcal{M}$, then s_1 asymmetrically c-commands s_2 at $\mathcal{S}$.

Elements of $\mathcal{M}$ are called, 'm_n', elements of $\mathcal{S}$, 's_n', and elements of $\mathcal{P}$, 'p_n'; identical indices indicate correspondence of elements, e.g., m_1 corresponds to s_1.

Similarly, there are mapping constraints of the $\mathcal{S} \leadsto \mathcal{P}$ family, requiring, for instance, asymmetric c-command to translate into precedence, sisterhood into adjacency, and syntactic phrases to translate into phonological

---

[3] In the definitions of the mapping constraints, $\mathcal{S}$ stands for $\mathcal{S}_O$, unless otherwise indicated. The role of $\mathcal{S}_I$ is in fact limited to constraints of the $\mathcal{S}_I \leadsto \mathcal{S}_O$ constraint family. Precedence in $\mathcal{M}$ refers to the standard assumption that argument structures are ordered tuples.

phrases, cf. Truckenbrodt (1999) for the latter. $\mathcal{M}\Rightarrow\mathcal{P}$ mapping governs the translation of information structure into prosodic structure, among others.

2.2 The typology of *wh*-movement

How can we account for ineffability with these mapping constraints? A very simple application of this idea is the typology of *wh*-movement, which, in the case of questions with a single *wh*-word, roughly divides languages into two large groups, namely, those that front the *wh*-phrase, and those that do not. This typology can be derived under the assumption that the *wh*-phrase is subject to conflicting $\mathcal{M}\Rightarrow\mathcal{S}$ mapping demands, the constraint in (8) conflicts with the one in (9):

(9) $\mathcal{M}\Rightarrow\mathcal{S}$(SCOPE):
        If an element m_1 has scope over another element m_2 at $\mathcal{M}$, then s_1 asymmetrically c-commands s_2 at $\mathcal{S}$.

In the case of an object *wh-phrase*, as in Table 3, $\mathcal{M}\Rightarrow\mathcal{S}$(ARG) requires the *wh*-phrase to remain behind the subject NP, but $\mathcal{M}\Rightarrow\mathcal{S}$(SCOPE) requires it to be located before the subject:[4]

$\mathcal{M}$ = Qx.bought(john,x)		$\mathcal{M}\Rightarrow\mathcal{S}$(ARG)	$\mathcal{M}\Rightarrow\mathcal{S}$(SCOPE)
wh-in-situ	*John bought what*		*
wh-fronting	*What bought John*	*	

Table 3. Wh-fronting vs. wh-in-situ languages

As can easily be seen from Table 3, whether a language is of the wh-in-situ or the wh-fronting type is a matter of the relative ranking of the two constraints. *Wh*-fronting is then ill-formed in in-situ languages and *wh*-in-situ is ill-formed in fronting languages.

It is possible that additional factors come into play that introduce more options. One example is Turkish, where focus is another semantic factor relevant for *wh*-placement:

[...] It should be noted that, although Turkish is an SOV language, the basic word order is overridden by various other factors. For example, the most unmarked position for a WH-element is to the immediate left of the

---

[4]I am abstracting from a couple of issues here, for instance, the fact that *do*-support is necessary in English to form an English object question.

verb, irrespective of the grammatical relation. The second-best alternative is for the WH-element to be placed in its original position; [. . .] (Kornfilt 1997)

(10)   Optional '*wh*-lowering' in Turkish subject questions:

a.   bu kitab-ı   **kim** oku-du?
        this book-ACC who read-Past

b.   **kim** bu kitab-ı   oku-du?
        who this book-ACC read-Past

The position left adjacent to the verb is the focus position in Turkish. Under the assumption that the *wh*-phrase bears focus in simple questions, unless some other element is contrastively focused, it is easy to integrate Turkish into our alternative account, just by adding an additional constraint of the $\mathcal{M}\Rightarrow\mathcal{S}$ family which is concerned with focus:

(11)   Constraint Ranking for Turkish:
        $\mathcal{M}\Rightarrow\mathcal{S}$(FOCUS) $\gg$ $\mathcal{M}\Rightarrow\mathcal{S}$(ARG) $\gg$ $\mathcal{M}\Rightarrow\mathcal{S}$(SCOPE)

The actual formulation of the focus placement constraint might be prosodic in nature. Thus, it might rather be an element of the $\mathcal{M}\Rightarrow\mathcal{P}$ mapping family, requiring, presumably, a focus to be left aligned in its phonological phrase. In addition, a prosodic well-formedness constraint might be needed which requires that the phonological phrase which is the head of the intonation phrase is aligned with the intonation phrase's right edge.

A further question is whether the linear order represented in $\mathcal{P}$ should also be required to fully reflect $\mathcal{S}$. Note that the system allows for mismatches between $\mathcal{S}$ and $\mathcal{P}$, such that the linear order observed in (10) might not exactly reflect the c-command relations in the underlying constituent tree. For ease of exposition, this whole interaction is abbreviated here with the constraint $\mathcal{M}\Rightarrow\mathcal{S}$(FOCUS).[5]

The optionality of wh-in-situ and wh-in-focus position might result from the possibility that a constituent other than the *wh*-phrase bears focus. In that case, the focused element is in focus position and the *wh*-element will occupy its argument position.

Before we proceed, it has to be noted that the picture is complicated by another factor introduced by the model I gave in (3). The fact that $\mathcal{S}$ is contained both in the input and in the output makes it possible for the worse structure to survive independent of the ranking of our $\mathcal{M}\Rightarrow\mathcal{S}$ constraints.

---

[5]See Schmid and Vogel (2004); Vogel (2004a, 2006b) for several analyses exploiting the option of $\mathcal{S}\Rightarrow\mathcal{P}$ mismatches.

Highly ranked $\mathscr{S}_I \diamond \mathscr{S}_O$ faithfulness lets both structures survive if specified in the input. Thus, it is predicted that there are languages with more than one option for *wh*-phrase placement. One example in case is French, which has both in situ and fronting.

2.3 *Wh*-movement in OT Syntax

A couple of OT accounts of *wh*-movement have been proposed in the past already, among others, Grimshaw (1997a); Ackema and Neeleman (1998); Legendre et al. (1998). A feature that they share, which differentiates them from the strictly representational account which I defend here, is that the fronting vs. in situ split is accounted for by the interaction of a constraint requiring wh-fronting (similar to our $\mathscr{M} \diamond \mathscr{P}(\text{SCOPE})$) and a constraint that bans syntactic movement, STAY, originally introduced by Grimshaw (1997a), importing the idea of derivational economy from minimalist syntax.

At first sight, the two ways of accounting for wh-movement seem to be equivalent. But the solution based on derivational economy needs to rule out the following structure from the candidate set:

(12)

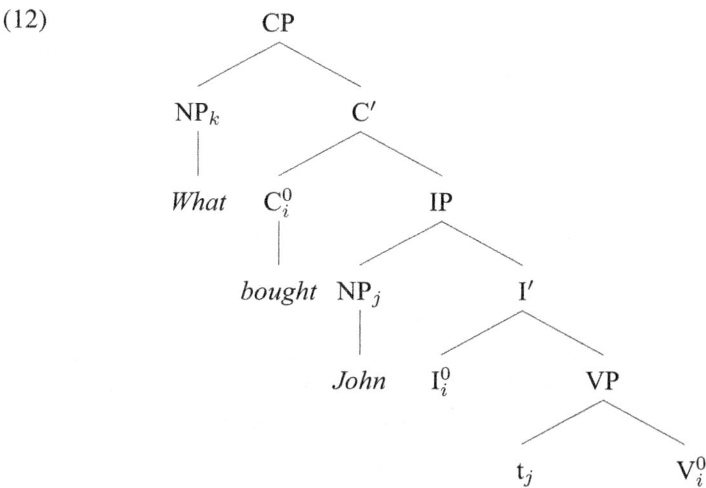

A violation of STAY can be avoided by simply inserting the *wh*-phrase directly in [Spec,CP]. This candidate also fulfils the *wh*-fronting constraint. Hence, it should be optimal even (wrongly) in in-situ languages.

In our approach, however, this structure still violates $\mathscr{M} \diamond \mathscr{S}(\text{ARG})$. So, it does not cause additional problems.

In a derivational system, like minimalism and its predecessors, structure (12) is usually ruled out by interpretive and case requirements: The NP is assigned its Θ-role inside VP, and uninterpretable otherwise. Likewise, case is assigned into that position, or another one designated for object case assignment, hence an NP inserted into [Spec, CP] has no case, or its case feature unchecked.

These options are not as straightforwardly applicable in OT. The OT syntax approaches which use STAY, following Grimshaw (1997a), agree in another architectural aspect: the input contains an argument structure specification.

For this reason, an argument against the structure in (12) in terms of a violation of the Θ-criterion is much less forceful than in a purely derivational system: omitted merge into Θ-position does not lead to a loss of semantic information. It is still there, in the input.

A constraint on case assignment, on the other hand, should be as violable as a constraint requiring *wh*-movement. So obligatory insertion into case position can hardly be motivated.

Hence, if one assumes STAY, it has to be *stipulated* that arguments of a verb are inserted into their VP-internal position — an arbitrary restriction on the candidate generator. As already mentioned, this stipulation is superfluous in the account that I am advocating.[6]

3   Wh-Islands

German is a language in which the extraction of a *wh*-element is possible in principle, as (13a) shows, but where this is impossible, if the *wh*-item is extracted out of a *wh*-clause (13b):

(13)   German:

      a.   Was   glaubt Maria, dass sie gekauft hat?
             What thinks M.   that she bought has
             'What does Maria think that she bought?'

      b.   *Was   fragt sich Maria, wer gekauft hat?
             What asks SELF M.   who bought has
             intended reading: 'What is the thing such that Maria wonders who bought it?'

---

[6]This issue and related problems in designing an OT syntax grammar are discussed more deeply in Vogel (2006a).

How can we account for this contrast? Let us have a look at the simplified semantic representation for (13b) in (14). The question operator is symbolised by 'Q' here.

(14)   Qy.wonder(maria, (Qx.bought(x,y)))

We have two *wh*-operators with different semantic scope, although both belong to the embedded clause. These operators are subject to the constraint ℳ⇨𝒮(SCOPE), which requires the syntactic correspondents of the operators, the noun phrases 'was' and 'wer', to c-command the elements in their scope. While 'wer' in (13b) (corresponding to 'Qx' in (14)), having embedded scope, only needs to occur in the specifier of the embedded CP in order to fulfil ℳ⇨𝒮(SCOPE), 'was' (corresponding to 'Qy' in (14)) has to occur in the specifier of the main clause CP, outside the embedded clause where it originates.

As illustrated in the semantic representation in (14), an operator always binds a variable, the operator 'Qx' binds 'x', and 'Qy' binds 'y'. Let us assume that the noun phrases 'was' and 'wer' are the syntactic correspondents of both the operator and the variable at the same time. Fulfilling ℳ⇨𝒮(SCOPE) for Qy now requires that the NP 'was' c-commands the NP 'wer' (because Qy has scope over Qx and x), but fulfilling ℳ⇨𝒮(SCOPE) for Qx requires that 'wer' c-commands 'was' (because Qx has scope over y). Therefore, if 'was' moves out of the embedded clause in order to fulfil ℳ⇨𝒮(SCOPE), that same constraint becomes violated for 'wer'.

Hence, it is impossible to satisfy ℳ⇨𝒮(SCOPE) for both operators at the same time. This dilemma, I contend, lies at the heart of *wh*-island phenomena.

Extraction of 'was' leads to a violation of further constraints, for instance, the constraint ℳ⇨𝒮(PRED), defined as in (15):

(15)   ℳ⇨𝒮(PRED): If m_1 is a predicate of m_2, then s_1 and s_2 are dominated by the same CP nodes.[7]

This constraint requires two elements which are semantically related by predication to be clause-mates, it thus penalises extraction across clause boundaries.

It seems, therefore, that structure (13b) is harmonically bounded by a structure like (16) where 'was' remains in situ — provided that no other constraint makes a distinction between the two structures.

---

[7]This constraint has been formulated as a constraint on clause-mateness in Vogel (2004a) in a less formal way.

(16)   Maria fragt sich, wer was gekauft hat?
       M.   asks SELF who what bought has
       'Maria wonders who bought what'

A third candidate structure that performs even better than (16) has a resumptive pronoun in place of the variable and the 'extracted' *wh*-phrase is base generated in its operator position, accompanied by a preposition to assign case to the *wh*-phrase:

(17)   **Von was** fragt sich Maria, wer **es** gekauft hat?
       Of **what** asks SELF M.   who **it** bought has
       'For what does Maria wonder who bought it?'

This structure circumvents the problem posed by the *wh*-island completely, by using unique syntactic correspondents for 'Qy' and 'y'.

The constraint violations for the three competing candidates are as illustrated in Table 4.

Qy.wonder(m, (Qx.buy(x,y)))	$\mathcal{M} \leftrightarrow \mathcal{S}$(SCOPE)	$\mathcal{M} \leftrightarrow \mathcal{S}$(PRED)
(13b)	*('*wer*')	*('*was*')
(16)	*('*was*')	
(17)		

Table 4. German wh-islands by harmonic bounding

(17) differs from (13b) and (16) in its lexical material. Whether that structure is able to block the other two in a language, is also a matter of the ranking of syntactic faithfulness. If the syntactic structure of (13b) is specified in the input, then (16) must already be considered as unfaithful, but (17) is even less faithful.

We have to keep in mind, though, that these two constraints individually *can* be violated in German. In multiple questions, only one of the *wh*-items can fulfil $\mathcal{M} \leftrightarrow \mathcal{S}$(SCOPE) (18). Likewise, as seen in (13a), extraction across clause boundaries is possible, if the extraction site is not a *wh*-island.

(18)   Wer   hat was   gesagt?
       who-NOM has what-ACC said

Thus, only a violation of both constraints leads to ungrammaticality. This cumulative effect is captured by a local constraint conjunction:

(19) $\mathcal{M} \diamond \mathcal{S}$ (SCOPE) &$_{\mathrm{CP}}$ $\mathcal{M} \diamond \mathcal{S}$ (PRED) (**WHISL**):
No simultaneous violation of $\mathcal{M} \diamond \mathcal{S}$ (SCOPE) and $\mathcal{M} \diamond \mathcal{S}$ (PRED) within the same CP.

This constraint describes *wh*-islands in a classical way: extraction out of a clause is ruled out, if this leads to a violation of $\mathcal{M} \diamond \mathcal{S}$ (SCOPE). WHISL is ranked higher than its two component constraints. The division between grammatical and ungrammatical is expressed by ranking the syntactic faithfulness constraint $\mathcal{S}_I \diamond \mathcal{S}_O$ between them:

(20)   WHISL $\gg$ $\mathcal{S}_I \diamond \mathcal{S}_O$ $\gg$ $\mathcal{M} \diamond \mathcal{S}$ (SCOPE) $\mathcal{M} \diamond \mathcal{S}$ (PRED)

A structure S_1 which is given in the input and violates WHISL will be neutralised to a different structure which fulfils that constraint.

The analysis also carries over to relative clauses, which behave on a par with embedded questions, as already shown by Ross (1967). A variant of (13b) where the extracted element is a relative pronoun is also ungrammatical:

(21)   *Dies ist das Buch, das   sich Maria fragt, wer gekauft hat.
This is the book which SELF M.   asks who bought has
'This is the book for which Maria wonders who bought it.'

The only grammatical version of such a clause uses a resumptive pronoun:

(22)   Dies ist das Buch, von dem   sich Maria fragt, wer es gekauft hat.
This is the book of which SELF M.   asks who it bought has
'This is the book for which Maria wonders who bought it.'

Semantically, the relative pronoun is treated as an operator, which turns the relative clause into a modifier, i.e., a predicate of the modified noun, as expressed by the lambda operator in (23):

(23) λx(wonder(m, Qy.buy(y,x))) (book)

The constraint $\mathcal{M} \diamond \mathcal{S}$ (SCOPE) therefore applies to relative pronouns in the same way as it does to *wh*-pronouns.

4 Exceptions to the *wh*-island constraint

If all languages were as strict as German with respect to *wh*-island effects, we could stop here. Unfortunately, English already provides some exceptions. The classical example is the contrast in (24):

(24)   (Sabel 2002: 274):

    a.   ??[$_{CP}$ What do you [$_{VP}$ t''wonder [$_{CP}$ how John could [$_{VP}$ t' [$_{VP}$ fix t]]]]]?

    b.   *[$_{CP}$ How do you [$_{VP}$ t'' wonder [$_{CP}$ what John could [$_{VP}$ t' [$_{VP}$ fix t]]]]]?

    c.   *[CP Who do you [VP t' wonder [CP how [IP t could fix the car]]]]?

Sabel (2002) and other authors before him claim that extraction out of a *wh*-island is possible from a Θ-position, typically the complement position of a verb phrase hosting a direct object, as in (24a). However, the clause is only slightly better than the two ungrammatical clauses. This lead Chomsky and Lasnik (1993) to an analysis in terms of chain licensing. Only uniform chains are legitimate at LF: either all members of a movement chain are A- or L-related,[8] or non-A- (or non-L-) related. In an A-chain, intermediate traces in non-A positions are deleted. This holds of t' and t'' in (24a).

The deletion of t', in particular, makes the difference to the other two structures. This trace is created by a movement step which violates the economy principle 'Minimise Chain Links' (MCL) which requires movement steps to be as short as possible: the long extracted *wh*-phrases in (24) have to skip the already filled specifier positions of IP and CP of the embedded clause. But as this offending trace is deleted in order to yield a uniform LF chain, the violation of MCL is cancelled out with the offending trace. Nevertheless, the MCL violation leads to slight deviance.

Violations of MCL also occur for t' in (24b) and t in (24c). But these traces cannot be deleted, as they are part of uniform chains. In (24b), we have a non-A chain, and all chain links are in appropriate positions, so trace deletion is not licensed. In (24c), on the other hand, the offending trace t is in an A-position, it represents the variable and cannot be deleted for semantic reasons anyway. Thus, in these two cases the MCL violation cannot be cancelled out, and this causes the ungrammaticality of the two sentences.

This whole mechanism has a very technical, and partly stipulative nature. Sabel's (2002) improvements do not change this impression significantly. In particular, typological differences are accounted for by him in a quite ad hoc manner: for those languages where the counterpart of (24a) is ill-formed, it is assumed that the starting position for wh-movement is the

---

[8]A-related positions are positions where an argument is assigned case or thematic role, and L-related positions are positions which are governed by lexical categories.

case position (where the trace is not deletable, by stipulation). Likewise, for a language like Spanish, which has a well-formed counterpart of (24b), it is assumed that the movement originates in a position which is both a Θ- and a case position. Also, it remains in the dark, why it is Θ-positions which are relevant here.

From an OT perspective, it is also important to consider which the alternative candidate structures are that clauses like (24c) lose against. As we will see, the most likely candidates are the structures with a resumptive pronoun which we already discussed in the previous section. A brief look at corpus data will confirm this. I found the following examples in the world wide web via a *google* search (all highlightings by me, R.V.).

(25)   "Jerry Hall is one of those models, along with so many nowadays (including her daughter) <u>who I wonder how **they** ever made it.</u>"
`chat.dailymail.co.uk/dailymail/threadnonInd.`
`jsp?forum=82&thread=9689929&message=10932031`

(26)   "I have a couple of friends who I've lost touch with <u>who I wonder what gender **they** are now</u>"
`forum.genderpeace.com/index.php?t=msg&goto=`
`158034&`

(27)   "I too have seen CMTs <u>who I wonder how **they** ever passed that test.</u>"
`archives.mtstars.com/main/13766.html`

Here we have three examples for the extraction of a *wh*-subject out of a *wh*-island, where the trace position is now occupied by a resumptive pronoun, '*they*'. For a minimalist analysis, the question arises, why such structures are well-formed at all, if the resumptive pronoun does nothing more than spelling out a movement trace — which still violates the principle MCL under the analysis of Chomsky and Lasnik (1993).

From the perspective of correspondence theory, it is not necessary to assume a derivational relation between the *wh*-phrase and the resumptive pronoun. We simply have a situation where operator and variable both have a syntactic correspondent of their own. That there might be a nonderivational relation between the two is also suggested by examples like the following which I also found at the WWW. The possibility of such structures has already been noticed by Ross (1967), describing their acceptability status as outside the norm, but nevertheless common in spoken American English.

(28)   "I realize Nursing is an important job, but I see many Nurses <u>who I</u>
         <u>wonder how accurate is **their** opinion?!!"</u>
         `allnurses.com/forums/showthread.php?t=109128`

(29)   "There are some super-fast DB players out there, tremendous musicians,
         <u>who I wonder what **their** ambitions were."</u>
         `www.talkbass.com/forum/showthread.php?t=124023`

(30)   "I welcome questions if you have any pertaining to my mother, the def-
         inite P, her husband <u>who I wonder what **his** motives may be with my</u>
         <u>daughter, ... "</u>
         `www.psychopath-research.com/ubbthreads/showflat`
         `.php?Cat=&Board=PSYCHOP_MAIN_FORUM&Number=195`

Here, the resumptive pronoun and the extracted *wh*-pronoun are incompatible in their case features. Even worse, if the extracted '*who*' is
assigned case, the question is: which element is its case assigner? Usually,
case assignment and assignment of thematic roles go hand in hand. But
here, the resumptive pronoun is assigned both inside the embedded clause.
For the examples in (25)–(27) we could simply assume that the extracted
wh-phrase has case by agreement with the resumptive pronoun. This cannot be the answer in (28)–(30). Nevertheless, the least likely answer is that
who is moved from the position of the resumptive pronoun. One reason is
that such movement is ruled out in general:

(31)   *Whose did you buy [$_{NP}$ t books] ?

In the following two examples the extracted *wh*-pronoun is in the accusative ('*whom*'), while the resumptive pronoun is nominative.

(32)   "and I have come to realize That there are quite a few folks with Nursing
         licenses <u>whom I wonder how the hell **they** ever got them."</u>
         `www.urban-living.org/new-1556448-697.html`

(33)   "I spend a good deal of my time cruising through other people's blogs
         ... some people I know <u>(whom I wonder how **they**'d feel if they knew I</u>
         <u>was reading)..."</u>
         `mylifeinretrospect.blog.com/2005/4/`

These examples suggest that the *wh*-phrases can be assigned accusative
case by '*wonder*'. This could also be the answer to (28)–(30). Examples
where a preposition is inserted to assign case to the 'extracted' *wh*-pronoun
can also be found:

(34)   "Obvious bug, **for** which I wonder how **it** slipped the Opera quality control."
```
list.opera.com/pipermail/opera-users/2001-Novem
ber/006894.html
```

(35)   "... have a lot of confidence in most of the material, although there are a few sketches **for** which I wonder how an audience will react."
```
annekenstein.typepad.com/monster/2005/07/index.
html
```

(36)   "they somehow managed to get two volunteers, **of** whom I wonder if **they** are still together?!"
```
www.byrnerobotics.com/forum/forum_posts.asp?TID=
6690&PN=1&TPN=1
```

(37)   "My body has painfull feelings **of** which I wonder what emotional state causes **them** ..."
```
www.palikanon.com/diverses/guestbook/guest-03_0
1-04_04.htm
```

We have evidence, thus, that an alternative analysis of the structure of *wh*-island configurations is available which does not rely on syntactic movement at all:

(38)   [$_{CP1}$ WH$_1$ ... *wonder* [$_{CP2}$ WH$_2$ ... pronoun$_1$ ...]]
   1.   WH$_1$ is directly inserted into CP1.
   2.   CP2 is a *wh*-clause which has another *wh*-pronoun or *wh*-complementiser (WH$_2$) in initial position, and a resumptive pronoun that correlates with WH$_1$.

This point of view also sheds some light on exceptions to the wh-island constraint in Spanish (and, likewise, Italian, cf. Rizzi 1982), as illustrated in (39), after Sabel (2002):

(39)   ?Quién no sabes   qué compró ?
        who   not know-you what bought
        'Who don't you know bought what'

Spanish and Italian are pro-drop languages, which means that subject pronouns usually remain unrealised, unless they are focused, or otherwise information structurally prominent. This also holds of resumptive pronouns. Thus, instead of an exceptional movement analysis, structure (39) could as well be interpreted as a structure with a resumptive pronoun inside the *wh*-island, with the perhaps irritating property that the resumptive subject pronoun is the null pronoun. From this perspective, there is no exception to the *wh*-island constraint to be accounted for.

I postulate that the exceptions to the *wh*-island constraint that we observe in English are of the same kind: what has taken place here, is not exceptional syntactic movement out of the *wh*-clause, but rather the exceptional use of a resumptive null pronoun.

The crucial task is now to determine the conditions under which it is possible to realise $pronoun_1$ as null pronoun in English. In terms of our correspondence theoretic analysis, the relevant structures have a syntactically present resumptive pronoun which has no $\mathscr{P}$ correspondent.

The description of such structures that has been given by Sabel (2002), among others, is that the resumptive pronoun can be omitted in a position where a thematic role is assigned. It is not a pure case position. Example (40) is of this kind:

(40)   "met some new people last night <u>who i wonder how i didn't meet before.</u>"
        `chainedlightning.blogspot.com/`

The pronominal gap is not obligatory, though. An example with a resumptive pronoun is the following one:[9]

(41)   "I meet people everyday <u>who I wonder how their parents could love **them**</u> not TO mention a partner."
        `supernaturale.com/glitter/viewtopic.php?p=2077`
        `95&sid=6f3fd91ce2635dec876dabfeb19be8ba`

Typical positions for the pronominal gap are also sisters to prepositions:

(42)   "There are lots more examples of that in my life; people that were cool, and unique, and <u>who I wonder how things have worked out for.</u>"
        `homepage.mac.com/dvorak/Journal.html`

(43)   "he is like a long lost sister <u>who I wonder How I ever lived without.</u>"
        `onefuckedupgirl.blogspot.com/2004_11_01_onefucke`
        `dupgirl_archive.html`

What these examples share is that the 'gap' is at the right edge of the verb phrase. However, as the following example shows, it need not necessarily be the right edge:

---

[9]But examples like (40) are rather rarely to be found at the WWW. With direct objects and objects of prepositions the gap seems to the preferred option. This preference seems to be even stronger with '*whether*'-clauses as *wh*-islands.

(44)   "Lately I feel an ever so slight tug toward things <u>which I wonder whether</u>
<u>I have truely left behind</u>."
`www.livejournal.com/users/martian2b/2003/03/05/`

Here the pronoun would have to occur between the verb and the particle:

(45)   ... left (them) behind (*them)

Nevertheless, the position after the particle is a legitimate position for
an object, as in (46):

(46)   She left behind her rival.

In Vogel (2006b), I gave an explanation of the contrast between (45)
and (46) in terms of prosody-syntax interaction, based on the account of
the prosodic properties of English weak function words by Selkirk (1996).
She shows that function words may only occur in a prosodically strong
form in particular positions within the sentence. Consider the following
example:

(47)   I can$_i$ eat more than Sara *cán$_j$*
[kæn],[kən],[kn̩]   [kæn],*[kən],*[kn̩]

The modal verb '*can*' may appear in a prosodically weak form ([kən],[kn̩]),
if it stands in a medial position, like '*can$_i$*' above. However, for '*can$_j$*',
standing in final position, the weak forms are excluded. Selkirk shows that
the relevant constraint is prosodic: in English, the right edge of a phonological phrase has to be aligned with the right edge of a prosodic word. She
postulates the prosodic alignment constraint ALIGNPPHR:

(48)   **ALIGNPPhR**:
Align(PPh, R; PWd, R)

Weak function words lack word stress. Only their strong forms count
as prosodic words, so only the strong form of '*can$_j$*', [kæn], is possible in
(47), to fulfil ALIGNPPHR.
I argue in Vogel (2006b) that there is a difference between pronouns
and modal verbs like '*can*': pronouns do not have a semantically neutral
strong form. If pronouns are stressed, they bear focus. This explains why
an unfocused pronoun is ungrammatical in the final position in (45). Given
that there exists a syntactically legitimate alternative — the pronoun might
stand between verb and particle –, leaving the pronoun in final position is

odd. On the other hand, there are cases like (49) where a weak pronoun does stand in final position:

(49)   We need'm (= 'We need him/them')

Contrary to Selkirk (1996), I assume in (Vogel 2006b) that this is a case where ALIGNPPHR is violated. This violation is due to the absence of a syntactically legitimate alternative that avoids this constraint violation. Contrary to a language like French, see (50), it is impossible to move an object pronoun in front of the finite verb.

(50)   a.   Marie le   voit.
                 M.   him sees
         b.   *Mary'm/him sees

That ALIGNPPHR can control the placement of weak pronouns in English can be seen with minimal pairs like (51). An NP might precede or follow a verbal particle, but if it is a pronoun, as in (51c,d), it has to precede the particle (51d) in order to avoid a violation of ALIGNPPHR:

(51)   a.   I gave up the plan.
         b.   I gave the plan up.
         c.   *I gave up it.
         d.   I gave it up.

The relation between these cases and the apparent exceptions to the *wh*-island constraint is fairly obvious: all such cases documented for English in the literature are cases where the resumptive pronoun would occur at the right edge of a phonological phrase. Resumptive pronouns are necessarily unfocused, therefore they can only appear in a weak form, and hence, their occurrence would violate ALIGNPPHR.

I assume that in these cases, it is legitimate in English to use the resumptive null pronoun. The details of the OT formulation of this approach are discussed in the following section.

5   Exceptions to *wh*-islands within OT

How can the account sketched in the previous section be implemented within OT? First of all, let us consider the structure of the candidates like (52).

(52)   What do you wonder how John could fix?

The semantics of this structure can be paraphrased as in (53), simplifying the interpretation of the adverbial *wh*-phrase.

(53) $\mathcal{M}$: Qx. wonder(you, Qy. (could-fix(john,x) & mode(y)))

For the syntactic analysis, let us assume that no syntactic movement has taken place. Thus, '*what*' is base-generated in the position of WH_x in (54). The verb '*fix*' nevertheless has a syntactic complement within its VP, the resumptive pronoun.

(54) $\mathcal{S}$: [$_{CP1}$ WH_x ... [$_{CP2}$ WH_y ... [$_{VP}$ could [$_{VP}$ fix pro_x]]]]

The surface form P roughly has the following structure:

(55) $\mathcal{P}$: (*what*$_x$)$_{PhP}$ ... (*how*$_y$ *John*)$_{PhP}$ (could <u>fix</u>)$_{PhP}$

The null realisation of the pronoun is an instance of 'underparsing' in the mapping from $\mathcal{S}$ to $\mathcal{P}$. It violates the constraint $\mathcal{S} \leftrightarrow \mathcal{P}$(MAX), which is defined in (56) in the spirit of OT correspondence theory (McCarthy and Prince 1995).

(56) $\mathcal{S} \leftrightarrow \mathcal{P}$(MAX):
         For every element s_i in $\mathcal{S}$, there is a corresponding p_i in $\mathcal{P}$.

As we saw above, the null realisation of the resumptive pronoun is optional. I assume that $\mathcal{S} \leftrightarrow \mathcal{P}$(MAX) is ranked on a par with ALIGNPPHR. In particular, I assume that the two constraints are globally tied, i.e., there are two parallel co-grammars of English, one where ALIGNPPHR immediately dominates $\mathcal{S} \leftrightarrow \mathcal{P}$(MAX), and another one where it is the other way around. However, we have to take care that null realisation of weak pronouns is not licensed in general, otherwise (57b) would be well-formed:

(57)   a.   I saw it
         b.   *I saw (meaning 'I saw it')

We have to restrict the null realisation of resumptive pronouns to those cases, where such pronouns are indeed resumptive, i.e., where they denote a discourse referent that has already been denoted by another element within the sentence. In our cases, this other element is the *wh*-pronoun. In terms of our correspondence theoretic framework, we can formulate this as an $\mathcal{M} \leftrightarrow \mathcal{P}$ mapping constraint: every discourse referent that occurs in $\mathcal{M}$ should have a correspondent in $\mathcal{P}$.

(58) $\mathcal{M} \leftrightsquigarrow \mathcal{P}$(MAX):
          For every element m_i in $\mathcal{M}$, there is a corresponding p_i in $\mathcal{P}$.

$\mathcal{M} \leftrightsquigarrow \mathcal{P}$(MAX) is fulfilled when we have a *resumptive* null pronoun, but not, for instance, in (57b), where the only element denoting the theme argument of the verb 'buy' would be left out at $\mathcal{P}$. Hence, to exclude (57b) we have to rank $\mathcal{M} \leftrightsquigarrow \mathcal{P}$(MAX) on top of the constraint tie:

(59) $\mathcal{M} \leftrightsquigarrow \mathcal{P}$(MAX) $\gg$ ALIGNPPHR $\circ$ $\mathcal{S} \leftrightsquigarrow \mathcal{P}$(MAX)

This sub-ranking has to be integrated with the constraint sub-ranking for the *wh*-island effect in (20) to yield the English ranking. As there is no phenomenon observable that would provide hints for the exact ranking, any ranking will do for our purposes, as long as the two sub-rankings are preserved.

6 Conclusion

The *wh*-island effect occurs in a configuration with two *wh*-operators that originate within the same finite clause, but one of them has a scope which is wider than that of the other one. A rough semantic characterisation might look like (60):

(60)   Qx [... Qy [... x y ...]]

In the syntactic structure, the two operators correspond to two *wh*-phrases WH_x and WH_y. To fulfil scoping for Qx, WH_x has to c-command/-precede WH_y. However, because the variable x is in the scope of Qy, WH_x is at the same time required to *be* c-commanded/preceded by WH_y, if WH_x counts as the syntactic correspondent of x. This dilemma is unavoidable. Scoping can therefore only be fulfilled for one of the two operators. Because extraction out of a clause is marked as such, it is preferred to fulfil scoping for WH_y. WH_x then appears syntactically at the position that conforms to the variable x, violating scoping for WH_x.

The result is the phenomenon we know as *wh*-island. The optimal syntactic structure for the expression of (60) uses a resumptive pronoun in the place of 'x'. Now Qx and x both have a correspondent of their own and the constraints on scoping can be fulfilled for both operators.

In the analysis that I developed here, the *wh*-island restriction results from a cumulation of constraint violations which independently are often tolerated. An OT implementation of this analysis requires a constraint interaction where a conjoined constraint outranks a faithfulness constraint, which in turn outranks the component constraints of the conjunction:

(61) $C_1 \& C_2 \gg \textrm{FAITH} \gg C_1 \; C_2$

In accounting for the exceptions to the *wh*-island constraint that we found in English, I argued that a prosodic constraint plays a crucial role here, which could already be shown to play an important role in the English grammar (Selkirk 1996; Vogel 2006b): the resumptive pronoun may be omitted if it would appear at the right edge of a phonological phrase, as this would violate a prosodic well-formedness constraint.

Syntactic wellformedness conditions account for the ineffability of *wh*-island "extraction" without a resumptive pronoun. But syntactic wellformedness can be overridden by a syntax-external factor like prosodic wellformedness. This aspect of the analysis brings into perspective a further dimension of the ineffability problem: we usually speak of ineffability *within the limits* of a certain level of linguistic description, or abstraction.

Bibliography

Ackema, P. and Neeleman, A. (1998) Whot. In Barbosa et al. (1998) 15–34.

Baković, E. and Keer, E. (2001) Optionality and ineffability. In G. Legendre, J. Grimshaw, and S. Vikner (eds.) *Optimality Theoretic Syntax* 97–112. Cambridge, MA: MIT Press.

Barbosa, P., Fox, D., Hagstrom, P., McGinnis, M. and Pesetsky, D. (eds.) (1998) *Is the best good enough? Optimality and competition in syntax.* Cambridge, Massachusetts: MIT Press.

Chomsky, N. and Lasnik, H. (1993) Principles and parameters theory. In J. Jacobs, A. Stechow, W. Sternefeld, and T. Vennemann (eds.) *Syntax. Ein internationales Handbuch zeitgenössischer Forschung* 506–69. Berlin: Walter De Gruyter.

Culicover, P. W. and Jackendoff, R. (2005) *Simpler Syntax.* Oxford, New York: Oxford University Press.

Fanselow, G. (1991) Minimale syntax. *Groninger Arbeiten zur Germanistischen Linguistik* 32.

Grimshaw, J. (1997) Projection, heads, and optimality. *Linguistic Inquiry* 28: 373–422.

Haider, H. (1996) Towards a superior account of superiority. In U. Lutz and G. Müller (eds.) *Papers on Wh-Scope Marking* 317–29. Arbeitspapiere des SFB 340, Bericht Nr. 76, Universität Tübingen.

Haider, H. (2000) Towards a superior account of superiority. In U. Lutz, G. Müller, and A. von Stechow (eds.) *Wh-Scope Marking*, Linguistik aktuell/Linguistics Today 231–48. Amsterdam, Philadelphia: John Benjamins.

Jackendoff, R. (1997) *The Architecture of the Language Faculty*, Volume 28 of *Linguistic Inquiry Monographs*. Cambridge, Massachusetts: MIT Press.

Kornfilt, J. (1997) *Turkish*. London: Routledge.

Legendre, G., P. Smolensky, and C. Wilson (1998) When is less more? faithfulness and minimal links in wh-chains. In Barbosa et al. (1998) 249–289.

McCarthy, J. and A. Prince (1995) Faithfulness and reduplicative identity. In J. Beckman, L. Walsh-Dickie, and S. Urbanczyk (eds.) *Papers in Optimality Theory*, Volume 18 249–384. Amherst, Massachussetts: UMass Occasional Papers in Linguistics.

Rizzi, L. (1982) *Issues in Italian Syntax*. Dordrecht: Foris.

Ross, J. R. (1967) *Constraints on Variables in Syntax*. Ph. D. thesis, MIT, Cambridge, Massachusetts. Appeared as Ross (1986): *Infinite Syntax*. Ablex Publishing Corporation, Norwood, New Jersey.

Sabel, J. (2002) A minimalist analysis of syntactic islands. *The Linguistic Review* 19: 271–315.

Schmid, T. and Vogel, R. (2004) Dialectal variation in German 3-verb clusters. a surface oriented ot account. *Journal of Comparative Germanic Linguistics* 7: 235–74.

Selkirk, E. (1996) The prosodic structure of function words. In J. Morgan and K. Demuth (eds.) *Signal to Syntax: Bootstrapping from Speech to Grammar in Early Acquisition* 187–213. Mahwah, New Jersey: Lawrence Erlbaum Associates.

Truckenbrodt, H. (1999) On the relation between syntactic phrases and phonological phrases. *Linguistic Inquiry* 30: 219–55.

Vogel, R. (2001) Case conflict in german free relative constructions. an optimality theoretic treatment. In G. Müller and W. Sternefeld (eds.) *Competition in Syntax* 341–75. Berlin: Mouton de Gruyter.

Vogel, R. (2002) Free relative constructions in ot syntax. In G. Fanselow and C. Féry (eds.) *Resolving Conflicts in Grammars: Optimality Theory in Syntax, Morphology, and Phonology. Linguistische Berichte Sonder-heft 11* 119–62. Hamburg: Helmut Buske Verlag.

Vogel, R. (2004a) Correspondence in ot syntax and minimal link effects. In A. Stepanov, G. Fanselow, and R. Vogel (eds.) *Minimality Effects in Syntax* 401–41. Berlin: Mouton de Gruyter.

Vogel, R. (2004b) Remarks on the architecture of optimality theoretic syntax grammars. In R. Blutner and H. Zeevat (eds.) *Optimality Theory and Pragmatics* 211–27. Houndmills, Basingstoke, Hampshire, England: Palgrave MacMillan.

Vogel, R. (2006a) The simple generator. In H. Broekhuis and R. Vogel (eds.) *Optimality Theory and Minimalism: A possible Convergence?*, Linguistics in Potsdam 25, 99–136. Potsdam: Institute of Linguistics, University of Potsdam.

Vogel, R. (2006b) Weak function word shift. *Linguistics* 44: 1059–93.

Williams, E. (2003) *Representation Theory*. Cambridge MA: MIT Press.

Language index

Author index

CPSIA information can be obtained at www.ICGtesting.com
Printed in the USA
BVOW06s0326271215

431002BV00007B/72/P